MODERN ESSAYS:

A RHETORICAL APPROACH

Second Edition

JAMES G. HEPBURN

ROBERT A. GREENBERG

MODERN ESSAYS:

A RHETORICAL APPROACH

Second Edition

THE MACMILLAN COMPANY, NEW YORK

FOREWORD

The aim of this text is to provide examples of the best American and British essays of the twentieth century so that students can learn from them something of the art and quality of good writing. The essays cover a wide range of subjects and types, from watching a bullfight with Ernest Hemingway to ridiculing Switzerland with Max Beerbohm, from the radical social analysis of Norman Mailer to the poetical reverie of Virginia Woolf. The selections are fairly equally divided between American and British authors, and they cover the whole of the last sixty-eight years. Seven writers are represented by two or three essays apiece.

The text is divided into an introductory section, *Fact and Thought,* and four rhetorical sections: *Unity, Transition, and Development; Organization; Point of View and Assumptions;* and *Style and Tone.* Each section has an introductory discussion, and each essay is followed by questions that are directed mainly to the subject of the section. There are also questions that anticipate other sections or look back, and among all the questions are some that are appropriate for theme topics. The essays within each section have been chosen as much to provide variety as to supply appropriate examples for analysis. Throughout the whole collection, though, the reader will find several essays on similar topics such as childhood, social problems, and national character. Such a topic may be useful for long themes, which also can be assigned on individual writers represented by more than one essay.

J. G. H.
R. A. G.

CONTENTS

Contents

FACT AND THOUGHT

The ordinary task of writing in college requires first of all that the student have some coherent facts and thoughts at his disposal. There are areas of investigation where facts seem to be clear and easy to come by. Water freezes at thirty-two degrees Fahrenheit, boils at two hundred and twelve, and weighs a certain amount (all under certain conditions). When we try to get behind these facts to other facts, such as what happens when water freezes, we come to areas where facts are difficult to find: what ultimate particles are involved in the freezing of water, and what are their precise movements and relationships to one another? To try to get at these facts, the twentieth century scientist relies on conventional scientific theories about atomic and subatomic structure, and if he works hard enough he may come up with new theories of his own. His facts and theories fit together. In other areas like history there are similarly multitudes of facts available for the asking. When was the Battle of Waterloo? Who were the leaders of the opposing forces? How large were those forces? Where did the main engagements take place? How effective was the artillery? Any encyclopedia will offer such facts of the case. But there are more slippery facts behind these facts. Was the French defeat inevitable? Did Napoleon lose his nerve? How much of the victory belonged to the English? Anyone trying to get at these facts is likely to rely on certain ideas about national character, Napoleon's character, and military strategy; and he may devise some new ideas of his own.

There is one area where a student in college has the facts at hand more readily than in science or history, and that is in his own life. Moreover, he is likely to know some of the facts behind the facts: he knows not only that he went to college in such and such a year to study political science but also that he went because he didn't know what else to do. The pressures of the family, the problem of the draft, the prestige of a college education—such matters floated in the background. A true account of why he went to college will rely on certain thoughts about family relations, free will, and social forces. The facts and the thoughts will go together.

Of course no account is ever entirely true. No one ever knows all the facts even about his own case, and his thoughts about the facts he does have may be half-baked, foolish, wild, or over-subtle. His facts and thoughts will always be questionable to someone else. Suppose that a newspaper reporter investigates a student riot in San Francisco. In the first place, he has a deadline to meet, and he cannot try to obtain the truth by interviewing everyone involved, even if all were available and could tell him everything perfectly in twenty minutes apiece. He finds a few people who are willing to talk, and tries to get their individual slants on the riot. He intends to take into account the likelihood that some of them are lying and others were so excited during the riot that they have only a fuzzy notion of what happened. He makes an educated guess that both sides are somewhat right and somewhat wrong. He has to think about whether the unseasonably hot month was partly to blame or whether a long history of riots at the college (of which he has no firsthand knowledge at all) was relevant. The next day the citizens of San Francisco can read his factual report, just as they can read factual reports on battles in Vietnam, corruption in labor unions, the newest miracle drugs, and lung cancer caused by smoking. But some of the students read the report and say: he must have gone to another city; that was not our riot. And yet they do not entirely agree among themselves as to what the riot was like or about, for they were all in slightly different places at the time, and none of them was in the dean's shoes.

Of course, the newspaper reporter has to write his article, and it would not necessarily be either a better or a worse article if he spent a year gathering his facts and thinking about them. He has a responsibility to be honest and to keep his wits about him and to take the plunge. Very possibly what will prevent the plunge from being disastrous is that he has the experience of a lifetime behind him, in which he has seen other riots, other angry people, other people justifying their own actions and blackening someone else's; he may have gone to college himself and had particular acquaintance with student and administration ways; and more fundamentally, he has a character of his own, radical or conservative, emotional or reserved, sardonic or detached. When he interviews the leader of the riot, he interprets the boy's facial expression and gestures as well as his words, and they tell him that he is dealing with a young politician, a young innocent, a young thug, or a young idealist. He may like the boy in spite of the boy's views, or vice versa. When he talks to the dean, he sees a man who is living in the nineteenth century or a man who is jealous of his power or a man who is a goodhearted fool or a man who is a shrewd manager of a potentially more explosive situation. In a few minutes he fills in a general picture of the boy and the dean, and infers something of the probable nature and course of the riot. (He may be wrong.) He binds his facts together with his whole awareness of life.

In a sense, then, a writer comes to every subject with the preparation of a lifetime, and if he uses that preparation well, and applies himself capably to his immediate task, he will have his head full enough of good facts and thoughts to serve himself quite adequately. The problem then is to put pen to paper. In subsequent sections of this text, some of the individual aspects of that problem will be discussed. In the present section there are several essays to examine in a broad way for the presence of fact and thought.

THE WORLD IN A WALL

GERALD DURRELL

Born in India, of English parentage, Gerald Durrell (1925—) was reared and educated in various parts of Europe. His zoological interests, as the following selection indicates, are of long standing, and he has either conducted or been a member of many expeditions on several continents in pursuit of zoological specimens. A further sense of his work and its excitements can be found in such of his books as *The Bafut Beagles, The Drunken Forest,* and *The Whispering Land.*

(1) The crumbling wall that surrounded the sunken garden along-side the house was a rich hunting ground for me. It was an ancient brick wall that had been plastered over, but now this outer skin was green with moss, bulging and sagging with the damp of many winters. The whole surface was an intricate map of cracks, some several inches wide, others as fine as hairs. Here and there large pieces had dropped off and revealed the rows of rose-pink bricks lying beneath like ribs. There was a whole landscape on this wall if you peered closely enough to see it; the roofs of a hundred tiny toadstools, red, yellow, and brown, showed in patches like villages on the damper portions; mountains of bottle-green moss grew in tuffets so symmetrical that they might have been planted and trimmed; forests of small ferns sprouted from cracks in the shady places, drooping languidly like little green fountains. The top of the wall was a desert land, too dry for anything except a few rust-red mosses to live in it, too hot for anything except sun-bathing by the dragon-flies. At the

base of the wall grew a mass of plants, cyclamen, crocus, asphodel, thrusting their leaves among the piles of broken and chipped roof-tiles that lay there. This whole strip was guarded by a labyrinth of blackberry hung, in season, with fruit that was plump and juicy and black as ebony.

(2) The inhabitants of the wall were a mixed lot, and they were divided into day and night workers, the hunters and the hunted. At night the hunters were the toads that lived among the brambles, and the geckos, pale, translucent with bulging eyes, that lived in the cracks higher up the wall. Their prey was the population of stupid, absent-minded crane-flies that zoomed and barged their way among the leaves; moths of all sizes and shapes, moths striped, tessellated, checked, spotted, and blotched, that fluttered in soft clouds along the withered plaster; the beetles, rotund and neatly clad as business men, hurrying with portly efficiency about their night's work. When the last glow-worm had dragged his frosty emerald lantern to bed over the hills of moss, and the sun rose, the wall was taken over by the next set of inhabitants. Here it was more difficult to differentiate between the prey and the predators, for everything seemed to feed indiscriminately off everything else. Thus the hunting wasps searched out caterpillars and spiders; the spiders hunted for flies; the dragon-flies, big, brittle, and hunting-pink, fed off the spiders and the flies; and the swift, lithe, and multicoloured wall lizards fed off everything.

(3) But the shyest and most self-effacing of the wall community were the most dangerous; you hardly ever saw one unless you looked for it, and yet there must have been several hundred living in the cracks of the wall. Slide a knife-blade carefully under a piece of the loose plaster and lever it gently away from the brick, and there, crouching beneath it, would be a little black scorpion an inch long, looking as though he were made out of polished chocolate. They were weird-looking things, with their flattened, oval bodies, their neat, crooked legs, the enormous crab-like claws, bulbous and neatly jointed as armour, and the tail like a string of brown beads ending in a sting like a rose-thorn. The scorpion would lie there quite quietly as you examined him, only raising his tail in an almost apologetic gesture of warning if you breathed too hard on him. If you kept him in the sun too long he would simply turn his back on you and

walk away, and then slide slowly but firmly under another section of plaster.

(4) I grew very fond of these scorpions. I found them to be pleasant, unassuming creatures with, on the whole, the most charming habits. Provided you did nothing silly or clumsy (like putting your hand on one) the scorpions treated you with respect, their one desire being to get away and hide as quickly as possible. They must have found me rather a trial, for I was always ripping sections of the plaster away so that I could watch them, or capturing them and making them walk about in jam-jars so that I could see the way their feet moved. By means of my sudden and unexpected assaults on the wall I discovered quite a bit about the scorpions. I found that they would eat bluebottles (though how they caught them was a mystery I never solved), grass-hoppers, moths, and lacewing flies. Several times I found them eating each other, a habit I found most distressing in a creature otherwise so impeccable.

(5) By crouching under the wall at night with a torch, I managed to catch some brief glimpses of the scorpions' wonderful courtship dances. I saw them standing, claws clasped, their bodies raised to the skies, their tails lovingly entwined; I saw them waltzing slowly in circles among the moss cushions, claw in claw. But my view of these performances was all too short, for almost as soon as I switched on the torch the partners would stop, pause for a moment, and then, seeing that I was not going to extinguish the light, they would turn round and walk firmly away, claw in claw, side by side. They were definitely beasts that believed in keeping themselves *to* themselves. If I could have kept a colony in captivity I would probably have been able to see the whole of the courtship, but the family had forbidden scorpions in the house, despite my arguments in favour of them.

Questions

1. Durrell does not mention certain facts about his wall, and he is very likely not interested in them. What might some of them be? Likewise, he ignores many facts about scorpions. What would they concern? What sorts of facts does he focus upon?

2. Durrell's leading idea is that his wall presents a miniature world. Point out several phrases throughout the passage that indicate the presence of this idea.

3. What special feeling does Durrell evince toward his subject? Is he absorbed or detached? Amused or serious? Sympathetic or disgusted? Aesthetically inclined or practical? Point to phrases and passages here and there that help to define his particular perspective.

4. Can you infer from the passage a few ideas Durrell probably holds about the large-scale world—about human beings, society, and nations?

5. Durrell describes his scorpions as though they were human beings dancing. Would you say that such a description is factual or fanciful, subjective or objective? Explain.

HOW WEALTH ACCUMULATES
AND MEN DECAY

GEORGE BERNARD SHAW

Though known principally as a playwright, George Bernard Shaw (1856–1950) produced a substantial body of prose, much of it, like the plays, polemical in character. Born in Dublin, he moved to London at the age of twenty, took to journalism, wrote unusually good music and drama criticism, wrote several unimpressive novels, and finally turned to playwriting. Meanwhile, he joined the Fabian Society, a socialist group opposed to revolutionary action, debated its principles publicly, and wrote economic and political tracts. His views found expression in his plays—*Widowers' Houses, Major Barbara, Man and Superman*—and though he advocated many causes and theories during a long life, his general orientation remained that of the Fabians. In 1925 he received a Nobel Prize in Literature. Offered below is a chapter from a study of socialism and capitalism, written when Shaw was in his early seventies.

(1) I want to stress this personal helplessness we are all stricken with in the face of a system that has passed beyond our knowledge and control. To bring it nearer home, I propose that we switch off from the big things like empires and their wars to little familiar things. Take pins for example! I do not know why it is that I so seldom use a pin when my wife cannot get on without boxes of them at hand; but it is so; and I will therefore take pins as being for some reason specially important to women.

(2) There was a time when pinmakers could buy the material;

From *The Intelligent Woman's Guide to Socialism and Capitalism* by George Bernard Shaw. Reprinted by permission of The Public Trustee and The Society of Authors, London.

shape it; make the head and the point; ornament it; and take it to market or to your door and sell it to you. They had to know three trades: buying, making, and selling; and the making required skill in several operations. They not only knew how the thing was done from beginning to end, but could do it. But they could not afford to sell you a paper of pins for a farthing. Pins cost so much that a woman's dress allowance was called pin money.

(3) By the end of the eighteenth century Adam Smith boasted that it took eighteen men to make a pin, each man doing a little bit of the job and passing the pin on to the next, and none of them being able to make a whole pin or to buy the materials or to sell it when it was made. The most you could say for them was that at least they had some idea of how it was made, though they could not make it. Now as this meant that they were clearly less capable and knowledgeable men than the old pinmakers, you may ask why Adam Smith boasted of it as a triumph of civilization when its effect was so clearly a degrading effect. The reason was that by setting each man to do just one little bit of the work and nothing but that, over and over again, he became very quick at it. The men, it is said, could turn out nearly five thousand pins a day each; and thus pins became plentiful and cheap. The country was supposed to be richer because it had more pins, though it had turned capable men into mere machines doing their work without intelligence, and being fed by the spare food of the capitalist as an engine is fed with coal and oil. That was why the poet Goldsmith, who was a far-sighted economist as well as a poet, complained that "wealth accumulates, and men decay."

(4) Nowadays Adam Smith's eighteen men are as extinct as the diplodocus. The eighteen flesh-and-blood machines are replaced by machines of steel which spout out pins by the hundred million. Even sticking them into pink papers is done by machinery. The result is that with the exception of a few people who design the machines, nobody knows how to make a pin or how a pin is made: that is to say, the modern worker in pin manufacture need not be one-tenth so intelligent and skillful and accomplished as the old pinmaker; and the only compensation we have for this deterioration is that pins are so cheap that a single pin has no expressible

value at all. Even with a big profit stuck on to the cost-price you can buy dozens for a farthing; and pins are so recklessly thrown away and wasted that verses have to be written to persuade children (without success) that it is a sin to steal a pin.

(5) Many serious thinkers, like John Ruskin and William Morris, have been greatly troubled by this, just as Goldsmith was, and have asked whether we really believe that it is an advance in wealth to lose our skill and degrade our workers for the sake of being able to waste pins by the ton. We shall see later on, when we come to consider the Distribution of Leisure, that the cure for this is not to go back to the old ways; for if the saving of time by modern machinery were equally divided among us, it would set us all free for higher work than pinmaking or the like. But in the meantime the fact remains that pins are now made by men and women who cannot make anything by themselves, and could not arrange between themselves to make anything even in little bits. They are ignorant and helpless, and cannot lift their finger to begin their day's work until it has all been arranged for them by their employers, who themselves do not understand the machines they buy, and simply pay other people to set them going by carrying out the machine maker's directions.

(6) The same is true of clothes. Formerly the whole work of making clothes, from the shearing of the sheep to the turning out of the finished and washed garment ready to put on, had to be done in the country by the men and women of the household, especially the women; so that to this day an unmarried woman is called a spinster. Nowadays nothing is left of all this but the sheep-shearing; and even that, like the milking of cows, is being done by machinery, as the sewing is. Give a woman a sheep today and ask her to produce a woollen dress for you; and not only will she be quite unable to do it, but you are as likely as not to find that she is not even aware of any connection between sheep and clothes. When she gets her clothes, which she does by buying them at a shop, she knows that there is a difference between wool and cotton and silk, between flannel and merino, perhaps even between stockinet and other wefts; but as to how they are made, or what they are made of, or how they came to be in the shop ready for her to buy, she knows hardly

anything. And the shop assistant from whom she buys is no wiser. The people engaged in the making of them know even less; for many of them are too poor to have much choice of materials when they buy their own clothes.

(7) Thus the capitalist system has produced an almost universal ignorance of how things are made and done, whilst at the same time it has caused them to be made and done on a gigantic scale. We have to buy books and encyclopedias to find out what it is we are doing all day; and as the books are written by people who are not doing it, and who get their information from other books, what they tell us is from twenty to fifty years out of date, and unpractical at that. And of course most of us are too tired of our work when we come home to want to read about it: what we need is a cinema to take our minds off it and feed our imagination.

(8) It is a funny place, this world of Capitalism, with its astonishing spread of ignorance and helplessness, boasting all the time of its spread of education and enlightenment. There stand the thousands of property owners and the millions of wage workers, none of them able to make anything, none of them knowing what to do until somebody tells them, none of them having the least notion of how it is that they find people paying them money, and things in the shops to buy with it. And when they travel they are surprised to find that savages and Esquimaux and villagers who have to make everything for themselves are more intelligent and resourceful! The wonder would be if they were anything else. We should die of idiocy through disuse of our mental faculties if we did not fill our heads with romantic nonsense out of illustrated newspapers and novels and plays and films. Such stuff keeps us alive; but it falsifies everything for us so absurdly that it leaves us more or less dangerous lunatics in the real world.

(9) Excuse my going on like this; but as I am a writer of books and plays myself, I know the folly and peril of it better than you do. And when I see that this moment of our utmost ignorance and helplessness, delusion and folly, has been stumbled on by the blind forces of Capitalism as the moment for giving votes to everybody, so that the few wise women are hopelessly overruled by the thousands whose political minds, as far as they can be said to have any

political minds at all, have been formed in the cinema, I realize that I had better stop writing plays for a while to discuss political and social realities in this book with those who are intelligent enough to listen to me.

Questions

1. Most of Shaw's facts support his main contention in one way or another. What is that contention, and at what point or points in the essay do you find it stated?

2. Can you justify Shaw's use of such facts as the derivations of *pin money* and *spinster*? Or is he just showing off his knowledge?

3. Shaw offers no facts in contradiction to his argument. Even if you agree with him, you ought to be able to suggest possible facts that he ignores.

4. If you have had any experience in an industrial organization, write an account of the work there either to support or contradict Shaw's account of the ignorance and helplessness bred by the modern manufacture of pins.

5. Shaw offers as a fact that savages and Eskimos are more intelligent and resourceful than the average person in the civilized world. What is the relationship of this "fact" to his main contention (Question 1)? What does your answer suggest about the connection between fact and idea?

6. What the future will be like is anyone's guess, but on the basis of Shaw's facts, do you think socialism is required for civilized man to regain his intelligence? See especially Paragraphs 5 and 7 through 9.

7. Does Shaw seem outraged or amused, orderly or impassioned, humble or arrogant in dealing with his subject? Explain and illustrate.

NOTTINGHAM AND THE
MINING COUNTRY

D. H. LAWRENCE

The son of a coal miner, D. H. Lawrence (1885–1930) spent his youth amid the poverty and brutality of an English mining town, taught for a time in a secondary school, but early dedicated himself to writing. His first novel, *The White Peacock,* appeared when he was twenty-six; three more followed in rapid succession, including the largely autobiographical *Sons and Lovers,* and also several volumes of poetry. With the end of World War I, he began a life of restless travel, settling for a time in Italy and Sicily and then in Australia and New Mexico. He passed his last years in different parts of Europe, dying in southern France at the age of forty-four of the tuberculosis he had contracted as a child. (Further information on Lawrence appears on pp. 271, 382.)

(1) I was born nearly forty-four years ago, in Eastwood, a mining village of some three thousand souls, about eight miles from Nottingham, and one mile from the small stream, the Erewash, which divides Nottinghamshire from Derbyshire. It is hilly country, looking west to Crich and towards Matlock, sixteen miles away, and east and north-east towards Mansfield and the Sherwood Forest district. To me it seemed, and still seems, an extremely beautiful countryside, just between the red sandstone and the oak-trees of Nottingham, and the cold limestone, the ash-trees, the stone fences

From *The Portable D. H. Lawrence,* edited by Diana Trilling. Copyright 1936 by Frieda Lawrence, © 1964 by Estate of the late Frieda Lawrence Ravagli. Reprinted by permission of The Viking Press, Inc.

of Derbyshire. To me, as a child and a young man, it was still the old England of the forest and agricultural past; there were no motor-cars, the mines were, in a sense, an accident in the landscape, and Robin Hood and his merry men were not very far away.

(2) The string of coal-mines of B.W. & Co. had been opened some sixty years before I was born, and Eastwood had come into being as a consequence. It must have been a tiny village at the beginning of the nineteenth century, a small place of cottages and fragmentary rows of little four-roomed miners' dwellings, the homes of the old colliers of the eighteenth century, who worked in the bits of mines, foot-hill mines with an opening in the hillside into which the miners walked, or windlass mines, where the men were wound up one at a time, in a bucket, by a donkey. The windlass mines were still working when my father was a boy—and the shafts of some were still there, when I was a boy.

(3) But somewhere about 1820 the company must have sunk the first big shaft—not very deep—and installed the first machinery of the real industrial colliery. Then came my grandfather, a young man trained to be a tailor, drifting from the south of England, and got the job of company tailor for the Brinsley mine. In those days the company supplied the men with the thick flannel vests, or singlets, and the moleskin trousers lined at the top with flannel, in which the colliers worked. I remember the great rolls of coarse flannel and pit-cloth which stood in the corner of my grandfather's shop when I was a small boy, and the big, strange old sewing-machine, like nothing else on earth, which sewed the massive pit-trousers. But when I was only a child the company discontinued supplying the men with pit-clothes.

(4) My grandfather settled in an old cottage down in a quarry-bed, by the brook at Old Brinsley, near the pit. A mile away, up at Eastwood, the company built the first miners' dwellings—it must be nearly a hundred years ago. Now Eastwood occupies a lovely posi-tion on a hilltop, with the steep slope towards Derbyshire and the long slope towards Nottingham. They put up a new church, which stands fine and commanding, even if it has no real form, looking across the awful Erewash Valley at the church of Heanor, similarly commanding, away on a hill beyond. What opportunities, what

opportunities! These mining villages *might* have been like the lovely
hill-towns of Italy, shapely and fascinating. And what happened?

(5) Most of the little rows of dwellings of the old-style miners
were pulled down, and dull little shops began to rise along the
Nottingham Road, while on the down-slope of the north side the company erected what is still known as the New Buildings, or the
Square. These New Buildings consist of two great hollow squares of
dwellings planked down on the rough slope of the hill, little four-
room houses with the 'front' looking outward into the grim, blank
street, and the 'back,' with a tiny square brick yard, a low wall, and a
w.c. and ash-pit, looking into the desert of the square, hard, uneven,
jolting black earth tilting rather steeply down, with these little back
yards all around, and openings at the corners. The squares were
quite big, and absolutely desert, save for the posts for clothes lines,
and people passing, children playing on the hard earth. And they
were shut in like a barracks enclosure, very strange.

(6) Even fifty years ago the squares were unpopular. It was
'common' to live in the Square. It was a little less common to live
in the Breach, which consisted of six blocks of rather more pretentious dwellings erected by the company in the valley below, two
rows of three blocks, with an alley between. And it was most 'common,' most degraded of all to live in Dakins Row, two rows of the
old dwellings, very old, black four-roomed little places, that stood
on the hill again, not far from the Square.

(7) So the place started. Down the steep street between the
squares, Scargill Street, the Wesleyans' chapel was put up, and I
was born in the little corner shop just above. Across the other side
of the Square the miners themselves built the big, barn-like Primitive Methodist chapel. Along the hill-top ran the Nottingham Road,
with its scrappy, ugly mid-Victorian shops. The little market-place,
with a superb outlook, ended the village on the Derbyshire side, and
was just here left bare, with the Sun Inn on one side, the chemist
across, with the gilt pestle-and-mortar, and a shop at the other
corner, the corner of Alfreton Road and Nottingham Road.

(8) In this queer jumble of the old England and the new, I
came into consciousness. As I remember, little local speculators
already began to straggle dwellings in rows, always in rows, across

the fields: nasty red-brick, flat-faced dwellings with dark slate roofs. The bay-window period only began when I was a child. But most of the country was untouched.

(9) There must be three or four hundred company houses in the squares and the streets that surround the squares, like a great barracks wall. There must be sixty or eighty company houses in the Breach. The old Dakins Row will have thirty to forty little holes. Then counting the old cottages and rows left with their old gardens down the lanes and along the twitchells, and even in the midst of Nottingham Road itself, there were houses enough for the population, there was no need for much building. And not much building went on when I was small.

(10) We lived in the Breach, in a corner house. A field-path came down under a great hawthorn hedge. On the other side was the brook, with the old sheep-bridge going over into the meadows. The hawthorn hedge by the brook had grown tall as tall trees, and we used to bathe from there in the dipping-hole, where the sheep were dipped, just near the fall from the old mill-dam, where the water rushed. The mill only ceased grinding the local corn when I was a child. And my father, who always worked in Brinsley pit, and who always got up at five o'clock, if not at four, would set off in the dawn across the fields at Coney Grey, and hunt for mushrooms in the long grass, or perhaps pick up a skulking rabbit, which he would bring home at evening inside the lining of his pit-coat.

(11) So that the life was a curious cross between industrialism and the old agricultural England of Shakespeare and Milton and Fielding and George Eliot. The dialect was broad Derbyshire, and always 'thee' and 'thou.' The people lived almost entirely by instinct, men of my father's age could not really read. And the pit did not mechanize men. On the contrary. Under the butty system, the miners worked underground as a sort of intimate community, they knew each other practically naked, and with curious close intimacy, and the darkness and the underground remoteness of the pit 'stall,' and the continual presence of danger, made the physical, instinctive, and intuitional contact between men very highly developed, a contact almost as close as touch, very real and very powerful. This physical awareness and intimate *togetherness* was at its strongest down pit.

When the men came up into the light, they blinked. They had, in a measure, to change their flow. Nevertheless, they brought with them above ground the curious dark intimacy of the mine, the naked sort of contact, and if I think of my childhood, it is always as if there was a lustrous sort of inner darkness, like the gloss of coal, in which we moved and had our real being. My father loved the pit. He was hurt badly, more than once, but he would never stay away. He loved the contact, the intimacy, as men in the war loved the intense male comradeship of the dark days. They did not know what they had lost till they lost it. And I think it is the same with the young colliers of to-day.

(12) Now the colliers had also an instinct of beauty. The colliers' wives had not. The colliers were deeply alive, instinctively. But they had no daytime ambition, and no daytime intellect. They avoided, really, the rational aspect of life. They preferred to take life instinctively and intuitively. They didn't even care very profoundly about wages. It was the women, naturally, who nagged on this score. There was a big discrepancy, when I was a boy, between the collier who saw, at the best, only a brief few hours of daylight—often no daylight at all during the winter weeks—and the collier's wife, who had all the day to herself when the man was down pit.

(13) The great fallacy is, to pity the man. He didn't dream of pitying himself, till agitators and sentimentalists taught him to. He was happy: or more than happy, he was fulfilled. Or he was fulfilled on the receptive side, not on the expressive. The collier went to the pub and drank in order to continue his intimacy with his mates. They talked endlessly, but it was rather of wonders and marvels, even in politics, than of facts. It was hard facts, in the shape of wife, money, and nagging home necessities, which they fled away from, out of the house to the pub, and out of the house to the pit.

(14) The collier fled out of the house as soon as he could, away from the nagging materialism of the woman. With the women it was always: This is broken, now you've got to mend it! or else: We want this, that, and the other, and where is the money coming from? The collier didn't know and didn't care very deeply—his life was otherwise. So he escaped. He roved the countryside with his dog, prowling for a rabbit, for nests, for mushrooms, anything. He loved the countryside, just the indiscriminating feel of it. Or he loved just

to sit on his heels and watch—anything or nothing. He was not intellectually interested. Life for him did not consist in facts, but in a flow. Very often, he loved his garden. And very often he had a genuine love of the beauty of flowers. I have known it often and often, in colliers.

(15) Now the love of flowers is a very misleading thing. Most women love flowers as possessions, and as trimmings. They can't look at a flower, and wonder a moment, and pass on. If they see a flower that arrests their attention, they must at once pick it, pluck it. Possession! A possession! Something added on to *me!* And most of the so-called love of flowers to-day is merely this reaching out of possession and egoism: something I've *got:* something that embellishes *me.* Yet I've seen many a collier stand in his back garden looking down at a flower with that odd, remote sort of contemplation which shows a *real* awareness of the presence of beauty. It would not even be admiration, or joy, or delight, or any of those things which so often have a root in the possessive instinct. It would be a sort of contemplation: which shows the incipient artist.

(16) The real tragedy of England, as I see it, is the tragedy of ugliness. The country is so lovely: the man-made England is so vile. I know that the ordinary collier, when I was a boy, had a peculiar sense of beauty, coming from his intuitive and instinctive consciousness, which was awakened down pit. And the fact that he met with just cold ugliness and raw materialism when he came up into daylight, and particularly when he came to the Square or the Breach, and to his own table, killed something in him, and in a sense spoiled him as a man. The woman almost invariably nagged about material things. She was taught to do it; she was encouraged to do it. It was a mother's business to see that her sons 'got on,' and it was the man's business to provide the money. In my father's generation, with the old wild England behind them, and the lack of education, the man was not beaten down. But in my generation, the boys I went to school with, colliers now, have all been beaten down, what with the din-din-dinning of Board Schools, books, cinemas, clergymen, the whole national and human consciousness hammering on the fact of material prosperity above all things.

(17) The men are beaten down, there is prosperity for a time, in their defeat—and then disaster looms ahead. The root of all disaster

is disheartenment. And men are disheartened. The men of England, the colliers in particular, are disheartened. They have been betrayed and beaten.

(18) Now though perhaps nobody knew it, it was ugliness which betrayed the spirit of man, in the nineteenth century. The great crime which the moneyed classes and promoters of industry committed in the palmy Victorian days was the condemning of the workers to ugliness, ugliness, ugliness: meanness and formless and ugly surroundings, ugly ideals, ugly religion, ugly hope, ugly love, ugly clothes, ugly furniture, ugly houses, ugly relationship between workers and employers. The human soul needs actual beauty even more than bread. The middle classes jeer at the colliers for buying pianos—but what is the piano, often as not, but a blind reaching out for beauty? To the woman it is a possession and a piece of furniture and something to feel superior about. But see the elderly colliers trying to learn to play, see them listening with queer alert faces to their daughter's execution of *The Maiden's Prayer,* and you will see a blind, unsatisfied craving for beauty. It is far more deep in the men than in the women. The women want show. The men want beauty, and still want it.

(19) If the company, instead of building those sordid and hideous Squares, then, when they had that lovely site to play with, there on the hill top: if they had put a tall column in the middle of the small market-place, and run three parts of a circle of arcade round the pleasant space, where people could stroll or sit, and with the handsome houses behind! If they had made big, substantial houses, in apartments of five and six rooms, and with handsome entrances. If above all, they had encouraged song and dancing—for the miners still sang and danced—and provided handsome space for these. If only they had encouraged some form of beauty in dress, some form of beauty in interior life—furniture, decoration. If they had given prizes for the handsomest chair or table, the loveliest scarf, the most charming room that the men or women could make! If only they had done this, there would never have been an industrial problem. The industrial problem arises from the base forcing of all human energy into a competition of mere acquisition.

(20) You may say the working man would not have accepted such a form of life: the Englishman's home is his castle, etc., etc.—

'my own little home.' But if you can hear every word the next-door-people say, there's not much castle. And if you can see everybody in the square if they go to the w.c.! And if your one desire is to get out of the 'castle' and your 'own little home'!—well, there's not much to be said for it. Anyhow it's only the woman who idolizes 'her own little home'—and it's always the woman at her worst, her most greedy, most possessive, most mean. There's nothing to be said for the 'little home' any more: a great scrabble of ugly pettiness over the face of the land.

(21) As a matter of fact, till 1800 the English people were strictly a rural people—very rural. England has had towns for centuries, but they have never been real towns, only clusters of village streets. Never the real *urbs*. The English character has failed to develop the real *urban* side of a man, the civic side. Siena is a bit of a place, but it is a real city, with citizens intimately connected with the city. Nottingham is a vast place sprawling towards a million, and it is nothing more than an amorphous agglomeration. There *is* no Nottingham, in the sense that there is Siena. The Englishman is stupidly undeveloped, as a citizen. And it is partly due to his 'little home' stunt, and partly to his acceptance of hopeless paltriness in his surrounding. The new cities of America are much more genuine cities, in the Roman sense, than is London or Manchester. Even Edinburgh used to be more of a true city than any town England ever produced.

(22) That silly little individualism of 'the Englishman's home is his castle' and 'my own little home' is out of date. It would work almost up to 1800, when every Englishman was still a villager, and a cottager. But the industrial system has brought a great change. The Englishman still likes to think of himself as a 'cottager'—'my home, my garden.' But it is puerile. Even the farm labourer to-day is psychologically a town-bird. The English are town-birds through and through, to-day, as the inevitable result of their complete industrialization. Yet they don't know how to build a city, how to think of one, or how to live in one. They are all suburban, pseudo-cottagy, and not one of them knows how to be truly urban—the citizens as the Romans were citizens—or the Athenians—or even the Parisians, till the war came.

(23) And this is because we have frustrated that instinct of com-

munity which would make us unite in pride and dignity in the
bigger gesture of the citizen, not the cottager. The great city means
beauty, dignity, and a certain splendour. This is the side of the
Englishman that has been thwarted and shockingly betrayed. England is a mean and petty scrabble of paltry dwellings called 'homes.'
I believe in their heart of hearts all Englishmen loathe their little
homes—but not the women. What we want is a bigger gesture, a
greater scope, a certain splendour, a certain grandeur, and beauty,
big beauty. The American does far better than we, in this.

(24) And the promoter of industry, a hundred years ago, dared
to perpetrate the ugliness of my native village. And still more
monstrous, promoters of industry to-day are scrabbling over the face
of England with miles and square miles of red-brick 'homes,' like
horrible scabs. And the men inside these little red rat-traps get more
and more helpless, being more and more humiliated, more and more
dissatisfied, like trapped rats. Only the meaner sort of women go on
loving the little home which is no more than a rat-trap to her man.

(25) Do away with it all, then. At no matter what cost, start in
to alter it. Never mind about wages and industrial squabbling. Turn
the attention elsewhere. Pull down my native village to the last
brick. Plan a nucleus. Fix the focus. Make a handsome gesture of
radiation from the focus. And then put up big buildings, handsome,
that sweep to a civic centre. And furnish them with beauty. And
make an absolute clean start. Do it place by place. Make a new
England. Away with little homes! Away with scrabbling pettiness
and paltriness. Look at the contours of the land, and build up from
these, with a sufficient nobility. The English may be mentally or
spiritually developed. But as citizens of splendid cities they are more
ignominious than rabbits. And they nag, nag, nag all the time about
politics and wages and all that, like mean narrow housewives.

Questions

1. Almost all of Lawrence's facts concern two or three subjects. Industrialism is one of them. What are the others?

2. Lawrence returns to the past, both historically and in terms of his
personal experience. Are his facts in the one instance more or less reliable
than in the other? To what extent does the difference affect his argument?

3. What ideas govern the essay? Show how their relative importance shifts in the course of the essay.

4. What qualities do you suppose Lawrence would like in a woman? Argue on the basis of what he dislikes.

5. Is it surprising and convincing when Lawrence says that men who work in a coal pit are more sensitive, more alive, than their women? Does his opinion suggest that the members of the college football team are likely to be more sensitive and alive than the average sweetly studious coed? Discuss.

6. What are the general values that underlie Lawrence's likes and dislikes about men, women, industrialism, architecture, and so forth?

7. Would Lawrence have liked the American city of today? Discuss the issue with reference to the one American city you know best. Base your discussion on the things he says in his essay.

8. Have you witnessed an example of urban renewal, where the old was swept away and "an absolute clean start" made? Did it work out as happily as Lawrence suggests it can? Write an account of it.

9. Sometimes Lawrence is objective, as in most of his account of the beginnings of Eastwood. Sometimes he is personal, as in his expression of likes and dislikes. What is the range of feeling that he displays in the essay? What sort of person does he seem to be?

AUDUBON'S HAPPY LAND

KATHERINE ANNE PORTER

Katherine Anne Porter (1894——) was born in Indian Creek, a small town in Texas, was reared there and in Louisiana, and received her education in small convent schools. She admits to being the great-great-great-granddaughter of Daniel Boone, and to having begun writing stories as soon as she could put words to paper. Since then she has established herself as one of the most meticulous and distinguished short-story writers of her time. Her stories, often set in the Southwest, have been collected in *Flowering Judas, Pale Horse, Pale Rider,* and *The Leaning Tower.* In addition to her novel, *Ship of Fools,* she has written essays and movie scripts and has done several translations.

(1) The center of St. Francisville is ugly as only small towns trying frantically to provide gasoline and sandwiches to passing motorists can be, but its lane-like streets unfold almost at once into grace and goodness. On the day of our visit, the only sign of special festivity was a splendid old Negro, in top hat, frock coat with nose-gay in buttonhole, a black cotton umbrella shading his venerable head, seated before the casually contrived small office where we bought our tickets for the Audubon pilgrimage and were joined by our guide. The old Negro rose, bowed, raised his hat at arm's length to an angle of forty-five degrees more or less, playing his role in the ceremonies not only as a detail of the scene, but as part also of its history. Our guide appeared in a few minutes, tying a flowered kerchief under her chin, *babushka* fashion, as she came. She was dark and thin and soft-voiced, so typically Louisiana French that

we thought she must be from New Orleans, or the Bayou Teche country. It turned out that she was from Idaho, lately married to a cousin of the Percys at "Greenwood." No matter; she belonged also, by virtue of love and attachment, as well as appearance, to the scene and its history.

(2) Saint Francis, who preached to the birds, and Audubon, who painted them as no one before or since, are both commemorated in this place. In 1779, the monks of Saint Francis founded the town and christened it. Spain ruled the territory then, though the brothers Le Moyne—Iberville and Bienville—had claimed it three-quarters of a century before for France. The Spanish government made a classical error with the classical result. It invited wealthy foreign investors to help settle the country, and the foreign investors ended by taking final possession. These particular foreigners bore such names as Ratliff, Barrow, Wade, Hamilton, Percy; they were all men of substance and of worldly mind, mostly from Virginia and the Carolinas, who obtained by Spanish grant splendid parcels of land of about twelve thousand acres each. These acres formed a subtropical jungle to the very banks of the Mississippi. A man could not, said an old woodsman, sink his hunting knife to the hilt in it anywhere.

(3) The newcomers had on their side the strong arm of slave labor, and definite views on caste, property, morals, and manners. They pushed back the Louisiana jungle mile by mile, uncovered rich lands, and raised splendid crops. They built charming houses and filled them with furniture from France and England. Their silver and porcelain and linen were such as befitted their pride, which was high, and their tastes, which were delicate and expensive. Their daughters sang, danced, and played the harpsichord; their sons played the flute and fought duels; they collected libraries, they hunted and played chess, and spent the winter season in New Orleans. They traveled much in Europe, and brought back always more and more Old World plunder. Everywhere, with ceaseless, intensely personal concern, they thought, talked, and played politics.

(4) In a few short years, these wealthy, nostalgic Americans were, in the phrase of the day, "groaning under the galling yoke of Spain." They forgathered evening after evening in one or another

of their mansions and groaned; that is to say, discussed the matter
with shrewdness, realism, and a keen eye to the possibilities. They
called upon President Madison to lend a hand in taking this territory
from Spain, which continued to hold it for some reason long after
the Louisiana Purchase. "President Madison," says a local historian
of that day, "remained deaf to their cries." The Feliciana planters
then stopped crying, organized a small army, and marched on the
Spanish capital, Baton Rouge. Harsh as it sounds in such a gentle-
manly sort of argument, they caused the Spanish Commandant to
be killed as proof of the seriousness of their intentions. They then
declared for themselves the Independent Republic of West Florida,
with St. Francisville as its capital. A certain Mr. Fulwar Skipwith
was elected President. All was done in form, with a Constitution, a
Body of Laws, and a flag designed for the occasion. The strategy
was a brilliant success. President Madison sent friendly troops to
annex the infant republic to the United States of America. This
Graustarkian event took place in 1810.

(5) The next year, a Roosevelt (Nicholas), partner in an Eastern
steamship company, sent the first steamboat into the Mississippi,
straight past St. Francisville and her sister town, Bayou Sara. The
days of opulence and glory began in earnest, based solidly on land,
money crops, and transportation, to flourish for just half a century.

(6) It is quite finished as to opulence, and the glory is now a
gentle aura, radiating not so much from the past as from the present,
for St. Francisville lives with graceful competence on stored wealth
that is not merely tangible. The legend has, in fact, magnified the
opulence into something more than it really was, to the infinite
damage of a particular truth: that wealth in the pre-War South was
very modest by present standards, and it was not ostentatious, even
then. The important thing to know about St. Francisville, as perhaps a typical survivor of that culture, is this: no one there tells
you about steamboat wealth, or wears the air of poverty living on
its memories, or (and this is the constant, rather tiresome accusa-
tion of busy, hasty observers) "yearns for the good old days."

(7) The town's most treasured inhabitant was Audubon, and its
happiest memory. This is no afterthought, based on his later repu-

tation. And it is the more interesting when we consider what kind of reputation Audubon's was, almost to the end; nothing at all that a really materialistic society would take seriously. He was an artist, but not a fashionable one, never successful by any worldly standards; but the people of St. Francisville loved him, recognized him, took him to themselves when he was unknown and almost in despair. And now in every house, they will show you some small souvenir of him, some record that he was once a guest there. The Pirries, of New Orleans and Oakley, near St. Francisville, captured him in New Orleans at the moment when he was heading East, disheartened, and brought him to Oakley for the pleasant employment of teaching their young daughter, Miss Eliza, to dance and draw, of mornings. His afternoons, and some of his evenings, he spent in the Feliciana woods, and we know what he found there.

(8) The Feliciana country is not a jungle now, nor has it been for a great while. The modest, occasional rises of earth, called hills, are covered with civilized little woods, fenced grazing-fields for fine cattle, thatches of sugar cane, of corn, and orchards. Both Felicianas, east and west, are so handsome and amiable you might mistake them for one, instead of twins. For fear they will be confounded in the stranger's eye, the boundaries are marked plainly along the highway. The difference was to me that West Feliciana was holding a spring festival in honor of Audubon, and I, a returned Southerner, in effect a tourist, went straight through East Feliciana, which had not invited visitors, to West Feliciana, which had.

(9) You are to think of this landscape as an April garden, flowering with trees and shrubs of the elegant, difficult kind that live so securely in this climate: camellias, gardenias, crêpe myrtle, fine oldfashioned roses; with simpler things, honeysuckle, dogwood, wisteria, magnolia, bridal-wreath, oleander, redbud, leaving no fence or corner bare. The birds of Saint Francis and of Audubon fill the air with their light singing and their undisturbed flight. The great, dark oaks spread their immense branches fronded with moss; the camphor and cedar trees add their graceful shapes and their dry, spicy odors; and yes, as you have been told, perhaps too often, there are the white, pillared houses seated in dignity, glimpsed first at a distance through their park-like gardens.

(10) The celebrated oak *allées* are there at "Live Oak," at "Waverly," at "Rosedown," perhaps the finest grove of all at "Highland"—the wide, shaded driveways from the gate to the great door, all so appropriately designed for the ritual events of life, a wedding or a funeral procession, the christening party, the evening walks of betrothed lovers. W. B. Yeats causes one of his characters to reflect, in face of a grove of ancient trees, "that a man who planted trees, knowing that no descendant nearer than his great-grandson could stand under their shade, had a noble and generous confidence." That kind of confidence created this landscape, now as famous, as banal, if you like, as the horse-chestnuts along the Champs Elysées, as the perfume gardens of Grasse, as the canals of Venice, as the lilies-of-the-valley in the forest of Saint-Cloud. It possesses, too, the appeal of those much-visited scenes, and shares their nature, which is to demand nothing by way of arranged tribute; each newcomer may discover it for himself; but this landscape shares its peculiar treasure only with such as know there is something more here than mere hungry human pride in mahogany staircases and silver doorknobs. The real spirit of the place planted those oaks, and keeps them standing.

(11) The first thing that might strike you is the simplicity, the comparative smallness of even the largest houses (in plain figures, "Greenwood" is one hundred feet square; there is a veranda one hundred and ten feet long at "The Myrtles," a long, narrow house), compared not only to the grandeur of their legend, but to anything of corresponding fame you may have seen, such as the princely houses of Florence or the Spanish palaces in Mexico, or, as a last resort, the Fifth Avenue museums of the fantastically rich of two or three generations ago. Their importance is of another kind—that of the oldest New York houses, or the Patrizieren houses in Basel; with a quality nearly akin to the Amalienburg in the forest near Munich, quite the loveliest house I ever saw, or expect to see. These St. Francisville houses are examples of pure domestic architecture, somehow urban in style, graceful, and differing from city houses in this particular, that they sit in landscapes designed to show them

off; they are meant to be observed from every point of view. No two of them are alike, but they were all built to be lived in, by people who had a completely aristocratic sense of the house as a dwelling-place.

(12) They are ample and their subtle proportions give them stateliness not accounted for in terms of actual size. They are placed in relation to the south wind and the morning sun. Their ceilings are high, because high ceilings are right for this kind of architecture, and this kind of architecture is right for a hot climate. Their fireplaces are beautiful, well placed, in harmony with the rooms, and meant for fine log fires in the brief winters. Their windows are many, tall and rightly spaced for light and air, as well as for the view outward. All of them, from "Live Oak," built in 1779, to "The Myrtles," built in the 1840's, have in common the beauty and stability of cypress, blue poplar, apparently indestructible brick made especially for the chimneys and foundations, old methods of mortising and pinning, hand-forged nails.

(13) "Live Oak" stands on a green knoll, and, from the front door, one looks straight through the central room to the rolling meadow bordered with iris in profuse bloom. This house is really tired, worn down to the bare grain, the furniture just what might have been left from some remote disaster, but it is beautiful, a place to live in, with its wide, double porches and outside staircase in the early style of the Spanish in Louisiana, its dark paneling, and its air of gentle remoteness.

(14) "Waverly" is another sort of thing altogether, a bright place full of color, where the old furniture is set off with gaily flowered rugs, and the heavy old Louisiana four-poster beds—of a kind to be found nowhere else—are dressed sprucely in fresh curtains. The white pillars of "Waverly" are flat and slender, and the graceful fan-lights of the front door are repeated on the second floor, with an especially airy effect. The vestiges of the old boxwood maze are being coaxed back to life there, and gardenias grow in hedges, as they should.

(15) At "The Myrtles," the flowery iron grille of the long veranda sets the Victorian tone; the long dining-room still wears, between the thin moldings, its French wallpaper from 1840—sepia-colored pan-

els from floor to ceiling of game birds and flowers. The cypress floor is honey-colored, the Italian marble mantelpiece was that day banked with branches of white dogwood. All the rooms are long, full of the softest light lying upon the smooth surfaces of old fruit-wood and mahogany. From the back veranda, an old-fashioned back yard, full of country living, lay in the solid shade of grape arbors and trees rounded like baskets of flowers. Chickens roamed and picked there; there was a wood-pile with a great iron wash-pot up-ended against it, near the charred spot where the fire is still built to heat the water.

(16) At "Virginia," we saw George Washington's account-book, made, I believe, at Valley Forge, with all the detailed outlay of that troublesome episode. "Virginia" is by way of being an inn now— that is to say, if travelers happen along they will be put up in tall, canopied beds under fine old quilted coverlets. The large silver spoons in the dining-room came from an ancestor of the Fisher family—Baron de Würmser, who had them as a gift from Frederick the Great. Generous-sized ladles they are, too, paper-thin and flexible. Like so many old coin silver spoons, they appear to have been chewed, and they have been. A thin silver spoon was once considered the ideal object for an infant to cut his teeth upon. But there were dents in a de Würmser soup ladle which testified that some Fisher infant must have been a saber-toothed tiger. "Surely no teething child did that," I remarked. "No," said the hostess, a fleeting shade of severity on her brow. "It was thrown out with the dish-water once, and the pigs got it." Here is the French passport for a Fisher grandfather, dated 1836. It was then he brought back the splendid flowered wallpaper, even now fresh in its discreet colors, the hand-painted mauve linen window-shades on rollers, then so fashionable, replacing the outmoded Venetian blinds; the ornate, almost mor-bidly feminine drawing-room chairs and sofas.

(17) At "Greenwood," the host was engaged with a group of oil prospectors, for, beneath their charming, fruitful surfaces, the Feli-cianas are suspected of containing the dark, the sinister new treas-ure more powerful than gold. If so, what will become of the oaks

and the flourishing fields and the gentle cattle? What will become
of these lovely houses? "They make syrup and breed cattle here,"
said our guide; "that keeps 'Greenwood' going very well. Some
people (she named them) wanted Mr. Percy to make a dude ranch
of this place, but he wouldn't hear of it."

(18) We mentioned our premonitions about St. Francisville if oil
should be discovered. Our guide spoke up with the quiet reckless-
ness of faith. "It wouldn't do any harm," she said. "The Feliciana
people have had what money can buy, and they have something
money can't buy, and they know it. They have nothing to sell.
Tourists come here from all over and offer them thousands of dollars for their little things, just little things they don't need and
hardly ever look at, but they won't sell them."

(19) "Greenwood" is the typical Southern mansion of too many
songs, too many stories—with the extravagant height of massive,
round pillar, the too-high ceiling, the gleaming sweep of central hall,
all in the 1830 Greek, gilded somewhat, but lightly. There is bare-
ness; space dwarfing the human stature and breathing a faint bleak-
ness. Yet the gentle groves and small hills are framed with overwhelming effect between those columns; effect grandiose beyond
what the measuring eye knows is actually there.

(20) It seems now that the builders should have known that this
house was the end, never the beginning. It is quite improbable that
anyone should again build a house like "Greenwood" to live in.
But there it is, with the huge beams of the gallery being replaced,
oil prospectors roaming about, and the hostess sitting in her drawing-
room with the green-and-gold chairs, the lace curtains fine as bride
veils drifting a little; the young girls in jodhpurs are going out to
ride. Here, as everywhere else, there were no radios or gramophones
going, no telephones visible or ringing; and it seemed to me suddenly that this silence, the silence of a house in order, of people at
home, the silence of leisure, is the most desirable of all things we
have lost.

(21) At "Highland," descendants in the fourth generation stand
in the shade of the oaks planted, as the old House Book records, in
January 1832. The house is older. It has its share of drum tables,
fiddle-backed chairs, carved door-frames and wainscoting, but its

real beauty lies in the fall of light into the ample, square rooms, the rise of the stair tread, the energy and firmness of its structure. The paneled doors swing on their hand-forged hinges as they did the day they were hung there; the edge of the first doorstep—an immense log of cypress square-hewn—is as sharp as though feet had not stepped back and forth over it for one hundred and forty years.

(22) "Rosedown" is more formal, with its fish pool and eighteenth-century statuary set along the *allée,* and in a semicircle before the conventionally planted garden. The office still stands there, and the "slave bell" in its low wooden frame. The "slave bell" was the dinner-bell for the whole plantation. Above all, at "Rosedown," the Ancestors still rule, still lend their unquenchable life to a little world of fabulous old ladies and a strange overgrowth of knick-knacks sprouting like small, harmless fungi on a tree-trunk. Their portraits—Sully seems to have been the preferred painter—smile at you, or turn their attentive heads toward one another; as handsome and as gallant and elegantly dressed a set of young men and women as you would be apt to find blood-kin under one roof. "My great-great-grandfather," said the old, old lady, smiling back again at the high-headed, smooth-cheeked young beau in the frilled shirt-bosom and deep blue, sloping-shouldered coat. His eyes are the same bright hazel as her own. This was the only house in which the past lay like a fine dust in the air.

(23) Steamboats brought wealth and change to St. Francisville once, and oil may do it again. In that case, we are to suppose that new grand pianos would replace the old, square, black Steinways of 1840, as they had in turn replaced the harpsichords. There would be a great deal of shoring up, replacement, planting, pruning, and adding. There would be travel again, and humanistic education. The young people who went away cannot, alas, come back young, but the young there now would not have to go away.

(24) And what else would happen to this place, so occupied, so self-sufficient, so reassuringly solid and breathing? St. Francisville is not a monument, nor a *décor,* nor a wailing-wall for mourners for the past. It is a living town, moving at its own pace in a familiar

world. But it was comforting to take a last glance backward as we turned into the main highway, at Audubon's Happy Land, reflecting that, for the present, in the whole place, if you except the fruits of the earth and the picture postcards at "Rosedown," there was nothing, really nothing, for sale.

Questions

1. Which, if any, of the facts in the essay suggest that a woman rather than a man observed and selected the material?

2. Miss Porter says in Paragraph 11 that the mansions are "to be observed from every point of view," but she observes them from a particular one. What architectural standards are implicit in such phrases as "subtle proportions," "right for a hot climate," and "harmony" (Paragraph 12)? What values attach to such phrases as "fine log fires," "indestructible brick," and "old methods of mortising" (Paragraph 12)? Show that the same standards apply to Miss Porter's descriptions of "Waverly" and "Greenwood."

3. By what aesthetic, social, and moral standards might one condemn Southern mansions?

4. Why is oil a "sinister new treasure" to Miss Porter (Paragraph 17)? Is she merely a sentimentalist who is able to look at old-fashioned ways of making money—via slave labor and political murder—through rose-colored glasses?

5. Miss Porter implies that St. Francisville will not sell out to the oil prospectors and other money-makers. What is the evidence that it will?

6. Characterize Miss Porter's feelings about her scene. Are they solemn, restrained, or enthusiastic about the things she likes? Are they outraged, sardonic, flippant, or aloof about the things she doesn't like?

7. Read Norman Mailer's essay in this section, and describe one of Miss Porter's mansions in the way he would presumably see it.

8. Here is a modern house for Miss Porter. What are the things she would not like about it, and why? It has picture windows, front and back, looking out on the Connecticut Turnpike and on a private swimming pool. The interior is open-plan and spacious, and is all on one floor. The kitchen is furnished with automatic dish and clothes washers, garbage-disposal unit, and television set. The furniture is covered with dustproof plastic. There is an extremely efficient oil-heating system, with air-conditioner attached.

EQUAL IN PARIS

JAMES BALDWIN

James Baldwin (1924——) was born and raised in Harlem, and though he found it necessary to enter a period of self-imposed exile in Europe, mainly in Paris, it was to Harlem that he returned. His identity, as Negro and man, was to be discovered, he felt, in America. The record of that search, with its many frustrations and its remarkable insights into American life, is provided to some extent in his fiction (*Go Tell It on the Mountain, Giovanni's Room, Another Country*) but mainly in his essays, many of them autobiographical. They have been collected in *Notes of a Native Son, Nobody Knows My Name,* and *The Fire Next Time.*

(1) On the 19th of December, in 1949, when I had been living in Paris for a little over a year, I was arrested as a receiver of stolen goods and spent eight days in prison. My arrest came about through an American tourist whom I had met twice in New York, who had been given my name and address and told to look me up. I was then living on the top floor of a ludicrously grim hotel on the rue du Bac, one of those enormous dark, cold, and hideous establishments in which Paris abounds that seem to breathe forth, in their airless, humid, stone-cold halls, the weak light, scurrying chambermaids, and creaking stairs, an odor of gentility long long dead. The place was run by an ancient Frenchman dressed in an elegant black suit which was green with age, who cannot properly be described as bewildered or even as being in a state of shock, since he had really stopped breathing around 1910. There he sat at his desk in the

weirdly lit, fantastically furnished lobby, day in and day out, greeting each one of his extremely impoverished and *louche* lodgers with a stately inclination of the head that he had no doubt been taught in some impossibly remote time was the proper way for a *propriétaire* to greet his guests. If it had not been for his daughter, an extremely hardheaded *tricoteuse*—the inclination of *her* head was chilling and abrupt, like the downbeat of an ax—the hotel would certainly have gone bankrupt long before. It was said that this old man had not gone farther than the door of his hotel for thirty years, which was not at all difficult to believe. He looked as though the daylight would have killed him.

(2) I did not, of course, spend much of my time in this palace. The moment I began living in French hotels I understood the necessity of French cafés. This made it rather difficult to look me up, for as soon as I was out of bed I hopefully took notebook and fountain pen off to the upstairs room of the Flore, where I consumed rather a lot of coffee and, as evening approached, rather a lot of alcohol, but did not get much writing done. But one night, in one of the cafés of St. Germain des Près, I was discovered by this New Yorker and only because we found ourselves in Paris we immediately established the illusion that we had been fast friends back in the good old U.S.A. This illusion proved itself too thin to support an evening's drinking, but by that time it was too late. I had committed myself to getting him a room in my hotel the next day, for he was living in one of the nest of hotels near the Gare St. Lazare, where, he said, the *propriétaire* was a thief, his wife a repressed nymphomaniac, the chambermaids "pigs," and the rent a crime. Americans are always talking this way about the French and so it did not occur to me that he meant what he said or that he would take into his own hands the means of avenging himself on the French Republic. It did not occur to me, either, that the means which he *did* take could possibly have brought about such dire results, results which were not less dire for being also comic-opera.

(3) It came as the last of a series of disasters which had perhaps been made inevitable by the fact that I had come to Paris originally with a little over forty dollars in my pockets, nothing in the bank, and no grasp whatever of the French language. It developed,

shortly, that I had no grasp of the French character either. I considered the French an ancient, intelligent, and cultured race, which indeed they are. I did not know, however, that ancient glories imply, at least in the middle of the present century, present fatigue and, quite probably, paranoia; that there is a limit to the role of the intelligence in human affairs; and that no people come into possession of a culture without having paid a heavy price for it. This price they cannot, of course, assess, but it is revealed in their personalities and in their institutions. The very word "institutions," from my side of the ocean, where, it seemed to me, we suffered so cruelly from the lack of them, had a pleasant ring, as of safety and order and common sense; one had to come into contact with these institutions in order to understand that they were also outmoded, exasperating, completely impersonal, and very often cruel. Similarly, the personality which had seemed from a distance to be so large and free had to be dealt with before one could see that, if it was large, it was also inflexible and, for the foreigner, full of strange, high, dusty rooms which could not be inhabited. One had, in short, to come into contact with an alien culture in order to understand that a culture was not a community basket-weaving project, nor yet an act of God; was something neither desirable nor undesirable in itself, being inevitable, being nothing more or less than the recorded and visible effects on a body of people of the vicissitudes with which they had been forced to deal. And their great men are revealed as simply another of these vicissitudes, even if, quite against their will, the brief battle of their great men with them has left them richer.

(4) When my American friend left his hotel to move to mine, he took with him, out of pique, a bedsheet belonging to the hotel and put it in his suitcase. When he arrived at my hotel I borrowed the sheet, since my own were filthy and the chambermaid showed no sign of bringing me any clean ones, and put it on my bed. The sheets belonging to *my* hotel I put out in the hall, congratulating myself on having thus forced on the attention of the Grand Hôtel du Bac the unpleasant state of its linen. Thereafter, since, as it turned out, we kept very different hours—I got up at noon, when, as I gathered by meeting him on the stairs one day, he was only just getting in—my new-found friend and I saw very little of each other.

(5) On the evening of the 19th I was sitting thinking melancholy thoughts about Christmas and staring at the walls of my room. I imagine that I had sold something or that someone had sent me a Christmas present, for I remember that I had a little money. In those days in Paris, though I floated, so to speak, on a sea of acquaintances, I knew almost no one. Many people were eliminated from my orbit by virtue of the fact that they had more money than I did, which placed me, in my own eyes, in the humiliating role of a free-loader; and other people were eliminated by virtue of the fact that they enjoyed their poverty, shrilly insisting that this wretched round of hotel rooms, bad food, humiliating concierges, and unpaid bills was the Great Adventure. It couldn't, however, for me, end soon enough, this Great Adventure; there was a real question in my mind as to which would end soonest, the Great Adventure or me. This meant, however, that there were many evenings when I sat in my room, knowing that I couldn't work there, and not knowing what to do, or whom to see. On this particular evening I went down and knocked on the American's door.

(6) There were two Frenchmen standing in the room, who immediately introduced themselves to me as policemen; which did not worry me. I had got used to policemen in Paris bobbing up at the most improbable times and places, asking to see one's *carte d'identité*. These policemen, however, showed very little interest in my papers. They were looking for something else. I could not imagine what this would be and, since I knew I certainly didn't have it, I scarcely followed the conversation they were having with my friend. I gathered that they were looking for some kind of gangster and since I wasn't a gangster and knew that gangsterism was not, insofar as he had one, my friend's style, I was sure that the two policemen would presently bow and say *Merci, messieurs,* and leave. For by this time, I remember very clearly, I was dying to have a drink and go to dinner.

(7) I did not have a drink or go to dinner for many days after this, and when I did my outraged stomach promptly heaved everything up again. For now one of the policemen began to exhibit the most vivid interest in me and asked, very politely, if he might see my room. To which we mounted, making, I remember, the most civilized small talk on the way and even continuing it for some

moments after we were in the room in which there was certainly
nothing to be seen but the familiar poverty and disorder of that
precarious group of people of whatever age, race, country, calling,
or intention which Paris recognizes as *les étudiants* and sometimes,
more ironically and precisely, as *les nonconformistes.* Then he moved
to my bed, and in a terrible flash, not quite an instant before he
lifted the bedspread, I understood what he was looking for. We
looked at the sheet, on which I read, for the first time, lettered in
the most brilliant scarlet I have ever seen, the name of the hotel
from which it had been stolen. It was the first time the word *stolen*
entered my mind. I had certainly seen the hotel monogram the day
I put the sheet on the bed. It had simply meant nothing to me. In
New York I had seen hotel monograms on everything from silver
to soap and towels. Taking things from New York hotels was practically a custom, though, I suddenly realized, I had never known
anyone to take a *sheet.* Sadly, and without a word to me, the in-
spector took the sheet from the bed, folded it under his arm, and
we started back downstairs. I understood that I was under arrest.

(8) And so we passed through the lobby, four of us, two of us
very clearly criminal, under the eyes of the old man and his daughter,
neither of whom said a word, into the streets where a light rain was
falling. And I asked, in French, "But is this very serious?"

(9) For I was thinking, it is, after all, only a sheet, not even new.

(10) "No," said one of them. "It's not serious."

(11) "It's nothing at all," said the other.

(12) I took this to mean that we would receive a reprimand at
the police station and be allowed to go to dinner. Later on I concluded that they were not being hypocritical or even trying to comfort
us. They meant exactly what they said. It was only that they spoke
another language.

(13) In Paris everything is very slow. Also, when dealing with the
bureaucracy, the man you are talking to is never the man you have
to see. The man you have to see has just gone off to Belgium, or is
busy with his family, or has just discovered that he is a cuckold;
he will be in next Tuesday at three o'clock, or sometime in the
course of the afternoon, or possibly tomorrow, or, possibly, in the
next five minutes. But if he is coming in the next five minutes he will

be far too busy to be able to see you today. So that I suppose I was not really astonished to learn at the commissariat that nothing could possibly be done about us before The Man arrived in the morning. But no, we could not go off and have dinner and come back in the morning. Of course he knew that we *would* come back—that was not the question. Indeed, there was no question: we would simply have to stay there for the night.

(14) We were placed in a cell which rather resembled a chicken coop. It was now about seven in the evening and I relinquished the thought of dinner and began to think of lunch.

(15) I discouraged the chatter of my New York friend and this left me alone with my thoughts. I was beginning to be frightened and I bent all my energies, therefore, to keeping my panic under control. I began to realize that I was in a country I knew nothing about, in the hands of a people I did not understand at all. In a similar situation in New York I would have had some idea of what to do because I would have had some idea of what to expect. I am not speaking now of legality which, like most of the poor, I had never for an instant trusted, but of the temperament of the people with whom I had to deal. I had become very accomplished in New York at guessing and, therefore, to a limited extent manipulating to my advantage the reactions of the white world. But this was not New York. None of my old weapons could serve me here. I did not know what they saw when they looked at me. I knew very well what Americans saw when they looked at me and this allowed me to play endless and sinister variations on the role which they had assigned me; since I knew that it was, for them, of the utmost importance that they never be confronted with what, in their own personalities, made this role so necessary and gratifying to them, I knew that they could never call my hand or, indeed, afford to know what I was doing; so that I moved into every crucial situation with the deadly and rather desperate advantages of bitterly accumulated perception, of pride and contempt. This is an awful sword and shield to carry through the world, and the discovery that, in the game I was playing, I did myself a violence of which the world, at its most ferocious, would scarcely have been capable, was what had driven me out of New York. It was a strange feeling, in this situation, after a year in Paris,

to discover that my weapons would never again serve me as they had.

(16) It was quite clear to me that the Frenchmen in whose hands I found myself were no better or worse than their American counterparts. Certainly their uniforms frightened me quite as much, and their impersonality, and the threat, always very keenly felt by the poor, of violence, was as present in that commissariat as it had ever been for me in any police station. And I had seen, for example, what Paris policemen could do to Arab peanut vendors. The only difference here was that I did not understand these people, did not know what techniques their cruelty took, did not know enough about their personalities to see danger coming, to ward it off, did not know on what ground to meet it. That evening in the commissariat I was not a despised black man. They would simply have laughed at me if I had behaved like one. For them, I was an American. And here it was they who had the advantage, for that word, *Américain,* gave them some idea, far from inaccurate, of what to expect from me. In order to corroborate none of their ironical expectations I said nothing and did nothing—which was not the way any Frenchman, white or black, would have reacted. The question thrusting up from the bottom of my mind was not *what* I was, but *who.* And this question, since a *what* can get by with skill but a *who* demands resources, was my first real intimation of what humility must mean.

(17) In the morning it was still raining. Between nine and ten o'clock a black Citroën took us off to the Ile de la Cité, to the great, gray Préfecture. I realize now that the questions I put to the various policemen who escorted us were always answered in such a way as to corroborate what I wished to hear. This was not out of politeness, but simply out of indifference—or, possibly; an ironical pity—since each of the policemen knew very well that nothing would speed or halt the machine in which I had become entangled. They knew I did not know this and there was certainly no point in their telling me. In one way or another I would certainly come out at the other side—for they also knew that being found with a stolen bedsheet in one's possession was not a crime punishable by the guillotine. (They had the advantage over me there, too, for there were certainly moments later on when I was not so sure.) If I did *not* come out at

the other side—well, that was just too bad. So, to my question, put while we were in the Citroën—"Will it be over today?"—I received a *"Oui, bien sûr."* He was not lying. As it turned out, the *procès-verbal* was over that day. Trying to be realistic, I dismissed, in the Citroën, all thoughts of lunch and pushed my mind ahead to dinner.

(18) At the Préfecture we were first placed in a tiny cell, in which it was almost impossible either to sit or to lie down. After a couple of hours of this we were taken down to an office, where, for the first time, I encountered the owner of the bedsheet and where the *procès-verbal* took place. This was simply an interrogation, quite chillingly clipped and efficient (so that there was, shortly, no doubt in one's own mind that one *should* be treated as a criminal), which was recorded by a secretary. When it was over, this report was given to us to sign. One had, of course, no choice but to sign it, even though my mastery of written French was very far from certain. We were being held, according to the law in France, incommunicado, and all my angry demands to be allowed to speak to my embassy or to see a lawyer met with a stony *"Oui, oui. Plus tard."* The *procès-verbal* over, we were taken back to the cell, before which, shortly, passed the owner of the bedsheet. He said he hoped we had slept well, gave a vindictive wink, and disappeared.

(19) By this time there was only one thing clear: that we had no way of controlling the sequence of events and could not possibly guess what this sequence would be. It seemed to me, since what I regarded as the high point—the *procès-verbal*—had been passed and since the hotel-keeper was once again in possession of his sheet, that we might reasonably expect to be released from police custody in a matter of hours. We had been detained now for what would soon be twenty-four hours, during which time I had learned only that the official charge against me was *receleur.* My mental shifting, between lunch and dinner, to say nothing of the physical lack of either of these delights, was beginning to make me dizzy. The steady chatter of my friend from New York, who was determined to keep my spirits up, made me feel murderous; I was praying that some power would release us from this freezing pile of stone before the impulse became the act. And I was beginning to wonder what was happening in that beautiful city, Paris, which lived outside these walls. I won-

dered how long it would take before anyone casually asked, "But where's Jimmy? He hasn't been around"—and realized, knowing the people I knew, that it would take several days.

(20) Quite late in the afternoon we were taken from our cells; handcuffed, each to a separate officer; led through a maze of steps and corridors to the top of the building; fingerprinted; photographed. As in movies I had seen, I was placed against a wall, facing an old-fashioned camera, behind which stood one of the most completely cruel and indifferent faces I had ever seen, while someone next to me and, therefore, just outside my line of vision, read off in a voice from which all human feeling, even feeling of the most base description, had long since fled, what must be called my public characteristics —which, at that time and in that place, seemed anything but that. He might have been roaring to the hostile world secrets which I could barely, in the privacy of midnight, utter to myself. But he was only reading off my height, my features, my approximate weight, my color—that color which, in the United States, had often, odd as it may sound, been my salvation—the color of my hair, my age, my nationality. A light then flashed, the photographer and I staring at each other as though there was murder in our hearts, and then it was over. Handcuffed again, I was led downstairs to the bottom of the building, into a great enclosed shed in which had been gathered the very scrapings off the Paris streets. Old, old men, so ruined and old that life in them seemed really to prove the miracle of the quickening power of the Holy Ghost—for clearly their life was no longer their affair, it was no longer even their burden, they were simply the clay which had once been touched. And men not so old, with faces the color of lead and the consistency of oatmeal, eyes that made me think of stale *café-au-lait* spiked with arsenic, bodies which could take in food and water—any food and water—and pass it out, but which could not do anything more, except possibly, at midnight, along the riverbank where rats scurried, rape. And young men, harder and crueler than the Paris stones, older by far than I, their chronological senior by some five to seven years. And North Africans, old and young, who seemed the only living people in this place because they yet retained the grace to be bewildered. But they were not bewildered by being in this shed: they were simply bewildered

because they were no longer in North Africa. There was a great hole in the center of this shed, which was the common toilet. Near it, though it was impossible to get very far from it, stood an old man with white hair, eating a piece of camembert. It was at this point, probably, that thought, for me, stopped, that physiology, if one may say so, took over. I found myself incapable of saying a word, not because I was afraid I would cry but because I was afraid I would vomit. And I did not think any longer of the city of Paris but my mind flew back to that home from which I had fled. I was sure that I would never see it any more. And it must have seemed to me that my flight from home was the cruelest trick I had ever played on myself, since it had led me here, down to a lower point than any I could ever in my life have imagined—lower, far, than anything I had seen in that Harlem which I had so hated and so loved, the escape from which had soon become the greatest direction of my life. After we had been here an hour or so a functionary came and opened the door and called out our names. And I was sure that *this* was my release. But I was handcuffed again and led out of the Préfecture into the streets—it was dark now, it was still raining—and before the steps of the Préfecture stood the great police wagon, doors facing me, wide open. The handcuffs were taken off, I entered the wagon, which was peculiarly constructed. It was divided by a narrow aisle, and on each side of the aisle was a series of narrow doors. These doors opened on a narrow cubicle, beyond which was a door which opened onto another narrow cubicle: three or four cubicles, each private, with a locking door. I was placed in one of them; I remember there was a small vent just above my head which let in a little light. The door of my cubicle was locked from the outside. I had no idea where this wagon was taking me and, as it began to move, I began to cry. I suppose I cried all the way to prison, the prison called Fresnes, which is twelve kilometers outside of Paris.

(21) For reasons I have no way at all of understanding, prisoners whose last initial is A, B, or C are always sent to Fresnes; everybody else is sent to a prison called, rather cynically it seems to me, La Santé. I will, obviously, never be allowed to enter La Santé, but I was told by people who certainly seemed to know that it was infinitely more unbearable than Fresnes. This arouses in me, until today, a

positive storm of curiosity concerning what I promptly began to think of as The Other Prison. My colleague in crime, occurring lower in the alphabet, had been sent there and I confess that the minute he was gone I missed him. I missed him because he was not French and because he was the only person in the world who knew that the story I told was true.

(22) For, once locked in, divested of shoelaces, belt, watch, money, papers, nailfile, in a freezing cell in which both the window and the toilet were broken, with six other adventurers, the story I told of *l'affaire du drap de lit* elicited only the wildest amusement or the most suspicious disbelief. Among the people who shared my cell the first three days no one, it is true, had been arrested for anything much more serious—or, at least, not serious in my eyes. I remember that there was a boy who had stolen a knitted sweater from a *monoprix,* who would probably, it was agreed, receive a six-month sentence. There was an older man there who had been arrested for some kind of petty larceny. There were two North Africans, vivid, brutish, and beautiful, who alternated between gaiety and fury, not at the fact of their arrest but at the state of the cell. None poured as much emotional energy into the fact of their arrest as I did; they took it, as I would have liked to take it, as simply another unlucky happening in a very dirty world. For, though I had grown accustomed to thinking of myself as looking upon the world with a hard, penetrating eye, the truth was that they were far more realistic about the world than I, and more nearly right about it. The gap between us, which only a gesture I made could have bridged, grew steadily, during thirty-six hours, wider. I could not make any gesture simply because they frightened me. I was unable to accept my imprisonment as a fact, even as a temporary fact. I could not, even for a moment, accept my present companions as *my* companions. And they, of course, felt this and put it down, with perfect justice, to the fact that I was an American.

(23) There was nothing to do all day long. It appeared that we would one day come to trial but no one knew when. We were awakened at seven-thirty by a rapping on what I believe is called the Judas, that small opening in the door of the cell which allows the guards to survey the prisoners. At this rapping we rose from the

floor—we slept on straw pallets and each of us was covered with one thin blanket—and moved to the door of the cell. We peered through the opening into the center of the prison, which was, as I remember, three tiers high, all gray stone and gunmetal steel, precisely that prison I had seen in movies, except that, in the movies, I had not known that it was cold in prison. I had not known that when one's shoelaces and belt have been removed one is, in the strangest way, demoralized. The necessity of shuffling and the necessity of holding up one's trousers with one hand turn one into a rag doll. And the movies fail, of course, to give one any idea of what prison food is like. Along the corridor, at seven-thirty, came three men, each pushing before him a great garbage can, mounted on wheels. In the garbage can of the first was the bread—this was passed to one through the small opening in the door. In the can of the second was the coffee. In the can of the third was what was always called *la soupe,* a pallid paste of potatoes which had certainly been bubbling on the back of the prison stove long before that first, so momentous revolution. Naturally, it was cold by this time and, starving as I was, I could not eat it. I drank the coffee—which was not coffee—because it was hot, and spent the rest of the day, huddled in my blanket, munching on the bread. It was not the French bread one bought in bakeries. In the evening the same procession returned. At ten-thirty the lights went out. I had a recurring dream, each night, a nightmare which always involved my mother's fried chicken. At the moment I was about to eat it came the rapping at the door. Silence is really all I remember of those first three days, silence and the color gray.

(24) I am not sure now whether it was on the third or the fourth day that I was taken to trial for the first time. The days had nothing, obviously, to distinguish them from one another. I remember that I was very much aware that Christmas Day was approaching and I wondered if I was really going to spend Christmas Day in prison. And I remember that the first trial came the day before Christmas Eve.

(25) On the morning of the first trial I was awakened by hearing my name called. I was told, hanging in a kind of void between my mother's fried chicken and the cold prison floor, *"Vous préparez. Vous êtes extrait"*—which simply terrified me, since I did not know

what interpretation to put on the word *"extrait,"* and since my cellmates had been amusing themselves with me by telling terrible
stories about the inefficiency of French prisons, an inefficiency so
extreme that it had often happened that someone who was supposed
to be taken out and tried found himself on the wrong line and was
guillotined instead. The best way of putting my reaction to this is to
say that, though I knew they were teasing me, it was simply not
possible for me to totally *dis*believe them. As far as I was concerned,
once in the hands of the law in France, anything could happen. I
shuffled along with the others who were *extrait* to the center of the
prison, trying, rather, to linger in the office, which seemed the only
warm spot in the whole world, and found myself again in that dreadful wagon, and was carried again to the Ile de la Cité, this time to
the Palais de Justice. The entire day, except for ten minutes, was
spent in one of the cells, first waiting to be tried, then waiting to be
taken back to prison.

(26) For I was *not* tried that day. By and by I was handcuffed
and led through the halls, upstairs to the courtroom where I found
my New York friend. We were placed together, both stage-whisper-
ingly certain that this was the end of our ordeal. Nevertheless, while
I waited for our case to be called, my eyes searched the courtroom,
looking for a face I knew, hoping, anyway, that there was someone
who knew *me,* who would carry to someone outside the news that I
was in trouble. But there was no one I knew there and I had had
time to realize that there was probably only one man in Paris who
could help me, an American patent attorney for whom I had worked
as an office boy. He could have helped me because he had a quite
solid position and some prestige and would have testified that, while
working for him, I had handled large sums of money regularly,
which made it rather unlikely that I would stoop to trafficking in
bedsheets. However, he was somewhere in Paris, probably at this
very moment enjoying a snack and a glass of wine and as far as
the possibility of reaching him was concerned, he might as well
have been on Mars. I tried to watch the proceedings and to make
my mind a blank. But the proceedings were not reassuring. The boy,
for example, who had stolen the sweater *did* receive a six-month
sentence. It seemed to me that all the sentences meted out that day

were excessive; though, again, it seemed that all the people who were sentenced that day had made, or clearly were going to make, crime their career. This seemed to be the opinion of the judge, who scarcely looked at the prisoners or listened to them; it seemed to be the opinion of the prisoners, who scarcely bothered to speak in their own behalf; it seemed to be the opinion of the lawyers, state lawyers for the most part, who were defending them. The great impulse of the courtroom seemed to be to put these people where they could not be seen—and not because they were offended at the crimes, unless, indeed, they were offended that the crimes were so petty, but because they did not wish to know that their society could be counted on to produce, probably in greater and greater numbers, a whole body of people for whom crime was the only possible career. Any society inevitably produces its criminals, but a society at once rigid and unstable can do nothing whatever to alleviate the poverty of its lowest members, cannot present to the hypothetical young man at the crucial moment that so-well-advertised right path. And the fact, perhaps, that the French are the earth's least sentimental people and must also be numbered among the most proud aggravates the plight of their lowest, youngest, and unluckiest members, for it means that the idea of rehabilitation is scarcely real to them. I confess that this attitude on their part raises in me sentiments of exasperation, admiration, and despair, revealing as it does, in both the best and the worst sense, their renowned and spectacular hard-headedness.

(27) Finally our case was called and we rose. We gave our names. At the point that it developed that we were American the proceedings ceased, a hurried consultation took place between the judge and what I took to be several lawyers. Someone called out for an interpreter. The arresting officer had forgotten to mention our nationalities and there was, therefore, no interpreter in the court. Even if our French had been better than it was we would not have been allowed to stand trial without an interpreter. Before I clearly understood what was happening, I was handcuffed again and led out of the courtroom. The Trial had been set back for the 27th of December.

(28) I have sometimes wondered if I would *ever* have got out of prison if it had not been for the older man who had been arrested for the mysterious petty larceny. He was acquitted that day and when he

returned to the cell—for he could not be released until morning—he found me sitting numbly on the floor, having just been prevented, by the sight of a man, all blood, being carried back to *his* cell on a stretcher, from seizing the bars and screaming until they let me out. The sight of the man on the stretcher proved, however, that screaming would not do much for me. The petty-larceny man went around asking if he could do anything in the world outside for those he was leaving behind. When he came to me I, at first, responded, "No, nothing" —for I suppose I had by now retreated into the attitude, the earliest I remember, that of my father, which was simply (since I had lost his God) that nothing could help me. And I suppose I will remember with gratitude until I die the fact that the man now insisted: *"Mais, êtes-vous sûr?"* Then it swept over me that he was going *outside* and he instantly became my first contact since the Lord alone knew how long with the outside world. At the same time, I remember, I did not really believe that he would help me. There was no reason why he should. But I gave him the phone number of my attorney friend and my own name.

(29) So, in the middle of the next day, Christmas Eve, I shuffled downstairs again, to meet my visitor. He looked extremely well fed and sane and clean. He told me I had nothing to worry about any more. Only not even he could do anything to make the mill of justice grind any faster. He would, however, send me a lawyer of his acquaintance who would defend me on the 27th, and he would himself, along with several other people, appear as a character witness. He gave me a package of Lucky Strikes (which the turnkey took from me on the way upstairs) and said that, though it was doubtful that there would be any celebration in the prison, he would see to it that I got a fine Christmas dinner when I got out. And this, somehow, seemed very funny. I remember being astonished at the discovery that I was actually laughing. I was, too, I imagine, also rather disappointed that my hair had not turned white, that my face was clearly not going to bear any marks of tragedy, disappointed at bottom, no doubt, to realize, facing him in that room, that far worse things had happened to most people and that, indeed, to paraphrase my mother, if this was the worst thing that ever happened to me I could consider myself among the luckiest people ever to be born. He injected—my visitor—into my

solitary nightmare common sense, the world, and the hint of blacker things to come.

(30) The next day, Christmas, unable to endure my cell, and feeling that, after all, the day demanded a gesture, I asked to be allowed to go to Mass, hoping to hear some music. But I found myself, for a freezing hour and a half, locked in exactly the same kind of cubicle as in the wagon which had first brought me to prison, peering through a slot placed at the level of the eye of an old Frenchman, hatted, overcoated, muffled, and gloved, preaching in this language which I did not understand, to this row of wooden boxes, the story of Jesus Christ's love for men.

(31) The next day, the 26th, I spent learning a peculiar kind of game, played with match-sticks, with my cellmates. For, since I no longer felt that I would stay in this cell forever, I was beginning to be able to make peace with it for a time. On the 27th I went again to trial and, as had been predicted, the case against us was dismissed. The story of the *drap de lit,* finally told, caused great merriment in the courtroom, whereupon my friend decided that the French were "great." I was chilled by their merriment, even though it was meant to warm me. It could only remind me of the laughter I had often heard at home, laughter which I had sometimes deliberately elicited. This laughter is the laughter of those who consider themselves to be at a safe remove from all the wretched, for whom the pain of the living is not real. I had heard it so often in my native land that I had resolved to find a place where I would never hear it any more. In some deep, black, stony, and liberating way, my life, in my own eyes, began during that first year in Paris, when it was borne in on me that this laughter is universal and never can be stilled.

Questions

1. One fact lies at the heart of this essay. What is it, and what, briefly, is both its importance and unimportance?

2. Baldwin does not tell us such facts as the sort of writing that he did, the individual character of the French police officers, the details of the conduct of the second trial. Justify these omissions.

3. In his account of his experience in New York (Paragraph 15), Bald-

win does not give any precise details about his conversations with white people. What do you suppose those conversations, and the thoughts behind them, were like?

4. Paragraph 20 consists largely of factual details about the photographing process, the prisoners, and the police wagon. What feelings on Baldwin's part are connected to these facts—created by them, or expressed by them?

5. Describe Baldwin's mental experience—what he thought, felt, and learned. Avoid entirely, if possible, any reference to the external facts of his situation, arrest, and trial.

6. Do you think that Baldwin would subscribe to either of the following propositions: prisons are built by people who are able to laugh; slum hotels are run by people who are able to laugh.

7. Baldwin had reason to be angry about his experience with the French police. What is the chief feeling that comes through? Illustrate.

8. The controlling thought of the essay concerns the images people have of themselves and of others. What different types of people does Baldwin mention, and what does he suggest are their individual images of themselves and of others? Write a discussion of the issue.

MINORITIES

NORMAN MAILER

Norman Mailer (1923—) was born in New York City and was educated at Harvard. While serving in World War II, he began writing *The Naked and the Dead,* a long and impressive first novel. His subsequent fiction includes *Barbary Shore, The Deer Park,* and *An American Dream.* But much of his energy has gone into other prose forms, which, between novels, have allowed him, as he has said, a continuous confrontation with the reader. When collecting this work—in *Advertisements for Myself, The Presidential Papers,* and *Cannibals and Christians*— Mailer provides a series of linking essays to give coherence to the individual volumes. One such essay is presented here.

(1) The modern American politician—read: the Democratic or Republican liberal—often begins his career with a modest passion to defend the rights of minorities. By the time he is successful, his passion has been converted to platitude.

(2) Minority groups are the artistic nerves of a republic, and like any phenomenon which has to do with art, they are profoundly divided. They are both themselves and the mirror of their culture as it reacts upon them. They are themselves and the negative truth of themselves. No white man, for example, can hate the Negro race with the same passionate hatred and detailed detestation that each Negro feels for himself and for his people; no anti-Semite can begin to comprehend the malicious analysis of his soul which every Jew indulges every day.

(3) For decades the Jews have been militant for their rights, since the Second War the Negroes have emerged as an embattled and disci-

Reprinted by permission of G. P. Putnam's Sons from *The Presidential Papers* by Norman Mailer. © 1960, 1961, 1962, 1963 by Norman Mailer.

plined minority. It is thus characteristic of both races that they have a more intense awareness of their own value and their own lack of value than the awareness of the white Anglo-Saxon Protestant for himself. Unlike the Protestant of the center, minorities have a nature which is polarized. So it is natural that their buried themes, precisely those preoccupations which are never mentioned by minority action groups like the Anti-Defamation League or the NAACP, are charged with paradox, with a search for psychic extremes. To a Protestant, secure in the middle of American life, God and the Devil, magic, death and eternity, are matters outside himself. He may contemplate them but he does not habitually absorb them into the living tissue of his brain. Whereas the exceptional member of any minority group feels as if he possesses God and the Devil within himself, that the taste of his own death is already in his cells, that his purchase on eternity rises and falls with the calm or cowardice of his actions. It is a life exposed to the raw living nerve of anxiety, and rare is the average Jew or Negro who can bear it for long—so the larger tendency among minorities is to manufacture a mediocre personality which is a dull replica of the manners of the white man in power. Nothing can be more conformist, more Square, more profoundly depressing than the Jew-in-the-suburb, or the Negro as member of the Black Bourgeoisie. It is the price they pay for the fact that not all self-hatred is invalid—the critical faculty turned upon oneself can serve to create a personality which is exceptional, which mirrors the particular arts and graces of the white gentry, but this is possible only if one can live with one's existential nerve exposed. Man's personality rises to a level of higher and more delicate habits only if he is willing to engage a sequence of painful victories and cruel defeats in his expedition through the locks and ambushes of social life. One does not copy the manner of someone superior; rather one works an art upon it which makes it suitable for oneself. Direct imitation of a superior manner merely produces a synthetic manner. The collective expression of this in a minority group is nothing other than assimilation.

(4) To the degree each American Jew and American Negro is assimilated he is colorless, a part of a collective nausea which is encysted into the future. The problem in a democracy is not to assimilate minorities but to avoid stifling them as they attain their equality. If the Jews and Negroes attain a brilliant equality with the white Anglo-Saxon

Protestant and the Irish Catholic, then America will be different. Whatever it will become, it will be different from anything we can conceive. Whereas if the Negro and Jew are assimilated into the muted unimaginative level of present-day American life, then America will be very much like it is now, only worse. The problem is similar to the difficulty in dealing with juvenile delinquents—one can pacify them by any one of a number of unimaginative programs and be left with a human material which is apathetic if indeed not anchored to moronic expectations; or one can search for arts which transmute violence into heroic activity. An inflammation or rent in the body can heal in such a way that the limb or organ offers new powers of coordination which did not exist before; equally the inflammation can subside to a chronic leaden dullness of function.

(5) So with minorities, one must look for more than the insurance of their rights—one must search to liberate the art which is trapped in the thousand acts of perception which embody their self-hatred, for self-hatred ignored must corrode the roots of one's past and leave one marooned in an alien culture. The liberal premise—that Negroes and Jews are like everybody else once they are given the same rights—can only obscure the complexity, the intensity, and the psychotic brilliance of a minority's inner life.

(6) The pieces which follow [in *The Presidential Papers*] involve certain preoccupations of the minority, but what they have to say about Jews and Negroes is special, for they deal with the extreme ends of the spectrum. The Hasidim embodied the most passionate and individual expression of Jewish life in many centuries, the Negro as an actor, or to anticipate the next paper, the Negro as heavyweight champion and contender is certainly as exceptional. But the argument of existential politics might be that one never understands a people or a time by contemplating a common denominator, for the average man in a minority group is no longer a member of that minority—he is instead a social paste which has been compounded out of the grinding stone of the society which contains him. He is not his own authentic expression. By this logic, the average Negro or Jew is not so much a black man or a Semite as a mediocre ersatz Protestant. That does not mean he is altogether an inferior man of the center—in his suppressed nerve, in his buried heart, exist the themes which the exceptional man

of the minority can embody. So a responsible politician, a President, let us say, professionally sensitive to minority groups, cannot begin to be of real stature to that minority until he becomes aware of what is most extraordinary in a people as well as what is most pressing and ubiquitous in their need. The Jews have staggered along for centuries wondering to their primitive horror whether they have betrayed God once in the desert or again twice with Christ: so they are obsessed in their unconscious nightmare with whether they belong to a God of righteousness or a Devil of treachery—their flight from this confrontation has rushed to produce a large part of that mechanistic jargon which now rules American life in philosophy, psychoanalysis, social action, productive process, and the arts themselves. The Negro, secretly fixed upon magic—that elixir of nature which seems to mediate between God and Devil—has never made his peace with Christianity, or mankind. The Negro in the most protected recesses of his soul still does not know if he is a part of mankind, or a special embodiment of nature suspended between society and the gods. As the Negro enters civilization, Faust may be his archetype, even as the Jew has fled Iago * as the despised image of himself.

Questions

1. Mailer deals in ideas (opinions) that he presents as facts. Nevertheless he offers many unquestionable facts, such as the emergence of Negroes as a disciplined minority since World War II. Isolate the major unquestionable facts in the first three paragraphs and decide to what extent the argument is built upon them.

2. Mailer says that "minority groups are the artistic nerves of a republic." This is an often-heard opinion, based upon facts such as the profusion and importance of Negro music in American culture. Select two of Mailer's other opinions and back them up with the sort of factual detail you assume he had in mind.

3. Choose a well-known liberal politician of recent years, and try to discover from an extended biographical account of him whether the course of his career follows the pattern that Mailer describes in his first paragraph. Possibilities: Robert F. Kennedy, J. William Fulbright, Richard Neuberger.

* Not Shylock. *Iago.*

4. A few very general ideas cover the individual ideas that Mailer is discussing. One of them is that artistic creativity depends to an important extent upon social conditions. What are one or two others?

5. Mailer's views are probably offensive to many Jews, Negroes, and white Anglo-Saxon Protestants of the center. Does he seem to want to ram his ideas down their throats, to sugarcoat these ideas, or what? Describe the general tone of his discussion.

6. From the views he expresses here, what would you imagine Mailer's attitudes to be toward the admission of China to the United Nations, the United Nations itself, aid to underdeveloped countries? Explain.

7. Read James Baldwin's essay in this section. Does it suggest that Mailer is correct in his opinion of how Negroes feel about themselves? Write a discussion of the issue.

IMAGINATION

GEORGE SANTAYANA

Born in Madrid, of Spanish parents, George Santayana (1863–1952) was brought to the United States at the age of nine, attended public schools in Boston, and then studied at Harvard, where he subsequently taught philosophy for twenty-two years, until his resignation in 1912. From then until his death, he lived in different parts of Europe, much of the time in Rome, lecturing and writing on literature, aesthetics, metaphysics, religion, and politics. Among his better-known works are *The Sense of Beauty, The Life of Reason* (in five volumes), and *Persons and Places,* a series of autobiographical essays. He also wrote several volumes of poetry, one long novel, *The Last Puritan,* and a number of translations.

(1) Men are ruled by imagination: imagination makes them into men, capable of madness and of immense labors. We work dreaming. Consider what dreams must have dominated the builders of the Pyramids—dreams geometrical, dreams funereal, dreams of resurrection, dreams of outdoing the pyramid of some other Pharaoh! What dreams occupy that fat man in the street, toddling by under his shabby hat and bedraggled rain-coat? Perhaps he is in love; perhaps he is a Catholic, and imagines that early this morning he has partaken of the body and blood of Christ; perhaps he is a revolutionist, with the millennium in his heart and a bomb in his pocket. The spirit bloweth where it listeth; the wind of inspiration carries our dreams before it and constantly refashions them like clouds. Nothing could be madder, more irresponsible, more dangerous than this guidance of men by dreams. What saves us is the fact that our imaginations, groundless and chimerical

From *Soliloquies in England* by George Santayana. Reprinted by permission of Constable & Co., Ltd.

as they may seem, are secretly suggested and controlled by shrewd old instincts of our animal nature, and by continual contact with things. The shock of sense, breaking in upon us with a fresh irresistible image, checks wayward imagination and sends it rebounding in a new direction, perhaps more relevant to what is happening in a world outside.

(2) When I speak of being governed by imagination, of course I am indulging in a figure of speech, in an ellipsis; in reality we are governed by that perpetual latent process within us by which imagination itself is created. Actual imaginings—the cloud-like thoughts drifting by—are not masters over themselves nor over anything else. They are like the sound of chimes in the night; they know nothing of whence they came, how they will fall out, or how long they will ring. There is a mechanism in the church tower; there was a theme in the composer's head; there is a beadle who has been winding the thing up. The sound wafted to us, muffled by distance and a thousand obstacles, is but the last lost emanation of this magical bell-ringing. Yet in our dream it is all in all; it is what first entertains and absorbs the mind. Imagination, when it chimes within us, apparently of itself, is no less elaborately grounded; it is a last symptom, a rolling echo, by which we detect and name the obscure operation that occasions it; and not this echo in its aesthetic impotence, but the whole operation whose last witness it is, receives in science the name of imagination, and may be truly said to rule the human world.

(3) This extension of names is inevitable although unfortunate, because language and perception are poetical before they become scientific, if they ever do; as Aristotle observes that the word anger is used indifferently for two different things: dialectically, or as I call it, imaginatively, for the desire for revenge, but physically for a boiling of the humours. And utterly different as these two things are in quality, no great inconvenience results from giving them the same name, because historically they are parts of the same event. Nature has many dimensions at once, and whenever we see anything happen, much else is happening there which we cannot see. Whilst dreams entertain us, the balance of our character is shifting beneath: we are growing while we sleep. The young think in one way, the drunken in another, and the dead not at all; and I imagine—for I have imagination myself—that they do not die because they stop thinking, but they stop thinking be-

cause they die. How much veering and luffing before they make that
port! The brain of man, William James used to say, has a hair-trigger
organization. His life is terribly experimental. He is perilously dependent on the oscillations of a living needle, imagination, that never
points to the true north.

(4) There are books in which the footnotes, or the comments
scrawled by some reader's hand in the margin, are more interesting
than the text. The world is one of these books. The reciprocal interference of magnetic fields (which I understand is the latest conception
of matter) may compose a marvellous moving pattern; but the chief
interest to us of matter lies in its fertility in producing minds and pre-
senting recognizable phenomena to the senses; and the chief interest
of any scientific notion of its intrinsic nature lies in the fact that, if not
literally true, it may liberate us from more misleading conceptions.
Did we have nothing but electrical physics to think of, the nightmare
would soon become intolerable. But a hint of that kind, like a hasty
glance into the crater of a volcano, sends a wholesome shudder
through our nerves; we realize how thin is the crust we build on, how
mythical and remote from the minute and gigantic scale of nature are
the bright images we seem to move among, all cut out and fitted to our
human stature. Yet these bright images are our natural companions,
and if we do not worship them idolatrously nor petrify them into sub-
stances, forgetting the nimble use of them in mental discourse, which
is where they belong, they need not be more misleading to us, even for
scientific purposes, than are words or any other symbols.

(5) It is fortunate that the material world, whatever may be its intrinsic structure or substance, falls to our apprehension into such
charming units. There is the blue vault of heaven, there are the twin-
kling constellations, there are the mountains, trees, and rivers, and
above all those fascinating unstable unities which we call animals and
persons; magnetic fields I am quite ready to believe them, for such in
a vast vague way I feel them to be, but individual bodies they will
remain to my sensuous imagination, and dramatic personages to my
moral sense. They, too, are animate: they, too, compose a running
commentary on things and on one another, adding their salacious
footnotes to the dull black letter of the world. Many of them are hardly

aware of their own wit; knowing they are but commentators, they are intent on fidelity and unconscious of invention. Yet against their will they gloss everything, willy-nilly we are all scholiasts together. Heaven forbid that I should depreciate this prodigious tome of nature, or question in one jot or tittle the absolute authority of its Author; but it is like an encyclopedia in an infinite number of volumes, or a directory with the addresses of everybody that ever lived. We may dip into it on occasion in search of some pertinent fact, but it is not a book to read; its wealth is infinite, but so is its monotony; it is not composed in our style nor in our language, we could not have written one line of it. Yet the briefest text invites reflection, and we may spin a little homily out of it in the vernacular for our own edification.

(6) In the *Mahabharata,* a learned friend tells me, a young champion armed for the combat and about to rush forward between the two armies drawn up in battle array, stops for a moment to receive a word of counsel from his spiritual adviser—and that word occupies the next eighteen books of the epic; after which the battle is allowed to proceed. These Indian poets had spiritual minds, they measured things by their importance to the spirit, not to the eye. They despised verisimilitude and aesthetic proportion; they despised existence, the beauties of which they felt exquisitely nevertheless, and to which their imagination made such stupendous additions. I honor their courage in bidding the sun stand still, not that they might thoroughly vanquish an earthly enemy, but that they might wholly clarify their own soul. For this better purpose the sun need not stand still materially. For the spirit, time is an elastic thing. Fancy is quick and brings the widest vistas to a focus in a single instant. After the longest interval of oblivion and death, it can light up the same image in all the greenness of youth; and if cut short, as it were at Pompeii, in the midst of a word, it can, ages after, without feeling the break, add the last syllable. Imagination changes the scale of everything, and makes a thousand patterns of the woof of nature, without disturbing a single thread. Or rather—since it is nature itself that imagines—it turns to music what was only strain; as if the universal vibration, suddenly ashamed of having been so long silent and useless, had burst into tears and laughter at its own folly, and in so doing had become wise.

Questions

1. In his first paragraph Santayana discusses the relationship between imagination and the "world outside." Restate that relationship in your own words.

2. In Paragraphs 2 and 3, Santayana explains what he means by imagination. How does his definition differ from the ordinary definition? What specifically does he mean by "sensuous imagination" (Paragraph 5), and what relationship does he see between sensuous imagination and the material world?

3. Why is it that for Santayana the world is a book "in which the footnotes, or the comments scrawled by some reader's hand in the margin, are more interesting than the text"?

4. Santayana alludes to a lot of facts (in the ordinary sense), but in a generalized, condensed way. It is not to the specific lover, Catholic, or revolutionary that he refers with specific facts about his individual belief and behavior but rather to stereotyped figures. Point out other instances of this.

5. Santayana's essay is one of thought more than of fact. What are some of his chief ideas—aside from his main idea that the world is ruled by imagination—and what are some of the facts by which he supports those ideas?

6. If Santayana were to report on a student riot, what do you suppose his account would be like? Why? Write an opening paragraph of such an account.

7. Assume that someone else holds the same general views as Santayana. What distinguishes the way in which Santayana holds them—is he intense or detached? Amused or cynical? Objective or subjective? Argue from evidence in the essay.

REMINISCENCES OF CHILDHOOD

Dylan Thomas (1914–1953) published his first book of poetry
when he was twenty and his second two years later. He then
did odd jobs, spent some time as a journalist, and worked for
the British Broadcasting Company. In marked contrast to the
intellectualized manner of many of his contemporaries, his
writings are impassioned and highly subjective; often they
show the influence of his native South Wales. By the time of
his early death, he had established himself as a poet of importance and as an erratic and flamboyant public figure, with a
particularly large following in the United States, where he is
remembered for his exuberant public readings. His prose has
been collected in *Portrait of the Artist As a Young Dog* and
Quite Early One Morning. Shortly before his death he wrote a
verse play, *Under Milk Wood*.

(1) I like very much people telling me about their childhood, but
they'll have to be quick or else I'll be telling them about mine.

(2) I was born in a large Welsh town at the beginning of the Great
War—an ugly, lovely town (or so it was and is to me), crawling,
sprawling by a long and splendid curving shore where truant boys and
sandfield boys and old men from nowhere, beachcombed, idled and
paddled, watched the dock-bound ships or the ships steaming away
into wonder and India, magic and China, countries bright with or-
anges and loud with lions; threw stones into the sea for the barking
outcast dogs; made castles and forts and harbours and race tracks in
the sand; and on Saturday summer afternoons listened to the brass

band, watched the Punch and Judy, or hung about on the fringes of the crowd to hear the fierce religious speakers who shouted at the sea, as though it were wicked and wrong to roll in and out like that, white-horsed and full of fishes.

(3) One man, I remember, used to take off his hat and set fire to his hair every now and then, but I do not remember what it proved, if it proved anything at all, except that he was a very interesting man.

(4) This sea-town was my world; outside a strange Wales, coal-pitted, mountained, river-run, full, so far as I knew, of choirs and football teams and sheep and storybook tall hats and red flannel petticoats, moved about its business which was none of mine.

(5) Beyond that unknown Wales with its wild names like peals of bells in the darkness, and its mountain men clothed in the skins of animals perhaps and always singing, lay England which was London and the country called the Front, from which many of our neighbours never came back. It was a country to which only young men travelled.

(6) At the beginning, the only "front" I knew was the little lobby before our front door. I could not understand how so many people never returned from there, but later I grew to know more, though still without understanding, and carried a wooden rifle in the park and shot down the invisible unknown enemy like a flock of wild birds. And the park itself was a world within the world of the sea-town. Quite near where I lived, so near that on summer evenings I could listen in my bed to the voices of older children playing ball on the sloping paper-littered bank, the park was full of terrors and treasures. Though it was only a little park, it held within its borders of old tall trees, notched with our names and shabby from our climbing, as many secret places, caverns and forests, prairies and deserts, as a country somewhere at the end of the sea.

(7) And though we would explore it one day, armed and desperate, from end to end, from the robbers' den to the pirates' cabin, the high-wayman's inn to the cattle ranch, or the hidden room in the under-growth, where we held beetle races, and lit the wood fires and roasted potatoes and talked about Africa, and the makes of motor cars, yet still the next day, it remained as unexplored as the Poles—a country just born and always changing.

(8) There were many secret societies but you could belong only to one; and in blood or red ink, and a rusty pocketknife, with, of course, an instrument to remove stones from horses' feet, you signed your name at the foot of a terrible document, swore death to all the other societies, crossed your heart that you would divulge no secret and that if you did, you would consent to torture by slow fire, and undertook to carry out by yourself a feat of either daring or endurance. You could take your choice: would you climb to the top of the tallest and most dangerous tree, and from there hurl stones and insults at grown-up passers-by, especially postmen, or any other men in uniform? Or would you ring every doorbell in the terrace, not forgetting the doorbell of the man with the red face who kept dogs and ran fast? Or would you swim in the reservoir, which was forbidden and had angry swans, or would you eat a whole old jam jar full of mud?

(9) There were many more alternatives. I chose one of endurance and for half an hour, it may have been longer or shorter, held up off the ground a very heavy broken pram we had found in a bush. I thought my back would break and the half hour felt like a day, but I preferred it to braving the red face and the dogs, or to swallowing tadpoles.

(10) We knew every inhabitant of the park, every regular visitor, every nursemaid, every gardener, every old man. We knew the hour when the alarming retired policeman came in to look at the dahlias and the hour when the old lady arrived in the Bath chair with six Pekinese, and a pale girl to read aloud to her. I think she read the newspaper, but we always said she read the *Wizard*. The face of the old man who sat summer and winter on the bench looking over the reservoir, I can see clearly now and I wrote a poem long long after I'd left the park and the sea-town called:

The Hunchback in the Park

The hunchback in the park
A solitary mister
Propped between trees and water
From the opening of the garden lock
That lets the trees and water enter
Until the Sunday sombre ball at dark

Eating bread from a newspaper
Drinking water from the chained cup
That the children filled with gravel
In the fountain basin where I sailed my ship
Slept at night in a dog kennel
But nobody chained him up.

Like the park birds he came early
Like the water he sat down
And Mister they called Hey mister
The truant boys from the town
Running when he had heard them clearly
On out of sound

Past lake and rockery
Laughing when he shook his paper
Hunchbacked in mockery
Through the loud zoo of the willow groves
Dodging the park-keeper
With his stick that picked up leaves.

And the old dog sleeper
Alone between nurses and swans
While the boys among willows
Made the tigers jump out of their eyes
To roar on the rockery stones
And the groves were blue with sailors

Made all day until bell-time
A woman figure without fault
Straight as a young elm
Straight and tall from his crooked bones
That she might stand in the night
After the locks and the chains

All night in the unmade park
After the railings and shrubberies

The birds the grass the trees and the lake
And the wild boys innocent as strawberries
Had followed the hunchback
To his kennel in the dark.

(11) And that park grew up with me; that small world widened as I learned its secrets and boundaries, as I discovered new refuges and ambushes in its woods and jungles; hidden homes and lairs for the multitudes of imagination, for cowboys and Indians, and the tall terrible half-people who rode on nightmares through my bedroom. But it was not the only world—that world of rockery, gravel path, play-bank, bowling green, bandstands, reservoir, dahlia garden, where an ancient keeper, known as Smoky, was the whiskered snake in the grass one must keep off. There was another world where with my friends I used to dawdle on half holidays along the bent and Devon-facing seashore, hoping for gold watches or the skull of a sheep or a message in a bottle to be washed up with the tide; and another where we used to wander whistling through the packed streets, stale as station sandwiches, round the impressive gasworks and the slaughter house, past by the blackened monuments and the museum that should have been in a museum. Or we scratched at a kind of cricket on the bald and cindery surface of the recreation ground, or we took a tram that shook like an iron jelly down to the gaunt pier, there to clamber under the pier, hanging perilously onto its skeleton legs or to run along the end where patient men with the seaward eyes of the dockside unemployed capped and mufflered, dangling from their mouths pipes that had long gone out, angled over the edge for unpleasant tasting fish.

(12) Never was there such a town as ours, I thought, as we fought on the sandhills with rough boys or dared each other to climb up the scaffolding of half-built houses soon to be called Laburnum Beaches. Never was there such a town, I thought, for the smell of fish and chips on Saturday evenings; for the Saturday afternoon cinema matinees where we shouted and hissed our threepences away; for the crowds in the streets with leeks in their hats on international nights; for the park, the inexhaustible and mysterious, bushy red-Indian hiding park where the hunchback sat alone and the groves were blue with sailors.

The memories of childhood have no order, and so I remember that never was there such a dame school as ours, so firm and kind and smelling of galoshes, with the sweet and fumbled music of the piano lessons drifting down from upstairs to the lonely schoolroom, where only the sometimes tearful wicked sat over undone sums, or to repeat a little crime—the pulling of a girl's hair during geography, the sly shin kick under the table during English literature. Behind the school was a narrow lane where only the oldest and boldest threw pebbles at windows, scuffled and boasted, fibbed about their relations—

(13) "My father's got a chauffeur."

(14) "What's he want a chauffeur for? He hasn't got a car."

(15) "My father's the richest man in the town."

(16) "My father's the richest man in Wales."

(17) "My father owns the world."

(18) And swapped gob-stoppers for slings, old knives for marbles, kite strings for foreign stamps.

(19) The lane was always the place to tell your secrets; if you did not have any, you invented them. Occasionally now I dream that I am turning out of school into the lane of confidences when I say to the boys of my class, "At last, I have a real secret."

(20) "What is it—what is it?"

(21) "I can fly."

(22) And when they do not believe me, I flap my arms and slowly leave the ground only a few inches at first, then gaining air until I fly waving my cap level with the upper windows of the school, peering in until the mistress at the piano screams and the metronome falls to the ground and stops, and there is no more time.

(23) And I fly over the trees and chimneys of my town, over the dockyards skimming the masts and funnels, over Inkerman Street, Sebastopol Street, and the street where all the women wear men's caps, over the trees of the everlasting park, where a brass band shakes the leaves and sends them showering down on to the nurses and the children, the cripples and the idlers, and the gardeners, and the shouting boys: over the yellow seashore, and the stone-chasing dogs, and the old men, and the singing sea.

(24) The memories of childhood have no order, and no end.

Questions

1. The facts that Thomas uses in his essay include lies, beliefs, fears, misunderstanding, and dreams. Explain and illustrate.

2. Thomas is writing about both the outer and the inner worlds of his childhood. Do the following items belong to one or both worlds: "dockbound ships" (Paragraph 2); "football teams and sheep and storybook tall hats" (Paragraph 4); "secret places, caverns and forests" (Paragraph 6); "my father's got a chauffeur" (Paragraph 13)?

3. Thomas says at the end that "the memories of childhood have no order, and no end." Does his material really illustrate this idea? Explain.

4. Thomas remembers his childhood with affection. Show that this feeling governs the description even of material that might ordinarily seem unpleasant.

5. Does Thomas think childhood is mainly painful, romantic, disordered, thoughtless, absurd, or what? Choose one or two adjectives (not necessarily from those given) that seem most adequate to express his view, and show how they cover several aspects of his material.

6. Thomas' language and sentence structure are both distinctive. Determine their primary characteristics, and consider what the essay would have been like had it been written in an opposite manner.

7. In the essay preceding this one, George Santayana says that "men are ruled by imagination." Do you suppose that he and Thomas are essentially in agreement? Read Santayana's essay if you have not already, and write a discussion of this point.

UNITY, TRANSITION, AND DEVELOPMENT

The writer who has prepared his subject thoroughly still has to write his essay. And if writing an essay were like filling a bag, his task would be easy. But an essay has to be composed, and its parts have to be composed. One of those parts is the paragraph, and knowing how to write a good paragraph will take the writer a long way toward writing a good essay. A well-written paragraph will display certain qualities—unity, transition, and development are usually among them. Unity in a paragraph means singleness of subject. Consider the following paragraph in which John Millington Synge describes some islanders off Ireland.

It is likely that much of the intelligence and charm of these people is due to the absence of any division of labor, and to the correspondingly wide development of each individual, whose varied knowledge and skill necessitates considerable activity of mind. Each man can speak two languages. He is a skilled fisherman, and can manage a curragh with extraordinary nerve and dexterity. He can farm simply, burn kelp, cut out pampooties, mend nets, build and thatch a house, and make a cradle or a coffin. His work changes with the seasons in a way that keeps him free from the dullness that comes to people who have always the same occupation. The danger of his life on the sea gives him the alertness of the primitive hunter, and the long nights he spends fishing in his curragh bring him some of the emotions that are thought peculiar to men who have lived with the arts.*

The first sentence asserts that the islanders possess intelligence and charm in part because there is no division of labor. The second sentence illustrates intelligence in language. The third sentence illustrates intelligence in fishing and suggests both intelligence and charm in the nerve and dexterity of the activity. The fourth sentence illustrates intelligence in several land activities, and in so doing it also illustrates the variety of tasks at which the islanders labor. The fifth sentence illustrates variety of labor and generally restates the first sentence in saying that the seasonal changes in labor make for freedom from dullness.

* From *The Complete Works of John M. Synge.* Copyright © 1935 by The Modern Library, Inc. Reprinted by permission of Random House, Inc.

The last sentence repeats, with some elaboration, the illustration in the third sentence. Thus the paragraph as a whole consists of an assertion and illustrations to support it. It is a unified paragraph, with a single subject, which is expressed by the assertion in the first sentence. A sentence that contains the idea of a paragraph is called a *topic sentence*. As the topic sentence, Synge's first sentence provides the broad statement of the view that is restated in the fifth sentence, and it is the basis for the illustrations in the second, third, fourth, and last sentences.

Topic sentences are indicators of paragraph unity. Sometimes they occur in the middle or at the end of the paragraph instead of at the beginning. Sometimes they exist as fragments of a sentence or may comprise two or three sentences, each one covering part of a paragraph. Occasionally they turn up in the last line of the preceding paragraph or in the first line of the next one. Or sometimes they are not found at all. A skillful writer rarely thinks about topic sentences when he uses them, but the beginner will find them helpful in establishing the unity of his paragraphs. They can guide the reader in keeping the general idea of a paragraph in focus.

A unified paragraph has several parts. Synge's paragraph conducts a small argument. He makes an assertion and illustrates it with several examples, reasserts it, and illustrates it again. That his sentences fit together well is due not only to the fact that they concern a single subject but also to the presence of transitional (linking) devices that hold the parts of the thought together. The major transitional devices to link sentences are the following: repeated words, synonyms, and other substitutes; parallel phrasing; and conjunctive and directive words. In his first sentence Synge speaks of the *people* of the islands and later of *each individual*. The second sentence substitutes *each man* for *each individual*, and implies *each man of these people*. The third sentence substitutes the pronoun *he* for *man* and *individual*. The fourth sentence repeats *he*. The fifth substitutes *his* and *him*, and refers to the *people* of the islands indirectly by its reference to other *people*. The last sentence repeats *his*, *him*, and *he*. In a similar way the words *intelligence, charm, development, knowledge, skill*, and *activity of the mind* in the first sentence are repeated or substituted for by a multitude of words and phrases: *can speak, skilled, can manage, nerve, dexterity, can farm*, and so forth. Sometimes Synge employs virtual opposites, as when he uses *freedom from dullness* instead of *intelligence and charm.* The other important transitional device that Synge employs is parallel phrasing. The form of the second sentence, *Each man can speak . . . ,* is closely paralleled in the third and fourth with *He is . . . and can manage . . .* and *He can farm . . . .* The last two sentences retain the same simple opening—subject and verb of the main thought—as the three preceding sentences.

Transitional devices can of course be used badly. Had Synge begun all his sentences after the first one with *he can,* his phrasing would have been tiresome even though straightforward and clear. Had he begun the second sentence with *in the first place,* the third with *secondly,* the next with *furthermore* (all three, conjunctions), the passage would have become tedious. The writer needs to make transitions, but he ought to avoid boring his reader with unnecessary directions. It also should be noted that transitional devices usually do more than merely connect. All of the substitutes for *intelligence* in the passage are in part repetitions of *intelligence* without being tedious, but they are also variations that help to define what Synge means by intelligence. The people of the islands might not be able to pass college examinations, but Synge is thinking of a broad sort of intelligence that is defined by skill, nerve, dexterity, alertness, and aesthetic emotion.

By the time a writer has written a unified paragraph whose parts are adequately connected, he has probably also performed his other task—that of development. In order to develop a paragraph—that is, to develop the idea that a topic sentence suggests—a writer has to illuminate, explain, justify, exemplify, elaborate. He cannot simply repeat his topic sentence five different ways. The means of developing a paragraph are various, and an understanding of them can make a writer conscious of the kinds and quality of material that he possesses or lacks. His freedom to use one or another means of development is an opportunity to choose the most effective approach in a given context. The most common means of development is the one that Synge relies on in his paragraph: *illustration,* or *example.* He uses three basic illustrations: language, sea activity, and land activity, breaking up to some extent his mention of the last two. He also uses *repetition,* or *restatement,* the fifth sentence being in large part a repetition of the first. Repetition is a term that hardly suggests development, but some amount of repetition is essential in the development of an idea, especially when the idea is complex. Some techniques of development that Synge might have employed, but did not, include the following. An *anecdote* is an illustration enlarged to become a complete small tale. Synge might have argued his case with an anecdote about a single islander he knew, who in the course of a day displayed several of the talents that the paragraph mentions. *Comparison and contrast* usually involve illustration and may involve anecdote; this method sets two or more things side by side so that the individual qualities of one or both become clearer. Synge might have done what his fifth sentence hints at—written a few sentences describing some people who always follow the same occupation, so as to describe his islanders by contrast. An *analogy* is a comparison of one thing with something very different. Synge says that it is likely that the intelligence and charm of his islanders is due to variety of labor, and he might have supported his supposition with an analogy about the muscles in the human arm: give such muscles a single task to do, and you will soon have a musclebound person; but give them a variety of tasks, and they will be healthy. Had Synge poured out several more illustrations in his paragraph, his method of development might additionally have been described as *accumulation of detail.* Had he referred the reader to similar judgments about South Sea islanders by two sociologists, he would have been employing *supporting data,* which might have included *quotation.* Had he applied some research on the development of the human brain, he might have been employing *reason* in a fairly formal sense—just as he does employ reason in a looser sense in arguing his assertion with his evidence of various intelligent activity. And he might have written another paragraph in which he tried to give all the causes for the intelligence and charm of the islanders instead of one of the causes, in which case he might have employed *classification and analysis* (on a reduced scale, *division and enumeration*), offering four categories of causes: absence of division of labor, heredity, climate and geography, and traditional culture.

Paragraph development inevitably involves the question of paragraph order or arrangement. Do we want to begin with a topic sentence or do we want to lead up to it? If we have three examples, in what order do we offer them? Insofar as an answer to these questions concerns the relationship of the individual paragraph to the rest of the essay, it will be considered in Section III. The purely internal problem of order can be met in a variety of ways. In some instances, especially in very brief paragraphs, no preferred order emerges, and none may be necessary or desirable. But usually some sort of ordering is called for. The Synge paragraph shows on the surface a rather loose ordering of material, and we may wonder why the third sentence, about fishing, was not followed immediately by the last sentence, which is about fishing too. But one thing is certain: if we took the last sentence and put it with the third, and then took the second sentence, about language, and put it last, we would have a badly arranged paragraph. Why? Synge's main point is that the absence of a division of labor produces intelligence and charm, and the fact that each man speaks Gaelic and English (necessary in his selling of fish and other goods) is perhaps the least significant and certainly the least dramatic aspect of his various labor. To put this detail last would be to end the paragraph lamely and almost irrelevantly. It is a small detail that Synge tucks in unobtrusively near the beginning. As the paragraph stands, it closes appropriately and convincingly with attention on the most important part of the islanders' life. If we review the discussion of the unity of the paragraph on page 73, we see that the ordering of material is, in fact, quite careful. The first sentence provides the topic; each of the next three focuses on an aspect of the islander's life (language, sea activity, land activity); the next sentence restates the topic; and the last sentence offers a single, more dramatic illustration that replaces the three brief illustrations earlier. The paragraph has a neat, two-part organization that moves forward easily.

Every paragraph makes its own demands in the way of materials, and much of what can be said on the subject will emerge in the discussion of organization in Section III. Some common patterns of ordering, to be considered later, may be mentioned here: chronology, order of importance, spatial order, visual order, procedure (as in a physics experiment), narrative sequence, and logic. Most of these patterns can be used in the normal order they suggest or in reverse order, and sometimes—as with the flashback in chronology—they can be usefully interrupted.

After a writer has written a unified and well-developed paragraph, he writes others of the same quality until he completes a unified and well-developed essay. His several paragraphs in the essay will deal with the same subject, just as the several sentences within each paragraph do. His transitions from paragraph to paragraph will be made in the same ways as those from sentence to sentence. And together, his paragraphs will show a development similar to the development within each paragraph. If a writer knows how to write a good paragraph, he probably knows how to write a good essay.

NEW YORK

E. B. White

E. B. White (1899—) was born in Mount Vernon, New York, and studied at Cornell University. After a variety of jobs, including newspaper and advertising work as well as a stint at sea, he joined the staff of *The New Yorker* and began an association that has persisted in one form or another since the early 1920's. In addition to giving shape to and writing much of the "Talk of the Town" column, he has contributed essays and commentary on a wide range of subjects. Their variety can be sampled in *Is Sex Necessary?* (with James Thurber), *Quo Vadimus?* and *The Second Tree from the Corner*. (Further information on White appears on pp. 137, 248.)

(1) The oft-quoted thumbnail sketch of New York is, of course: "It's a wonderful place, but I'd hate to live there." I have an idea that people from villages and small towns, people accustomed to the convenience and the friendliness of neighborhood over-the-fence living, are unaware that life in New York follows the neighborhood pattern. The city is literally a composite of tens of thousands of tiny neighborhood units. There are, of course, the big districts and big units: Chelsea and Murray Hill and Gramercy (which are residential units), Harlem (a racial unit), Greenwich Village (a unit dedicated to the arts and other matters), and there is Radio City (a commercial development), Peter Cooper Village (a housing unit), the Medical Center (a sickness unit) and many other sections each of which has some distinguishing characteristic. But the curious thing about New York is that each large geographical unit is composed of countless small neighborhoods. Each

neighborhood is virtually self-sufficient. Usually it is no more than two or three blocks long and a couple of blocks wide. Each area is a city within a city within a city. Thus, no matter where you live in New York, you will find within a block or two a grocery store, a barbershop, a newsstand and shoeshine shack, an ice-coal-and-wood cellar (where you write your order on a pad outside as you walk by), a dry cleaner, a laundry, a delicatessen (beer and sandwiches delivered at any hour to your door), a flower shop, an undertaker's parlor, a movie house, a radio-repair shop, a stationer, a haberdasher, a tailor, a drugstore, a garage, a tearoom, a saloon, a hardware store, a liquor store, a shoe-repair shop. Every block or two, in most residential sections of New York, is a little main street. A man starts for work in the morning and before he has gone two hundred yards he has completed half a dozen missions: bought a paper, left a pair of shoes to be soled, picked up a pack of cigarettes, ordered a bottle of whiskey to be dispatched in the opposite direction against his home-coming, written a message to the unseen forces of the wood cellar, and notified the dry cleaner that a pair of trousers awaits call. Homeward bound eight hours later, he buys a bunch of pussy willows, a Mazda bulb, a drink, a shine—all between the corner where he steps off the bus and his apartment. So complete is each neighborhood, and so strong the sense of neighborhood, that many a New Yorker spends a lifetime within the confines of an area smaller than a country village. Let him walk two blocks from his corner and he is in a strange land and will feel uneasy till he gets back.

(2) Storekeepers are particularly conscious of neighborhood boundary lines. A woman friend of mine moved recently from one apartment to another, a distance of three blocks. When she turned up, the day after the move, at the same grocer's that she had patronized for years, the proprietor was in ecstasy—almost in tears—at seeing her. "I was afraid," he said, "now that you've moved away I wouldn't be seeing you any more." To him, *away* was three blocks, or about seven hundred and fifty feet.

Questions

1. Both paragraphs have topic phrases or sentences. What are they? The first paragraph can be broken down into three or four smaller units.

Identify these units and their topic phrases or sentences. Explain the relationship of these smaller units to the main topic of the paragraph.

2. What is the relationship between sentences one and two and between sentences two and three in Paragraph 1? Identify the key transitional words and phrases in sentences two and three, and sentences four through nine.

3. To what elements in Paragraph 1 do "conscious" and "boundary lines" in the first sentence of Paragraph 2 relate? What is the broad relationship of the second paragraph to the first?

4. Point out the accumulation of detail, anecdote, example, and comparison through which White develops the two paragraphs.

5. What seems to you to be the most convincing piece of evidence that New York is a neighborly place? What distinguishes it from the other evidence?

6. Examine the lists of "big districts and big units," small neighborhood stores, and missions that the man performs going to and from work. What basis do you see for the ordering of each of the lists? What feeling or attitude towards New York does White seem to express through the general degree of orderliness that he gives to the lists?

THE ALMIGHTY DOLLAR

W. H. AUDEN

W. H. Auden (1907—) was born in York, England, and received his education at Oxford. His presence was first felt in the 1930's, when he seemed the most promising poet of his generation. Ironical, witty, full of verbal inventiveness, his poetry was both a response to and analysis of the difficulties brought on by the economic and spiritual depression of the decade. In 1939 he emigrated to the United States, becoming a citizen in 1946. He is the author of many volumes of poetry (*The Age of Anxiety, Nones*); his prose, on literary and cultural subjects, is gathered in *The Dyer's Hand*.

(1) Political and technological developments are rapidly obliterating all cultural differences and it is possible that, in a not remote future, it will be impossible to distinguish human beings living on one area of the earth's surface from those living on any other, but our different pasts have not yet been completely erased and cultural differences are still perceptible. The most striking difference between an American and a European is the difference in their attitudes towards money. Every European knows, as a matter of historical fact, that, in Europe, wealth could only be acquired at the expense of other human beings, either by conquering them or by exploiting their labor in factories. Further, even after the Industrial Revolution began, the number of persons who could rise from poverty to wealth was small; the vast majority took it for granted that they would not be much richer nor poorer than their fathers. In consequence, no European associates wealth with personal merit or poverty with personal failure.

(2) To a European, money means power, the freedom to do as he likes, which also means that, consciously or unconsciously, he says: "I want to have as much money as possible myself and others to have as little money as possible."

(3) In the United States, wealth was also acquired by stealing, but the real exploited victim was not a human being but poor Mother Earth and her creatures who were ruthlessly plundered. It is true that the Indians were expropriated or exterminated, but this was not, as it had always been in Europe, a matter of the conqueror seizing the wealth of the conquered, for the Indian had never realized the potential riches of his country. It is also true that, in the Southern states, men lived on the labor of slaves, but slave labor did not make them fortunes; what made slavery in the South all the more inexcusable was that, in addition to being morally wicked, it didn't even pay off handsomely.

(4) Thanks to the natural resources of the country, every American, until quite recently, could reasonably look forward to making more money than his father, so that, if he made less, the fault must be his; he was either lazy or inefficient. What an American values, therefore, is not the possession of money as such, but his power to make it as a proof of his manhood; once he has proved himself by making it, it has served its function and can be lost or given away. In no society in history have rich men given away so large a part of their fortunes. A poor American feels guilty at being poor, but less guilty than an American *rentier* who has inherited wealth but is doing nothing to increase it; what can the latter do but take to drink and psychoanalysis?

(5) In the Fifth Circle on the Mount of Purgatory, I do not think that many Americans will be found among the Avaricious; but I suspect that the Prodigals may be almost an American colony. The great vice of Americans is not materialism but a lack of respect for matter.

Questions

1. What is the relation between the first sentence and the rest of the essay?

2. There is a topic sentence in Paragraph 1. Show in detail what part of the essay it covers.

3. Locate or provide a topic phrase for Paragraph 3. What preceding material does this paragraph parallel? What preceding material does Paragraph 4 parallel?

4. Analyze the means of transition from sentence to sentence in the first paragraph.

5. The overall means of development in the essay are comparison and contrast. What are the individual means employed in Paragraphs 3 and 4?

6. Does the means of development in Paragraph 3 also determine the ordering of sentences in it? Does the means of development in Paragraph 4 determine the ordering of sentences in it? Compare the two paragraphs.

7. In his last sentence Auden says that Americans have "a lack of respect for matter." Aside from what Auden takes to be their lack of respect for nature, can you think of any other ways in which his assertion seems true? Or does American admiration for cars, for instance, suggest it is untrue? Discuss.

SEEING LIFE

ARNOLD BENNETT

Like many English novelists before him, Arnold Bennett (1867–1931) was also a famous journalist. His political articles written during World War I and his literary criticism written during the 1920's were notable for their lucidity and intelligence. As a novelist, Bennett is known as a realistic portrayer of English provincial life (*The Old Wives' Tale, Clayhanger, These Twain*—works that have their setting in the potteries of Staffordshire, where he lived as a youth). Of equal merit are his fantasies (*The Glimpse*), impressionistic sketches (*The Pretty Lady*), and psychological portraits (*Lord Raingo*). Bennett was content that the public should think of him as a realist; privately he described all of his novels as "variations on the theme of beauty." The following selection is the opening of a discussion on writing that was intended for a popular audience.

(1) A young dog, inexperienced, sadly lacking in even primary education, ambles and frisks along the footpath of Fulham Road, near the mysterious gates of a Marist convent. He is a large puppy, on the way to be a dog of much dignity, but at present he has little to recommend him but that gawky elegance, and that bounding gratitude for the gift of life, which distinguish the normal puppy. He is an ignorant fool. He might have entered the convent of nuns and had a fine time, but instead he steps off the pavement into the road, the road being a vast and interesting continent imperfectly explored. His confidence in his nose, in his agility, and in the goodness of God is touching, abso-

lutely painful to witness. He glances casually at a huge, towering ver-
milion construction that is whizzing towards him on four wheels,
preceded by a glint of brass and a wisp of steam; and then with disdain
he ignores it as less important than a mere speck of odorous matter in
the mud. The next instant he is lying inert in the mud. His confidence
in the goodness of God had been misplaced. Since the beginning of
time God had ordained him a victim.

(2) An impressive thing happens. The motor-bus reluctantly slack-
ens and stops. Not the differential brake, nor the footbrake, has arrested the motor-bus, but the invisible brake of public opinion, acting
by administrative transmission. There is not a policeman in sight. Theoretically, the motor-bus is free to whiz onward in its flight to the paradise of Shoreditch, but in practice it is paralysed by dread. A man in
brass buttons and a stylish cap leaps down from it, and the blackened
demon who sits on its neck also leaps down from it, and they move
gingerly towards the puppy. A little while ago the motor-bus might
have overturned a human cyclist or so, and proceeded nonchalant on
its way. But now even a puppy requires a post-mortem: such is the
force of public opinion aroused. Two policemen appear in the distance.

(3) "A street accident" is now in being, and a crowd gathers with
calm joy and stares, passive and determined. The puppy offers no sign
whatever; just lies in the road. Then a boy, destined probably to a
great future by reason of his singular faculty of initiative, goes to the
puppy and carries him by the scruff of the neck, to the shelter of the
gutter. Relinquished by the boy, the lithe puppy falls into an easy horizontal attitude, and seems bent upon repose. The boy lifts the puppy's
head to examine it, and the head drops back wearily. The puppy is
dead. No cry, no blood, no disfigurement! Even no perceptible jolt of
the wheel as it climbed over the obstacle of the puppy's body! A won-
derfully clean and perfect accident!

(4) The increasing crowd stares with beatific placidity. People
emerge impatiently from the bowels of the throbbing motor-bus and
slip down from its back, and either join the crowd or vanish. The two
policemen and the crew of the motor-bus have now met in parley. The
conductor and the driver have an air at once nervous and resigned;
their gestures are quick and vivacious. The policemen, on the other
hand, indicate by their slow and huge movements that eternity is theirs.

And they could not be more sure of the conductor and the driver if they had them manacled and leashed. The conductor and the driver admit the absolute dominion of the elephantine policemen; they admit that before the simple will of the policemen inconvenience, lost minutes, shortened leisure, docked wages, count as less than naught. And the policemen are carelessly sublime, well knowing that magistrates, jails, and the very Home Secretary on his throne—yes, and a whole system of conspiracy and perjury and brutality—are at their beck in case of need. And yet occasionally in the demeanour of the policemen towards the conductor and the driver there is a silent message that says: "After all, we, too, are working men like you, over-worked and under-paid and bursting with grievances in the service of the pitiless and dishonest public. We, too, have wives and children and privations and frightful apprehensions. We, too, have to struggle desperately. Only the awful magic of these garments and of the garter which we wear on our wrists sets an abyss between us and you." And the conductor writes and one of the policemen writes, and they keep on writing while the traffic makes beautiful curves to avoid them.

(5) The still increasing crowd continues to stare in the pure blankness of pleasure. A close-shaved, well-dressed, middle-aged man, with a copy of *The Sportsman* in his podgy hand, who has descended from the motor-bus, starts stamping his feet. "I was knocked down by a taxi last year," he says fiercely. "But nobody took no notice of *that*! Are they going to stop here all the blank morning for a blank tyke?" And for all his respectable appearance, his features become debased, and he emits a jet of disgusting profanity and brings most of the Trinity into the thunderous assertion that he has paid his fare. Then a man passes wheeling a muck-cart. And he stops and talks a long time with the other uniforms, because he, too, wears vestiges of a uniform. And the crowd never moves nor ceases to stare. Then the new arrival stoops and picks up the unclaimed, masterless puppy, and flings it, all soft and yielding, into the horrid mess of the cart, and passes on. And only that which is immortal and divine of the puppy remains behind, floating perhaps like an invisible vapour over the scene of the tragedy.

(6) The crowd is tireless, all eyes. The four principals still converse and write. Nobody in the crowd comprehends what they are about. At length the driver separates himself, but is drawn back, and

a new parley is commenced. But everything ends. The policemen turn on their immense heels. The driver and conductor race towards the motor-bus. The bell rings, the motor-bus, quite empty, disappears snorting round the corner into Walham Green. The crowd is now lessening. But it separates with reluctance, many of its members continuing to stare with intense absorption at the place where the puppy lay or the place where the policemen stood. An appreciable interval elapses before the "street accident" has entirely ceased to exist as a phenomenon.

(7) The members of the crowd follow their noses, and during the course of the day remark to acquaintances:

(8) "Saw a dog run over by a motor-bus in the Fulham Road this morning! Killed dead!"

(9) And that is all they do remark. That is all they have witnessed. They will not, and could not, give intelligible and interesting particulars of the affair (unless it were as to the breed of the dog or the number of the bus-service). They have watched a dog run over. They analyse neither their sensations nor the phenomenon. They have witnessed it whole, as a bad writer uses a *cliché*. They have observed—that is to say, they have really seen—nothing.

Questions

1. Identify the subject of each of the first three paragraphs. To what extent is the subject of Paragraph 2 prepared for in the first? To what extent is the subject of Paragraph 3 prepared for beforehand? What topic phrases or sentences—if any—do the three paragraphs have?

2. What words in the second sentence of the sketch link it to the first sentence? Identify the words and phrases in the rest of the first paragraph that link to *inexperienced* in the first sentence (as synonym, antonym, example, consequence, etc.).

3. What is the most obvious transitional device that Bennett employs in the first paragraph? What effect does he achieve by its repetition? Where do you find the same device employed in the opening sentences of succeeding paragraphs?

4. What elements in Paragraphs 3 and 5 stand parallel to each other? What is the essential contrast between the two paragraphs? What relationship do the two paragraphs bear to Paragraph 4?

5. What pattern dominates the arrangement of most of the material in the sketch? Point out in Paragraphs 3 and 4 the transitional words related to this pattern.

6. From whose point of view is Fulham Road "a vast and interesting continent" (Paragraph 1)? To whom is the accident "impressive" (Paragraph 2)? Who thinks that the boy is "destined probably to a great future" (Paragraph 3)? To whom are the policemen "carelessly sublime" (Paragraph 4)? On the basis of your answers, would you say that Bennett stands apart from the scene he describes? Does other evidence support or contradict your answer? Would you say that Bennett is present more in the scene or in the essay?

7. By what means does Bennett imply that the scene he describes is typical rather than unique? (Note, for example, the fact that, except for the boy and the middle-aged man, Bennett gives no individual qualities to members of the crowd.) By what means does he achieve the vividness of a unique scene?

8. At the end of the sketch Bennett asserts that the crowd has observed nothing except a few details. Can you classify the kinds of things that Bennett himself has seen? Consider "glint of brass and a wisp of steam" (Paragraph 1), "blackened demon" (Paragraph 2), "whole system of conspiracy and perjury and brutality" (Paragraph 4), "while the traffic makes beautiful curves" (Paragraph 4).

THE KITCHEN

ALFRED KAZIN

Alfred Kazin (1915—) was born in New York City and received his education at the City College of New York and
Columbia University. His comprehensive study of modern
American prose, *On Native Grounds,* appeared when he was
twenty-seven. Since then he has published innumerable essays
and reviews, collected in *The Inmost Leaf* and *Contemporaries,*
and edited books of criticism on Theodore Dreiser and F. Scott
Fitzgerald. He has lectured and taught at many colleges and
universities and is generally considered one of the best of those
critics who appraise literature from a social-historical point of
view. The prose that follows is from his autobiography, of
which two volumes have now been published—*A Walker in
the City, Starting Out in the Thirties.*

(1) In Brownsville tenements the kitchen is always the largest
room and the center of the household. As a child I felt that we
lived in a kitchen to which four other rooms were annexed. My
mother, a "home" dressmaker, had her workshop in the kitchen.
She told me once that she had begun dressmaking in Poland at
thirteen; as far back as I can remember, she was always making
dresses for the local women. She had an innate sense of design, a
quick eye for all the subtleties in the latest fashions, even when she
despised them, and great boldness. For three or four dollars she would
study the fashion magazines with a customer, go with the customer
to the remnants store on Belmont Avenue to pick out the material,
argue the owner down—all remnants stores, for some reason, were

supposed to be shady, as if the owners dealt in stolen goods—and then for days would patiently fit and baste and sew and fit again. Our apartment was always full of women in their housedresses sitting around the kitchen table waiting for a fitting. My little bedroom next to the kitchen was the fitting room. The sewing machine, an old nut-brown Singer with golden scrolls painted along the black arm and engraved along the two tiers of little drawers massed with needles and thread on each side of the treadle, stood next to the window and the great coal-black stove which up to my last year in college was our main source of heat. By December the two outer bedrooms were closed off, and used to chill bottles of milk and cream, cold borscht and jellied calves' feet.

(2) The kitchen held our lives together. My mother worked in it all day long, we ate in it almost all meals except the Passover *seder,* I did my homework and first writing at the kitchen table, and in winter I often had a bed made up for me on three kitchen chairs near the stove. On the wall just over the table hung a long horizontal mirror that sloped to a ship's prow at each end and was lined in cherry wood. It took up the whole wall, and drew every object in the kitchen to itself. The walls were a fiercely stippled whitewash, so often rewhitened by my father in slack seasons that the paint looked as if it had been squeezed and cracked into the walls. A large electric bulb hung down the center of the kitchen at the end of a chain that had been hooked into the ceiling; the old gas ring and key still jutted out of the wall like antlers. In the corner next to the toilet was the sink at which we washed, and the square tub in which my mother did our clothes. Above it, tacked to the shelf on which were pleasantly ranged square, blue-bordered white sugar and spice jars, hung calendars from the Public National Bank on Pitkin Avenue and the Minsker Progressive Branch of the Workman's Circle; receipts for the payment of insurance premiums, and household bills on a spindle; two little boxes engraved with Hebrew letters. One of these was for the poor, the other to buy back the Land of Israel. Each spring a bearded little man would suddenly appear in our kitchen, salute us with a hurried Hebrew blessing, empty the boxes (sometimes with a sidelong look of disdain if they were not full), hurriedly bless us again for remembering our less fortunate Jewish brothers and sisters,

and so take his departure until the next spring, after vainly trying to persuade my mother to take still another box. We did occasionally remember to drop coins in the boxes, but this was usually only on the dreaded morning of "midterms" and final examinations, because my mother thought it would bring me luck. She was extremely superstitious, but embarrassed about it, and always laughed at herself whenever, on the morning of an examination, she counseled me to leave the house on my right foot. "I know it's silly," her smile seemed to say, "but what harm can it do? It may calm God down."

(3) The kitchen gave a special character to our lives; my mother's character. All my memories of that kitchen are dominated by the nearness of my mother sitting all day long at her sewing machine, by the clacking of the treadle against the linoleum floor, by the patient twist of her right shoulder as she automatically pushed at the wheel with one hand or lifted the foot to free the needle where it had got stuck in a thick piece of material. The kitchen was her life. Year by year, as I began to take in her fantastic capacity for labor and her anxious zeal, I realized it was ourselves she kept stitched together. I can never remember a time when she was not working. She worked because the law of her life was work, work and anxiety; she worked because she would have found life meaningless without work. She read almost no English; she could read the Yiddish paper, but never felt she had time to. We were always talking of a time when I would teach her how to read, but somehow there was never time. When I awoke in the morning she was already at her machine, or in the great morning crowd of housewives at the grocery getting fresh rolls for breakfast. When I returned from school she was at her machine, or conferring over *McCall's* with some neighborhood woman who had come in pointing hopefully to an illustration—"Mrs. Kazin! Mrs. Kazin! Make me a dress like it shows here in the picture!" When my father came home from work she had somehow mysteriously interrupted herself to make supper for us, and the dishes cleared and washed, was back at her machine. When I went to bed at night, often she was still there, pounding away at the treadle, hunched over the wheel, her hands steering a piece of gauze under the needle with a finesse that always contrasted sharply with her swollen hands and broken nails. Her left

hand had been pierced through when as a girl she had worked in the infamous Triangle Shirtwaist Factory on the East Side. A needle had gone straight through the palm, severing a large vein. They had sewn it up for her so clumsily that a tuft of flesh always lay folded over the palm.

(4) The kitchen was the great machine that set our lives running; it whirred down a little only on Saturdays and holy days. From my mother's kitchen I gained my first picture of life as a white, over-heated, starkly lit workshop redolent with Jewish cooking, crowded with women in housedresses, strewn with fashion magazines, patterns, dress material, spools of thread—and at whose center, so lashed to her machine that bolts of energy seemed to dance out of her hands and feet as she worked, my mother stamped the treadle hard against the floor, hard, hard, and silently, grimly at war, beat out the first rhythm of the world for me.

(5) Every sound from the street roared and trembled at our windows—a mother feeding her child on the doorstep, the screech of the trolley cars on Rockaway Avenue, the eternal smash of a handball against the wall of our house, the clatter of *"der Italyéner"* 's cart packed with watermelons, the sing-song of the old-clothes men walking Chester Street, the cries *"Árbes! Árbes! Kinder! Kinder! Heyse gute árbes!"* All day long people streamed into our apartment as a matter of course—"customers," upstairs neighbors, downstairs neighbors, women who would stop in for a half-hour's talk, sales-men, relatives, insurance agents. Usually they came in without ringing the bell—everyone knew my mother was always at home. I would hear the front door opening, the wind whistling through our front hall, and then some familiar face would appear in our kitchen with the same bland, matter-of-fact inquiring look: no need to stand on ceremony: my mother and her kitchen were available to everyone all day long.

(6) At night the kitchen contracted around the blaze of light on the cloth, the patterns, the ironing board where the iron had burned a black border around the tear in the muslin cover; the finished dresses looked so frilly as they jostled on their wire hangers after all the work my mother had put into them. And then I would get that strangely ominous smell of tension from the dress fabrics and

the burn in the cover of the ironing board—as if each piece of cloth
and paper crushed with light under the naked bulb might suddenly
go up in flames. Whenever I pass some small tailoring shop still lit up
at night and see the owner hunched over his steam press; whenever
in some poorer neighborhood of the city I see through a window
some small crowded kitchen naked under the harsh light glittering
in the ceiling, I still smell that fiery breath, that warning of imminent
fire. I was always holding my breath. What I must have felt most
about ourselves, I see now, was that we ourselves were like kindling
—that all the hard-pressed pieces of ourselves and all the hard-used
objects in that kitchen were like so many slivers of wood that might
go up in flames if we came too near the white-blazing filaments in
that naked bulb. Our tension itself was fire, we ourselves were forever
burning—to live, to get down the foreboding in our souls, to make
good.

(7) Twice a year, on the anniversaries of her parents' deaths, my
mother placed on top of the ice-box an ordinary kitchen glass
packed with wax, the *yortsayt,* and lit the candle in it. Sitting at the
kitchen table over my homework, I would look across the threshold
to that mourning-glass, and sense that for my mother the distance
from our kitchen to *der heym,* from life to death, was only a flame's
length away. Poor as we were, it was not poverty that drove my
mother so hard; it was loneliness—some endless bitter brooding over
all those left behind, dead or dying or soon to die; a loneliness
locked up in her kitchen that dwelt every day on the hazardousness
of life and the nearness of death, but still kept struggling in the
lock, trying to get us through by endless labor.

(8) With us, life started up again only on the last shore. There
seemed to be no middle ground between despair and the fury of
our ambition. Whenever my mother spoke of her hopes for us, it
was with such unbelievingness that the likes of us would ever come
to anything, such abashed hope and readiness for pain, that I finally
came to see in the flame burning on top of the ice-box death itself
burning away the bones of poor Jews, burning out in us everything
but courage, the blind resolution to live. In the light of that mourn-
ing-candle, there were ranged around me how many dead and dying
—how many eras of pain, of exile, of dispersion, of cringing before
the powers of this world!

(9) It was always at dusk that my mother's loneliness came home most to me. Painfully alert to every shift in the light at her window, she would suddenly confess her fatigue by removing her pince-nez, and then wearily pushing aside the great mound of fabrics on her machine, would stare at the street as if to warm herself in the last of the sun. "How sad it is!" I once heard her say. "It grips me! It grips me!" Twilight was the bottommost part of the day, the chillest and loneliest time for her. Always so near to her moods, I knew she was fighting some deep inner dread, struggling against the returning tide of darkness along the streets that invariably assailed her heart with the same foreboding— Where? Where now? Where is the day taking us now?

(10) Yet one good look at the street would revive her. I see her now, perched against the windowsill, with her face against the glass, her eyes almost asleep in enjoyment, just as she starts up with the guilty cry—"What foolishness is this in me!"—and goes to the stove to prepare supper for us: a moment, only a moment, watching the evening crowd of women gathering at the grocery for fresh bread and milk. But between my mother's pent-up face at the window and the winter sun dying in the fabrics—"Alfred, see how beautiful!" —she has drawn for me one single line of sentience.

Questions

1. What do the first two sentences suggest will be the subject of Paragraph 1? To what extent does the subject shift in the rest of the paragraph?

2. To what extent does the first sentence of Paragraph 2 serve as topic sentence? What chief divisions of subject do you see in the paragraph?

3. Examine the opening sentences of Paragraphs 2 through 8. Compare the sorts of links that they establish with previous material. What broad movement of subject-matter do they suggest?

4. Point out the chief transitional words and phrases within Paragraph 6. Then trace the shifts in subject from sentence to sentence. What broad means of development governs the movement? What relationship does the final sentence in the paragraph bear to Paragraphs 7 and 8?

5. What means of development does Kazin employ in Paragraph 9? What elements in the last paragraph link it to this one?

6. What are the four or five chief qualities that Kazin ascribes to his mother? Why do you suppose he presents them in the order he does?

7. On the basis of your answers to the first six questions, define the general degree of orderliness of Kazin's writing. What quality do you think it lends to the sketch: energy, seriousness, wit, openness, or something else? What general mood does Kazin display?

8. What is Kazin's mother like, and what are the various means by which he describes her? What particular influences upon him does Kazin ascribe to her?

9. What is Kazin's sketch primarily about—the kitchen, his mother, something else, or something more? Base your answer on an analysis of the chief topics of each paragraph and upon the general direction that the several paragraphs take.

10. If you have read the essay by Dylan Thomas in Section I, compare his treatment of childhood with Kazin's. Does memory operate in the same manner for both men?

GERMAN RELATIONS

ROBERT GRAVES

Born at Wimbledon, England, and educated at Oxford, Robert
Graves (1895——) has made his home for the last thirty-five
years on the island of Majorca. During a long and often con-
troversial literary career, he has written poetry, essays, and
historical novels (*I, Claudius*), has translated the classics (*Iliad,
The Golden Ass*), and has made original contributions in anthropology and poetics (*The Greek Myths, The White Goddess*). His autobiography, *Goodbye to All That,* from which
the following is a chapter, shocked the literary world on its
appearance in 1929, and it has since come to be judged a
minor classic of candid irreverence.

(1) My mother took us abroad to stay at my grandfather's house
in Germany five times between my second and twelfth year. Then he
died, and we never went again. He owned a big old manor-house
at Deisenhofen, ten miles from Munich; by name "Laufzorn," which
means "Begone, anger!" Our summers there were easily the best
things of my early childhood. Pine forests and hot sun, red deer,
black and red squirrels, acres of blueberries and wild strawberries;
nine or ten different kinds of edible mushrooms which we went
into the forest to pick, and unfamiliar flowers in the fields—Munich
lies high—and outcrops of Alpine flowers occur here and there; a
farm with all the usual animals except sheep; drives through the
countryside in a brake behind my grandfather's greys; and bathing
in the Isar under a waterfall. The Isar was bright green, and said

to be the fastest river of Europe. We used to visit the uncles who
kept a peacock farm a few miles away; and a grand-uncle, Johannes
von Ranke, the ethnologist, who lived on the lake shores of Tegern-
see, where everyone had buttercup-blond hair; and occasionally my
Aunt Agnes, Freifrau Baronin von Aufsess, of Aufsess Castle, some
hours away by train, high up in the Bavarian Alps.

(2) Aufsess, built in the ninth century, stood so remote that it
had never been sacked, but remained Aufsess property ever since.
To the original building, a keep with only a ladder-entrance half-way
up, a mediaeval castle had been added. Its treasures of plate and
armour were amazing. My Uncle Siegfried showed us children the
chapel: its walls hung with enamelled shields of each Aufsess baron,
impaled with the arms of the noble family into which he had married. He pointed to a stone in the floor which pulled up by a ring,
and said: "That is the family vault where all Aufsesses go when
they die. I'll be down there one day." He scowled comically. (But
he got killed in the War as an officer of the Imperial German Staff
and, I believe, they never found his body.) Uncle Siegfried had a
peculiar sense of humour. One day we children saw him on the
garden path, eating pebbles. He told us to go away, but of course
we stayed, sat down, and tried to eat pebbles too; only to be told
very seriously that children should not eat pebbles: we would break
our teeth. We agreed, after trying one or two; so he found us each
a pebble which looked just like all the rest, but which crushed
easily and had a chocolate centre. This was on condition that we
went away and left him to his picking and crunching. When we
returned, later in the day, we searched and searched, but found only
the ordinary hard pebbles. He never once let us down in a joke.

(3) Among the castle treasures were a baby's lace cap that had
taken two years to make; and a wine glass which my uncle's old
father had found in the Franco-Prussian War standing upright in the
middle of the square in an entirely ruined French village. For dinner,
when we went there, we ate some enormous trout. My father, a
practised fisherman, asked my uncle in astonishment where they
came from. He explained that an underground river welled up close
to the castle, and the fish which emerged with it were quite white
from the darkness, of extraordinary size, and stone-blind.

(4) They also gave us jam made of wild rose-berries, which they called "Hetchi-Petch," and showed us an iron chest in a small, thick-walled, whitewashed room at the top of the keep—a tremendous chest, twice the size of the door, and obviously made inside the room, which had no windows except arrow-slits. It had two keys, and must have been twelfth- or thirteenth-century work. Tradition ruled that it should never be opened, unless the castle stood in the most extreme danger. The baron held one key; his steward, the other. The chest could be opened only by using both keys, and nobody knew what lay inside; it was even considered unlucky to speculate. Of course, we speculated. It might be gold; more likely a store of corn in sealed jars; or even some sort of weapon—Greek fire, perhaps. From what I know of the Aufsesses and their stewards, it is inconceivable that the chest ever got the better of their curiosity. A ghost walked the castle, the ghost of a former baron known as the "Red Knight"; his terrifying portrait hung half-way up the turret staircase which led to our bedrooms. We slept on feather-beds for the first time in our lives.

(5) Laufzorn, which my grandfather had bought and restored from a ruinous condition, could not compare in tradition with Auf-sess, though it had for a time been a shooting lodge of the Bavarian kings. Still, two ghosts went with the place; the farm labourers used to see them frequently. One of them was a carriage which drove furiously along without horses and, before the days of motor cars, spread real horror. Not having visited the banqueting hall since childhood, I find it difficult to recall its true dimensions. It seemed as big as a cathedral, with stained-glass armorial windows, and bare floor-boards were furnished only at the four corners with small islands of tables and chairs; swallows had built rows of nests all along the sides of the ceiling. There were roundels of coloured light from the windows, the many-tined stags' heads (shot by my grandfather) mounted on the walls, swallow-droppings under the nests, and a little harmonium in one corner where we sang Ger-man songs. These concentrate my memories of Laufzorn. The bot-tom storey formed part of the farm. A carriage-drive ran right through it, with a wide, covered courtyard in the centre, where cattle were once driven to safety in times of baronial feud. On one

side of the drive lay the estate steward's quarters, on the other the farm servants' inn and kitchen. In the middle storey lived my grandfather and his family. The top storey was a store for corn, apples, and other farm produce; and up here my cousin Wilhelm—later shot down in an air battle by a school-fellow of mine—used to lie for hours picking off mice with an air-gun.

(6) Bavarian food had a richness and spiciness that we always missed on our return to England. We loved the rye bread, the dark pine honey, the huge ice-cream puddings made with fresh raspberry juice and the help of snow stored during the winter in an ice-house, my grandfather's venison, the honey cakes, the pastries, and particularly the sauces rich with different kinds of mushrooms. Also the pretzels, the carrots cooked in sugar, and summer pudding of cranberries and blueberries. In the orchard, close to the house, we could eat as many apples, pears, and greengages as we liked. There were also rows of black-currant and gooseberry bushes in the garden. The estate, despite the recency of my grandfather's tenure, his liberalism, and his experiments in modern agricultural methods, remained feudalistic. The poor, sweaty, savage-looking farm servants, who talked a dialect we could not understand, frightened us. They ranked lower even than the servants at home; and as for the colony of Italians, settled about half a mile from the house, whom my grandfather had imported as cheap labour for his brick factory—we associated them in our minds with "the gipsies in the wood" of the song. My grandfather took us over the factory one day and made me taste a lump of Italian *polenta*. My mother told us afterwards—when milk pudding at Wimbledon came to table burned, and we complained—"Those poor Italians in your grandfather's brick yard used to burn their *polenta* on purpose, sometimes, just for a change of flavour."

(7) Beyond the farm buildings at Laufzorn lay a large pond, fringed with irises and full of carp; my uncles netted it every three or four years. Once we watched the fun, and shouted when we saw the net pulled closer and closer to the shallow landing corner. It bulged with wriggling carp, and a big pike threshed about among them. I waded in to help, and came out with six leeches, like black rubber tubes, fastened to my legs; salt had to be put on their tails

before they would leave go. The farm labourers grew wildly excited; one of them gutted a fish with his thumb, and ate it raw. I also remember the truck line between the railway station, two miles away, and the brick yard. Since the land had a fall of perhaps one in a hundred between the factory and the station, the Italians used to load the trucks with bricks; then a squad of them would give the trucks a hard shove and run along the track pushing for twenty or thirty yards; after which the trucks sailed off all by themselves down to the station.

(8) We were allowed to climb up into the rafters of the big hay barn, and jump down into the springy hay; we gradually increased the height of the jumps. It was exciting to feel our insides left behind us in the air. Once we visited the Laufzorn cellar, not the ordinary beer cellar, but another into which one descended from the court-yard—quite dark except for a little slit window. A huge heap of potatoes lay on the floor; to get to the light, they had put out a twisted mass of long white feelers. In one corner was a dark hole closed by a gate: a secret passage from the house to a ruined monas-tery, a mile away—so we were told. My uncles had once been down some distance, but the air got bad and they came back; the gate had been put up to prevent others from trying it and losing their senses. Come to think of it, they were probably teasing us, and the hole led to the bottom of the *garde-robe*—which is a polite name for a mediaeval earth-closet.

(9) When we drove out with my grandfather, he was acclaimed with *"Grüss Gott, Herr Professor!"* by the principal personages of each village we went through. It always had a big inn with a rumbling skittle-alley, and a tall Maypole, banded like a barber's pole with blue and white, the Bavarian national colours. Apple and pear trees lined every road. The idea of these unguarded public fruit trees astonished us. We could not understand why any fruit remained on them. On Wimbledon Common even the horse-chestnut trees were pelted with sticks and stones, long before the chestnuts ripened, and in defiance of an energetic common keeper. What we least liked in Bavaria were the wayside crucifixes with their realistic blood and wounds, and the *ex-voto* pictures, like sign-boards, of naked souls in purgatory, grinning with anguish among high red and yellow

flames. Though taught to believe in hell, we did not like to be reminded of it.

(10) Munich we found sinister—disgusting fumes of beer and cigar smoke, and intense sounds of eating in the restaurants; the hotly dressed, enormously stout population in trams and trains; the ferocious officials. Then the terrifying Morgue, which children were not allowed to visit. Any notable who died was taken to the Morgue, they told us, and put in a chair, to sit in state for a day or two. If a general, he had his uniform on; or if a burgomaster's wife, she had on her silks and jewels. Strings were tied to their fingers, and the slightest movement of a single string would ring a great bell, in case any life remained in the corpse after all. I have never verified the truth of this, but it was true enough to me. When my grandfather died, about a year after our last visit, I pictured him in the Morgue with his bushy white hair, his morning coat, his striped trousers, his decorations, and his stethoscope. And perhaps, I thought, a silk hat, gloves, and cane on a table beside him. Trying, in a nightmare, to be alive; but knowing himself dead.

(11) The Headmaster of Rokeby School, who caned me for forgetting my gymnastic shoes, loved German culture, and impressed this feeling on the school, so that it stood to my credit that I could speak German and had visited Germany. At my other preparatory schools this German connexion seemed something at least excusable, and perhaps even interesting. Only at Charterhouse did it rank as a social offence. My history from the age of fourteen, when I went to Charterhouse, until just before the end of the War, when I began to think for myself, is a forced rejection of the German in me. I used to insist indignantly on being Irish, and took my self-protective stand on the technical point that solely the father's nationality counted. Of course, I also accepted the whole patriarchal system of things, convinced of the natural supremacy of male over female. My mother took the "love, honour, and obey" contract literally; my sisters were brought up to wish themselves boys, to be shocked at the idea of woman's suffrage, and not to expect so expensive an education as their brothers. The final decision in any domestic matter always rested with my father. My mother would say: "If two ride together, one must ride behind."

(12) We children did not talk German well; our genders and

minor parts of speech were shaky, and we never learned to read Gothic characters or script. Yet we had the sense of German so strongly that I feel I know German far better than French, though able to read French almost as fast as I can read English, and German only very painfully and slowly, with the help of a dictionary. I use different parts of my mind for the two languages. French is a surface acquirement which I could forget quite easily if I had no reason to speak it every now and then.

Questions

1. What topic phrases or sentences cover most of Paragraph 2? What material do they fail to cover?

2. Show that Paragraphs 3 and 4 lack unity. Do Paragraphs 2 through 4 form a unified whole? If so, devise a topic sentence that covers them all.

3. Does the general degree of unity in the first four paragraphs seem in or out of keeping with the overall character of Graves' essay? Explain.

4. Show how the opening phrase in each of Paragraphs 2 through 6 links to preceding material. What kinds of transitions are involved?

5. Identify the chief means of development in Paragraphs 6 through 10. Are they the probable means that Graves' overall subject in the essay suggests?

6. What general qualities of German culture emerge in the essay up through Paragraph 10 on Munich? What qualities of life in Munich, if any, are echoed in German country life? Does the comparison suggest chiefly differences, or underlying similarities, between the urban and rural aspects of the culture?

7. In Paragraph 4, Graves refers to the "terrifying portrait" of a former baron. Obviously the portrait is terrifying only from a child's point of view. Where in the essay do you find the child's point of view most clearly developed, and where do you find a point of view that could just as easily be an adult's as a child's? Compare the passages. (Do not consider the last two paragraphs.)

8. How distinguishable is Graves as a child from the other children in the essay? Discuss. How individual does he seem as a man writing an essay?

9. If you have read James Baldwin's essay in Section I, compare the qualities he finds in the French character with those Graves finds in the German character.

WAXWORKS AT THE ABBEY

VIRGINIA WOOLF

Though rather less esteemed than she once was, Virginia Woolf (1882–1941) remains one of the more important of modern novelists. A tireless experimenter, she reveals in such novels as *Mrs. Dalloway, To the Lighthouse,* and *The Waves* a sensibility alert to the most fleeting impression and nuance, and a style delicate, intense, and thoroughly subjective. Similar qualities, somewhat subdued, are present in many of her essays, which may be read in a number of collections, including *The Common Reader* (in two volumes), *The Death of the Moth,* and *The Captain's Death Bed.* Among her other nonfiction are *A Room of One's Own* and *Three Guineas,* both of which champion the rights of woman, and *A Writer's Diary,* a posthumous culling, by her husband, from her private journals. (Further information on Virginia Woolf appears on p. 368.)

(1) Nobody but a very great man could have worn the Duke of Wellington's top hat. It is as tall as a chimney, as straight as a ramrod, as black as a rock. One could have seen it a mile off advancing indomitably down the street. It must have been to this emblem of incorruptible dignity that the Duke raised his two fingers when passers-by respectfully saluted him. One is almost tempted to salute it now.

(2) The connexion between the waxworks in the Abbey and the Duke of Wellington's top hat is one that the reader will discover if he goes to the Abbey when the waxworks are shut. The waxworks have their hours of audience like other potentates. And if that hour

From *Granite and Rainbow* by Virginia Woolf. Copyright 1958, by Leonard Woolf. Reprinted by permission of Harcourt, Brace & World, Inc., and Leonard Woolf.

is four and it is now a trifle past two, one may spend the intervening moments profitably in the United Services Museum in Whitehall, among cannon and torpedoes and gun-carriages and helmets and spurs and faded uniforms and the thousand other objects which piety and curiosity have saved from time and treasured and numbered and stuck in glass cases forever. When the time comes to go, indeed, there is not as much contrast as one would wish, perhaps, between the Museum at one end of Whitehall and the Abbey at the other. Too many monuments solicit attention with outstretched hands; too many placards explain this and forbid that; too many sightseers shuffle and stare for the past and the dead and the mystic nature of the place to have full sway. Solitude is impossible. Do we wish to see the Chapels? We are shepherded in flocks by gentlemen in black gowns who are for ever locking us in or locking us out; round whom we press and gape; from whom drop raucously all kinds of dry unappetizing facts; how much beauty this tomb has; how much age that; when they were destroyed; by whom they were restored and what the cost was—until everybody longs to be let off a tomb or two and is thankful when the lesson hour is over. However, if one is very wicked, and very bored, and lags a little behind; if the key is left in the door and turns quite easily, so that after all it is an open question whether one has broken one's country's laws or not, then one can slip aside, run up a little dark staircase and find oneself in a very small chamber alone with Queen Elizabeth.

(3) The Queen dominates the room as she once dominated England. Leaning a little forward so that she seems to beckon you to come to her, she stands, holding her sceptre in one hand, her orb in the other. It is a drawn, anguished figure, with the pursed look of someone who goes in perpetual dread of poison or of trap; yet forever braces herself to meet the terror unflinchingly. Her eyes are wide and vigilant; her nose thin as the beak of a hawk; her lips shut tight; her eyebrows arched; only the jowl gives the fine drawn face its massiveness. The orb and the sceptre are held in the long thin hands of an artist, as if the fingers thrilled at the touch of them. She is immensely intellectual, suffering, and tyrannical. She will not allow one to look elsewhere.

(4) Yet in fact the little room is crowded. There are many hands here holding other sceptres and orbs. It is only beside Queen Elizabeth that the rest of the company seems insignificant. Flowing in velvet they fill their glass cases, as they once filled their thrones, with dignity. William and Mary are an amiable pair of monarchs; bazaar-opening, hospital-inspecting, modern; though the King, unfortunately, is a little short in the legs. Queen Anne fondles her orb in her lap with plump womanly hands that should have held a baby there. It is only by accident that they have clapped a great crown on her hair and told her to rule a kingdom, when she would so much rather have flirted discreetly—she was a pretty woman; or run to greet her husband smiling—she was a kindly one. Her type of beauty in its homeliness, its domesticity, comes down to us less impaired by time than the grander style. The Duchess of Richmond, who gave her face to Britannia on the coins, is out of fashion now. Only the carriage of the little head on the long neck, and the simper and the still look of one who has always stood still to be looked at assure us that she was beautiful once and had lovers beyond belief. The parrot sitting on its perch in the corner of the case seems to make its ironical comment on all that. Once only are we reminded of the fact that these effigies were moulded from the dead and that they were laid upon coffins and carried through the streets. The young Duke of Buckingham who died at Rome of consumption is the only one of them who has resigned himself to death. He lies very still with the ermine on his shoulders and the coronet on his brows, but his eyes are shut; his nose is a great peak between two sunk cheeks; he has succumbed to death and lies steeped in its calm. His aloofness compares strangely with the carnality of Charles the Second round the corner. King Charles still seems quivering with the passions and the greeds of life. The great lips are still pouting and watering and asking for more. The eyes are pouched and creased with all the long nights they have watched out—the torches, the dancing, and the women. In his dirty feathers and lace he is the very symbol of voluptuousness and dissipation, and his great blue-veined nose seems an irreverence on the part of the modeller, as if to set the crowd, as the procession comes by,

nudging each other in the ribs and telling merry stories of the monarch.

(5) And so from this garish bright assembly we run downstairs again into the Abbey, and enter that strange muddle and miscellany of objects both hallowed and ridiculous. Yet now the impression is less tumultuous than before. Two presences seem to control its incoherence, as sometimes a chattering group of people is ordered and quieted by the entry of someone before whom, they know not why, they fall silent. One is Elizabeth, beckoning; the other is an old top-hat.

Questions

1. Devise a topic sentence for Paragraph 1. What phrase in the paragraph defines the topic most adequately?

2. Try to devise a topic sentence for Paragraph 2. If it does not seem possible to devise a satisfactory one, divide the paragraph into smaller parts and see whether topic sentences can be devised for them. What holds the paragraph together?

3. Examine the opening sentences of Paragraphs 2 through 5. What sorts of links do they establish with earlier material? Compare and contrast their forcefulness and smoothness as transitions.

4. By what means does Mrs. Woolf develop Paragraph 1? Contrast it with the means by which she develops Paragraph 3.

5. What pattern—if any—determines the order in which Mrs. Woolf describes the several wax figures in the room with Queen Elizabeth? What pattern—or patterns—predominate in the broad arrangement of material in the sketch?

6. What are the two main connections between the Duke of Wellington and Queen Elizabeth discussed in the essay?

7. "Straight as a ramrod" (Paragraph 1) is a cliché. What makes it more than a cliché here? Rocks are perhaps not characteristically black. What justifies "black as a rock" (Paragraph 1)?

8. Point out the irony and exaggeration in the first three sentences in the first paragraph. What sort of man is the Duke of Wellington made to seem in the fourth sentence? Is there any material in the first four sentences that suggests that Mrs. Woolf means to be taken seriously in the

fifth? To what extent do her irony and exaggeration serve to ridicule the Duke of Wellington? To what extent do they do something else?

9. The dramatic relationship between Paragraphs 1 and 2 is similar to that between Paragraphs 3 and 4. Explain the relationship. What comment does the final paragraph make upon the relationship?

10. Is the essay mainly about the waxworks, about Elizabeth and Wellington, or something else? Base your answer upon a discussion of the chief topics of the several paragraphs and upon the general development of the essay.

11. Mrs. Woolf leaves behind as strong an impression of herself as of Queen Elizabeth. What qualities does she reveal? What aspects of the essay particularly suggest a woman writer instead of a man?

MARRAKECH

GEORGE ORWELL

George Orwell—in real life Eric Blair (1903–1950)—was born in Bengal, of English parents. Sent to England for his education, he returned to India before he was twenty, served for five years with the Imperial Police in Burma, and then lived a vagrant's existence in Europe. He settled finally in England, where he wrote his best-known books, *Animal Farm*, a satire on Soviet history, and *1984*, a frighteningly vivid image of life in a totalitarian society. But his best work is probably in the essay form, whose length and relative openness he found particularly suitable to his perceptions on society. His essays have been gathered in *Dickens, Dali, and Others; Shooting an Elephant;* and *Such, Such Were the Joys*. The prose that follows was composed in 1939, on the eve of World War II. (Further information on Orwell appears on pp. 235, 373.)

(1) As the corpse went past the flies left the restaurant table in a cloud and rushed after it, but they came back a few minutes later.

(2) The little crowd of mourners—all men and boys, no women —threaded their way across the market-place between the piles of pomegranates and the taxis and the camels, wailing a short chant over and over again. What really appeals to the flies is that the corpses here are never put into coffins, they are merely wrapped in a piece of rag and carried on a rough wooden bier on the shoulders of four friends. When the friends get to the burying-ground they hack an oblong hole a foot or two deep, dump the body in it and fling over it a little of the dried-up, lumpy earth, which is like

broken brick. No gravestone, no name, no identifying mark of any kind. The burying-ground is merely a huge waste of hummocky earth, like a derelict building-lot. After a month or two no one can even be certain where his own relatives are buried.

(3) When you walk through a town like this—two hundred thousand inhabitants, of whom at least twenty thousand own literally nothing except the rags they stand up in—when you see how the people live, and still more how easily they die, it is always difficult to believe that you are walking among human beings. All colonial empires are in reality founded upon that fact. The people have brown faces—besides, there are so many of them! Are they really the same flesh as yourself? Do they even have names? Or are they merely a kind of undifferentiated brown stuff, about as individual as bees or coral insects? They rise out of the earth, they sweat and starve for a few years, and then they sink back into the nameless mounds of the graveyard and nobody notices that they are gone. And even the graves themselves soon fade back into the soil. Sometimes, out for a walk, as you break your way through the prickly pear, you notice that it is rather bumpy underfoot, and only a certain regularity in the bumps tells you that you are walking over skeletons.

(4) I was feeding one of the gazelles in the public gardens.

(5) Gazelles are almost the only animals that look good to eat when they are still alive, in fact, one can hardly look at their hindquarters without thinking of mint sauce. The gazelle I was feeding seemed to know that this thought was in my mind, for though it took the piece of bread I was holding out it obviously did not like me. It nibbled rapidly at the bread, then lowered its head and tried to butt me, then took another nibble and then butted again. Probably its idea was that if it could drive me away the bread would somehow remain hanging in mid-air.

(6) An Arab navvy working on the path nearby lowered his heavy hoe and sidled slowly towards us. He looked from the gazelle to the bread and from the bread to the gazelle, with a sort of quiet amazement, as though he had never seen anything quite like this before. Finally he said shyly in French:

(7) "I could eat some of that bread."

(8) I tore off a piece and he stowed it gratefully in some secret place under his rags. This man is an employee of the Municipality.

(9) When you go through the Jewish quarters you gather some idea of what the medieval ghettoes were probably like. Under their Moorish rulers the Jews were only allowed to own land in certain restricted areas, and after centuries of this kind of treatment they have ceased to bother about overcrowding. Many of the streets are a good deal less than six feet wide, the houses are completely windowless, and sore-eyed children cluster everywhere in unbelievable numbers, like clouds of flies. Down the centre of the street there is generally running a little river of urine.

(10) In the bazaar huge families of Jews, all dressed in the long black robe and little black skull-cap, are working in dark fly-infested booths that look like caves. A carpenter sits crosslegged at a prehistoric lathe, turning chair-legs at lightning speed. He works the lathe with a bow in his right hand and guides the chisel with his left foot, and thanks to a lifetime of sitting in this position his left leg is warped out of shape. At his side his grandson, aged six, is already starting on the simpler parts of the job.

(11) I was just passing the coppersmiths' booths when somebody noticed that I was lighting a cigarette. Instantly, from the dark holes all round, there was a frenzied rush of Jews, many of them old grandfathers with flowing grey beards, all clamouring for a cigarette. Even a blind man somewhere at the back of one of the booths heard a rumour of cigarettes and came crawling out, groping in the air with his hand. In about a minute I had used up the whole packet. None of these people, I suppose, works less than twelve hours a day, and every one of them looks on a cigarette as a more or less impossible luxury.

(12) As the Jews live in self-contained communities they follow the same trades as the Arabs, except for agriculture. Fruit-sellers, potters, silversmiths, blacksmiths, butchers, leatherworkers, tailors, water-carriers, beggars, porters—whichever way you look you see nothing but Jews. As a matter of fact there are thirteen thousand of them, all living in the space of a few acres. A good job Hitler wasn't there. Perhaps he was on his way, however. You hear the

usual dark rumours about the Jews, not only from the Arabs but from the poorer Europeans.

(13) "Yes, mon vieux, they took my job away from me and gave it to a Jew. The Jews! They're the real rulers of this country, you know. They've got all the money. They control the banks, finance —everything."

(14) "But," I said, "isn't it a fact that the average Jew is a labourer working for about a penny an hour?"

(15) "Ah, that's only for show! They're all moneylenders really. They're cunning, the Jews."

(16) In just the same way, a couple of hundred years ago, poor old women used to be burned for witchcraft when they could not even work enough magic to get themselves a square meal.

(17) All people who work with their hands are partly invisible, and the more important the work they do, the less visible they are. Still, a white skin is always fairly conspicuous. In northern Europe, when you see a labourer ploughing a field, you probably give him a second glance. In a hot country, anywhere south of Gibraltar or east of Suez, the chances are that you don't even see him. I have noticed this again and again. In a tropical landscape one's eye takes in everything except the human beings. It takes in the dried-up soil, the prickly pear, the palm tree and the distant mountain, but it always misses the peasant hoeing at his patch. He is the same colour as the earth, and a great deal less interesting to look at.

(18) It is only because of this that the starved countries of Asia and Africa are accepted as tourist resorts. No one would think of running cheap trips to the Distressed Areas. But where the human beings have brown skins their poverty is simply not noticed. What does Morocco mean to a Frenchman? An orange-grove or a job in Government service. Or to an Englishman? Camels, castles, palm trees, Foreign Legionnaires, brass trays, and bandits. One could probably live there for years without noticing that for nine-tenths of the people the reality of life is an endless, back-breaking struggle to wring a little food out of an eroded soil.

(19) Most of Morocco is so desolate that no wild animal bigger

than a hare can live on it. Huge areas which were once covered with forest have turned into a treeless waste where the soil is exactly like broken-up brick. Nevertheless a good deal of it is cultivated, with frightful labour. Everything is done by hand. Long lines of women, bent double like inverted capital L's, work their way slowly across the fields, tearing up the prickly weeds with their hands, and the peasant gathering lucerne for fodder pulls it up stalk by stalk instead of reaping it, thus saving an inch or two on each stalk. The plough is a wretched wooden thing, so frail that one can easily carry it on one's shoulder, and fitted underneath with a rough iron spike which stirs the soil to a depth of about four inches. This is as much as the strength of the animals is equal to. It is usual to plough with a cow and a donkey yoked together. Two donkeys would not be quite strong enough, but on the other hand two cows would cost a little more to feed. The peasants possess no harrows, they merely plough the soil several times over in different directions, finally leaving it in rough furrows, after which the whole field has to be shaped with hoes into small oblong patches to conserve water. Except for a day or two after the rare rainstorms there is never enough water. Along the edges of the fields channels are hacked out to a depth of thirty or forty feet to get at the tiny trickles which run through the subsoil.

(20) Every afternoon a file of very old women passes down the road outside my house, each carrying a load of firewood. All of them are mummified with age and the sun, and all of them are tiny. It seems to be generally the case in primitive communities that the women, when they get beyond a certain age, shrink to the size of children. One day a poor old creature who could not have been more than four feet tall crept past me under a vast load of wood. I stopped her and put a five-sou piece (a little more than a farthing) into her hand. She answered with a shrill wail, almost a scream, which was partly gratitude but mainly surprise. I suppose that from her point of view, by taking any notice of her, I seemed almost to be violating a law of nature. She accepted her status as an old woman, that is to say as a beast of burden. When a family is travelling it is quite usual to see a father and a grown-up son riding ahead on donkeys, and an old woman following on foot, carrying the baggage.

(21) But what is strange about these people is their invisibility. For several weeks, always at about the same time of day, the file of old women had hobbled past the house with their firewood, and though they had registered themselves on my eyeballs I cannot truly say that I had seen them. Firewood was passing—that was how I saw it. It was only that one day I happened to be walking behind them, and the curious up-and-down motion of a load of wood drew my attention to the human being beneath it. Then for the first time I noticed the poor old earth-coloured bodies, bodies reduced to bones and leathery skin, bent double under the crushing weight. Yet I suppose I had not been five minutes on Moroccan soil before I noticed the overloading of the donkeys and was infuriated by it. There is no question that the donkeys are damnably treated. The Moroccan donkey is hardly bigger than a St. Bernard dog, it carries a load which in the British Army would be considered too much for a fifteen-hands mule, and very often its packsaddle is not taken off its back for weeks together. But what is peculiarly pitiful is that it is the most willing creature on earth, it follows its master like a dog and does not need either bridle or halter. After a dozen years of devoted work it suddenly drops dead, whereupon its master tips it into the ditch and the village dogs have torn its guts out before it is cold.

(22) This kind of thing makes one's blood boil, whereas—on the whole—the plight of the human beings does not. I am not commenting, merely pointing to a fact. People with brown skins are next door to invisible. Anyone can be sorry for the donkey with its galled back, but it is generally owing to some kind of accident if one even notices the old woman under her load of sticks.

(23) As the storks flew northward the Negroes were marching southward—a long, dusty column, infantry, screw-gun batteries, and then more infantry, four or five thousand men in all, winding up the road with a clumping of boots and a clatter of iron wheels.

(24) They were Senegalese, the blackest Negroes in Africa, so black that sometimes it is difficult to see whereabouts on their necks the hair begins. Their splendid bodies were hidden in reach-me-down

khaki uniforms, their feet squashed into boots that looked like blocks of wood, and every tin hat seemed to be a couple of sizes too small. It was very hot and the men had marched a long way. They slumped under the weight of their packs and the curiously sensitive black faces were glistening with sweat.

(25) As they went past a tall, very young Negro turned and caught my eye. But the look he gave me was not in the least the kind of look you might expect. Not hostile, not contemptuous, not sullen, not even inquisitive. It was the shy, wide-eyed Negro look, which actually is a look of profound respect. I saw how it was. This wretched boy, who is a French citizen and has therefore been dragged from the forest to scrub floors and catch syphilis in garrison towns, actually has feelings of reverence before a white skin. He has been taught that the white race are his masters, and he still believes it.

(26) But there is one thought which every white man (and in this connection it doesn't matter twopence if he calls himself a socialist) thinks when he sees a black army marching past. "How much longer can we go on kidding these people? How long before they turn their guns in the other direction?"

(27) It was curious, really. Every white man there had this thought stowed somewhere or other in his mind. I had it, so had the other onlookers, so had the officers on their sweating chargers and the white N.C.O.'s marching in the ranks. It was a kind of secret which we all knew and were too clever to tell; only the Negroes didn't know it. And really it was like watching a flock of cattle to see the long column, a mile or two miles of armed men, flowing peacefully up the road, while the great white birds drifted over them in the opposite direction, glittering like scraps of paper.

Questions

1. The objects of Orwell's attention are corpses, a gazelle, a hungry Arab, Jews, laborers, etc. In what single respect is Orwell interested in them? What, then, is the subject of the essay? In what passage or passages do you find the subject most explicitly stated?

2. Orwell does not always follow customary practice in paragraph development and in transition between paragraphs. Point out two or three

examples of his particular practice, and discuss the effects he achieves thereby. What other aspects of the essay, if any, have a similar character?

3. Orwell uses the device of a walk through Marrakech. How careful is he to keep the course of his walk before the reader? Do you see any special benefits he derives from using the walk and from using it the way he does?

4. In context, what does the word "invisible" mean (first sentence, Paragraph 17)? What sort of work is "important" work (same sentence)?

5. If you were reading the essay aloud, what would be the difference in tone with which you would read "Are they really the same flesh as yourself?" (Paragraph 3) and "How much longer can we go on kidding these people?" (Paragraph 26) What is the significance of the difference?

6. In terms of Orwell's subject, what is the difference in implication of the processions with which he begins and ends the essay?

7. What is the distinguishing characteristic of the material in each of the three sections? Could the first and third sections be reversed easily? Why or why not?

8. Orwell's essay is a kind of argument, but it is not a lawyer's argument or a philosopher's. What are the main points he is making, and why are they so effective?

9. What sort of man does Orwell seem? Consider what he says of himself, the things he does, the feelings he expresses, and what he says of other people.

THE REAL SECRET OF PILTDOWN

Loren Eiseley (1907—) has taught at a variety of colleges and universities, including the University of Pennsylvania, where he is professor of anthropology and the history of science. As in the essay that follows (from *The Immense Journey*), much of Eiseley's writing has sought to point up the relevance of scientific work not normally accessible to the nonspecialized reader. Among his other books are *Darwin's Century, The Firmament of Time,* and *Mind as Nature,* and he has also published verse and prose, not as yet collected, of a nonscientific nature.

(1) How did man get his brain? Many years ago Charles Darwin's great contemporary, and co-discoverer with him of the principle of natural selection, Alfred Russel Wallace, propounded that simple question. It is a question which has bothered evolutionists ever since, and when Darwin received his copy of an article Wallace had written on this subject he was obviously shaken. It is recorded that he wrote in anguish across the paper, "No!" and underlined the "No" three times heavily in a rising fervor of objection.

(2) Today the question asked by Wallace and never satisfactorily answered by Darwin has returned to haunt us. A skull, a supposedly very ancient skull, long used as one of the most powerful pieces of evidence documenting the Darwinian position upon human evolution, has been proven to be a forgery, a hoax perpetrated by an unscrupulous but learned amateur. In the fall of 1953 the famous Piltdown cranium, known in scientific circles all over the world since its dis-

covery in a gravel pit on the Sussex Downs in 1911, was jocularly dismissed by the world's press as the skull that had "made monkeys out of the anthropologists." Nobody remembered in 1953 that Wallace, the great evolutionist, had protested to a friend in 1913, "The Piltdown skull does not prove much, if anything!"

(3) Why had Wallace made that remark? Why, almost alone among the English scientists of his time, had he chosen to regard with a dubious eye a fossil specimen that seemed to substantiate the theory to which he and Darwin had devoted their lives? He did so for one reason: he did not believe what the Piltdown skull appeared to reveal as to the nature of the process by which the human brain had been evolved. He did not believe in a skull which had a modern brain box attached to an apparently primitive face and given, in the original estimates, an antiquity of something over a million years.

(4) Today we know that the elimination of the Piltdown skull from the growing list of valid human fossils in no way affects the scientific acceptance of the theory of evolution. In fact, only the circumstance that Piltdown had been discovered early, before we had a clear knowledge of the nature of human fossils and the techniques of dating them, made the long survival of this extraordinary hoax possible. Yet in the end it has been the press, absorbed in a piece of clever scientific detection, which has missed the real secret of Piltdown. Darwin saw in the rise of man, with his unique, time-spanning brain, only the undirected play of such natural forces as had created the rest of the living world of plants and animals. Wallace, by contrast, in the case of man, totally abandoned this point of view and turned instead toward a theory of a divinely directed control of the evolutionary process. The issue can be made clear only by a rapid comparison of the views of both men.

(5) As everyone who has studied evolution knows, Darwin propounded the theory that since the reproductive powers of plants and animals potentially far outpace the available food supply, there is in nature a constant struggle for existence on the part of every living thing. Since animals vary individually, the most cleverly adapted will survive and leave offspring which will inherit, and in their turn enhance, the genetic endowment they have received from their ancestors. Because the struggle for life is incessant, this unceasing process

promotes endless slow changes in bodily form, as living creatures are subjected to different natural environments, different enemies, and all the vicissitudes against which life has struggled down the ages.

(6) Darwin, however, laid just one stricture on his theory: it could, he maintained, "render each organized being only as perfect or a little more perfect than other inhabitants of the same country." It could allow any animal only a relative superiority, never an absolute perfection—otherwise selection and the struggle for existence would cease to operate. To explain the rise of man through the slow, incremental gains of natural selection, Darwin had to assume a long struggle of man with man and tribe with tribe.

(7) He had to make this assumption because man had far outpaced his animal associates. Since Darwin's theory of the evolutionary process is based upon the practical value of all physical and mental characters in the life struggle, to ignore the human struggle of man with man would have left no explanation as to how humanity by natural selection alone managed to attain an intellectual status so far beyond that of any of the animals with which it had begun its competition for survival.

(8) To most of the thinkers of Darwin's day this seemed a reasonable explanation. It was a time of colonial expansion and ruthless business competition. Peoples of primitive cultures, small societies lost on the world's margins, seemed destined to be destroyed. It was thought that Victorian civilization was the apex of human achievement and that other races with different customs and ways of life must be biologically inferior to Western man. Some of them were even described as only slightly superior to apes. The Darwinians, in a time when there were no satisfactory fossils by which to demonstrate human evolution, were unconsciously minimizing the abyss which yawned between man and ape. In their anxiety to demonstrate our lowly origins they were throwing modern natives into the gap as representing living "missing links" in the chain of human ascent.

(9) It was just at this time that Wallace lifted a voice of lonely protest. The episode is a strange one in the history of science, for Wallace had, independently of Darwin, originally arrived at the same general conclusion as to the nature of the evolutionary process. Nevertheless, only a few years after the publication of Darwin's work,

The Origin of Species, Wallace had come to entertain a point of view which astounded and troubled Darwin. Wallace, who had had years of experience with natives of the tropical archipelagoes, abandoned the idea that they were of mentally inferior cast. He did more. He committed the Darwinian heresy of maintaining that their mental powers were far in excess of what they really needed to carry on the simple food-gathering techniques by which they survived.

(10) "How, then," Wallace insisted, "was an organ developed so far beyond the needs of its possessor? Natural selection could only have endowed the savage with a brain a little superior to that of an ape, whereas he actually possesses one but little inferior to that of the average member of our learned societies."

(11) At a time when many primitive peoples were erroneously assumed to speak only in grunts or to chatter like monkeys, Wallace maintained his view of the high intellectual powers of natives by insisting that "the capacity of uttering a variety of distinct articulate sounds and of applying to them an almost infinite amount of modulation . . . is not in any way inferior to that of the higher races. An instrument has been developed in advance of the needs of its possessor."

(12) Finally, Wallace challenged the whole Darwinian position on man by insisting that artistic, mathematical, and musical abilities could not be explained on the basis of natural selection and the struggle for existence. Something else, he contended, some unknown spiritual element, must have been at work in the elaboration of the human brain. Why else would men of simple cultures possess the same basic intellectual powers which the Darwinists maintained could be elaborated only by competitive struggle?

(13) "If you had not told me you had made these remarks," Darwin said, "I should have thought they had been added by someone else. I differ grievously from you and am very sorry for it." He did not, however, supply a valid answer to Wallace's queries. Outside of murmuring about the inherited effects of habit—a contention without scientific validity today—Darwin clung to his original position. Slowly Wallace's challenge was forgotten and a great complacency settled down upon the scientific world.

(14) For seventy years after the publication of *The Origin of*

Species in 1859, there were only two finds of fossil human skulls which seemed to throw any light upon the Darwin-Wallace controversy. One was the discovery of the small-brained Java Ape Man, the other was the famous Piltdown or "dawn man." Both were originally dated as lying at the very beginning of the Ice Age, and, though these dates were later to be modified, the skulls, for a very long time, were regarded as roughly contemporaneous and very old.

(15) Two more unlike "missing links" could hardly be imagined. Though they were supposed to share a million-year antiquity, the one was indeed quite primitive and small-brained; the other, Piltdown, in spite of what seemed a primitive lower face, was surprisingly modern in brain. Which of these forms told the true story of human development? Was a large brain old? Had ages upon ages of slow, incremental, Darwinian increase produced it? The Piltdown skull seemed to suggest such a development.

(16) Many were flattered to find their anthropoid ancestry seemingly removed to an increasingly remote past. If one looked at the Java Ape Man, one was forced to contemplate an ancestor, not terribly remote in time, who still had a face and a brain which hinted strongly of the ape. Yet, when by geological evidence this "erect walking ape-man" was finally assigned to a middle Ice Age antiquity, there arose the immediate possibility that Wallace could be right in his suspicion that the human brain might have had a surprisingly rapid development. By contrast, the Piltdown remains seemed to suggest a far more ancient and slow-paced evolution of man. The Piltdown hoaxer, in attaching an ape jaw to a human skull fragment, had, perhaps unwittingly, created a creature which supported the Darwinian idea of man, not too unlike the man of today, extending far back into pre-Ice Age times.

(17) Which story was the right one? Until the exposé of Piltdown in 1953, both theories had to be considered possible and the two hopelessly unlike fossils had to be solemnly weighed in the same balance. Today Piltdown is gone. In its place we are confronted with the blunt statement of two modern scientists, M. R. A. Chance and A. P. Mead.

(18) "No adequate explanation," they confess over eighty years after Darwin scrawled his vigorous "No!" upon Wallace's paper,

"has been put forward to account for so large a cerebrum as that found in man."*

(19) We have been so busy tracing the tangible aspects of evolution in the *forms of animals* that our heads, the little globes which hold the midnight sky and the shining, invisible universes of thought, have been taken about as much for granted as the growth of a yellow pumpkin in the fall.

(20) Now a part of this mystery as it is seen by the anthropologists of today lies in the relation of the brain to time. "If," Wallace had said, "researches in all parts of Europe and Asia fail to bring to light any proofs of man's presence far back in the Age of Mammals, *it will be at least a presumption that he came into existence at a much later date and by a more rapid process of development.*" If human evolution should prove to be comparatively rapid, "explosive" in other words, Wallace felt that his position would be vindicated, because such a rapid development of the brain would, he thought, imply a divinely directed force at work in man. In the 1870's when he wrote, however, human prehistory was largely an unknown blank. Today we can make a partial answer to Wallace's question. Since the exposure of the Piltdown hoax all of the evidence at our command —and it is considerable—points to man, in his present form, as being one of the youngest and newest of all earth's swarming inhabitants.

(21) The Ice Age extends behind us in time for, at most, a million years. Though this may seem long to one who confines his studies to the written history of man, it is, in reality, a very short period as the student of evolution measures time. It is a period marked more by the extinction of some of the last huge land animals, like the hairy mammoth and the saber-toothed tiger, then it is by the appearance of new forms of life. To this there is only one apparent exception: the rise and spread of man over the Old World land mass.

(22) Most of our knowledge of him—even in his massive-faced, beetle-browed stage—is now confined, since the loss of Piltdown, to the last half of the Ice Age. If we pass backward beyond this point we can find traces of crude tools, stone implements which hint that some earlier form of man was present here and there in Europe, Asia,

* *Symposia of the Society for Experimental Biology,* VII, Evolution (New York: Academic Press, 1953), p. 395.

and particularly Africa in the earlier half of Ice Age time, but to the scientist it is like peering into the mists floating over an unknown landscape. Here and there through the swirling vapor one catches a glimpse of a shambling figure, or a half-wild primordial face stares back at one from some momentary opening in the fog. Then, just as one grasps at a clue, the long gray twilight settles in and the wraiths and the half-heard voices pass away.

(23) Nevertheless, particularly in Africa, a remarkable group of human-like apes have been discovered: creatures with small brains and teeth of a remarkably human cast. Prominent scientists are still debating whether they are on the direct line of ascent to man or are merely near relatives of ours. Some, it is now obvious, existed too late in time to be our true ancestors, though this does not mean that their bodily characters may not tell us what the earliest anthropoids who took the human turn of the road were like.

(24) These apes are not all similar in type or appearance. They are men and yet not men. Some are frailer-bodied, some have great, bone-cracking jaws and massive gorilloid crests atop their skulls. This fact leads us to another of Wallace's remarkable perceptions of long ago. With the rise of the truly human brain, Wallace saw that man had transferred to his machines and tools many of the alterations of parts that in animals take place through evolution of the body. Unwittingly, man had assigned to his machines the selective evolution which in the animal changes the nature of its bodily structure through the ages. Man of today, the atomic manipulator, the aeronaut who flies faster than sound, has precisely the same brain and body as his ancestors of twenty thousand years ago who painted the last Ice Age mammoths on the walls of caves in France.

(25) To put it another way, it is man's ideas that have evolved and changed the world about him. Now, confronted by the lethal radiations of open space and the fantastic speeds of his machines, he has to invent new electronic controls that operate faster than his nerves, and he must shield his naked body against atomic radiation by the use of protective metals. Already he is physically antique in this robot world he has created. All that sustains him is that small globe of gray matter through which spin his ever-changing conceptions of the universe.

(26) Yet, as Wallace, almost a hundred years ago, glimpsed this timeless element in man, he uttered one more prophecy. When we come to trace out history into the past, he contended, sooner or later we will come to a time when the body of man begins to differ and diverge more extravagantly in its appearance. Then, he wrote, we shall know that we stand close to the starting point of the human family. In the twilight before the dawn of the human mind, man will not have been able to protect his body from change and his remains will bear the marks of all the forces that play upon the rest of life. He will be different in his form. He will be, in other words, as variable in body as we know the South African man-apes to be.

(27) Today, with the solution of the Piltdown enigma, we must settle the question of the time involved in human evolution in favor of Wallace, not Darwin; we need not, however, pursue the mystical aspects of Wallace's thought—since other factors yet to be examined may well account for the rise of man. The rapid fading out of archaeological evidence of tools in lower Ice Age times—along with the discovery of man-apes of human aspect but with ape-sized brains, yet possessing a diverse array of bodily characters—suggests that the evolution of the human brain was far more rapid than that conceived of in early Darwinian circles. At that time it was possible to hear the Eskimos spoken of as possible survivals of Miocene men of several million years ago. By contrast to this point of view, man and his rise now appear short in time—explosively short. There is every reason to believe that whatever the nature of the forces involved in the production of the human brain, a long slow competition of human group with human group or race with race would not have resulted in such similar mental potentialities among all peoples everywhere. Something—some other factor—has escaped our scientific attention.

(28) There are certain strange bodily characters which mark man as being more than the product of a dog-eat-dog competition with his fellows. He possesses a peculiar larval nakedness, difficult to explain on survival principles; his periods of helpless infancy and childhood are prolonged; he has aesthetic impulses which, though they vary in intensity from individual to individual, appear in varying manifestations among all peoples. He is totally dependent, in

the achievement of human status, upon the careful training he receives in human society.

(29) Unlike a solitary species of animal, he cannot develop alone. He has suffered a major loss of precise instinctive controls of behavior. To make up for this biological lack, society and parents condition the infant, supply his motivations, and promote his long-drawn training at the difficult task of becoming a normal human being. Even today some individuals fail to make this adjustment and have to be excluded from society.

(30) We are now in a position to see the wonder and terror of the human predicament: man is totally dependent on society. Creature of dream, he has created an invisible world of ideas, beliefs, habits, and customs which buttress him about and replace for him the precise instincts of the lower creatures. In this invisible universe he takes refuge, but just as instinct may fail an animal under some shift of environmental conditions, so man's cultural beliefs may prove inadequate to meet a new situation, or, on an individual level, the confused mind may substitute, by some terrible alchemy, cruelty for love.

(31) The profound shock of the leap from animal to human status is echoing still in the depths of our subconscious minds. It is a transition which would seem to have demanded considerable rapidity of adjustment in order for human beings to have survived, and it also involved the growth of prolonged bonds of affection in the subhuman family, because otherwise its naked, helpless offspring would have perished.

(32) It is not beyond the range of possibility that this strange reduction of instincts in man in some manner forced a precipitous brain growth as a compensation—something that had to be hurried for survival purposes. Man's competition, it would thus appear, may have been much less with his own kind than with the dire necessity of building about him a world of ideas to replace his lost animal environment. . . .

(33) Modern science would go on to add that many of the characters of man, such as his lack of fur, thin skull, and globular head, suggest mysterious changes in growth rates which preserve, far into human maturity, foetal or infantile characters which hint that the forces creat-

ing man drew him fantastically out of the very childhood of his brutal forerunners. Once more the words of Wallace come back to haunt us: "We may safely infer that the savage possesses a brain capable, if cultivated and developed, of performing work of a kind and degree far beyond what he ever requires it to do."

(34) As a modern man, I have sat in concert halls and watched huge audiences floating dazed on the voice of a great singer. Alone in the dark box I have heard far off as if ascending out of some black stairwell the guttural whisperings and bestial coughings out of which that voice arose. Again, I have sat under the slit dome of a mountain observatory and marveled, as the great wheel of the galaxy turned in all its midnight splendor, that the mind in the course of three centuries has been capable of drawing into its strange, nonspatial interior that world of infinite distance and multitudinous dimensions.

(35) Ironically enough, science, which can show us the flints and the broken skulls of our dead fathers, has yet to explain how we have come so far so fast, nor has it any completely satisfactory answer to the question asked by Wallace long ago. Those who would revile us by pointing to an ape at the foot of our family tree grasp little of the awe with which the modern scientist now puzzles over man's lonely and supreme ascent. As one great student of paleoneurology, Dr. Tilly Edinger, recently remarked, "If man has passed through a Pithecanthropus phase, the evolution of his brain has been unique, not only in its result but also in its tempo. . . . Enlargement of the cerebral hemispheres by 50 per cent seems to have taken place, speaking geologically, within an instant, and without having been accompanied by any major increase in body size."

(36) The true secret of Piltdown, though thought by the public to be merely the revelation of an unscrupulous forgery, lies in the fact that it has forced science to reëxamine carefully the history of the most remarkable creation in the world—the human brain.

Questions

1. The opening sentence provides the topic of the whole essay. Show that Eiseley paraphrases this sentence four or five times later.

2. Where in the essay is the first succinct expression of Darwin's explanation of how man got his brain? For which subsequent paragraphs, if

any, will this phrase or sentence serve as the topic? Where is the first expression of Wallace's explanation? For which subsequent paragraphs, if any, will this phrase or sentence serve as the topic?

3. Analyze the transitions within Paragraphs 3 and 4. What is the single most obvious device in each paragraph, and why are both devices particularly appropriate for the sort of essay Eiseley is writing?

4. Analyze the means of development in Paragraph 5. To what extent in this paragraph is the means of development also a transitional device?

5. Paragraph 13 repeats the opening paragraph and the first sentence in Paragraph 2. What is the reason for this repetition?

6. The phrase "the relation of the brain to time" in the opening sentence of Paragraph 20 is a topic phrase for one or more of the succeeding paragraphs. How many does it in fact cover? Explain.

7. Eiseley eventually gets around to suggesting his own answer to the question of where man got his brain. What sentence opens his discussion, and what sentence most succinctly expresses his view?

8. Review the essay and reconsider Questions 2, 3, 6, and 7. You should be able to decide whether Eiseley's view is fundamentally closer to Darwin's or Wallace's. Discuss.

9. Eiseley describes man as a "creature of dream." Read George Santayana's essay in Section I, and write a discussion of whether Santayana means the same thing when he says that "men are ruled by imagination."

section **III**

ORGANIZATION

If a person is writing up a physics experiment or explaining how to refine sugar, he usually has no trouble in organizing his writing. He has followed a prescribed or obvious order in making the experiment and observed a fixed order in the refining process. All he has to do is transfer the pattern to the page. With most other writing, though, his task is not so easy, and he may have to make a choice among several organizational patterns or he may have to devise a scheme of his own.

Suppose a writer is going to describe Times Square in New York City, where Broadway slants across the intersection of Seventh Avenue and 42nd Street. He knows the place thoroughly—the movie houses, restaurants, lights, streets, people—everything. Where does he begin, where does he end, and where is the middle? What he could do is to take an imaginary walk over to Times Square from Sixth Avenue and describe everything as it struck his eye. Or he could walk up from 38th Street and describe everything that struck his ear. Or he could walk over from Eighth Avenue and concentrate on the odors. Just to think about such possibilities suggests one fact about organizing the ordinary piece of writing: to begin with, you can't put everything in, not every sight, sound, and odor. Deciding what you want to leave out is one of the first stages of organizing an essay. So the writer decides that he wants to focus on the sights and include a few sounds. He still has to decide whether he wants to walk over from Eighth Avenue or possibly drop down in a helicopter. He is likely to make this decision according to whether he has ever seen Times Square from a helicopter and what it is about the sights of Times Square that he finds interesting. Perhaps the most striking thing from his own experience in Times Square is not the huge advertisements or the mad traffic or the Hindus and Arabs and Chinese who walk side by side with black and white Americans, but instead the restaurant that has tables and chairs outside where people sit comfortably eating and drinking and talking as though they were living in a quiet village. Well, then, how to organize such an

essay? The answer may come easily. The person does not want to begin with the restaurant; he wants to end with it. In a broad way he
wants, in the first part, to describe some of the most obvious, blatant
aspects of the center of the big city—the tall buildings, the masses of
people, the noise, and so forth; and then he wants to present the restaurant by way of contrast. In thinking this over he may decide that
he has a particular point to make: Times Square is not all it seems—
or beneath the surface, life in Times Square is much like life elsewhere—or Times Square has everything, including the opposite of
what it is supposed to have. With one of these points in mind, the
person now has his broad organizational pattern: he will use many
details about the huge city center to lead to the contradiction of the
restaurant. There will still be incidental problems of organization for
him to face; and he may decide that, given the point he wants to make,
he will begin at 50th Street and walk down to Times Square as though
he were on his first visit, observing all the obvious sights and sounds
of Times Square as they occur and then stumbling upon the restaurant
at 42nd Street.

   In general, then, organizing an essay means not merely adopting a
pattern, but adopting a pattern that is appropriate to one's intentions.
Until the writer knows what he wants to say in his essay, he is unlikely
to know what his best organizational pattern is. In fact, the organization of an essay becomes part of the idea of the essay. Suppose that
the person who wants to discuss the strangeness of an outdoor restaurant in Times Square puts his description of the restaurant first, and
then goes on to describe the noise and bustle around it. The chances
are that he will not make his point—even if he states it baldly—for an
effective contrast requires that the reader have the noise and bustle in
mind while he contemplates the restaurant, instead of trying to recall
the restaurant while he is told about the noise and bustle. This is not
to say that no one should begin a description of Times Square with the
restaurant, only that an essay so organized would very likely achieve a
different effect and have a different point. Perhaps to one person the
striking thing about Times Square is that it is the most public of places.
He begins with the restaurant, and shows a diner whose private
thoughts are interrupted by a car backfiring, a rubber-necking tourist,

a waiter who wants the table for another customer and another tip. When the diner leaves and walks up toward 50th Street, his thoughts disintegrate under the barrage of sights and sounds.

In many cases, a writer will find that the sort of audience he is writing for will affect his organization, just as the sort of audience may affect what he has to say. If the person describing Times Square is a New Yorker writing for New Yorkers, it is unlikely that he is going to risk boring them by trudging up one street or down another. They know too much. He may want to begin his essay as he enters the restaurant, with a glance over his shoulder at all the familiar sights, and then take his seat and linger over the village atmosphere. Or if he begins in the restaurant—trying to show how public Times Square is— he may feel no need to leave at all.

Organizing an essay ought never to be a mechanical process. If everything is in order, but the order is pointless, then the essay is badly organized. Following are descriptions of twelve familiar organizational patterns. Every one of them is a mechanical pattern unless the writer has good reason for following it.

Argumentation. Basically, an argument divides into three parts: assertion; evidence, illustration, or reasoning; and conclusion, or reassertion. Usually the pattern is complicated through the use, for example, of secondary illustration; and a well-argued piece of writing will take into account objections, counter-evidence, and so forth. If the writer is advocating an action, he will have to discuss the need for the action and the advantages of the particular action over other possible actions. The arrangement of the elements of an argument is not rigid, but need can be expected to precede evidence, and evidence can be expected to precede counter-evidence.

Cause-effect. This term more often describes the substance of an essay than the organizing principle behind it. If a writer deals with a single cause and its effect (for example, the raid on Harper's Ferry before the Civil War and its repercussions), cause-effect merely gives him a beginning for organizing his material. If he is dealing in multiple causes, he faces the problem of ordering them. Cause-effect is a significant organizing principle when the writer is dealing with a chain of several circumstances that he can link causally:

Northern anti-slavery sentiment, the Kansas aid movement, the attraction of John Brown to Kansas, John Brown's murder of pro-slavery men at Pottawatomie Creek, his raising of funds to continue such violence, his raid on Harper's Ferry, and the development of Northern sympathy for him.

Chronology. Unlike some other organizational patterns, chronology is a two-way street. A writer can begin at the beginning of a chronological sequence or he can begin at the end of it, and often enough in the first instance he may want to interrupt the sequence for a flashback. Chronology is frequently involved in other organizational patterns such as cause-effect and narrative sequence. The chain of causes described in the previous paragraph is chronological.

Classification (and Analysis). As a preliminary act in organizing an essay, classification can be of the greatest help. A welter of causes of the Civil War (the Depression of 1857, the Kansas–Nebraska Bill, economic inequality between North and South, the Dred Scott Decision, the election of Lincoln, the firing on Fort Sumter) could be arranged under the headings of economic, political, and moral causes. After such classification, the writer would still have to decide upon the ordering of the three main causes and the ordering of the causes subordinate to each of them.

Dramatic Organization. In dramatic literature one frequently sees a progressive raising of tension to a climax toward the end of the play, and sometimes a brief falling off afterward. Such a structure is occasionally a primary or secondary organizational pattern in essays. A writer who is interested in discussing the economic, political, and moral causes of the Civil War for a popular audience may decide that his main organizational scheme will be chronological so that he can also be dramatic and build his discussion to a climax with the firing on Fort Sumter.

Order of Importance. Especially in brief essays and occasionally in longer, serious ones, an arrangement of topics in order of importance is very useful. In the longer essay, the discussion usually builds toward the most important topic instead of beginning with the most important and descending—so as not to lose the reader along the way. Building toward the most important topic is, of course, to some extent dramatic.

Investigation and Conclusions. Less formally, this can be called *observation and inference.* Transferring to paper the order of investigation in a physics experiment provides the most rigid illustration of this sort of organization. But the journalist who observed a Civil War battle and drew certain conclusions about Northern generalship from it could have organized his newspaper report in broadly the same way.

Narrative Sequence. A connected series of events and actions is the basic order employed in short stories and novels, and it is often used in essays. Because events and actions occur in time, narrative sequence is chronological, and it can, of course, be interrupted or reversed for good reason.

Process. New methods of refining sugar, making steel, or taking inventory of army supplies are occasionally developed; but the new process usually becomes fixed for a time. The writer who wishes to report on the process can follow the fixed order if he wants. If he is writing for a popular audience instead of a technical one, he is likely to want to leave out steps of the process; he may try to shape the process dramatically or in some other way.

Spatial Order. A writer who is describing a fair may begin at the gate and walk along the main avenue. A writer who is describing the Mississippi may take a boat down it. A writer who is describing a person's character may set him off on a trip in order to do so.

Order of Thought. The order of thought can be logical, rational, erratic, emotional, irrational. A writer who is conducting an argument will want to make a logical or rational progression such as is suggested above under "Argumentation" and "Investigation and Conclusions"; he will not want to put down his ideas helter-skelter and justify his order by saying that was the way they came to mind. But a writer of a personal essay may combine some degree of rational order with some degree of stream of consciousness, for the presumed value of the personal essay lies, in large part, in its display of the writer's consciousness. The personal essay is perhaps the most difficult sort of essay to write successfully.

Visual Order. This sort of organization frequently goes with spatial order. It is especially useful in the personal essay where the perspective of the writer is most in evidence.

THE MOTORCAR

E. B. WHITE

Though he has published verse (*The Lady Is Cold, Fox of Peapack*) and several children's books (*Stuart Little, Charlotte's Web*), White is best known for his witty, informal, and very human essays on the passing scene. Though these are often personal and whimsical in manner, and almost any event can serve as stimulus, White's tendency is to move outward from the particular experience to some of its larger social and cultural implications. The purchase of a motorcar, as in the prose that follows, can prove to be more than one man's dilemma. (Further information on White appears on pp. 79, 248.)

A Pavilion near Jeffreys Hook, March 16, 1958

(1) The automobile industry, according to the newspaper that usurps my bed, is facing a period of crucial decisions. On the whole, this is good news. There is always the chance that during a time of crisis some car manufacturer will shake free from the vision of stratocruisers and rockets and at last see the automobile for what it is—a handy little four-wheeled contraption that moves along the surface of the earth carrying an American family on errands of an inconsequential nature, a vehicle requiring no wings for rising into the air, no fins for diving into the sea. The determination to resist the queer, corrupting conception of the automobile as a winged thing or a finny thing should be the first crucial decision the industry makes.

(2) For twenty-five years car makers have foolishly pursued two false and seductive ideas: first, that the stature of man is decreasing;

second, that the way to create beauty is to turn the matter over to a style department after consulting a few motivational-research monkeys and a covey of social psychologists. Everyone should know that the stature of man is *not* decreasing (if anything, men and women are somewhat taller than they used to be), and anyone who has eyes in his head should know that beauty is the child of truth, not to be had by last-minute scheming and conniving. I do not recall ever seeing a properly designed boat that was not also a beautiful boat. Purity of line, loveliness, symmetry—these arrive mysteriously whenever someone who knows and cares creates something that is perfectly fitted to do its work, whether the object is a grain scoop, a suspension bridge, or a guillotine. Nobody styled the orb web of a spider, nobody styled the sixteen-foot canoe. Both are beautiful, and for a common reason: each was designed to perform a special task under special conditions. I think it would be impossible to build a thoroughly honest and capable motor-car, correctly designed to meet the conditions a car must meet, and have it turn out to be anything but good-looking. But the method used in Detroit is to turn some engineers loose in one room and some stylists in another room, while the motivational pixies scamper back and forth whispering secrets in everybody's ear, and after months of such fooling and plotting and compromising and adjusting, then out comes the new automobile, and no wonder it carries the telltale marks of monstrosity on its poor tortured body. In many cases it looks as though the final licks had been given it by a group of emotionally disturbed children.

(3) Not only have car makers lacked faith in the essential truth of a motor vehicle but they have painted their lily so lavishly and so drunkenly that they have ruined its appearance and added greatly to its cost. A garbage scow carries a filthy cargo but it has clean lines—cleaner by far than the lines of the 1958 automobile.

(4) The mess the car makers find themselves in today bears a strong likeness to the pickle the motion-picture industry got into ten or a dozen years ago. That, too, was the direct result of indulging in dream life and underestimating the intelligence and stature of the people. The movie makers, if you remember, got so absorbed in the work of examining the entrails of pollsters and taking everybody's pulse in America to see what the average heartbeat was, they had no time to

examine their own innards for a subject worth filming. It took them a number of years to pull out of their queer preoccupation with the human circulatory system and get back into the simple creative life. Now it's the car makers whose fingers are wrapped around my wrist in what feels like the grip of death. If they really want to know the state of my health and the shape of my desires, I shall be happy to accommodate them, but I warn them it's not the way to go about designing and building an automobile.

(5) I sit here in this pavilion, running a low fever and looking out at the world from a high window. My view includes a small slice of the West Side Highway, southbound. The cars pass in an endless parade, and there is a terrible sameness to them—a litter of lively pigs from the brood sow in Detroit. Some are slightly upswept, some are slightly downcast (like the industry itself). But almost all of them seem to have been poured from the same mold: the Cadillac is blood brother to the Ford, the Lincoln and the Plymouth could lie down together in a field of daisies and you'd hardly know they weren't twins.

(6) My newspaper says that the atmosphere in the hub of the auto industry is one of gloom. The bedtime story I am about to tell, revealing my pulse rate, my prejudices, and the state of my dreams, is not calculated to lift the industry's spirits, but it is a true story, and it concerns a man and his search for a car, and on that account it does bear on the vexing problems of these troubled times. I'll begin at the beginning, it's so soothing to do it that way.

(7) In the summer of 1949, being then of sound mind and in good pocket, I purchased a four-door De Soto sedan in a pleasing shade of green—a green as rich as the new growth of a spruce tree in the spring. I mention the name of De Soto hesitantly, for I have no wish to send a convulsion of pain through the bodies of Harlow Curtice and Henry Ford II, and indeed the name of the car could as well be Oldsmobile or Mercury and make no difference; it's the year 1949 that is the pertinent fact here. At any rate, my new car seemed at the time a very agreeable and serviceable automobile, and so it turned out to be. For this beauty I paid the handsome sum, in cash, of two thousand four hundred and ninety-five dollars, a veritable pile. I took possession of the car in Bangor, Maine, a few blocks from the railroad station. Through the years that have intervened, having through God's grace

remained of sound mind, I have managed not to lose possession of the car, although there have been a couple of narrow squeaks in recent months.

(8) I now skip lightly over eight years and we come to the summer of 1957. Last August, when somebody else was at the wheel, my car met with a slight accident involving another vehicle. The whole affair was on a very low pitch of disaster: the other car was motionless at the time, and my own car was moving at the rate of about seven miles per hour. But despite the trivial nature of the encounter, my right front fender received a long, straight slash the whole length of it, raked fore and aft by the strong, sharp blade of the opponent's rear bumper. I was so impressed by the neatness of the stroke that I drove to a local garage and instructed the mechanic to finish the job off with his shears and then weld a temporary bracket to the frame, to support what was left of the fender; namely, its upper part. When this was accomplished, the first discovery I made was that the right, or damaged, side of my car presented a better appearance, on the whole, than the left, or un-damaged, side. The right front wheel had been exposed to view by the loss of the lower half of the fender, and I noted with satisfaction that a wheel revealed is more exciting to the eye than a wheel concealed.

(9) For a few days, neither my wife nor I paid any particular at-tention to the fact that our family automobile was now asymmetrical and beat up. Our minds were on other matters, and when we wanted to go somewhere we would simply get in the car and go, enjoying the same inward elegance to which we had long been accustomed. But then one day the subject came up, as it was bound to sooner or later, and the phrase "new car" escaped from our lips and went darting about the rooms like Tinker Bell. "New car"! What an intoxicating sound the words make—like the jingle of frogs! What hot thoughts course through the mind! Before embarking on the golden adventure of shopping for an automobile, however, we strolled out together one morning to take a long, hard look at what we had in mind (a 1949 De Soto) and size up the true situation in a mood of cold sobriety.

(10) The busted fender was, of course, a brilliant reality. And there was also the little matter of the torn upholstery on the front seat, which looked like the work of squirrels but was actually *my* work. I habitually carry a jackknife in my right-hand trousers pocket, and the

bony structure of this useful tool, working through to the cloth of the seat, had taken its toll over the years. Also, on one occasion I had deliberately cut a swatch from the seat, to give to an upholsterer as a sample. This was during a phase when we were entertaining the idea of reupholstering the car. Nothing came of the reupholstery project at the time; it died of its own weight, leaving the front seat with its swatch-hole as a reminder of our good intentions and untapped resourcefulness.

(11) After studying our car for a few minutes, we decided that the word for it was "shabby." Both of us knew, though, that we were looking at an automobile the likes of which (if we were to lose it) we might not see again, a car that had not given us a moment's anxiety or pain in the whole time we had owned it and that still served us in an almost perfect manner. Its paint, after eight years, compared favorably with the paint on the new crop of cars; its metal seemed somehow stronger and heavier; all the doors worked with precision; and the only rattle it had was one it had had from the very beginning—a built-in rattle caused by a small glass plate on the instrument panel framing the legend "DE LUXE." I had always rather enjoyed this rattle as a piece of audible irony; it made me chuckle to observe that the only cheap streak in the entire car was caused by the stylist's written proclamation of swank. Every now and again I'd tire of the noise and plug the glass plate with a paper match or a tiny wad of Kleenex, but sooner or later DE LUXE would sound off again. DE LUXE was all that ever broke the silence of De Soto.

(12) The upshot of our conference was this: Because of "shabbiness" we would look for a new car, but we would take our time about it. We were not faced with a crisis in transportation (the car ran fine), and we agreed that we would trade in our old automobile on a new one only if we could find a new one that seemed to be at least as good as what we had. We would not buy a new car merely because it bore the label "1957" or the label "1958." We would not let shabbiness embarrass us into doing anything foolish. That was the way we talked in our pride.

(13) My wife is the sort of woman who does not notice automobiles except during the infrequent periods when we are in the process of selecting one. She has never counted on an automobile to invest her

with prestige. (She was a distinguished woman at birth and needed no help from Detroit.) Motorcars simply do not attract her attention or excite her fancy, and I knew well enough that it was eight years since she'd last examined an automobile with eyes that see, and that she was in for a number of surprises, most of them unpleasant. The three things that especially interest her in a car are whether she can see out when at the wheel, whether she can ride in the front seat for any length of time without getting a pain in her back, and whether she can enter the car in a forthright manner, without turning around and going in backwards. She has never been willing to slink into an automobile fanny first, as millions of spineless and adjustable American women have learned to do, and I greatly respect this quality in her.

(14) To prepare for what lay ahead I went to my workbench, got a spirit level and a two-foot rule, and carefully measured the height of the driver's seat from the floor. It measured fourteen and three-quarters inches.

(15) From the end of August till the middle of January, whenever we could find a spare hour or two, we drove about the countryside, visiting nearby towns and cities in search of a car. We would pull in to a dealer's place with our naked right front wheel gleaming in the beautiful light and illuminating the car the way a cauliflower ear illuminates the face of an old fighter, and I would watch the dealer's eye rove furtively over the injured fender and see him make a mental note to knock an extra hundred dollars off the trade-in allowance. A new car would be trotted out for our inspection, and each of us in turn would sit in the driver's seat to get the feel of the thing. In most instances my wife lasted only a fraction of a minute at the wheel and came sliding and slithering out amid little stifled cries of alarm and disgust. Front seats had sunk in eight years, some of them a few inches, many of them without a trace. In several of the cars we looked at, the front seat was little more than a tilted hassock—a hassock that answered to the touch of a button, gliding forward and back, up and down, and leaving you either with your legs stretched straight out in front of you as though you were sitting on the floor, or with your knees pinned in a vicious grip under the steering wheel as though you were in the stocks.

(16) At first we were shown 1957 automobiles, but soon after Labor Day we began encountering cars that were called 1958, among

them the Edsel of great renown. It was an autumn rich in new experience for us. Everywhere we were courteously treated and everywhere we were bitterly disappointed. We ran through General Motors, we ran through Chrysler, we ran through Ford, we rambled through Rambler, and we poked around among foreign cars. A friend of ours who runs the general store where we trade let me drive his Lincoln, and another friend, just home from Germany, let me drive the Mercedes that he had brought back with him. (This last car, incidentally, felt more like our old 1949 sedan than anything else we had tried, but its manual gearshift seemed to me so delicately selective as to require the sandpapered fingers of a lock picker, and I felt fairly certain that even if I got together enough money to buy such a car, my wife would strip the gears out of it inside a day, unless I managed to beat her to it myself.)

(17) I usually carried my two-foot rule with me on our excursions and would make quick measurements of the front seat when nobody was looking, hoping to run across a car that could touch the fourteen-and-three-quarters-inch mark. The little Hillman, curiously enough, came close, and we were so impressed by this single fact we almost bought the car on the spot. But the same thing happened at the Hillman place that happened at all the other agencies: we took a short ride, with me at the wheel; then we thanked the man and said we wanted time to think it over; then we climbed back into the De Soto and started for home in an easy glide. Almost immediately the subtle superiority of our 1949 car to the one we had just been testing infected us, manifesting itself in a dozen indescribable ways and stirring our blood, and we felt relieved and happy and exhilarated by the rediscovery of old familiar virtues and properties, and this made us light-headed and gay, and I stepped down on the accelerator and gradually the old automobile responded to the surge of gasoline until we were rushing along at the speed of the wind (forty-five miles an hour), singing and clowning and admiring the wonderful sheen of the green hood that stretched out in front of us, a green as rich as the new growth of a spruce tree in the spring. Even the holes in the upholstery were in perfect concealment; I sat on the knife-hole, my bride on the swatch-hole. Not a sign of shabbiness was apparent, the missing section of the fender being well out of view over the curve of the machine.

(18) Sometime in January we tired of the rigmarole of buying a new car and decided to wait patiently for a turn in the automotive tide. I treated our sedan to a new front fender, had a few minor dents smoothed out, installed a pair of new front springs, and commissioned our upholsterer to re-cover the seats. (He told us that he was about to leave for Cape Canaveral to visit a son who is engaged in Space but that he would tend to our car when he returned to Maine and to terrestrial affairs.) I also arranged for another coat of Turtle Wax to be applied to the surface of Old Shabby. And that is where the matter stands now, and that is the end of my story.

(19) Thirty or forty years ago, when a man wanted a car, he had a fabulous assortment to choose from—everything from a jackrabbit to a bearcat. Big cars, small cars, medium-size cars, cheap cars, expensive cars, moderate-priced cars, high cars, low cars, open cars, closed cars, gas cars, steam cars, electric cars: it was paradise. The trend in manufacturing has been to standardize the automobile, as though the consumer were himself standard and fixed. Big cars have grown smaller, small cars have grown bigger, all cars have grown lower, all cars have gone up in price. Sales of most American cars are lagging; only the foreign cars are enjoying an active market.

(20) My newspaper says that Detroit is reappraising the scene. Car makers are asking, "Do people want expensive chrome-covered, prestige-laden big cars, or do they want smaller and more economical basic transportation?" I think the answer to that is, there is no such thing as "people" in the sense that the word is used here. Every person is different. Some want expensive chrome-covered, prestige-laden cars; some want plain undecorated inexpensive cars that carry no more prestige than an old umbrella. Some want a car that is spacious, to carry big loads long distances. Others want a small, economical car for light going on short hauls.

(21) For millions of men a motorcar is primarily a means of getting to and from work. For millions of wives it is primarily a means of getting to and from the nearby shops, churches, and schools. Yet from reading auto ads you would think that the primary function of the motorcar in America was to carry its owner first into a higher social stratum, then into an exquisite delirium of high adventure.

(22) In the New England village I live in, the automobile is used

chiefly for getting to and from a job and a store. The one car for which there is always a brisk demand in my town is the Model A Ford, now about thirty years old. Whenever a Model A comes on the market, it is snapped up in no time, and usually there is a waiting list. People actually advertise in the papers, wanting to buy a Model A. The reason the A is going strong today is simple: the car is a triumph of honest, unfussy design and superior materials. It doesn't look like a turbojet or like an elephant's ear, it drinks gasoline in moderation, it puts on no airs, and when something gets out of adjustment the owner can usually tinker it back to health himself. The car is not long, it is not low, but it works and it is extremely durable. It wouldn't fill the bill today for high-speed travel over superhighways, but I am quite sure of one thing—if Ford could suddenly produce a new batch of Model A's and put them up for sale some morning, at about double what they cost originally, they'd be gone by nightfall. I'd be strongly tempted to buy one myself. It isn't *exactly* what I'm looking for, but it's close. And the price would be so favorable I wouldn't have to turn in my old car but could keep it and become a two-car American, using the Ford for dashing to the store for a box of soap flakes and the De Soto for long-distance de-luxe occasions, such as running out to San Francisco to see the Giants play ball.

(23) Whenever the automobile industry is in trouble, it's a serious matter for the country. The motorcar is really our No. 1 consumer item; when it languishes, everything languishes. I have contributed my tiny bit to the sickness in Detroit, because I haven't bought a car in nine years—an un-American way to act. But the fault is not mine. I think manufacturers should take a deep breath and start over, on new principles. They should regard the American motorist as an individual, not a type. They should respect his honesty and his intellect and his physical stature. They should abandon the cult of "lowness," as though lowness were synonymous with beauty and performance. (Every car should have a low center of gravity, but it isn't hard to come by. Virtually everything that's heavy about an automobile is in a naturally low position—engine, wheels, axles, frame, drive shaft, transmission, differential.)

(24) The architect and his brother the engineer are perhaps the most valuable citizens we have. When they fail us, it affects our health

and our purse. I believe that in motordom architects and engineers are not permitted to work undisturbed; their elbow is constantly being jiggled by tipsters, pollsters, motivationalists, and dreammongers. To design a car is a responsible job, like designing a railroad bridge or a skyscraper. The motorcar is a killer and will always be a killer, but the death rate will always respond to responsible work at the drawing board. Where there are honesty and sincerity and technical skill and belief in the good traits of human beings, there is never any problem about beauty of form and line. The reason women's clothes are hideous this season is that the bag or sack is a betrayal of anatomy, and fails to translate the figure of a woman, merely caricaturing it. But it's one thing to pander to human foibles when creating a dress and quite another when creating a car. A car is a matter of life and death.

(25) I didn't carry a two-foot rule around the countryside in order to annoy dealers. I did it because I was afraid we might have a terrible accident if my wife was obliged to sit almost at floor level while driving a high-powered car. This was a more compelling consideration than the slight increment of prestige I might gain by owning a vehicle my neighbors would think was smart because it was low. I'd rather stay down on a low level of society with a living wife than be up with the best of them as a widower. During our days of searching, I noticed that although dealers don't like two-foot rules, many of the ones I encountered were sympathetic to my cry. None of them gave me much of an argument, and several of them said they agreed.

(26) I'll promise Detroit one thing: build me a car that's as comfortable, as safe, as durable, and as handsome as the one I have today, and I'll swap cars.

Questions

1. White's essay divides into three main parts. What is the broad relationship of each one to the others.

2. Analyze the organization of the first six paragraphs, defining the overall organization and explaining the position of the material on Hollywood.

3. White's account of his De Soto up to "the end of my story" (Para-

graph 18) proceeds chronologically. Justify the one or two breaks or modifications in the chronology.

4. White's manner is easy and casual. Would you say that his overall organization is easy and casual too, in keeping with his manner, or does it possess an underlying carefulness and formality? Discuss.

5. White says that American car manufacturers have been seduced into wrong ideas for twenty-five years, roughly from the early 1930's to the late 1950's; but he seems to think that his 1949 De Soto is a good car, in fact a "beauty." Is there a basic contradiction here? Discuss the issue.

6. White wrote his essay in 1958, when automobiles sported fins. Have the fins disappeared only to be replaced by an equal absurdity? Discuss one prominent stylistic feature of the newest cars in the light of White's essay.

7. If you recall the history of the Edsel (Paragraph 16), you may be able to comment upon the degree of exaggeration in the next to last sentence in Paragraph 2. Look up the matter in the *New York Times Index* or in a recent history of automobiles.

8. White's opinion that anything perfectly designed for its task is inevitably beautiful (Paragraph 2) is a familiar one. Would you say that television antennae fit the case? Write an essay on the general issue.

DEATH IN THE AFTERNOON

ERNEST HEMINGWAY

Ernest Hemingway (1898–1961) was one of the two or three most influential writers of fiction of his time. In a style terse and at times ironic, he fashioned his work from his own large and varied experiences, which in turn reflected some of the principal cultural shocks of the century: *A Farewell to Arms* derives from his experiences during World War I; *The Sun Also Rises,* from what he saw as an American expatriate in postwar Paris; *For Whom the Bell Tolls,* from the strife he witnessed as a newspaperman during the Spanish Civil War. He received the Nobel Prize in 1954, two years after the publication of *The Old Man and the Sea,* a moving short novel that celebrates man's powers of endurance. His one play and some of his many short stories have been collected in *The Fifth Column and the First Forty-Nine Stories;* his non-fiction includes *Green Hills of Africa,* on big-game hunting, and *Death in the Afternoon,* on bullfighting.

(1) In the modern formal bullfight or corrida de toros there are usually six bulls that are killed by three different men. Each man kills two bulls. The bulls by law are required to be from four to five years old, free from physical defects, and well armed with sharp-pointed horns. They are inspected by a municipal veterinary surgeon before the fight. The veterinary is supposed to reject bulls that are under age, insufficiently armed or with anything wrong with their eyes, their horns or any apparent disease or visible bodily defect such as lameness.

(2) The men who are to kill them are called matadors and which of the six bulls they are to kill is determined by lot. Each matador or killer, has a cuadrilla, or team, of from five to six men who are paid by him and work under his orders. Three of these men who aid him on foot with capes, and, at his orders place the banderillas, three-foot wooden shafts with harpoon points, are called peones or banderilleros. The other two, who are mounted on horses when they appear in the ring, are called picadors.

(3) No one is called a toreador in Spain. That is an obsolete word which was applied to those members of the nobility who, in the days before professional bullfighting, killed bulls from horseback for sport. Anyone who fights bulls for money, whether as a matador, banderillero or a picador is called a torero. A man who kills them on horseback with a javelin, using trained thoroughbred horses, is called a rejoneador or a caballero en plaza. A bullfight in Spanish is called a corrida de toros or a running of bulls. A bull ring is called a plaza de toros.

(4) In the morning before the bullfight the representatives of each matador, usually their oldest or most trusted banderilleros, meet at the corrals of the plaza de toros where the bulls that are to be fought that afternoon are quartered. They look over the bulls, compare their size, weight, height, the length of their horns, width of horns, sharpness of horns, and the condition of their coats. This last is as good an indication as any of their physical condition and probable bravery. There is no sure sign by which bravery may be determined although there are many indications of probable cowardice. The confidential banderilleros question the herder or vaquero who has travelled from the ranch with the bulls and who, while he is in charge of them, is called the mayoral, about the qualities and probable disposition of each bull. The bulls must be divided into three lots of two bulls each by common consent of the representatives assembled and the effort is to have one good bull and one bad bull, good and bad from the bullfighter's standpoint, in each lot. A good bull for the bullfighter is not too big, not too strong, not too much horns, not too much height at shoulder, but above all with good vision, good reaction to color and movement, brave and frank to charge. A bad bull, for the bullfighter, is too big a bull, too old a

bull, too powerful a bull, with too wide horns; but above all a bad bull is one with no reaction to color or movement or with defective courage and lack of sustained viciousness, so that the bullfighter cannot tell when, whether or how he will charge. The representatives, usually short men in caps, not yet shaven for the day, with a great variety of accents, but all with the same hard eyes, argue and discuss. They say the number 20 has more horns than the 42, but the 42 weighs two arrobas (fifty pounds) more than the 16. The 46 is as big as a cathedral, one calls to him and he raises his head from where he has been feeding, and the 18 is roan-colored and may be as cowardly as a steer. The lots are made up after much arguing and the numbers of two bulls, those branded on their flanks, are written on three different cigarette papers and the papers rolled up into balls and dropped into a cap. The roan-colored probable coward has been paired with a medium-weight, black bull with not too long horns and a glossy coat. The cathedral-size 46 is coupled with the 16 which, being just barely big enough to be passed by the veterinaries and without salient characteristics, is the ideal of the half-bull that looks like a bull but lacks the full development of muscle and knowledge of how to use his horns, that all the representatives have hoped to get for their bullfighter. The number 20 with the wide horns with the needle points is balanced by the 42 which is the next smallest to the 16. The man who holds the cap shakes it and each representative puts in a brown hand and draws out a tight-rolled cigarette paper. They unroll them, read them, perhaps take a final look at the two bulls they have drawn and go off to the hotel to find the matador and tell him what he has to kill.

(5) The matador decides in which order he prefers to take his bulls. He may take the worst one first and hope to rehabilitate himself with the second in case his work with the first turns out badly. Or if he is third in the order to kill he may take the best one first knowing that he will be killing the sixth bull and if it should be getting dark and the crowd wanting to leave he will be pardoned an attempt to finish quickly and in the easiest way possible should this bull turn out to be difficult.

(6) The matadors kill their bulls in turn in the order of their seniority; this dating from their presentation as a matador de toros

in the Plaza of Madrid. If any matador is gored so that he is unable to return from the infirmary his bulls were formerly all killed by the senior-ranking matador of those remaining in the ring. Now they are divided between the remaining matadors.

(7) The bullfight usually takes place at five o'clock or five-thirty in the afternoon. At a half-hour past noon of the day of the fight the apartado takes place. This is the sorting out of bulls in the corrals with the aid of steers and, by the use of swinging doors, runways and trap doors, separating them and trapping them into the individual pens or chiqueros where they are to stay and rest until they come out into the ring in the order in which it has been determined they are to be fought. Bulls are not deprived of food and water before fighting as one may read in various guides to Spain nor are they kept in a dark pen for several days. They are in the chiqueros in a dim light for not more than four hours before the bullfight commences. They are not fed there after they leave the corral any more than a boxer would be fed immediately before a fight, but the reason for placing them in the small dimly lighted pens is to have some way of getting them promptly into the ring, and to rest them and keep them quiet before the fight.

(8) Usually only the matadors, their friends and representatives, the bull ring management, the authorities, and a very few spectators attend the apartado. It is usually the first time the matador sees the bulls he is to kill that afternoon. The number of spectators is kept down in most places by putting the price of tickets at five pesetas. The bull ring management wants few people at the sorting in order that the bulls may not have their attention attracted by the spectators who want to see action and so call to the bulls to excite them that they may charge the doors or the walls or each other. If they charge in the corrals they run a risk of injuring their horns or of goring each other and the management would have to replace them in the ring at the expense of a couple of hundred dollars apiece. Many bullfight spectators and hangers-on have a belief that they can talk to the bulls as well or better than the bullfighters. Protected by the high fence or the wall of the corral they try to catch the bull's eye and they utter the guttural "huh!-huh!-huh!" that the herders and toreros use to call the bull's attention. If the bull in the

pen below raises his great head with the wide horns, solid-looking as wood and smoothly pointed, and the hump of muscle in his neck and shoulders, heavy and wide in repose, rises in a great swelling crest under the black, hairy sheen of his hide and his nostrils widen and he lifts and jerks his horns as he looks toward the spectator then the amateur speaker of bull talk has had a success. If the bull should really charge, driving his horns into the wood, or tossing his head at the talker it would be a triumph. To hold down the number of successes and avoid triumphs the management puts the tickets at five pesetas on the theory that anyone able to pay five pesetas to see bulls sorted will be too dignified to try to talk to bulls before bullfights.

(9) There is no way they can be sure of this, and at some places in the country where they have bulls only once a year you see men at the apartado who pay five pesetas only in order to have a better opportunity to exercise their powers as talkers to bulls. But in general the five pesetas reduce the amount of sober talking. The bulls pay little attention to a drunk. I have many times seen drunken men shout at bulls and never seen the bulls pay any attention. The five-peseta atmosphere of dignity in a town like Pamplona, where a man can be drunk twice and eat a meal at the horse fair on five pesetas, gives an almost religious hush to the apartado. No one spends five pesetas there to see the bulls sorted unless he is very rich and dignified. But the atmosphere of the sorting can be very different in other places. I have never seen it quite the same in any two towns. After the sorting everybody goes to the café.

(10) The bullfight itself takes place in a sand-covered ring enclosed by a red wooden fence a little over four feet high. This red wooden fence is called a barrera. Behind it is a narrow circular passageway that separates it from the first row of seats in the amphitheatre. This narrow runway is called the callejon. In it stand the sword-handlers with their jugs of water, sponges, piles of folded muletas and heavy leather sword cases, the bull ring servants, the vendors of cold beer and gaseosas, of iced fruits in nets that float in galvanized buckets full of ice and water, of pastries in flat baskets, of salted almonds, and of peanuts. In it also are the police, the bullfighters who are not in the ring at the moment, several plainclothes

policemen ready to arrest amateurs who may jump into the ring, the photographers, and on seats built in it and protected by shields of boards, are the doctors, the carpenters who repair the barrera if it is broken, and the delegates of the government. In some rings the photographers are allowed to circulate in the callejon; in others they must work from their seats.

(11) The seats of the bull ring are uncovered except for the boxes or palcos and the first gallery or grada. From the gallery the seats descend in circular rows to the edge of the ring. These rows of numbered places are called tendidos. The two rows nearest the ring, the front rows of all the seats, are called barreras and contra-barreras. The third row are known as delanteras de tendidos or the front row of the tendidos. The bull ring for numbering purposes is cut into sections as you would cut a pie, and these sections numbered tendidos 1, 2, 3, and so on up to 11 and 12 depending on the size of the ring.

(12) If you are going to a bullfight for the first time the best place for you to sit depends on your temperament. From a box or from the first row in the gallery details of sound and smell and those details of sight that make for the perception of danger are lost or minimized, but you see the fight better as a spectacle and the chances are that, if it is a good bullfight, you will enjoy it more. If it is a bad bullfight, that is, not an artistic spectacle, you will be better off the closer you are, since you can then, for lack of a whole to appreciate, learn and see all the details, the whys and the wherefores. The boxes and the gallery are for people who do not want to see things too closely for fear they may upset them, for people who want to see the bullfight as a spectacle or a pageant, and for experts who can see details even though a long way from them and want to be high enough up so they can see everything that happens in any part of the ring in order to be able to judge it as a whole.

(13) The barrera is the best seat if you want to see and hear what happens and to be so close to the bull that you will have the bull-fighter's point of view. From the barrera the action is so near and so detailed that a bullfight that would be soporific from the boxes or the balcony is always interesting. It is from the barrera that you see danger and learn to appreciate it. There too you have an un-

interrupted view of the ring. The only other seats, besides the first row in the gallery and the first row in the boxes, where you do not see people between you and the ring, are the sobrepuertas. These are the seats that are built over the doorways through which you enter the various sections of the ring. They are about half-way up to the sides of the bowl and from them you get a good view of the ring and a good perspective, yet you are not as distant as in the boxes or gallery. They cost about half as much as the barreras or the first row of gallery or boxes and they are very good seats.

(14) The west walls of the bull ring building cast a shadow and those seats that are in the shade when the fight commences are called seats of the sombra or shade. Seats that are in the sun when the fight commences but that will be in the shadow as the afternoon advances are called of sol y sombra. Seats are priced according to their desirability and whether they are shaded or not. The cheapest seats are those which are nearest the roof on the far sunny side and have no shade at all at any time. They are the andanadas del sol and on a hot day, close under the roof, they must reach temperatures that are unbelievable in a city like Valencia where it can be 104° Fahrenheit in the shade, but the better seats of the sol are good ones to buy on a cloudy day or in cold weather.

(15) At your first bullfight if you are alone, with no one to instruct you, sit in a delantra de grada or a sobrepuerta. If you cannot get these seats you can always get a seat in a box. They are the most expensive seats and the farthest from the ring, but they give a good panoramic view of the fight. If you are going with someone who really knows bullfighting and want to learn to understand it and have no qualms about details a barrera is the best seat, contrabarrera the next best and sobrepuerta the next.

(16) If you are a woman and think you would like to see a bullfight and are afraid you might be badly affected by it do not sit any closer than the gallery the first time. You might enjoy the fight from there where you will see it as a spectacle and not care for it at all if you sat closer so that the details destroyed the effect of the whole. If you have plenty of money, want not to see but to have seen a bullfight and plan no matter whether you like it or not to leave after the first bull, buy a barrera seat so that someone who

has never had enough money to sit in a barrera can make a quick rush from above and occupy your expensive seat as you go out taking your preconceived opinions with you.

(17) That is the way it used to happen at San Sebastian. Due to various grafts of ticket resale and the reliance of the management on the wealthy curiosity trade from Biarritz and the Basque Coast, the barreras, by the time you buy them, cost a hundred pesetas apiece or over. A man could live a week on that in a bullfighters' boarding-house in Madrid, go to the Prado four times a week, buy good seats in the sun for two bullfights, buy the papers afterwards and drink beer and eat shrimps in the Pasaje Alvarez off the Calle de Vitoria, and still have something left to get his shoes shined with. Yet by buying any sort of seat within diving range of the barrera at San Sebastian you could be sure of having a hundred-peseta seat to occupy when the citizens who knew they were morally bound to leave the bull ring after the first bull stand up to make their well-fed, skull and bones-ed, porcelain-ed, beach-tanned, flannelled, Panama-hatted, sport-shod exits. I've seen them go many times when the women with them wanted to stay. They could go to the bullfight, but they had to meet at the Casino after they had seen the first bull killed. If they didn't leave and liked it there was something wrong with them. Maybe they were queer. There was never anything wrong with them. They always left. That was until bullfights became respectable. In nineteen-thirty-one I did not see one leave within range and now it looks as though the good days of the free barreras at San Sebastian are over.

Questions

1. Hemingway begins with the bull and ends with the audience. What other subjects does he discuss? What does he not discuss that you would expect him to? What in fact is the general scope of the selection?

2. Hemingway uses at least three organizational patterns: chronological, processive, and spatial. Locate them. What other significant pattern, if any, do you see?

3. Describe the overall organization of the selection and justify it.

4. What is the effect of the arrangement of material in the sentence

that begins: "A good bull for the bullfighter is not too big . . ." (Paragraph 4)? What if the sentence began: "A good bull for the bullfighter is brave"? How do you respond to the sentence that begins: "If it is a bad bullfight, that is, not an artistic spectacle . . ." (Paragraph 12)? What do the two sentences together suggest about Hemingway's attitude towards bullfighting?

5. What would you say is the tone of voice in which Hemingway offers the first three paragraphs? What other tone would be a more obvious one to adopt in discussing bullfighting? Why do you suppose he adopts the particular tone that he does?

6. About two-thirds of the way through the selection Hemingway moves from third person to second. Can you justify his doing so? Has his subject-matter shifted, or his attitude toward his subject?

7. Try to define Hemingway's attitudes toward drunkards at the apartado, "rich and dignified" people at the apartado, women who "want not to see" the bullfight, and men who "had to meet at the Casino after they had seen the first bull killed."

8. Analyze the irony in the last seven sentences of the selection.

9. Describe the various aspects of Hemingway's attitude toward bullfighting. Is it likely that he would respond in similar terms to any other sport—prizefighting, perhaps, or baseball?

THE RETURN HOME

ROBERT PENN WARREN

Robert Penn Warren (1905—) has distinguished himself as poet, novelist, literary critic, and teacher. Born in Kentucky, he studied at Vanderbilt University, the University of California, and Oxford, where he was a Rhodes Scholar. He early identified himself with other Southern writers, and though he has made his home away from the South for the past twenty-five years, that region continues to influence most of his work. His novels include *Night Rider, All the King's Men* (which won a Pulitzer Prize), *World Enough and Time,* and *The Flood*. He has written a long narrative poem, *Brother to Dragons,* on the circumstances of the Lewis and Clarke expedition. What follows is the opening portion of a survey Warren made of Southern attitudes on the racial problem.

(1) "I'm glad it's you going," my friend, a Southerner, long resident in New York, said, "and not me." But I went back, for going back this time, like all the other times, was a necessary part of my life. I was going back to look at the landscapes and streets I had known—Kentucky, Tennessee, Arkansas, Mississippi, Louisiana—to look at the faces, to hear the voices, to hear, in fact, the voices in my own blood. A girl from Mississippi had said to me: "I feel it's all happening inside of me, every bit of it. It's all there."

(2) I know what she meant.

(3) To the right, the sun, cold and pale, is westering. Far off, a little yellow plane scuttles down a runway, steps awkwardly into

the air, then climbs busily, learning grace. Our big plane trundles ponderously forward, feeling its weight like a fat man, hesitates, shudders with an access of sudden, building power; and with a new roar in my ears, I see the ground slide past, then drop away, like a dream. I had not been aware of the instant we had lost that natural contact.

(4) Memphis is behind me, and I cannot see it, but yonder is the river, glittering coldly, and beyond, the tree-sprigged flats of Arkansas. Still climbing, we tilt eastward now, the land pivoting away below us, the tidy toy farms, white houses, silos the size of a spool of white thread, or smaller, the stock ponds bright like little pieces of gum wrapper dropped in brown grass, but that brown grass is really trees, the toy groves, with shadows precise and long in the leveling light.

(5) Arkansas has pivoted away. It is Mississippi I now see down there, the land slipping away in the long light, and in my mind I see, idly, the ruined, gaunt, classic clay hills, with the creek bottoms throttled long since in pink sand, or the white houses of Holly Springs, some of them severe and beautiful, or Highway 61 striking south from Memphis, straight as a knife edge through the sad and baleful beauty of the Delta country, south toward Vicksburg and the Federal cemeteries, toward the fantasia of Natchez.

(6) It seems like a thousand years since I first drove that road, more than twenty-five years ago, a new concrete slab then, dizzily glittering in the August sun-blaze, driving past the rows of tenant shacks, Negro shacks set in the infinite cotton fields, and it seems like a hundred years since I last drove it, last week, in the rain, then toward sunset the sky clearing a little, but clouds solid and low on the west like a black range of mountains frilled upward with an edge of bloody gold light, quickly extinguished. Last week, I noticed that more of the shacks were ruinous, apparently abandoned. More, but not many, had an electric wire running back from the road. But when I caught a glimpse, in the dusk, of the interior of a lighted shack, I usually saw the coal-oil lamp. Most shacks were not lighted. I wondered if it was too early in the evening. Then it was early no longer. Were that many of the shacks abandoned?

(7) Then we would pass in the dark some old truck grudging

and clanking down the concrete, and catch, in the split-second flick
of our headlamps, a glimpse of the black faces and the staring eyes.
Or the figure, sudden in our headlight, would rise from the roadside, dark and shapeless against the soaked blackness of the cotton
land: the man humping along with the croker sack on his shoulders
(containing what?), the woman with a piece of sacking or paper
over her head against the drizzle now, at her bosom a bundle that
must be a small child, the big children following with the same slow,
mud-lifting stride in the darkness. The light of the car snatches past,
and I think of them behind us in the darkness, moving up the track
beside the concrete, seeing another car light far yonder toward Memphis, staring at it perhaps, watching it grow, plunge at them, strike
them, flick past. They will move on, at their pace. Yes, they are still
here.

(8) I see a river below us. It must be the Tennessee. I wonder
on which side of us Shiloh is, and guess the right, for we must have
swung far enough north for that. I had two grandfathers at Shiloh,
that morning of April 6, 1862, young men with the other young men
in gray uniforms stepping toward the lethal spring thickets of dogwood and redbud, to the sound of bird song, "One hundred and
sixty men we took in the first morning, son. Muster the next night,
and it was sixteen answered." They had fallen back on Corinth, into
Mississippi.

(9) The man in the seat beside me on the plane is offering me a
newspaper. I see the thumb of the hand clutching the paper. The
nail is nearly as big as a quarter, split at the edges, grooved and
horny, yellowish, with irrevocable coal-black grime deep under the
nail and into the cuticle. I look at the man. He is a big man, very
big, bulging over the seat, bulging inside his blue serge. He is fiftyish,
hair graying. His face is large and raw-looking, heavy-jowled, thick
gray eyebrows over small, deep-set, appraising eyes. His name, which
he tells me, sounds Russian or Polish, something ending in -ski.

(10) I begin to read the paper, an article about the riots at the
University of Alabama. He notices what I am reading. "Bet you
thought I was from down here," he said. "From the way I talk. But

I ain't. I was born and raised in New York City, but I been in the
scrap business down here ten years. Didn't you think I was from
down here?"

(11) "Yes," I say, for that seems the sociable thing to say.

(12) He twists his bulk in the blue serge and reaches and stabs a
finger at the headline about Alabama. "Folks could be more gen'-
rous and fair-thinking," he says. "Like affable, you might say, and
things would work out. If folks get affable and contig'ous, you might
say, things sort of get worked out in time, but you get folks not being
affable-like and stirring things up and it won't work out. Folks on
both sides the question."

(13) He asks me if I don't agree, and I say, sure, I agree. Sure, if
folks were just affable-like.

(14) I am thinking of what a taxi driver had said to me in Memphis: "Looks like the Lucy girl wouldn't want to go no place where
people threw eggs at her and sich. But if they'd jist let her alone,
them Goodrich plant fellers and all, it would blow over. What few
niggers come would not have stayed no duration. Not when they
found she couldn't git the social stuff, and all."

(15) And what the school superintendent, in middle Tennessee,
had said: "You take a good many people around here that I know,
segregationists all right, but when they read about a thousand to
one, it sort of makes them sick. It is the unfairness in that way that
gets them."

(16) And an organizer of one of the important segregation groups,
a lawyer, when I asked him if Autherine Lucy wasn't acting under
law, he creaked his swivel chair, moved his shoulders under his
coat, and touched a pencil on his desk, before saying: "Yes—yes—
but it was just the Federal Court ruled it."

(17) And a taxi driver in Nashville, a back-country man come to
the city, a hard, lean, spare face, his lean, strong shoulders humped
forward over the wheel so that the clavicles show through the coat:
"A black-type person and a white-type person, they ain't alike. Now
the black-type person, all they think about is fighting and having
a good time and you know what. Now the white-type person is more
American-type, he don't mind fighting but he don't fight to kill for
fun. It's that cannibal blood you cain't git out."

(18) Now, on the plane, my companion observes me scribbling something in a notebook.

(19) "You a writer or something?" he asks. "A newspaper fellow, maybe?"

(20) I say yes.

(21) "You interested in that stuff?" he asks, and points to the article. "Somebody ought to tell 'em not to blame no state, not even Alabam' or Mississippi, for what the bad folks do. Like stuff in New York or Chicago. Folks in Mississippi got good hearts as any place. They always been nice and good-hearted to me, for I go up to a man affable. The folks down here is just in trouble and can't claw out. Don't blame 'em, got good hearts but can't claw out of their trouble. It is hard to claw out from under the past and the past way."

(22) He asks me if I have been talking to a lot of people.

(23) I had been talking to a lot of people.

(24) I had come to the shack at dusk, by the brimming bayou, in the sea of mud where cotton had been. The cold drizzle was still falling. In the shack, on the hickory chair, the yellow girl, thin but well made, wearing a salmon sweater and salmon denim slacks, holds the baby on her knee and leans toward the iron stove. On the table beyond her is an ivory-colored portable radio and a half-full bottle of Castoria. On the other side of the stove are her three other children, the oldest seven. Behind me, in the shadowy background, I know there are faces peering in from the other room of the shack, black faces, the half-grown boys, another girl I had seen on entering. The girl in the salmon sweater is telling how she heard her husband had been killed. "Livin in town then, and my sister, she come that night and tole me he was shot. They had done shot him dead. So I up and taken out fer heah, back to the plantation. Later, my sister got my chillen and brought 'em. I ain't gonna lie, mister. I tell you, I was scairt. No tellin if that man what done it was in jail or no. Even if they had arrest him, they might bon' him out and he come and do it to me. Be mad because they 'rest him. You caint never tell. And they try him and 'quit him, doan know as I kin stay

heah. Even they convick him, maybe I leave. Some good folks round heah and they helpin me, and I try to appreciate and be a prayin chile, but you git so bore down on and nigh ruint and sort of brainwashed, you don't know what. Things git to goin round in yore head. I could run out or somethin, but you caint leave yore chillen. But look like I might up and leave. He git 'quitted, that man, and maybe I die, but I die goin."

(25) This is the cliché. It is the thing the uninitiate would expect. It is the cliché of fear. It is the cliché come fresh, and alive.

(26) There is another image. It is morning in Nashville. I walk down Union Street, past the Negro barber shops, past the ruinous buildings plastered over with placards of old circuses and rodeos, buildings being wrecked now to make way for progress, going into the square where the big white stone boxlike, ugly and expensive Davidson County Court House now stands on the spot where the old brawling market once was. Otherwise, the square hasn't changed much, the same buildings, wholesale houses, liquor stores, pawn shops, quick lunches, and the same kind of people stand on the corners, countrymen, in khaki pants and mackinaw coats, weathered faces and hard, withdrawn eyes, usually pale eyes, lean-hipped men ("narrow-assted" in the country phrase) like the men who rode with Forrest, the farm wives, young with a baby in arms, or middle-aged and work-worn, with colored cloths over the head, glasses, false teeth, always the shopping bag.

(27) I walk down toward the river, past the Darling Display Distribution show window, where a wax figure stands in skirt and silk blouse, the fingers spread on one uplifted hand, the thin face lifted with lips lightly parted as though in eternal, tubercular expectation of a kiss. I see the power pylons rising above the river mist. A tug is hooting up-river in the mist.

(28) I go on down to the right, First Street, to the replica of Fort Nashborough, the original settlement, which stands on the river bank under the shadow of warehouses. The stockade looks so child-flimsy and jerry-built jammed against the massive, soot-stained warehouses. How could the settlers have ever taken such protection seriously? But it was enough, that and their will and the long rifles and the hunting knives and the bear-dogs they unleashed to help

them when they broke the Indians at the Battle of the Bluffs. They took the land, and remain.

(29) I am standing in the middle of the empty stockade when a boy enters and approaches me. He is about fifteen, strongly built, wearing a scruffed and tattered brown leather jacket, blue jeans, a faded blue stocking cap on the back of his head, with a mop of yellow hair hanging over his forehead. He is a fine-looking boy, erect, manly in the face, with a direct, blue-eyed glance. "Mister," he said to me, "is this foh't the way it was, or they done remodeled it?"

(30) I tell him it is a replica, smaller than the original and not on the right spot, exactly.

(31) "I'm glad I seen it, anyway," he says. "I like to go round seeing things that got history, and such. It gives you something to think about. Helps you in a quiz sometimes, too."

(32) I ask him where he goes to school.

(33) "Atlanta," he says. "Just come hitch-hiking up this a-way, looking at things for interest. Like this here foh't."

(34) "You all been having a little trouble down your way," I ask, "haven't you?"

(35) He looks sharply at me, hesitates, then says: "Niggers—you mean niggers?"

(36) "Yes."

(37) "I hate them bastards," he says, with a shuddering, automatic violence, and averts his face and spits through his teeth, a quick, viperish, cut-off expectoration.

(38) I say nothing, and he looks at me, stares into my face with a dawning belligerence, sullen and challenging, and suddenly demands: "Don't you?"

(39) "I can't say that I do," I reply. "I like some and I don't like some others."

(40) He utters the sudden obscenity, and removes himself a couple of paces from me. He stops and looks back over his shoulder. "I'm hitching on back to Atlanta," he declares in a flat voice, "this afternoon," and goes on out of the fort.

(41) This, too, is a cliché. The boy, standing on the ground of history and heroism, his intellect and imagination stirred by the fact, shudders with that other, automatic emotion which my question had

evoked. The cliché had come true: the cliché of hate. And somehow the hallowedness of the ground he stood on had vindicated, as
it were, that hate.

Questions

1. The second section of the sketch closes with mention of Warren's
grandfathers at Shiloh. What phrase in the first section does his mention of them recall? State the broad meaning of that phrase.

2. In the second section Warren describes the plane take-off and the
look of Highway 61. These things have nothing directly to do with the
subject of segregation. What justifies their inclusion?

3. Analyze Warren's use of chronology and geography as organizing
patterns in the second section.

4. How sympathetic is Warren to the man who sits beside him on the
plane? What does Warren achieve—apart from unity—by using his
conversation with the man as a frame for the viewpoints of four other
people? Can you see any basis for the order of the viewpoints?

5. Is there any reason for believing that Warren presents the two episodes in the fourth section in chronological order? In what respect does
the ordering of the two episodes parallel the ordering of material in the
third section? Would he lose anything by reversing the order?

6. The four sections of the sketch do not constitute an independent
unit of Warren's book, but they do display a certain development appropriate to their position as opening sections of it. What is that development?

7. What does Warren mean by the "cliché of fear" and the "cliché
of hate"? What does he mean when he says that the hallowedness of
the ground vindicated the boy's hate?

8. In some respects Warren is objective and dispassionate in his sketch;
in other respects he is subjective. Point out the clearest illustration of
each attitude. Why does he try to maintain both attitudes?

9. How does Warren feel about the South generally, past and present?
How does this feeling affect his responses to the particular situations he
describes?

10. Define as precisely as possible what you think Warren's attitude
is toward the Negro-white problem. Do you see any aspects of agreement
with the position argued in the essay by Norman Mailer included in
Section I?

A VAPOR MOVING NORTH-NORTHWEST

DANIEL LANG

Daniel Lang (1915—) has spent much of his life as a journalist, initially as a newspaper reporter and then, during World War II, as an overseas correspondent for *The New Yorker*. Though he has since written on a variety of subjects for many periodicals, he has been especially concerned with problems of nuclear science, in both its peaceful and wartime applications. His books include *Early Tales of the Atomic Age, The Man in the Thick Lead Suit,* and *From Hiroshima to the Moon.*

(1) A few moments after the underground nuclear blast known as Project Gnome went off, at noon on a Sunday, in December, 1961, in a flat and chilly stretch of desert southeast of Carlsbad, New Mexico, all of us who were watching the event from a mound of bulldozed earth four and a half miles due south of ground zero—some four hundred foreign observers, congressmen, government scientists, local citizens, photographers, and reporters—could tell that something had gone wrong. What gave us this impression was not the broad blanket of dust that the explosive—deep below in a formation of salt rock—had jolted out of the desert. Nor was it the bouncing we took—the result of a violent earth tremor that had been caused by the nuclear charge, which was one-fourth as powerful as the Hiroshima bomb. (In the immediate vicinity of the explosion, the desert leaped three feet, and it has yet to descend to its former level.) We had been told to expect these things. Rather, it was the sight of thick and steadily thickening white vapor at the scene of the firing that made us think

that plans had miscarried. The vapor was puffing up through an elevator shaft that dropped twelve hundred feet to an eleven-hundred-foot tunnel, at the end of which the explosive, and also much of the project's experimental equipment, had been installed. As we watched the vapor slowly begin to spread, like ground fog, and, rising, vanish into the air, we knew we were witnessing something that we had been practically assured wouldn't happen—venting, or the accidental escape of radioactivity into the atmosphere. "The probability of the experiment venting is so low as to approach the impossible," the Atomic Energy Commission had stated in a comprehensive pamphlet it had published on Project Gnome. Indeed, at a briefing held the previous evening in Carlsbad, where Gnome's headquarters were located, one of the speakers had warned that the shot was just a small one and might well disappoint us as a spectacle. It was the excitement of its underlying idea that made it worthwhile for us to be at the proving ground, we had been told, for Project Gnome marked the opening of the Plowshare Program—a series of nuclear blasts whose purpose, as the name implied, was to turn the atom to peaceful ways. Any number of benefits, we were informed, could flow from these blasts: harbors might be carved out of wasteland in Alaska; oil might be dislodged from shale; abundant sources of water under great mountains might be freed; diamonds might be made out of ordinary carbon.

(2) We were in no danger—the wind was blowing the vapor to the north-northwest of us—but the feeling seemed to take hold that this wasn't necessarily the Prophet Isaiah's day. Before the explosion, a gala mood had prevailed on our barren mound. Local ranchers, their big Stetsons bobbing, had heartily declared that it was a great day for these parts. The operators of nearby potash mines—the world's largest producers of this chemical—had agreed. Their wives, modishly clad, had greeted each other effusively. And Louis M. Whitlock, the manager of the Carlsbad Chamber of Commerce, had assured me, "This bomb is for the good of mankind, and we're for it," as we awaited the explosion. Representative Ben Franklin Jensen, of Iowa, a Republican member of the House Appropriations Committee, had also caught the proper spirit. "There are certain things you just have to spend money on, and Plowshare is one of them,"

he told me. The foreign visitors lent a certain glamour to the occasion. There was Professor Francis Perrin, for instance—a small, goateed man with elegant manners who was the High Commissioner of France's Commissariat á l'Energie Atomique. The science attaché of the Japanese Embassy was there, too—a young chemist named Dr. Seiichi Ishizaka. Chatting with him shortly before the venting, I had gathered that his government was of two minds about the wisdom of the day's explosion. "Japan is curious," he had told me, smiling politely. The bustle of the many journalists on the scene had added to the festive air. The local people had been fascinated by their activities, clustering around each time Dr. Edward Teller, the widely celebrated father of the H-bomb, who is also the father of Plowshare, posed for television crews. On the high-school platform in Carlsbad during the previous evening's briefing, he had, in response to a reporter's question, agreed that the Plowshare Program was "too little and too late," and referring to the recent resumption of atmospheric testing in the Soviet Union, had gone on to say, "Plowshare had to wait for permission from the Kremlin, which it is giving in a slightly ungracious manner."

(3) Now, as the insidious gases continued to escape from the shaft, the gala mood faded. An A.E.C. official, speaking over a public-address system from a crudely constructed lectern, announced that all drivers should turn their cars around to facilitate a speedy retreat from the test area. An evacuation, he said, might be in order. A short while later—about half an hour after the detonation—the same official, a calm, affable man by the name of Richard G. Elliott, announced that, according to word from a control point a hundred yards forward, the venting had created a radioactive cloud, low and invisible, which was moving in the general direction of Carlsbad, twenty-three miles away to the northwest. The invisible cloud, which was being tracked by an Air Force helicopter equipped with radiation counters, was expected to miss the town, but it would pass over a section of the highway on which we had driven from Carlsbad. The state police had consequently been instructed to throw up a roadblock there. Until further notice, the only way to reach Carlsbad would be to head southeast and follow a detour of a hundred and fifty miles. Some spectators left at once to take this roundabout route,

figuring that they might as well get the trip over and done with, rather than face an indefinite delay. Some other spectators also departed hurriedly; they suspected the A.E.C. of being excessively cautious, and hoped to use the direct highway to Carlsbad before the police could organize their blockade. As things turned out, a few of these motorists did elude the police, only to be intercepted eventually in Carlsbad itself. Seven cars were found to be contaminated; the A.E.C. paid to have them washed down. Two of the passengers, according to the A.E.C., showed slight, easily removable traces of radioactivity, one on his hand and the other on his clothing and hair. As for the cloud, the helicopter that had started tracking it had been forced to return to base when the craft's instruments showed that it was being contaminated. Another machine took its place, and the pilot of this kept the cloud under surveillance until darkness forced him to give up his mission; the cloud was then five miles north of a small town called Artesia, about sixty miles north-northwest of the test site; it had hovered briefly over the eastern edge of the town, and continued in its north-northwesterly path. At the time he took his leave of the cloud, the pilot reported, its radiation was diminishing steadily—a process attributed to nature, rather than to Gnome's artificers.

(4) Fortunately, the countryside over which this gaseous debris was being wafted was only sparsely populated. In fact, this was one of the reasons the explosive had been set off in this particular area. In spite of the reassurances about venting in the pamphlet, the A.E.C. and its chief contractor for Plowshare—the University of California's Lawrence Radiation Laboratory, in Livermore, California—had had this eventuality very much in mind when they planned Gnome. Many precautions had been taken. The tunnel was packed with bags of salt and blocks of concrete, designed to arrest the spread of radioactivity. Wind patterns had been analyzed by the United States Weather Bureau during the entire week before the shot. The day's detonation had, in fact, been delayed four hours until the winds were considered to be blowing in a safe direction. Ranchers for five miles around had been evacuated, tactfully, by being asked to join the Gnome spectators; their cattle, less privileged, had simply been driven off to roam different pastures for the day—or for however long it might

take the United States Public Health Service to certify the cleanliness of their familiar acres. The Federal Aviation Agency had been asked to order planes in the area to maintain a certain altitude until further notice. The dryness of the salt formation notwithstanding, the United States Geological Survey had made ground-water surveys of the surrounding area for six months before the shot and would continue to do so for at least a year afterward, in order to keep tabs on any underground movement of radioactive material. Seismic effects had also been anticipated. A special bill had been put through Congress to assure the potash industry of suitable indemnification in the event of damage. On the day of the detonation, no potash miners were on hand to chip at the rose-colored walls of their rough corridors. Nor were tourists permitted to explore the Carlsbad Caverns, thirty-four miles to the east of the detonation site. Acting on behalf of Project Gnome, the Coast and Geodetic Survey had placed a seismograph inside the Caverns. A member of the Caverns' staff—a naturalist from the National Park Service—was on hand to measure seismic effects in his own way; he watched to see if the blast would ripple one of the still, subterranean ponds that had been created over millennia, partly by drops of water from the cave's stalactites. (It didn't.) In retrospect, perhaps the most significant of all the precautions taken was the relatively last-minute reduction of the yield of the explosive from ten kilotons, as originally planned, to five kilotons. "Whoever made *that* decision, I'd like to shake his hand," an A.E.C. official told me the day after the shot.

(5) Those of us who, like me, were waiting for the roadblock to be lifted, passed the time as best we could. We discussed our reactions to the blast for a while, but, oddly, this soon began to pall. Some of us wandered over to a chuck wagon that the A.E.C. had thoughtfully laid on, and bought ourselves coffee and sandwiches. Now and then, we heard new announcements, of varying interest, on the public-address system. One dealt with the far-flung network of seismic recording stations that had been organized by the Department of Defense. A colonel mounted the lectern to tell us that the network appeared to have functioned well. (He didn't know then that Gnome's seismic signal had been recorded in Scandinavia and Japan.) The firing, the colonel added, had taken place "at exactly one four-

thousandth of a second after noon." Returning to the lectern, Elliott told us that, according to the instruments, the radiation at the bottom of the shaft now came to a million roentgens an hour, while on the ground at the top of the shaft the count was ten thousand roentgens an hour—twelve and a half times the lethal exposure for a healthy man.

(6) After a while, some of us went and sat in our cars to read or doze or just get out of the cold. Those who didn't could stare at the shaft, from which vapor was still issuing, or, if they preferred, scan the desert, stubbled with tumbleweed and greasewood and cactus. Only the distant sight of a potash refinery relieved the terrain. Bluish-white smoke was pouring from its tall chimney, its furnace having been left unbanked on this day of days. The refinery lay due northwest, near the Carlsbad road, so I knew that the radioactive gases were bound to mingle with the vapors of the tall chimney. Like my fellow-spectators, though, I had no idea when that would come to pass.

(7) The technical objectives of the day's blast, which were almost entirely in the hands of Livermore scientists, were well planned, it had been impressed on all of us in the course of the briefings before the shot. The central purpose was to see what happened when an atomic explosive was set off in a salt formation—what is called phenomenology. The Livermore people hadn't previously had a chance for such a test, their underground efforts thus far having been limited to military shots in the volcanic tuff of the Nevada test site— a substance that doesn't retain heat nearly as well as salt does. And heat was the key to much of what the researchers were seeking to learn. Gnome would enable them to carry out a heat-extraction experiment, for example—the general idea being to investigate the possibility of tapping for productive uses the inferno of superheated steam and other forms of energy that would result from the detonation. This energy, it was hoped, would be contained in a cavity in the salt that the explosive, low though its yield was, would create in about a tenth of a second. The cavity, if it didn't collapse, would be egg-shaped and glowing, and it would be about a hundred and ten

feet in diameter; six thousand tons of molten salt were expected to run down its sides and compose a pool thirty-five feet deep. The .cavity would also be "mined," by remote control, for radioactive isotopes—unstable atoms that are produced by a nuclear explosion, a fair percentage of which are valuable in scientific research, medical treatment, and industrial processes. (One of them, strontium 90, which is greatly feared in fallout, may some day be used in long-lived batteries to power unmanned weather stations in god-forsaken regions, a Livermore expert told me.)

(8) For pure researchers, it was thought, Gnome's most interesting data might be gained from the large numbers of neutrons—uncharged particles that are part of the atomic nucleus—that would be produced by the blast. In the instant of the explosion, I had been told, Gnome would release as many neutrons as a laboratory apparatus could release in several thousand years. So plentiful would they be, in fact, that only one out of ten million could be studied. Even so, much new light might be shed on such matters as the different velocities of neutrons and the interaction of these particles, which are usually emitted in bursts that last less than a hundred-millionth of a second, an interval of time that is known in scientific shoptalk as "a shake."

(9) But these technical objectives of Project Gnome were only a part of the Plowshare Program, and the Plowshare Program was something more than a scientific enterprise—a fact that had become apparent in the days immediately preceding the desert shot, when Carlsbad had been rife with briefings, interviews, and informative handouts. The case for Plowshare, in the opinion of some of the foreign observers and other people I talked with, seemed to rest on a variety of grounds. I learned, for example, that the proposed series of blasts had been approved by the A.E.C. four years before, which raised the question of why they were being started at this particular time. Plowshare officials readily acknowledged that the complete answer certainly included the state of international affairs. Was Plowshare, then, a solid program or a passing, virtuous response to the Russian resumption of atmospheric testing? Perhaps Plowshare's name

was partly to blame for this questioning attitude. "It sounds a little too much like magic," a foreign scientist remarked. "So many swords are being made just now."

(10) In any event, a day or two before the shot, I discussed Plowshare in Carlsbad with two of its overseers, both of whom were strongly in favor of the program, as one would expect, but in a fairly thoughtful, unmagical way. One of them was John S. Kelly, a bespectacled, mild-mannered man of thirty-nine who directed the A.E.C.'s Division of Peaceful Nuclear Explosives. He saw Plowshare's explosives as scientific and engineering tools. It excited him, he said, to contemplate the excavation jobs that might be performed in the future, like blasting lakes out of the wilderness and breaking up ore deposits that could be leached out. Plowshare represented a continuation of the whole history of explosives, Kelly said. Certainly explosives could be harmful, he conceded, but on the other hand gunpowder had done away with the feudal system and TNT had made possible the mining of fossil fuels.

(11) "But can we afford to guess wrong with nuclear explosives?" I asked. "Don't they represent an ultimate kind of energy?"

(12) "Why not use them for our ultimate good?" Kelly replied.

(13) For an undertaking concerned with the peaceful uses of the atom, I remarked, Plowshare appeared to have its ambiguities. The fissionable material and the equipment for the Gnome explosive, I mentioned, had been taken from our armaments stockpile; the explosive was being concealed from the public gaze, the same as a weapon is; men in uniform had come to Carlsbad for the shot, and were participating actively in its preparation; and among those prominently involved were people from Livermore, which was noted primarily as a center of weapons design.

(14) Kelly was quick to grant that the line between the peaceful and the military sides of the atom was fuzzy. It would be nice, he said, if the two functions could be neatly demarcated, for in that case the Plowshare Program, living up to its name more fully, could have postponed the blasts until war was an obsolete institution. But that wasn't the way things were, in Kelly's view. "We may have to take our peaceful uses when we can," he said.

(15) The other official I talked with was Dr. Gary H. Higgins,

the director of the Plowshare Division of the Lawrence Radiation Laboratory. Higgins was a soft-spoken chemist of thirty-four, whose desk in his Carlsbad office was adorned, when I saw it, with a small ceramic gnome he had bought in a department store. Like Kelly, he believed that nuclear explosives had a great peacetime future. "Within five to fifteen years, they'll be basic to our industrial economy," he told me. "They'll help us get at raw materials we need for our growing population. It may take us time to make use of them. After all, forest husbandry developed only when the nation was practically deforested." He was delighted that the United States was moving ahead with Plowshare, but not, he told me, because it relieved him of his weapons duties at Livermore. The two kinds of work, he felt, were not pure opposites; there was a difference between weapons and war, he said, just as there was between a police force and murder. But whether an idea like Plowshare or an arms race was to dominate our lives in the years ahead was another matter. It depended, Higgins thought, on whether mankind could eventually achieve an immense self-consciousness. "It would not cater to the oversimplified images that religion and ethics tend to give us," Higgins said. "It would enable us to recognize our weaknesses. We'd know our motives for acting the way we do, and what else is it that counts but intent, whether shots are called Plowshare or something else?"

(16) It was almost four hours after the detonation when I left the bulldozed mound in the desert. The roadblock hadn't yet been lifted, but to a number of us that didn't matter. We were chafing to get away, although not for any sensible reason I heard expressed. Perhaps the others felt, as I did, a sense of rebellion and indignation at being trapped by a mysterious, invisible antagonist. In the distance, the refinery's tall chimney continued to surrender its thick plume of smoke, giving no sign, of course, whether there had yet been any mingling with the radioactive cloud. Absurdly, I felt like going to the refinery to find out. Around us, shadows were beginning to fall on the desert, making it seem more limitless than ever, and underscoring our marooned condition.

(17) At any rate, when a rancher who was among the spectators

mentioned to some of us that certain back roads might bring one out on the Carlsbad highway three or four miles beyond the police block-ade, I was off at once, in a car with two other men—Ken Fujisaki, a young correspondent for a Tokyo newspaper, the *Sankei Shimbun,* and David Perlman, a reporter for the San Francisco *Chronicle.* The rancher, who himself was in no hurry to leave, had said he hadn't used those particular back roads in fifteen years, but at the time this remark had struck us as irrelevant. Our immediate goals were a windmill and a gas well—two landmarks that, the rancher had said, might soon guide us on our way to Carlsbad.

(18) "How would you like to spend two weeks in a fallout shel-ter?" Perlman, who was driving, asked me as he impatiently started the car.

(19) After a ten-minute drive over a bumpy, rutted road, we were at the gas well. We were also at a dead end. As we were looking at each other in puzzlement, we heard the honk of a car horn behind us, and discovered that we had been leaders of men. Nine other cars had followed us to the dead end; we had been too intent on our flight from safety to notice them. One of the vehicles was a small orange government truck, and another was a sports car—a dirty, white Triumph whose driver wore goggles. Some of us got out of our cars, conferred ignorantly, and decided to go back and follow a dirt road that had intersected the one we were on. This road also came to a dead end. Backtracking, we tried another, and then another. The fourth ran parallel to a ranch fence, on the other side of which were cattle and horses. Beyond the field they were in we could see the Carlsbad highway, only a couple of miles off. The fence seemed to run on endlessly, leading nowhere. Our caravan halted, and a few of us climbed a stile to seek advice at the ranch. We found a young Mexican hand, who obligingly corralled the animals, and opened a gate into a muddy, reddish road that crossed the field. In no time we were on the highway to Carlsbad. To get there, we had gone east, north, west, and northeast. Now we passed the potash refinery, its tall stack still smoking. I looked at it as long as I could. No police intercepted us. When we reached the Project Gnome office in Carls-bad, we learned that the roadblock had been called off fifteen min-utes after our departure. Perlman asked that he be gone over with

a radiation counter. He proved to be fine, which meant the rest of us were.

(20) When I arrived at my motel, the manager phoned me. He was a transplanted Englishman with whom I had made friends. Since I was leaving the next day, I thought perhaps he was calling to say goodbye, but it was Project Gnome that was on his mind.

(21) "I'm sick in bed, you see, so *I'm* quite all right, but it's the staff—" he began. A guest, he said, had told the cashier in the restaurant not to touch the money of anyone who had been to the test. The cashier had become hysterical. Then a policeman had come and collected two other members of the staff to have them "counted" at the Gnome office; the two had been spectators at the shot and had been among those who eluded the roadblock.

(22) "There's no need for any concern, is there?" the manager asked me uneasily. "I mean, those men out there know what they're doing, don't they?"

(23) I could hear him breathing at the other end of the phone, waiting for my answer.

(24) "Of course they do," I said. "Of course everything's all right."

Questions

1. Most of the first section of the essay has a chronological-narrative basis. Outline its major parts.

2. What organizing principle covers each of the succeeding sections?

3. No single term adequately describes the overall organization of the essay, but the organization is fairly simple, with sections one and four framing sections two and three. Describe the organization briefly.

4. Lang could very easily have written an essay using much the same material and built it to a dramatic conclusion with the faulty explosion. Why do you suppose he chose to begin with the explosion, and to end almost at a dead end as it were?

5. Lang's closing words in the essay express part of his opinion on the experiment. Explain. Where else do you find him expressing his opinion in a similar way?

6. Lang's opinions often come through solely by his selection and

arrangement of material, as when he sets the public-spirited clichés of local leaders against the polite scepticism of the Japanese chemist (Paragraph 2), both comments following his report of the actual mishap of the experiment. What opinion of his own does emerge here, and how do you know? Find and examine two other examples of the same sort.

7. Summarize Lang's opinions. They concern the roles of the government, scientists, politicians, technicians, and one or two other groups of people; they also concern nuclear explosions.

8. The manner in which Lang's opinions get expressed is part of the overall manner of the essay. How would you describe that manner? Does the organizational scheme seem to be in accord with it?

9. What has happened to the Plowshare Program since Project Gnome? The *New York Times Index* on the Atomic Energy Commission might provide information. Try one or two other likely sources.

ON CERTAIN MODERN WRITERS AND THE INSTITUTION OF THE FAMILY

G. K. CHESTERTON

Born in London, into a comfortable middle-class family, G. K. Chesterton (1874–1936) studied painting as a youth, but soon found his abilities better employed at writing. Through a long career he wrote continuously and in virtually every form —novels, biographies, histories, poetry, essays by the hundreds, mystery stories (whose hero-detective is Father Brown). For a time he even edited his own newspaper, *G. K.'s Weekly,* the better to protest the coldness and secularization of modern life, the largeness of modern business, the socialism of his arch-opponent George Bernard Shaw. Chesterton's work is often uneven, much of it journalistic ephemera, but at its best it expresses the energy and wit of a resourceful and imaginative controversialist.

(1) The family may fairly be considered, one would think, an ultimate human institution. Every one would admit that it has been the main cell and central unit of almost all societies hitherto, except, indeed, such societies as that of Lacedaemon, which went in for "efficiency," and has, therefore, perished, and left not a trace behind. Christianity, even enormous as was its revolution, did not alter this ancient and savage sanctity, it merely reversed it. It did not deny the trinity of father, mother, and child. It merely read it backwards, making it run child, mother, father. This it called, not the family, but the Holy Family, for many things are made holy by being turned upside down. But some sages of our decadence have

From *Heretics* by G. K. Chesterton. Reprinted by permission of The Bodley Head Ltd.

made a serious attack on the family. They have impugned it, as I think wrongly; and its defenders have defended it, and defended it wrongly. The common defence of the family is that, amid the stress and fickleness of life, it is peaceful, pleasant, and at one. But there is another defence of the family which is possible, and to me evident; this defence is that the family is not peaceful and not pleasant and not at one.

(2) It is not fashionable to say much nowadays of the advantages of the small community. We are told that we must go in for large empires and large ideas. There is one advantage, however, in the small state, the city, or the village, which only the wilfully blind can overlook. The man who lives in a small community lives in a much larger world. He knows much more of the fierce varieties and uncompromising divergences of men. The reason is obvious. In a large community we can choose our companions. In a small community our companions are chosen for us. Thus in all extensive and highly civilized societies groups come into existence founded upon what is called sympathy, and shut out the real world more sharply than the gates of a monastery. There is nothing really narrow about the clan; the thing which is really narrow is the clique. The men of the clan live together because they all wear the same tartan or are all descended from the same sacred cow; but in their souls, by the divine luck of things, there will always be more colours than in any tartan. But the men of the clique live together because they have the same kind of soul, and their narrowness is a narrowness of spiritual coherence and contentment, like that which exists in hell. A big society exists in order to form cliques. A big society is a society for the promotion of narrowness. It is a machinery for the purpose of guarding the solitary and sensitive individual from all experience of the bitter and bracing human compromises. It is, in the most literal sense of the words, a society for the prevention of Christian knowledge.

(3) We can see this change, for instance, in the modern transformation of the thing called a club. When London was smaller, and the parts of London more self-contained and parochial, the club was what it still is in villages, the opposite of what it is now in great cities. Then the club was valued as a place where a man could

be sociable. Now the club is valued as a place where a man can be unsociable. The more the enlargement and elaboration of our civilization goes on the more the club ceases to be a place where a man can have a noisy argument, and becomes more and more a place where a man can have what is somewhat fantastically called a quiet chop. Its aim is to make a man comfortable, and to make a man comfortable is to make him the opposite of sociable. Sociability, like all good things, is full of discomforts, dangers, and renunciations. The club tends to produce the most degraded of all combinations—the luxurious anchorite, the man who combines the self-indulgence of Lucullus with the insane loneliness of St. Simeon Stylites.

(4) If we were tomorrow morning snowed up in the street in which we live, we should step suddenly into a much larger and much wilder world than we have ever known. And it is the whole effort of the typically modern person to escape from the street in which he lives. First he invents modern hygiene and goes to Margate. Then he invents modern culture and goes to Florence. Then he invents modern imperialism and goes to Timbuctoo. He goes to the fantastic borders of the earth. He pretends to shoot tigers. He almost rides on a camel. And in all this he is still essentially fleeing from the street in which he was born; and of this flight he is always ready with his own explanation. He says he is fleeing from his street because it is dull; he is lying. He is really fleeing from his street because it is a great deal too exciting. It is exciting because it is exacting; it is exacting because it is alive. He can visit Venice because to him the Venetians are only Venetians; the people in his own street are men. He can stare at the Chinese because for him the Chinese are a passive thing to be stared at; if he stares at the old lady in the next garden, she becomes active. He is forced to flee, in short, from the too stimulating society of his equals—of free men, perverse, personal, deliberately different from himself. The street in Brixton is too glowing and overpowering. He has to soothe and quiet himself among tigers and vultures, camels and crocodiles. These creatures are indeed very different from himself. But they do not put their shape or color or custom into a decisive intellectual competition with his own. They do not seek to destroy his principles and assert their own; the stranger

monsters of the suburban street do seek to do this. The camel does not contort his features into a fine sneer because Mr. Robinson has not got a hump; the cultured gentleman at No. 5 does exhibit a sneer because Robinson has not got a dado. The vulture will not roar with laughter because a man does not fly; but the major at No. 9 will roar with laughter because a man does not smoke. The complaint we commonly have to make of our neighbours is that they will not, as we express it, mind their own business. We do not really mean that they will not mind their own business. If our neighbours did not mind their own business they would be asked abruptly for their rent, and would rapidly cease to be our neighbours. What we really mean when we say that they cannot mind their own business is something much deeper. We do not dislike them because they have so little force and fire that they cannot be interested in themselves. We dislike them because they have so much force and fire that they can be interested in us as well. What we dread about our neighbours, in short, is not the narrowness of their horizon, but their superb tendency to broaden it. And all aversions to ordinary humanity have this general character. They are not aversions to its feebleness (as is pretended), but to its energy. The misanthropes pretend that they despise humanity for its weakness. As a matter of fact, they hate it for its strength.

(5) Of course, this shrinking from the brutal vivacity and brutal variety of common men is a perfectly reasonable and excusable thing as long as it does not pretend to any point of superiority. It is when it calls itself aristocracy or aestheticism or a superiority to the bourgeoisie that its inherent weakness has in justice to be pointed out. Fastidiousness is the most pardonable of vices; but it is the most unpardonable of virtues. Nietzsche, who represents most prominently this pretentious claim of the fastidious, has a description somewhere—a very powerful description in the purely literary sense—of the disgust and disdain which consume him at the sight of the common people with their common faces, their common voices, and their common minds. As I have said, this attitude is almost beautiful if we may regard it as pathetic. Nietzsche's aristocracy has about it all the sacredness that belongs to the weak. When he makes us feel that he cannot endure the innumerable faces, the incessant

voices, the overpowering omnipresence which belongs to the mob, he will have the sympathy of anybody who has ever been sick on a steamer or tired in a crowded omnibus. Every man has hated mankind when he was less than a man. Every man has had humanity in his eyes like a blinding fog, humanity in his nostrils like a suffocating smell. But when Nietzsche has the incredible lack of humour and lack of imagination to ask us to believe that his aristocracy is an aristocracy of strong muscles or an aristocracy of strong wills, it is necessary to point out the truth. It is an aristocracy of weak nerves.

(6) We make our friends; we make our enemies; but God makes our next-door neighbour. Hence he comes to us clad in all the careless terrors of nature; he is as strange as the stars, as reckless and indifferent as the rain. He is Man, the most terrible of the beasts. That is why the old religions and the old scriptural language showed so sharp a wisdom when they spoke, not of one's duty towards humanity, but one's duty towards one's neighbour. The duty towards humanity may often take the form of some choice which is personal or even pleasurable. That duty may be a hobby; it may even be a dissipation. We may work in the East End because we are peculiarly fitted to work in the East End, or because we think we are; we may fight for the cause of international peace because we are very fond of fighting. The most monstrous martyrdom, the most repulsive experience, may be the result of choice or a kind of taste. We may be so made as to be particularly fond of lunatics or specially interested in leprosy. We may love Negroes because they are black or German Socialists because they are pedantic. But we have to love our neighbour because he is there—a much more alarming reason for a much more serious operation. He is the sample of humanity which is actually given us. Precisely because he may be anybody he is everybody. He is a symbol because he is an accident.

(7) Doubtless men flee from small environments into lands that are very deadly. But this is natural enough; for they are not fleeing from death. They are fleeing from life. And this principle applies to ring within ring of the social system of humanity. It is perfectly reasonable that men should seek for some particular variety of the human type, so long as they are seeking for that variety of the human type, and not for mere human variety. It is quite proper that a British

diplomatist should seek the society of Japanese generals, if what he wants is Japanese generals. But if what he wants is people different from himself, he had much better stop at home and discuss religion with the housemaid. It is quite reasonable that the village genius should come up to conquer London if what he wants is to conquer London. But if he wants to conquer something fundamentally and symbolically hostile and also very strong, he had much better remain where he is and have a row with the rector. The man in the suburban street is quite right if he goes to Ramsgate for the sake of Ramsgate—a difficult thing to imagine. But if, as he expresses it, he goes to Ramsgate "for a change," then he would have a much more romantic and even melodramatic change if he jumped over the wall into his neighbour's garden. The consequences would be bracing in a sense far beyond the possibilities of Ramsgate hygiene.

(8) Now, exactly as this principle applies to the empire, to the nation within the empire, to the city within the nation, to the street within the city, so it applies to the home within the street. The institution of the family is to be commended for precisely the same reasons that the institution of the nation, or the institution of the city, are in this matter to be commended. It is a good thing for a man to live in a family for the same reason that it is a good thing for a man to be besieged in a city. It is a good thing for a man to live in a family in the same sense that it is a beautiful and delightful thing for a man to be snowed up in a street. They all force him to realize that life is not a thing from outside but a thing from inside. Above all, they all insist upon the fact that life, if it be a truly stimulating and fascinating life, is a thing which, of its nature, exists in spite of ourselves. The modern writers who have suggested, in a more or less open manner, that the family is a bad institution, have generally confined themselves to suggesting, with much sharpness, bitterness, or pathos, that perhaps the family is not always very congenial. Of course the family is a good institution because it is uncongenial. It is wholesome precisely because it contains so many divergencies and varieties. It is, as the sentimentalists say, like a little kingdom, and, like most other little kingdoms, is generally in a state of something resembling anarchy. It is exactly because our brother George is not interested in our religious difficulties, but is

interested in the Trocadero Restaurant, that the family has some of the bracing qualities of the commonwealth. It is precisely because our uncle Henry does not approve of the theatrical ambitions of our sister Sarah that the family is like humanity. The men and women who, for good reasons and bad, revolt against the family, are, for good reasons and bad, simply revolting against mankind. Aunt Elizabeth is unreasonable, like mankind. Papa is excitable, like mankind. Grandpa is stupid, like the world; he is old, like the world.

(9) Those who wish, rightly or wrongly, to step out of all this, do definitely wish to step into a narrower world. They are dismayed and terrified by the largeness and variety of the family. Sarah wishes to find a world wholly consisting of private theatricals; George wishes to think the Trocadero a cosmos. I do not say, for a moment, that the flight to this narrower life may not be the right thing for the individual, any more than I say the same thing about flight into a monastery. But I do say that anything is bad and artificial which tends to make these people succumb to the strange delusion that they are stepping into a world which is actually larger and more varied than their own. The best way that a man could test his readiness to encounter the common variety of mankind would be to climb down a chimney into any house at random, and get on as well as possible with the people inside. And that is essentially what each one of us did on the day that he was born.

(10) This is, indeed, the sublime and special romance of the family. It is romantic because it is a toss-up. It is romantic because it is everything that its enemies call it. It is romantic because it is arbitrary. It is romantic because it is there. So long as you have groups of men chosen rationally, you have some special or sectarian atmosphere. It is when you have groups of men chosen irrationally that you have men. The element of adventure begins to exist; for an adventure is, by its nature, a thing that comes to us. It is a thing that chooses us, not a thing that we choose. Falling in love has been often regarded as the supreme adventure, the supreme romantic accident. In so much as there is in it something outside ourselves, something of a sort of merry fatalism, this is very true. Love does take us and transfigure and torture us. It does break our hearts with an unbearable beauty, like the unbearable beauty of music.

But in so far as we have certainly something to do with the matter; in so far as we are in some sense prepared to fall in love and in some sense jump into it; in so far as we do to some extent choose and to some extent even judge—in all this falling in love is not truly romantic, is not truly adventurous at all. In this degree the supreme adventure is not falling in love. The supreme adventure is being born. There we do walk suddenly into a splendid and startling trap. There we do see something of which we have not dreamed before. Our father and mother do lie in wait for us and leap out on us, like brigands from a bush. Our uncle is a surprise. Our aunt is, in the beautiful common expression, a bolt from the blue. When we step into the family, by the act of being born, we do step into a world which is incalculable, into a world which has its own strange laws, into a world which could do without us, into a world that we have not made. In other words, when we step into the family we step into a fairy-tale.

(11) This colour as of a fantastic narrative ought to cling to the family and to our relations with it throughout life. Romance is the deepest thing in life; romance is deeper even than reality. For even if reality could be proved to be misleading, it still could not be proved to be unimportant or unimpressive. Even if the facts are false, they are still very strange. And this strangeness of life, this unexpected and even perverse element of things as they fall out, remains incurably interesting. The circumstances we can regulate may become tame or pessimistic; but the "circumstances over which we have no control" remain god-like to those who, like Mr. Micawber, can call on them and renew their strength. People wonder why the novel is the most popular form of literature; people wonder why it is read more than books of science or books of metaphysics. The reason is very simple; it is merely that the novel is more true than they are. Life may sometimes legitimately appear as a book of science. Life may sometimes appear, and with a much greater legitimacy, as a book of metaphysics. But life is always a novel. Our existence may cease to be a song; it may cease even to be a beautiful lament. Our existence may not be an intelligible justice, or even a recognizable wrong. But our existence is still a story. In the fiery alphabet of every sunset is written "to be continued in our next." If we have sufficient intellect, we can

finish a philosophical and exact deduction, and be certain that we are finishing it right. With the adequate brain-power we could finish any scientific discovery, and be certain that we were finishing it right. But not with the most gigantic intellect could we finish the simplest or silliest story, and be certain that we were finishing it right. That is because a story has behind it, not merely intellect which is partly mechanical, but will, which is in its essence divine. The narrative writer can send his hero to the gallows if he likes in the last chapter but one. He can do it by the same divine caprice whereby he, the author, can go to the gallows himself, and to hell afterwards if he chooses. And the same civilization, the chivalric European civilization which asserted freewill in the thirteenth century, produced the thing called "fiction" in the eighteenth. When Thomas Aquinas asserted the spiritual liberty of man, he created all the bad novels in the circulating libraries.

(12) But in order that life should be a story of romance to us, it is necessary that a great part of it, at any rate, should be settled for us without our permission. If we wish life to be a system, this may be a nuisance; but if we wish it to be a drama, it is an essential. It may often happen, no doubt, that a drama may be written by somebody else which we like very little. But we should like it still less if the author came before the curtain every hour or so, and forced on us the whole trouble of inventing the next act. A man has control over many things in his life; he has control over enough things to be the hero of a novel. But if he had control over everything, there would be so much hero that there would be no novel. And the reason why the lives of the rich are at bottom so tame and uneventful is simply that they can choose the events. They are dull because they are omnipotent. They fail to feel adventures because they can make the adventures. The thing which keeps life romantic and full of fiery possibilities is the existence of these great plain limitations which force all of us to meet the things we do not like or do not expect. It is vain for the supercilious moderns to talk of being in uncongenial surroundings. To be in a romance is to be in uncongenial surroundings. To be born into this earth is to be born into uncongenial surroundings, hence to be born into a romance. Of all these great limitations and frameworks which fashion and create the poetry and

variety of life, the family is the most definite and important. Hence it is misunderstood by the moderns, who imagine that romance would exist most perfectly in a complete state of what they call liberty. They think that if a man makes a gesture it would be a startling and romantic matter that the sun should fall from the sky. But the startling and romantic thing about the sun is that it does not fall from the sky. They are seeking under every shape and form a world where there are no limitations—that is, a world where there are no outlines; that is, a world where there are no shapes. There is nothing baser than that infinity. They say they wish to be as strong as the universe, but they really wish the whole universe as weak as themselves.

Questions

1. Where in Paragraph 1 is the ostensible subject of the essay stated? What is the relationship of the rest of the paragraph to the subject?

2. What makes Chesterton's defense of the family unusual? Explain his distinction between clans and cliques. Why does he think next-door neighbors are more dangerous than vultures?

3. To what extent is the material in the first paragraph arranged chronologically? In what respect is Chesterton offering a chronological survey in Paragraph 2? Why does he focus in Paragraph 3 upon clubs of present and past rather than upon clubs of city and village?

4. In Paragraph 2 Chesterton says that "the man who lives in a small community lives in a much larger world." What does he mean by "larger"? With what other words in the rest of the paragraph—and in the rest of the essay—does it become equated?

5. Paragraphs 2, 3, and 4 form a unit. To what extent is their common subject defined by the phrase "advantages of the small community" (the opening of Paragraph 2)? On what rough basis are they ordered? What is their relationship to the first paragraph?

6. What is the special function of Paragraph 5? To what extent do Paragraphs 6 and 7 recapitulate earlier views? To what extent do they expand those views?

7. Chesterton comes to the subject of the family in Paragraph 8. Explain the broad relationship of the preceding material to it, and describe the general ordering of the discussion thus far.

8. Describe the broad ordering of material in Paragraphs 8 through 12. Describe the general organization of the essay.

9. Chesterton relies upon paradox to a considerable extent in his argument ("the man who lives in a small community lives in a much larger world"). Locate some paradoxes in the first four paragraphs and explain their meanings. What is the argumentative advantage of paradox over straightforward assertion?

10. Write an essay on the extent to which Mary McCarthy's autobiographical sketch, "The Blackguard," in this section illustrates the advantages of the small community as Chesterton sees them.

THE LAST PARADE

E. M. FORSTER

E. M. Forster (1879——) is highly esteemed both as novelist and essayist. Born in London, the son of an architect, he read classics and history at Cambridge, spent some time travelling in Italy and Greece, and on his return to England began writing in earnest. His first novel, *Where Angels Fear to Tread,* appeared when he was twenty-six; three more (most notably *Howards End*) appeared within the next five years. After a lapse of fourteen years he published his last and best novel, *A Passage to India,* based on two short stays in India. His essays, written over a long period and on many subjects, have been collected in *Abinger Harvest* and *Two Cheers for Democracy.* His short stories appear in two volumes, *The Celestial Omnibus and Other Stories* and *The Eternal Moment.* (Further information on Forster appears on pp. 280, 362.)

(1) Paris Exhibition, 1937: Palace of Discovery, Astronomical Section: model of the Earth in space. Yes, here is a model of this intimate object. It is a tidy size—so large that Europe or even France should be visible on it—and it revolves at a suitable rate. It does not take twenty-four hours to go round as in fact, nor does it whizz as in poetry. It considers the convenience of the observer, as an exhibit should. Staged in a solemn alcove, against a background of lamp-super-black, it preens its contours eternally, that is to say from opening to closing time, and allows us to see our home as others would see it, were there others who could see. Its colouring, its general appearance, accord with the latest deductions. The result is sur-

prising. For not France, not even Europe, is visible. There are great marks on the surface of the model, but they represent clouds and snows, not continents and seas. No doubt the skilled observer could detect some underlying fussiness, and infer our civilisation, but the average voyager through space would only notice our clouds and our snows; they strike the eye best. Natural boundaries, guns in action, beautiful women, pipe-lines—at a little distance they all wear the same veil. Sir Malcolm Campbell beats his own records till he sees his own back, Mr. Jack Hulbert cracks still cleaner jokes, forty thousand monkeys are born in Brazil and fifty thousand Italians in Abyssinia, the Palace of the Soviets rises even higher than had been planned, Lord Baden-Powell holds a yet larger jamboree, but all these exercises and the areas where they occur remain hidden away under an external shimmer. The moon—she shows her face. Throned in an adjacent room, the moon exhibits her pockmarks nakedly. But the Earth, because she still has atmosphere and life, is a blur.

(2) Paris Exhibition: the Spanish Pavilion, the Italian Pavilion. The other pavilions. The Palaces of Glass and of Peace. The Eiffel Tower. The last named occasionally sings. Moved by an emission of Roman Candles from its flanks, it will break of an evening into a dulcet and commanding melody. When this happens the pavilions fold their hands to listen, and are steeped for a little in shadow, so that the aniline fountains may play more brightly in the Seine. The melody swells, inciting the fireworks as they the melody, and both of them swell the crowd. O synchronisation! O splendour unequalled! Splendour ever to be surpassed? Probably never to be surpassed. The German and Russian Pavilions, the Chinese and Japanese Pavilions, the British and Italian Pavilions, any and all of the pavilions, will see to that. The Eiffel Tower sings louder, a scientific swan. Rosy chemicals stimulate her spine, she can scarcely bear the voltage, the joy, the pain. . . . The emotion goes to her tiny head, it turns crimson and vomits fiery serpents. All Paris sees them. They astonish the Pantheon and Montmartre. Even the Institut de France notices, heavy browed, dreaming of cardinals, laurels, and réclame in the past. O inspired giraffe! Whatever will the old thing turn into next?

Listen and see. The crisis is coming. The melody rises by slight and sure gradations, à la César Franck, spiralling easily upward upon the celestial roundabout. Bell pop popple crack, is the crisis, bell pop popple crack, the senses reel, music and light, lusic and might, the Eiffel Tower becomes a plesiosauros, flings out her arms in flame, and brings them back smartly to her vibrating sides, as one who should say "là!" Bell pop crack pop popple bell. The carillon dies away, the rockets fall, the senses disentangle. There is silence, there are various types of silences, and during one of them the Angel of the Laboratory speaks. "Au revoir, mes enfants," she says. "I hope you have enjoyed yourselves. We shall meet again shortly, and in different conditions." The children applaud these well-chosen words. The German Pavilion, the Russian Pavilion, confront one another again, and a small star shines out on the top of the Column of Peace.

(3) Paris Exhibition: Van Gogh. When the day breaks, Van Gogh can be found if wanted. He is housed in the corner of another palace between maps of Paris and intellectual hopes for the future, and the space suffices him. Well content with his half-dozen rooms, he displays his oddness and his misery to tired feet. "Sorrow is better than joy," he writes up upon the white walls of his cell. Here are pictures of potatoes and of miners who have eaten potatoes until their faces are tuberous and dented and their skins grimed and unpeeled. They are hopeless and humble, so he loves them. He has his little say, and he understands what he is saying, and he cuts off his own ear with a knife. The gaily painted boats of Saintes Maries sail away into the Mediterranean at last, and the Alpilles rise over St. Rémy for ever, but nevertheless "Sorrow is better than joy," for Van Gogh. What would the Eiffel Tower make of such a conclusion? Spinning in its alcove for millions of years, the earth brings a great artist to this. Is he just dotty, or is he failing to put across what is in his mind? Neither, if we may accept historical parallels. Every now and then people have preferred sorrow to joy, and asserted that wisdom and creation can only result from suffering. Half a mile off, Picasso has done a terrifying fresco in the Spanish Pavilion, a huge black and white thing called "Guernica." Bombs split bull's skull, woman's

trunk, man's shins. The fresco is indignant, and so it is less disquiet-
ing than the potato-feeders of Van Gogh. Picasso is grotesquely
angry, and those who are angry still hope. He is not yet wise, and
perhaps he is not yet a creator. Nevertheless, he too succeeds in
saying something about injustice and pain. Can one look through
pain or get round it? And can anything be done against money? On
the subject of money, Van Gogh becomes comprehensible and sound.
He has got round money because he has sought suffering and re-
nounced happiness. In the sizzle surrounding him, his voice stays
uncommercial, unscientific, pure. He sees the colour "blue," observes
that the colour "yellow" always occurs in it, and writes this preposterous postulate up upon the white walls. He has a home beyond
comfort and common sense with the saints, and perhaps he sees God.

(4) The Soviet Pavilion. This, bold and gleaming, hopes to solve
such problems for the ordinary man. And for the ordinary woman
too, who, of enormous size, leans forward on the roof beside her
gigantic mate. Seen from the side, they and the building upon which
they stand describe a hyperbola. They shoot into space, following
their hammer and sickle, and followed by the worker's world state.
The conception is satisfying, but a hyperbola is a mathematical line,
not necessarily an esthetic one, and the solid and ardent pair do not
group well when viewed from the banks of the bourgeois Seine.
Challenging injustice, they ignore good taste, indeed they declare
in their sterner moments that injustice and good taste are inseparable.
Their aims are moral, their methods disciplinary. Passing beneath
their sealed-up petticoats and trousers, we enter a realm which is
earnest, cheerful, instructive, constructive and consistent, but which
has had to blunt some of the vagrant sensibilities of mankind and
is consequently not wholly alive. Statistics, maps and graphs preach
a numerical triumph, but the art-stuff on the walls might as well
hang on the walls of the German Pavilion opposite: the incidents
and the uniforms in the pictures are different but the mentality of
the artists is the same, and is as tame. Only after a little thinking
does one get over one's disappointment and see the matter in perspective. For the Soviet Pavilion is a nudge to the blind. It is trying,

like Van Gogh, to dodge money and to wipe away the film of coins and notes which keeps forming on the human retina. One of the evils of money is that it tempts us to look at it rather than at the things that it buys. They are dimmed because of the metal and the paper through which we receive them. That is the fundamental deceitfulness of riches, which kept worrying Christ. That is the treachery of the purse, the wallet and the bank-balance, even from the capitalist point of view. They were invented as a convenience to the flesh, they have become a chain for the spirit. Surely they can be cut out, like some sorts of pain. Though deprived of them the human mind might surely still keep its delicacy unimpaired, and the human body eat, drink and make love. And that is why every bourgeois ought to reverence the Soviet Pavilion. Even if he is scared at Marxism he ought to realise that Russia has tried to put men into touch with things. She has come along with a handkerchief and wiped. And she has wiped close to the exhibition turnstiles and amid the chaos and carnage of international finance.

(5) Park of Attractions. I did enjoy myself here, I must say. That is the difficulty of considering the Exhibition: it is in so many pieces and so is oneself. After seeing the German Pavilion, which presents Valhalla as a telephone box, and the Belgian Pavilion, which is very lovely, and many other sacred and serious objects, I sought the Park of Attractions and went up to space in a pretence-balloon. A crane lifted me into the void while another crane lowered another balloon which filled with people when my balloon was up. Then my balloon came down and the other balloon went up. So I got out and walked over the surface of the earth to the Dervish Theatre. Then I watched other people play a game called "Deshabillez vos vedettes." I thought a vedette was a boat. Here it was a tin lady, naked except for a cincture of green feathers which the entrants tried to shoot off. Then I went to a booth advertising "Perversités. Images Troublantes." The entrance fee was a franc, which helped me to keep my head. Inside were some distorting mirrors, a little black savage who kept lashing herself or himself with a bunch of bootlaces, and some holes through which improper photographs should have been seen, but I got muddled and missed them. Oh,

the French, the French! Well pleased, I came out. It was a lovely evening. The moon, which had been trying various styles from Neon to Pantheon, now imitated a pretence-balloon. The Park of Attractions, which is extremely clever and pretty, was girt with a scenic railway, and at intervals the shrieks of voyagers through space rent the night. There was plenty to spend money on. Money, money, money! The crowd was what journalists call "good humoured"; and I, a journalist, was part of it. Tunisians and Moroccans strolled about and sometimes kissed one another. Oh, the French! Why are they so good at organizing these lighter happinesses? The English admire them, and themselves produce the suety dreariness, the puffed pretentiousness, of Wembley.

(6) Satan. Unexpected but unmistakable, he appears in the great entrance court of the Italian Pavilion, amongst the fragments of the lovely Italian past. These fragments are bent to his service—Garibaldi, St. Francis, Ravenna mosaics, Pompeian doves. He is to the left as one comes in, clothed all in black, and he dominates a large feeble picture of carnage. He is weakness triumphant—that is his rôle in the modern world. He presses a button and a bull bursts. He sprays savages with scent. He tilts his head back till his chin sticks out like a tongue and his eyeballs stare into his brain. Decent people take no notice of him or make fun of him, but presently something goes wrong with their lives; certain islands are inaccessible, a letter is unanswered, bonds confiscated, a friend takes a trip over the frontier and never returns. Elsewhere in this same pavilion are his instruments: things easily let off. He has only one remark to make: "I, I, I." He uses the symbols of the sacred and solemn past, but they only mean "I." Here, among superficial splendours of marble, he holds his court, and no one can withstand him except Van Gogh, and Van Gogh has nothing to lose. The rest of us are vulnerable, science is doing us in, the Angel of the Laboratory switches off the fireworks, and burns up the crowd without flame.

(7) Meanwhile, and all the while, the Earth revolves in her alcove, veiled in wool. She has sent samples of her hopes and lusts to Paris;

that they will again be collected there, or anywhere, is unlikely, but she herself will look much the same as soon as one stands a little back in space. Even if the Mediterranean empties into the Sahara it will not make much difference. It is our clouds and our snows that show.

Questions

1. Which items in the two series in the opening section of the essay, "Natural boundaries . . ." and "Sir Malcolm Campbell . . . ," are referred to—directly and indirectly—in later sections of the essay? To which other section is the main body of the first section most closely linked?

2. Identify the several direct and indirect references to peace and war in the second section. Which theme dominates the section? How do you know?

3. Of what relevance are the first and second sections to the implication of Forster's statement in the opening of the third section, "Van Gogh can be found if wanted"? How would you describe the organization of the first three sections?

4. What themes run through sections three and four? What differences does Forster see between Van Gogh and the Soviet citizens? With whom does he side? How do you know?

5. Identify four themes that Forster touches upon in sections four and five. In what ways do the themes in section five clarify or modify the themes in section four? What reverberation from an earlier section does Forster achieve with his phrase "shrieks of voyagers through space"?

6. At what points in the sixth section is Forster describing a physical image of Satan and at what points imagining things about him? Which of Satan's attributes has Forster alluded to earlier in the essay?

7. On the basis of your examination of the previous questions, answer the following ones. What are the major themes of the essay? What is the relationship of the first section to them? What is the relationship of Satan to them? Why does the section on Van Gogh follow the description of the Eiffel Tower rather than precede it? Why are Van Gogh and the Russian Pavilion juxtaposed? Why are the Park of Attractions and Satan juxtaposed? Why would it be undesirable to follow

the section on the Eiffel Tower with the section on Satan? What would you say is the organizing principle—or principles—governing the essay?

8. What advantages does Forster derive from the fragmentary and disjointed way in which he presents his material?

9. Identify the several ironic juxtapositions (such as "maps of Paris and intellectual hopes for the future") and apparent *non sequiturs* (such as "they are hopeless and humble, so he loves them") in Paragraph 3. Explain their meanings. Try to define the quality that they lend to the writing.

10. What is the difference in tone and implication in the descriptions of the earth in the first and last sections?

THE BLACKGUARD

MARY McCARTHY

Mary McCarthy (1912—) was born in Seattle, Washington, and studied at Vassar College (the subject of her novel, *The Group*). She taught for a time at Bard College and at Sarah Lawrence, but makes her home now in Paris. As the title, *Cast a Cold Eye* (a collection of short stories) intimates, hers is a detached, satirical, and occasionally merciless perspective. This is evident as much in her novels, which include *A Charmed Life* and *The Groves of Academe*—this last an assault on academic life—as in her essays, which are well represented in *On the Contrary*. She reviews her own early years in *Memories of a Catholic Childhood,* from which the following is a chapter.

(1) Were he living today, my Protestant grandfather would be displeased to hear that the fate of his soul had once been the occasion of intense theological anxiety with the Ladies of the Sacred Heart. While his mortal part, all unaware, went about its eighteen holes of golf, its rubber of bridge before dinner at the club, his immortal part lay in jeopardy with us, the nuns and pupils of a strict convent school set on a wooded hill quite near a piece of worthless real estate he had bought under the impression that Seattle was expanding in a northerly direction. A sermon delivered at the convent by an enthusiastic Jesuit had disclosed to us his danger. Up to this point, the disparity in religion between my grandfather and myself had given me no serious concern. The death of my parents, while it had drawn us together in many senses, including the legal one

(for I became his ward), had at the same time left the gulf of a generation between us, and my grandfather's Protestantism presented itself as a natural part of the grand, granite scenery on the other side. But the Jesuit's sermon destroyed this ordered view in a single thunderclap of doctrine.

(2) As the priest would have it, this honest and upright man, a great favorite with the Mother Superior, was condemned to eternal torment by the accident of having been baptized. Had he been a Mohammedan, a Jew, a pagan, or the child of civilized unbelievers, a place in Limbo would have been assured him; Cicero and Aristotle and Cyrus the Persian might have been his companions, and the harmless souls of unbaptized children might have frolicked about his feet. But if the Jesuit were right, all baptized Protestants went straight to Hell. A good life did not count in their favor. The baptismal rite, by conferring on them God's grace, made them also liable to His organizational displeasure. That is, baptism turned them Catholic whether they liked it or not, and their persistence in the Protestant ritual was a kind of asseverated apostasy. Thus my poor grandfather, sixty years behind in his Easter duty, actually reduced his prospects of salvation every time he sat down in the Presbyterian Church.

(3) The Mother Superior's sweet frown acknowledged me, an hour after the sermon, as I curtsied, all agitation, in her office doorway. Plainly, she had been expecting me. Madame MacIllvra, an able administrator, must have been resignedly ticking off the names of the Protestant pupils and parents all during the concluding parts of the morning's service. She had a faint worried air, when the conversation began, of depreciating the sermon: doctrinally, perhaps, correct, it had been wanting in delicacy; the fiery Jesuit, a missionary celebrity, had lived too long among the Eskimos. This disengaged attitude encouraged me to hope. Surely this lady, the highest authority I knew, could find a way out for my grandfather. She could see that he was a special case, outside the brutal rule of thumb laid down by the Jesuit. It was she, after all, in the convent, from whom all exemptions flowed, who created arbitrary holidays (called *congés* by the order's French tradition); it was she who permitted us to get forbidden books from the librarian and occasion-

ally to receive letters unread by the convent censor. (As a rule, all slang expressions, violations of syntax, errors of spelling, as well as improper sentiments, were blacked out of our friends' communications, so unless we moved in a circle of young Addisons or Burkes, the letters we longed for came to us as fragments from which the original text could only be conjectured.) To my twelve-year-old mind, it appeared probable that Madame MacIllvra, our Mother Superior, had the power to give my grandfather *congé,* and I threw myself on her sympathies.

(4) How could it be that my grandfather, the most virtuous person I knew, whose name was a byword among his friends and colleagues for a kind of rigid and fantastic probity—how could it be that this man should be lost, while I, the object of his admonition, the despair of his example—I, who yielded to every impulse, lied, boasted, betrayed—should, by virtue of regular attendance at the sacraments and the habit of easy penitence, be saved?

(5) Madame MacIllvra's full white brow wrinkled; her childlike blue eyes clouded. Like many headmistresses, she loved a good cry, and she clasped me to her plump, quivering, middle-aged bosom. She understood; she was crying for my grandfather and the injustice of it too. She and my grandfather had, as a matter of fact, established a very amiable relation, in which both took pleasure. The masculine line and firmness of his character made an aesthetic appeal to her, and the billowy softness and depth of the Mother Superior struck him favorably, but, above all, it was their difference in religion that salted their conversations. Each of them enjoyed, whenever they met in her straight, black-and-white little office, a sense of broadness, of enlightenment, of transcendent superiority to petty prejudice. My grandfather would remember that he wrote a check every Christmas for two Sisters of Charity who visited his office; Madame MacIllvra would perhaps recall her graduate studies and Hume. They had long, liberal talks which had the tone of *performances;* virtuoso feats of magnanimity were achieved on both sides. Afterward, they spoke of each other in nearly identical terms: "A very fine woman," "A very fine man."

(6) All this (and possibly the suspicion that her verdict might be repeated at home) made Madame MacIllvra's answer slow.

"Perhaps God," she murmured at last, "in His infinite mercy . . ." Yet this formulation satisfied neither of us. God's infinite mercy we believed in, but its manifestations were problematical. Sacred history showed us that it was more likely to fall on the Good Thief or the Woman Taken in Adultery than on persons of daily virtue and regular habits, like my grandfather. Our Catholic thoughts journeyed and met in a glance of alarmed recognition. Madame MacIllvra pondered. There were, of course, she said finally, other loopholes. If he had been improperly baptized . . . a careless clergyman . . . I considered this suggestion and shook my head. My grandfather was not the kind of man who, even as an infant, would have been guilty of a slovenly baptism.

(7) It was a measure of Madame MacIllvra's intelligence, or of her knowledge of the world, that she did not, even then, when my grandfather's soul hung, as it were, pleadingly between us, suggest the obvious, the orthodox solution. It would have been ridiculous for me to try to convert my grandfather. Indeed, as it turned out later, I might have dropped him into the pit with my innocent traps (the religious books left open beside his cigar cutter, or "Grandpa, won't you take me to Mass this Sunday? I am so tired of going alone"). "Pray for him, my dear," said Madame MacIllvra, sighing, "and I will speak to Madame Barclay. The point may be open to interpretation. She may remember something in the Fathers of the Church. . . ."

(8) A few days later, Madame MacIllvra summoned me to her office. Not only Madame Barclay, the learned prefect of studies, but the librarian and even the convent chaplain had been called in. The Benedictine view, it seemed, differed sharply from the Dominican, but a key passage in Saint Athanasius seemed to point to my grandfather's safety. The unbeliever, according to this generous authority, was not to be damned unless he rejected the true Church with sufficient knowledge and full consent of the will. Madame MacIllvra handed me the book, and I read the passage over. Clearly, he was saved. Sufficient knowledge he had not. The Church was foreign to him; he knew it only distantly, only by repute, like the

heathen Hiawatha, who had heard strange stories of missionaries, white men in black robes who bore a Cross. Flinging my arms about Madame MacIllvra, I blessed for the first time the insularity of my grandfather's character, the long-jawed, shut face it turned toward ideas and customs not its own. I resolved to dismantle at once the little altar in my bedroom at home, to leave off grace before meals, elaborate fasting, and all ostentatious practices of devotion, lest the light of my example shine upon him too powerfully and burn him with sufficient knowledge to a crisp.

(9) Since I was a five-day boarder, this project had no time to grow stale, and the next Sunday, at home, my grandfather remarked on the change in me, which my feeling for the dramatic had made far from unobtrusive. "I hope," he said in a rather stern and ironical voice, "that you aren't using the *irreligious* atmosphere of this house as an excuse for backsliding. There will be time enough when you are older to change your beliefs if you want to." The unfairness of this rebuke delighted me. It put me solidly in the tradition of the saints and martyrs; Our Lord had known something like it, and so had Elsie Dinsmore at the piano. Nevertheless, I felt quite angry and slammed the door of my room behind me as I went in to sulk. I almost wished that my grandfather would die at once, so that God could furnish him with the explanation of my behavior—certainly he would have to wait till the next life to get it; in this one he would only have seen in it an invasion of his personal liberties.

(10) As though to reward me for my silence, the following Wednesday brought me the happiest moment of my life. In order to understand my happiness, which might otherwise seem perverse, the reader must yield himself to the spiritual atmosphere of the convent. If he imagines that the life we led behind those walls was bare, thin, cold, austere, sectarian, he will have to revise his views; our days were a tumult of emotion. In the first place, we ate, studied, and slept in that atmosphere of intrigue, rivalry, scandal, favoritism, tyranny, and revolt that is common to all girls' boarding schools and that makes "real" life afterward seem a long and improbable armistice, a cessation of the true anguish of activity. But above the

tinkling of this girlish operetta, with its clink-clink of chanting friendships, its plot of smuggled letters, notes passed from desk to desk, secrets, there sounded in the Sacred Heart convent heavier, more solemn strains, notes of a great religious drama, which was also all passion and caprice, in which salvation was the issue and God's rather sultanlike and elusive favor was besought, scorned, despaired of, connived for, importuned. It was the paradoxical element in Catholic doctrine that lent this drama its suspense. The Divine Despot we courted could not be bought, like a piece of merchandise, by long hours at the *prie-dieu,* faithful attendance at the sacraments, obedience, reverence toward one's superiors. These solicitations helped, but it might well turn out that the worst girl in the school, whose pretty, haughty face wore rouge and a calm, closed look that advertised even to us younger ones some secret knowledge of men, was in the dark of her heart another Mary of Egypt, the strumpet saint in our midst. Such notions furnished a strange counterpoint to discipline; surely the Mother Superior never could have expelled a girl without recalling, with a shade of perplexity, the profligate youth of Saint Augustine and of Saint Ignatius of Loyola.

(11) This dark-horse doctrine of salvation, with all its worldly wisdom and riddling charm, was deep in the idiom of the convent. The merest lay sister could have sustained with spiritual poise her end of a conversation on the purification through sin with Mr. Auden, Herr Kafka, or *Gospodin* Dostoevski; and Madame Mac-Illvra, while she would have held it bad taste to bow down, like Father Zossima, before the murder in Dmitri Karamazov's heart, would certainly have had him in for a series of long, interesting talks in her office.

(12) Like all truly intellectual women, these were in spirit romantic desperadoes. They despised organizational heretics of the stamp of Luther and Calvin, but the great atheists and sinners were the heroes of the costume picture they taught as a subject called history. Marlowe, Baudelaire—above all, Byron—glowed like terrible stars above their literature courses. Little girls of ten were reciting "The Prisoner of Chillon" and hearing stories of Claire Clairmont, Caroline Lamb, the Segatti, and the swim across the Hellespont. Even M. Voltaire enjoyed a left-handed popularity. The nuns spoke of

him with horror and admiration mingled: "A great mind, an un-
conquerable spirit—and what fearful use they were put to." In
Rousseau, an unbuttoned, middle-class figure, they had no interest
whatever.

(13) These infatuations, shared by the pupils, were brought into
line with official Catholic opinion by a variety of stratagems. The
more highly educated nuns were able to accept the damnation of
these great Luciferian spirits. A simple young nun, on the other
hand, who played baseball and taught arithmetic to the sixth and
seventh grades, used to tell her pupils that she personally was convinced that Lord Byron in his last hours must have made an act of
contrition.

(14) It was not, therefore, unusual that a line from the works of
this dissipated author should have been waiting for us on the blackboard of the eighth-grade rhetoric classroom when we filed in that
Wednesday morning which remains still memorable to me. *"Zoe mou,
sas agapo":* the words of Byron's last assurance to the Maid of
Athens stood there in Madame Barclay's French-looking script,
speaking to us of the transiency of the passions. To me, as it happened, it spoke a twice-told tale. I had read the poem before, alone
in my grandfather's library; indeed, I knew it by heart, and I rather
resented the infringement on my private rights in it, the democrati-
zation of the poem which was about to take place. Soon, Madame
Barclay's pointer was rapping from word to word: "My . . . life . . .
I . . . love . . . you," she sharply translated. When the pointer started
back for its second trip, I retreated into hauteur and began drawing
a picture of the girl who sat next to me. Suddenly the pointer cracked
across my writing tablet.

(15) "You're just like Lord Byron, brilliant but unsound."

(16) I heard the pointer being set down and the drawing being
torn crisply twice across, but I could not look up. I had never felt
so flattered in my life. Throughout the rest of the class, I sat motionless, simulating meekness, while my classmates shot me glances
of wonder, awe, and congratulation, as though I had suddenly been
struck by a remarkable disease, or been canonized, or transfigured.
Madame Barclay's pronouncement, which I kept repeating to myself
under my breath, had for us girls a kind of final and majestic cer-

tainty. She was the severest and most taciturn of our teachers. Her
dark brows met in the middle; her skin was a pure olive; her upper
lip had a faint mustache; she was the iron and authority of the
convent. She tolerated no infractions, overlooked nothing, was utterly
and obdurately fair, had no favorites; but her rather pointed face
had the marks of suffering, as though her famous discipline had
scored it as harshly as one of our papers. She had a bitter and sarcastic
wit, and had studied, it was said, at the Sorbonne. Before this day,
I had once or twice dared to say to myself that Madame Barclay
liked me. Her dark, quiet handsome eyes would sometimes move in
my direction as her lips prepared an aphorism or a satiric gibe. Yet
hardly had I estimated the look, weighed and measured it to store
it away in my memory book of requited affections, when a stinging
penalty would recall me from my dream and I could no longer be
sure. Now, however, there was no doubt left. The reproof was a
declaration of love as plain as the sentence on the blackboard, which
shimmered slightly before my eyes. My happiness was a confused
exaltation in which the fact that I was Lord Byron and the fact that
I was loved by Madame Barclay, the most puzzling nun in the convent, blended in a Don Juanesque triumph.

(17) In the refectory that noon, publicity was not wanting to enrich this moment. Insatiable, I could hardly wait for the week end,
to take Madame Barclay's words home as though they had been
a prize. With the generosity of affluence, I spoke to myself of sharing
this happiness, this honor, with my grandfather. Surely, *this* would
make up to him for any worry or difficulty I had caused him. At
the same time, it would have the practical effect of explaining me
a little to him. Phrases about my prototype rang in my head: "that
unfortunate genius," "that turbulent soul," "that gifted and erratic
nature."

(18) My grandfather turned dark red when he heard the news.
His forehead grew knotty with veins; he swore; he looked strange
and young; it was the first time I had ever seen him angry. Argument
and explanation were useless. For my grandfather, history had inter-
posed no distance between Lord Byron and himself. Though the
incestuous poet had died forty years before my grandfather was
born, the romantic perspective was lacking. That insularity of my

grandfather's that kept him intimate with morals and denied the reality of the exotic made him judge the poet as he judged himself or one of his neighbors—that is, on the merit of his actions. He was on the telephone at once, asking the Mother Superior in a thundering, courtroom voice what right one of her sisters had to associate his innocent granddaughter with that degenerate blackguard, Byron. On Monday, Madame Barclay, with tight-drawn lips, told her class that she had a correction to make: Mary McCarthy did not resemble Lord Byron in any particular; she was neither brilliant, loose-living, nor unsound.

(19) The interviews between my grandfather and Madame Mac-Illvra came to an end. To that remarkable marriage of minds the impediment had at last been discovered. But from this time on, Madame Barclay's marks of favor to me grew steadily more distinct, while the look of suffering tightened on her face, till some said she had cancer (a theory supported by the yellowness of her skin) and some said she was being poisoned by an antipathy to the Mother Superior.

Questions

1. In the first two sections of this essay the basic organization is a combination of two related patterns. What are they?

2. What interruption or modification of the basic organizational patterns occurs in the first two sections?

3. The organization of section three is in large part the same as that in the opening sections, but the first four paragraphs depend upon another pattern or patterns. Analyze them.

4. What two or three themes of the first two sections are amplified in section three?

5. Although the two main organizational patterns are in evidence in the final section, this paragraph is hardly a direct conclusion to the rest of the essay. Justify it, without taking into account the presumed nature of the next essay in Miss McCarthy's book.

6. Although section three is somewhat related to the first two sections,

it stands easily enough by itself, and the first two sections can stand by themselves without it. Allowing for minor adjustments, could section three reasonably come first? If it could, justify the looseness of organization that would allow it to be so moved. If it could not, what organizational principle determines its present position?

7. Explain how "the reproof was a declaration of love" (Paragraph 16), relying upon the whole preceding discussion in that section to frame your answer.

8. In the third section, Miss McCarthy asserts that her nuns had considerable sympathy for great atheists and sinners. Apart from the obvious evidence of such phrases as "honest and upright man," what material in the first section suggests that Miss McCarthy herself, as a mature woman, sympathizes with the minor sinner, her grandfather?

9. Write an account of a conflict between feeling and belief in your own life.

10. What would you say are the chief reasons for Miss McCarthy's admiration and love for her nuns? Argue from evidence in the essay.

THE ABACUS AND THE BRAIN

JOSEPH WOOD KRUTCH

Joseph Wood Krutch (1893—) was for many years Professor of English and Dramatic Literature at Columbia University and also a distinguished drama critic for the *Nation*. He has written several important scholarly studies (*Thoreau, Samuel Johnson*), but he is perhaps best known for two sharply contrasting books, published twenty-five years apart. *The Modern Temper* (1929) reflects the despair of modern man in a world of lost values; *The Measure of Man* (1954) resumes the discussion of modern problems, but with some hopefulness. Since 1950, Krutch has lived most of the time in the Southwest and has been studying the natural life of the region (*The Desert Year, Voice of the Desert*). (Further information on Krutch appears on p. 322.)

(1) The statement that man behaves like a machine and that therefore he is one, involves two propositions which many physiologists as well as many psychologists appear to regard as demonstrated. It would seem unreasonable to ask that they clinch the argument by proving its obverse; that they conclude the demonstration by making a machine which behaves like a man. No one would really issue so unfair a challenge but many believe that it has been met already. "I think, therefore I am." The electronic calculator thinks, therefore it *is*. Is what? Is a man. Or at least the most important part of him, namely a brain.

(2) Now to understand just what this means and why the argument is dubious, we should really go back as far as the abacus,

though to most of us this ingenious device is only a harmless toy of wire and beads. Sometimes our Chinese laundryman plays with it for a few seconds before announcing, "Two dollars and thirty-five cents." We then go our way unaware of danger.

(3) Nobody seems to know who invented this prophetic gadget but whoever did started more than he knew. Arabic numerals came later into Europe and at first they seemed to relegate the abacus to the past. But it was only biding its time. About three hundred years ago John Napier with his "bones" taught the abacus how to be logarithmic instead of merely arithmetical and thus gave to the engineer the slide rule which can multiply or extract square roots faster than he can. Ever since then the human brain has been competing less and less successfully with the machine in the matter of calculation.

(4) When Marconi or De Forest—it was long a vexed question which—invented the grid radio tube, he had no idea that it would be able to figure. Neither, for that matter, did whoever invented the wheeled vehicle have any idea of using it to make pottery, though the anthropologists now tell us that the potter's wheel comes into every culture only after the cart. In other words, most fundamentally new gadgets turn out to be usable in fantastically disparate ways, and the man who made radio practical hit upon a device scarcely less adaptable than the wheel, the wedge or the lever. As everyone knows, contraptions which look rather like huge radios are now solving in minutes, or at most in weeks, problems either totally unsolvable by the human brain or so laborious that an individual would spend a large part of his lifetime with pencil, paper, and slide rule if he tried to work them out.

(5) As is usual when something like this comes along, the result is to make mechanists very happy and the rest of us uncomfortable. The abacus and the slide rule were merely tools. Man made them. They were a credit to his ingenuity. They proved how smart *he* was, not how smart *they* were; and nobody thought of them as having any significance or even any existence apart from him. But these electronic calculators are, we are now told, something quite different. They do not have the limitations which we commonly associate with mechanical devices because electricity has endowed them with a kind

of life. We are assured that they have memories or, as the followers
of Korzybski would say, that they are the first inorganic thing which
is capable of "time binding." Some people go even so far as to say
that they can exercise judgment, that they think for themselves. In
the opinion of their most ardent admirers they are less like a machine
and more like a human brain than anything man has ever succeeded
in making before.

(6) The poor deluded chemists have been working for a long
time learning to synthesize the amino acids in the hope that these
would lead to synthetic protein and that, in turn, to synthetic proto-
plasm. But suppose that at last they did succeed. What would they
have? An amoeba at best. Your engineer, on the other hand, brushes
aside all nonsense about the mysterious nature of life and, firm in his
conviction that all is mechanical, creates at one fell swoop life's highest manifestation, namely, thought.

(7) So at least some of them are telling us and we are ill equipped
to argue with them. The equations with which they juggle may seem
like mumbo jumbo to us but they have proved in many ways that
they are not. Mr. Einstein writes "$E = MC^2$" and (after a few merely
technological intermediary steps) Hiroshima goes up in smoke. Obviously these mathematicians know what they are talking about and
if they tell us that machines are now thinking—just like men only
better—perhaps we should marvel and keep silent.

(8) There is, however, a good deal at stake and it is hard not to
protest a little, not to hope that at least the metaphysical conclusions
of some mathematicians and engineers may not be incontrovertible.
It is bad enough to be caught up in a world which whizzes and
bangs; bad enough to be, ultimately, not merely blown up but dis-
integrated. That, however, we are beginning to get used to. Must
we also accept the conviction, not only that we are victims of the
machine, but also that we are merely machines ourselves? If, as is
obvious, contraptions are becoming more and more manlike, does it
necessarily follow that man must be assumed to be no more than a
contraption himself?

(9) According to the mechanists, the electronic calculator is the
best new evidence for their side in a long, long time. So far as I am

aware, no one has yet claimed that a calculator can have children, and the power of self-reproduction has long been on the biologist's list of the criteria for life. But biologists and engineers do not always see eye to eye, and the engineer would no doubt be eager to maintain that if a machine can think, that alone is sufficient to prove his point—namely that the so-called higher faculties of man are the result of the operation of physical forces and that the brain is, at most, no more different from a man-made machine than, say, the man-made electronic "valve" is different from the valve we turn on and off at our steam radiator.

(10) You can't see the wheels go round in the brain; but neither can you turn off an electronic valve by hand, though it is a mechanical device nonetheless. The calculator can remember and it can think. The first of these may be one of the lower capacities of the mind, but the second is, by common consent, the highest. Some, indeed, say that among all living things only man and, perhaps, the ape is capable of it. And if that is true, then the calculator is very far up the evolutionary scale, perhaps farther up than man himself. At least it can think better along certain lines than he can.

(11) Unfortunately for those of us who would like to resist this conclusion, it has been prepared for by the whole tendency of thought on such subjects during the last three hundred years. No one can deny that the study of the human body as a machine has been extremely fruitful of results, while theology and metaphysics have often seemed merely to march round and round in their familiar circles. The study of animal and of human *behavior* has led to apparently stable conclusions, while speculations about the soul, or even the mental processes, seemed to get nowhere.

(12) The psychologist, even though he was not clearly a mechanist by conviction, found it more and more advisable to concentrate his attention on instincts and conditioned reflexes. By consequence, we all fell into the habit of assuming that sooner or later all rational need for the consideration of anything else would vanish. What mechanism could not explain was assumed to be a mere residuum growing smaller and smaller. If the body is mostly a machine, then, it seemed, it is probably entirely a machine. And because we had been long prepared, most people were probably relieved to be told that the last objection to mechanism had been removed. Hitherto

machines couldn't think. But my new calculator, says the engineer, can. *Quod erat* (for a long time) *demonstrandum.*

(13) If we do not want to accept this demonstration, then it is evident that we cannot resist merely the last steps in the argument, but will have to go a long way back and begin to resist certain premises, long implicit and sometimes concealed. Again we shall have to point out that the very methods which scientists have chosen to use have prejudiced the conclusions; that to observe human or animal behavior *as though* it were merely mechanical, is inevitably to make it seem so; that to begin with the proposition "We cannot conveniently deal with consciousness and therefore we are justified in disregarding it," is simply to invite the confusions which have, in actual fact, arisen. It is to assume that what a given method finds intractable simply does not exist.

(14) Obviously, then, we have to begin by telling the mechanist that, however inconvenient he may find our insistence, we simply will not permit him to disregard any of the facts; not *any* of the facts and, especially, not so tremendous a fact as the fact of consciousness. Descartes, we shall say, was right. That we think—or rather that we are aware—is, of all things, the one which we know most directly and incontrovertibly. It may be a difficult fact to deal with but it is primary. Consciousness is the one thing which incontrovertibly *is,* and if there is one thing which we cannot afford to leave out of consideration it is that. To refuse to concern ourselves with it is to make the most monstrous error that could possibly be made.

(15) Certainly, then, we have a right to ask whether the electronic calculator is conscious. "Does it," we may also ask, "have ideas about itself?" Does it, for example, "believe" that mechanistic theories of life are "true"? These are some of the most important things that the human brain is capable of. No doubt some of the machine's admirers will scornfully reply that we can't prove that it doesn't. But that is hardly enough. If we are going to accept a conclusion so momentous as the conclusion that there is no important difference between us and a circuit of electronic tubes, then we may reasonably ask for more than merely negative evidence. The theory that consciousness is only an epiphenomenon is a theory not a fact. We have a right to say that awareness is the most important as well as the most obvious fact about us. Nothing which is not aware of itself

is anything like what we are. It has not been proved that we are machines until it has been proved that a machine can, to begin with —and it is only to begin with—say to itself, *"Cogito ergo sum."* If we are going to deal in mere guesses or probabilities, then some of us may guess that what goes on in a brain is not identical with what goes on in an electronic circuit.

(16) If there was no more to be said than this, it would still be worth saying. To some extent the air would be cleared and we would know where we stand. Those to whom a man is, first of all, a mere figuring machine, would be clearly separated from those to whom consciousness is the essential condition of all those activities which define the human being. But there is more to be said, and there are conclusions to be drawn.

(17) Let us remember that when Diogenes exhibited a plucked hen in the market place and called it "Plato's Man," no one supposed that he meant what he said. He was making it obvious to the meanest intelligence that "a two-legged animal without feathers" is an inadequate definition of man. Similarly when the mechanists exhibit a calculating machine as a contraption whose operations are essentially human, what we ought to conclude is precisely what the ancients concluded from Diogenes' demonstration. Obviously the mechanist's definition of the human being is as inadequate as Plato's definition of man. What he has done is not to prove his point but simply to achieve a glorious *reductio ad absurdum*. What we ought to do is to laugh first, and then to re-examine, not merely the definition so comically exposed, but also the whole long series of dubious assumptions and faulty methods which have led to so preposterous a conclusion. Only at the end of a long series of missteps could anyone be brought to the point where he would be compelled to entertain, even for the purpose of refuting it, the proposition that either a plucked hen or a calculating machine is the same thing as a man.

(18) Moreover definitions are, in this case, extremely important because we tend to cherish and to cultivate in the human race whatever traits and capacities enter into the definition of man which we, at the moment, accept. And it is evident enough that in recent centuries we have fixed our attention chiefly on those aspects of the

human being which most resemble, rather than those which least resemble, what a machine is capable of. Not only have we thought of man chiefly in terms of his anatomy, his instincts and his conditioned reflexes, but we have also talked as though the fact that he had an anatomy and had instincts was sufficient proof that the sum of these things was the whole of him.

(19) Even when we have gone beyond anatomy and reflexes to consider his mind, even when we have stopped short of the conviction that this mind was merely a refined manifestation of his ability to acquire habits and become conditioned, we have, nevertheless, tended to consider important chiefly the planning and the calculating powers of this mind. "Man," we have said, "is capable of reason"; not, as we might have said, "capable of hope," or of "doubt," or of "delight"—though all these capacities are certainly as important to him in his experience of living as reason; especially when "reason" means no more than the ability to scheme successfully.

(20) In "mental tests," those most characteristically limited manifestations of our concept of the criteria appropriate to the judgment of the human mind, the stress is chiefly upon the ability to analyze and to scheme, so that we put into the category of the most superior men those most likely to scheme successfully and we usually exhibit not the slightest concern over the question whether these "most superior" men are capable, to even an average extent, of the awarenesses, the emotions or the mental reactions which make men attractive, either to themselves or to others. And so, just as the economists have given us the ideal economic man who does nothing but produce and consume, so the mental testers have given us the ideal intelligent man who does nothing except scheme. Between them they have outlined a utopia in which creatures who are really only very flexible calculating machines do nothing except make goods which they then use up—living to eat and eating to live. For such creatures, living in such a world, most of the forms of consciousness would be not only unnecessary but also a burden. In a sense, therefore, the definition of man assumed by the tester prepares us for that definition of man in terms of which the calculator is human.

(21) If we stop to think, most of us do not really believe that the

Economic Man is more than a possibly useful methodological fiction, or that the Superior Man of the mental testers is more than simply the man most likely to succeed at tasks requiring the capacities which the tests do actually measure. The fact nevertheless remains that it is to the Economic Man and the I.Q. Man that our attention is directed far more often than on the whole man, who is something very different from either, something far less like anything the mechanists seem likely to be able to construct. And that fact has its consequences.

(22) Perhaps it is too soon, perhaps it will always be too soon, to try to formulate an adequate definition of man. Perhaps the fact that he is indefinable by his own mind is an essential fact about him. But we might, at least, consider more frequently than we do those of his characteristics which we have got into the habit of thinking about very seldom. We might, to begin with, ask concerning the calculating machine those questions posed earlier, and then add some more. Is it capable, we might ask, of imagination? Does it have any curiosity? Can it sympathize with anything? Can it be happy or miserable? Was it ever known to laugh, or even to show, by any unwonted flickerings in its tubes, that it considered something amusing? Does it—and this is most important of all—prefer one thing to another, or does it have its being in a universe where nothing has value, where all things are indifferent?

(23) Presumably we shall not get answers, though some of us may think we know what the answers would be if we could get them. But the real reason for asking is not that. The real reason is that even to ask is to be reminded how important is the "Yes" we get if we interrogate, not a machine, but a fellow creature; how defective, therefore, is that so called Science of Man which never really asks the questions at all and thus proves itself to be, not the Science of Man, but only the Science-of-What-Man-Would-Be-If-He-Were-Not-a-Man-But-a-Machine.

(24) In any event, to ask the questions either of the machine or of ourselves is to take the first step back in the direction of that

crossroads, passed perhaps three centuries ago, when we first began to diverge from the path of Wisdom into the path of Inadequate Knowledge. If we retrace our course, we shall be surprised to discover how much we have tended to forget about ourselves, how little we have studied, or even considered, the most remarkable of our capacities. We may even conclude that the ability to figure or to scheme is so far from being our only unique ability that it is not even the most important one—as indeed the possibility of making a machine which can do it for us sufficiently indicates. Perhaps man is not, first of all, a Reasoning Animal; perhaps something else that he does with his mind is even more obviously unique than reasoning. But what, then, shall we call this other thing; what is it that it is hardest to imagine a machine's doing for us?

(25) We might, I suppose, call it "wanting." Certainly even the stupidest man is capable of desiring something, and the cleverest of machines, no matter how brilliantly it may solve differential equations, is not. But the word "wanting" has a more refined and subtler cousin called "preference," which might do better. Man is an animal who not only wants something tangible but is capable also, even among things as insubstantial as ideas or beliefs, of *preferring* one thing to another. And when one has said that, one has arrived at the conventional terminology of metaphysics: Man has a Sense of Values. Other animals may or may not be capable of something out of which the Sense of Values develops. But a machine certainly is not. And there is the grandest of all the differences.

(26) When we think without reference to any preferences or "values" we think like a machine. That means also thinking without reference to joy, or laughter, or love. Very often nowadays we are urged by certain sociologists, political propagandists, and even anthropologists to do just that although they prefer to call it "thinking with detachment." But the thing from which we are asked to detach ourselves is, nevertheless, the state of being human, and the result of such thinking would be a world fit for machines, not for men.

(27) Perhaps, then, those wonderful electronic calculators are not, after all, anything like our brains. Perhaps the best of them is only a

super-abacus and therefore a triumph of human ingenuity but, no more than the laundryman's convenient device, a real challenge to the human being's uniqueness. To ask which it is—gadget or brain—is at least no academic question.

(28) To answer one way is to take what is perhaps the final step, not merely in the acceptance of mechanism as a philosophical doctrine, but in the direction of a civilization in which men will become more and more machinelike. To answer the other way is to choose instead the working conviction that man, as he was and as he can be, is neither the Economic Man nor the I.Q. Man but "The Animal Which Can Prefer." It is to believe that the most stupendous of his inventions was not the wheel, or the wedge, or the lever, but the values by which he has lived, and that the ability to act on, for example, the assumption that loyalty is better than treachery even when both seem to give a practical answer to a given problem, is more significant than any other ability he has ever manifested. It is also to believe that, in the future as in the past, what becomes of him will depend less on what machines he invents or what governments are imposed upon him than on what values he creates.

(29) Distrust of our mechanical age, fear that men will be destroyed by the engines which they have devised, is so widespread today that it has developed its own cant. But it often happens that men's fate overtakes them in the one way they had not sufficiently feared, and it may be that if we are to be destroyed by the machine it will not be in quite the manner we have been fearfully envisaging. Perhaps we are in no greater danger of being blown up by the atom bomb than we are of being destroyed by a wrong understanding of the abacus.

Questions

1. On what basis do Paragraphs 2, 3, and 4 form a unit? To what point in Paragraph 1 do they most directly refer? What is their relationship to Paragraph 5?

2. Explain the phrase "poor deluded chemists" that opens Paragraph 6. From whose standpoint are the chemists deluded? About what are they deluded?

3. Consider the following revision (Paragraph 7): Mr. Einstein writes "E = MC²" and (after a few merely technological intermediary steps) we have atomic power. What is the loss in implication? Relate the words *better* and *marvel* in the succeeding sentence to that implication.

4. Is Krutch more interested in disproving the view that men are like machines or the view that machines are like men? (Compare the first and last paragraphs in the first section.)

5. The second section of the essay divides broadly into three parts: Paragraphs 9 and 10, 11 and 12, and 13 through 15. Describe their relationship to each other, and then compare their ordering with the ordering of material in the first section. What is the general organizing principle at work in each section?

6. Supply the mechanist's definition of man that parallels Plato's definition (see Paragraph 17 in the third section). Where in the essay does Krutch first mention the mechanist's definition? What does he mean when he calls it a *reductio ad absurdum?* Explain the relationship of the "I.Q. Man" and the "Economic Man" to the *reductio ad absurdum.*

7. Krutch's final section contains a warning and a plea. State explicitly what they are. Contrast the tone of the warning here with the tone of the warning in Paragraph 2 of the essay. What is the effect of Krutch's concluding in this way?

8. Once you have seen the general ordering of material in the first two sections, you should be able to describe the general organization of the remainder of the essay. How clearly do the section divisions mark that organization?

9. Does the essay strike you as the thinking of a witty or a solemn person? Examine the first section for evidence to support your opinion.

10. Krutch alludes to several professional groups as mechanistic in their thinking. Identify the groups and discuss what makes their thinking seem mechanistic to Krutch. What groups of people do you suppose he would be inclined to see as antimechanistic? Explain.

11. Would you say that Krutch is wholly, largely, or only partly antiscientific in his outlook? Argue the point from evidence in the essay.

PROGRESS

CARL BECKER

Carl Becker (1873–1945) was born in Iowa and was educated at Cornell College and the University of Wisconsin. He subsequently taught at Dartmouth and the Universities of Kansas and Minnesota, and for the last twenty-eight years of his life was Professor of History at Cornell University, whose origins he treated in *Cornell University: Founders and the Founding*. From the first, his concern was with ideas and their role in history, a concern that may be seen in his best-known books, *The Declaration of Independence* and *The Heavenly City of the Eighteenth Century Philosophers,* both of which study certain major currents of eighteenth-century thought. Though never an easy optimist, Becker was sorely tried in the 1930's, as the following essay, written toward the middle of the decade, more than suggests. (Further information on Becker appears on p. 391.)

(1) "Thought," says Pascal, "makes the greatness of man." The universe can destroy an individual by a mere breath; but even if the entire force of the universe were employed to destroy a single man, the man "would still be more noble than that which destroys him, since he is aware of his own death and of the advantage which the universe has over him: of all this the universe knows nothing." This awareness of himself and of the universe is no doubt what chiefly distinguishes man from all other forms of life. Man alone is conscious in the sense that he alone can stand outside of himself, as it were, and watch himself functioning for a brief span in the

universe of which he is part. Man alone can coordinate memory of things past, perception of things present, anticipation of things to come, sufficiently so at least to know that he, like generations before him and after him, will live his brief span and will die. It is in virtue of this awareness, and somewhat in proportion to its intensity, that man alone asks the fundamental questions. Why and for what purpose this brief and precarious existence in a universe that endures? What is man's relation to the universe that is sometimes friendly, sometimes hostile, but in the end always fatal to him? How may he elude its hostility, win its favor, find compensations for the intolerable certainty of the death which it will inflict upon him? The answers which men have given to these questions are to be found in the various myths, religious doctrines, philosophical and ethical interpretations which they have accepted, and in those unconsciously held preconceptions which in every age so largely shape their thought and conduct. The modern idea of progress belongs in this category of answers to necessary but insoluble questions. Like the myths of primitive peoples and the religious and philosophical beliefs of more advanced societies, it springs from the nature of man as a conscious creature, who finds existence intolerable unless he can enlarge and enrich his otherwise futile activities by relating them to something more enduring and significant than himself.

(2) Although grounded in the nature of man as a conscious creature, the idea of progress belongs historically to the European tradition, and its origin may be derived from two sources. One of these is the classical conception of history as an endless series of cycles; the other is the Hebraic-Christian doctrine of messianic intervention and salvation.

(3) In Greek mythology the reign of Cronus was regarded as a golden age when men lived like gods free from toil and grief. The present appeared to be a period of degeneration, and improvement or progress could be conceived only in terms of regeneration—a return to the lost golden age. After the myth ceased to be believed, the Greeks continued to look back to the time of great lawgivers, such as Lycurgus and Solon, whose work they idealized, and forward to the time when other great lawgivers would appear and give them better laws again. "Until philosophers become kings . . . ,"

said Plato, "cities will not cease from ill." Yet however often restoration was accomplished by inspired lawgivers or philosopher-kings, fate and human frailty would again bring degeneration; so that, since "time is the enemy of man," most classical writers regarded human history as an endless series of cycles, a continual repetition of the familiar phenomena of recovery and degeneration. The rational mind, according to Marcus Aurelius, "stretches forth into the infinitude of Time, and comprehends the cyclical Regeneration of all things, and . . . discerns that our children will see nothing fresh, just as our fathers too never saw anything more than we" (*The Communings with Himself of Marcus Aurelius Antoninus,* tr. by C. R. Haines, Loeb Classical Library, London 1916, bk. XI, sect. I). To regenerate the Roman Empire was obviously less easy than to construct a constitution for a small city-state; and Marcus Aurelius, philosopher-king though he was, instead of giving new laws to society recommended that the individual cultivate resignation. The later centuries of the Roman Empire, when resignation became at once more necessary and more difficult, were therefore a suitable time for the hopeless classical doctrine of endless cycles to be replaced by the Hebraic-Christian doctrine of messianic intervention and salvation.

(4) The Jews like the Greeks looked back to a golden age, but it was identified with the creation of the world and with the Garden of Eden, in which the first men lived in innocence. Like the Greeks the Jews regarded the present as a period of degeneration, but they attributed the "fall" to Adam's disobedience to God's commands. God was at once the omniscient creator of the world and the supreme lawgiver, so that regeneration was identified with the coming of a God-inspired king of the house of David. Multiplied reverses and the destruction of the Hebraic state gave to this doctrine a less political, a more mystical and transcendent character. The once actual but now vanished kingdom was replaced by an ideal Israel, symbolized as the "son of man"; and the idea of a God-inspired king was replaced by the idea of a messiah who would effect a catastrophic intervention in the affairs of men and pronounce a doomlike judgment on the world. The Christian myth was but an elaboration of these ideas. Jesus, son of man, son of God, was the Messiah. But the end was not yet. The death of Jesus was expiation for the sins

of men, faith in Him the means of salvation. Jesus the man was dead, but Christ the Lord still lived and would come again; then the earthly city would be destroyed and all the faithful be gathered with God in the heavenly city, there to dwell in perfection forever.

(5) The weakness of the classical version of degeneration and recovery was that it offered no ultimate hope; of the Jewish, that its promise was for the chosen people only. The strength of the Christian version was that, conceiving human history as a cosmic drama in which all men played their predestined part, it offered to all the hope of eternal life as a compensation for the frustrations of temporal existence: by transferring the golden age from the past to the future it substituted an optimistic for a disillusioned view of human destiny. It is easily to be understood that such a view won wide assent in the Roman Empire during the centuries (300–500) of declining prosperity and increasing oppression or that it served so well to make existence tolerable in the relatively anarchic, isolated and static society of western Europe from the dissolution of the Roman Empire to the Renaissance of classical learning. But it lost its hold on the imaginations of men as a result of profound changes in the outward conditions of life which occurred in western Europe from the fourteenth to the nineteenth century. Among these changes were the rise of ordered secular governments, the growth of towns and industry, the geographical discoveries and the extension of commerce which brought western Europe into direct contact with alien customs and ideas, and above all the rise of an educated middle class whose interests were hampered by a form of society in which both the power and the doctrines of the Christian church supported the autocracy of kings and the privileges of a landed aristocracy. It was in this time of revolt against ecclesiastical and secular authority that the Christian doctrine of salvation was gradually transformed into the modern idea of progress.

(6) So long as Christian philosophy was little questioned, men could afford to ignore the factual experience of mankind since they were so well assured of its ultimate significance. But the declining influence of the church was accompanied by an increasing interest in the worldly activities of men in the past. Italian humanists turned to the study of classical writers; Protestant reformers appealed from

current theologians to the beliefs and practises of the primitive church. Thus was born the modern historical approach to problems, and human life came increasingly to be regarded rather as a historical process than as a finished drama to be played out according to a divine plan. Seen in historical perspective, classical civilization emerged for the humanists as a resplendent epoch from which the middle period of ecclesiastical ascendancy was manifestly a degeneration. Until the seventeenth century secular thought and learning turned for inspiration to the past—to the golden ages of Pericles and Augustus; and classical writers were idealized as models to be imitated, to be equaled if possible but hardly to be surpassed. In all this there was nothing that could not be found in the Greek notion of history with its cycles of recovery and degeneration, and but for two general influences modern thought might have been no more than a return to the classical view of human destiny.

(7) One of these influences was Christian philosophy itself. Although it was gradually discredited as an account of events historically verifiable, Christian philosophy had so thoroughly habituated men to the thought of an ultimate happy destiny that they could never be content with a pale imitation of Greek pessimism. The other influence was experimental science which, in proportion as it displaced the Christian notion of a utopian existence after death to be brought about by the miraculous intervention of God, opened up the engaging prospect of indefinite improvement in this life to be effected by the application of human reason to the mastery of the physical and social environment which determines men's lives for good or ill.

(8) In the seventeenth century Galileo and Newton made possible a new attitude toward nature. Nature was now seen to be friendly to man since the universe behaved in a uniform way according to universal natural laws—a behavior capable of being observed and measured and subjected to the uses of men. God was still the supreme lawgiver, the author of the universe; but His will was revealed in the great book of nature which men were to study in order to interpret, and to interpret in order that their ideas and customs might attain an increasing perfection by being brought into greater harmony with the laws of nature and of nature's God. God's revelation to men was thus made not through an inspired book or a divinely established

church but through His works, and man had been endowed with reason precisely that he might learn through the course of the centuries what that revelation was. It was therefore no longer so necessary to think of the golden age of Greece and Rome as unsurpassable. "Those whom we call the ancients were really those who lived in the youth of the world," said Pascal, and "as we have added the experience of the ages between us and them to what they knew, it is in ourselves that is to be found that antiquity which we venerate in others." In the ascription of antiquity to the race there is still the implication of degeneration; but if a continuously richer experience made the moderns wiser than the ancients, it was not difficult to hit upon the idea that future generations would, in virtue of the same advantages, surpass the moderns. "We have admired our ancestors less," said Chastellux, "but we have loved our contemporaries better, and have expected more of our descendants" (*De la félicité publique,* 2 vols., new ed. Paris 1822, vol. ii, p. 71). Thus in the eighteenth century the modern idea of progress was born. Under the pressure of social discontents the dream of perfection, that necessary compensation for the limitations of the present state, having long been identified with the golden age or the Garden of Eden or life eternal in the heavenly city of God, was at last projected into the temporal life of man on earth and identified with the desired and hoped for regeneration of society.

(9) As formulated by the *philosophes* the doctrine of progress was but a modification, however important, of the Christian doctrine of redemption; what was new in it was faith in the goodness of man and the efficacy of conscious reason to create an earthly utopia. The French Revolution was the outward expression of this faith. In the nineteenth century the doctrine of progress still reigned and won even a wider popular support, but it was somewhat differently conceived. After the disillusionment occasioned by the revolution and the Napoleonic conquests the prevailing desire was for social stability and national independence. The rationalization of this desire was provided by the historians and jurists who formulated the notion of historical continuity and deprecated the attempt to transform institutions according to a rational plan. Change was considered necessary but was thought to be beneficial only when it issued spontaneously

from national tradition; the concept of natural law was not abandoned, but it was regarded as implicit in historical evolution rather than as a conclusion from abstract reason. Law is not made by the legislator, said Savigny, any more than language is made by the grammarian. Ranke, who influenced three generations of historians, viewed progress as something to be discovered by tracing the history of each nation just as it had occurred and by noting the peculiar contribution which each nation at the appropriate moment had made to European civilization. Hegel formulated the point of view of early nineteenth century jurists and historians in the *Philosophie der Geschichte*. A reason of nature working over the heads of men, a transcendent *Vernunft* reconciling within its cloudy recesses innumerable and conflicting *Verstände,* progressively realized itself in the actual events of history.

(10) After the middle of the century natural science invested the doctrine of progress with a more materialistic implication. Progress was still regarded as the result of a force external to man; but the force was to be found not above but inherent in the phenomenal world. This view found support in the Darwinian theory of struggle for existence and survival of the fittest and in Schopenhauer's doctrine of the will as an aspect of a universal blind force. Guided by these preconceptions thinkers abandoned the effort to hasten progress by describing utopias and turned to the search for the inevitable law by which progress had been and would be achieved. Of the many efforts of this sort the most important were those of Auguste Comte and Karl Marx. Comte looked upon history as the result of the instinctive effort of men to ameliorate their condition—an effort which could be observed to fall into three stages of culture, the theological, the metaphysical and the positive, or scientific. Marx, interpreting the historic process in terms of Hegel's famous dialectic, found the determining force in the economic class conflict which, having substituted the nineteenth century capitalist competitive society for the aristocratic landed society of the Middle Ages and early modern times, would in turn replace the capitalist competitive society of the nineteenth century by the proletarian communist society of the future.

(11) Of the many theories of progress formulated in the nineteenth century the only one that had much influence on the thought

of common men was that of Marx. Yet the idea of progress, vaguely conceived as a rapid improvement in general prosperity and happiness, became a living force. The chief reason for this was no doubt the rapid changes in the outward conditions of life consequent upon the technological revolution. The common man, before whose eyes the marvels of science and invention were constantly displayed, noted the unprecedented increase in wealth, the growth of cities, the new and improved methods of transportation and communication, the greater security from disease and death and all the conveniences of domestic life unknown to previous generations, and accepted the doctrine of progress without question: the world was obviously better than it had been, obviously would be better than it was. The precise objective toward which the world was progressing remained, however, for the common man and for the intellectual, somewhat vague.

(12) Thus the nineteenth century doctrine of progress differed somewhat from that of the eighteenth. The difference may be expressed, with some exaggeration in the contrast, by saying that whereas the eighteenth century held that man can by taking thought add a cubit to his stature, the nineteenth century held that a cubit would be added to his stature whether he took thought or not. This latter faith that the stars were carrying men on to better things received a rude shock during the World War and subsequently; and there may be noted two significant changes in the present attitude toward the doctrine of progress. Certain thinkers, notably Spengler, are returning to the Greek notion of cycles, now formulated in terms of the rise, flourishing and decline of "cultures." Others are reverting to the eighteenth century idea that by deliberate purpose and the rational use of knowledge man can reconstruct society according to a more just and intelligible design. To this class belong those who have faith in communism, fascism and the planned capitalist society.

(13) The doctrine of progress is peculiarly suited to western society in modern times; that is, a highly dynamic society capable of seeing its achievements against a long historical background. From the practical and from the rational point of view there is no reason to suppose that it will have a more enduring virtue than other doctrines which it has supplanted. If, as may well happen, the possibili-

ties of scientific discovery and of technological invention should sometime be exhausted, the outward conditions of life might become sufficiently stabilized so that the idea of progress would cease to be
relevant. Rationally considered, the idea of progress is always at
war with its premises. It rests upon the notion of a universe in perpetual flux; yet the idea of progress has always carried the implication of finality, for it seems to be meaningless unless there is
movement toward some ultimate objective. The formal theories of
progress are all vitiated by this radical inconsistency. In Hegel's
scheme the objective was freedom, already realized in the Prussian
state. In Comte's theory the objective was the final positive stage
into which Europe had already entered. Marx criticized Hegel for
explaining history by a process which would not explain the future,
but he is himself open to the criticism of having explained history in
terms of a class conflict which would end with the establishment of a
classless society. It is easy to picture history as a process working
toward an ultimate good if the world is to come to an end when
that good is attained; but if the universe as presented by modern
science is to be accepted—a universe in perpetual flux—then a law
of history which at some determinate time ceases to apply leaves
much to be desired.

(14) Thus the final good, absolute standards of value, are sought
in vain; there is merely a universe in which the ideas of things as well
as the things themselves arise out of temporary conditions and are
transformed with the modification of the conditions out of which
they arose. On this assumption we must dispense with the notion of
finality, must suppose that the idea of progress and all of its special
formulations are but temporary insights useful for the brief moment
in which they flourish. "In escaping from the illusion of finality, is it
legitimate to exempt that dogma itself? Must not it, too, submit to
its own negation of finality? Will not that process of change, for
which Progress is the optimistic name, compel 'Progress' too to fall
from the commanding position in which it is now, with apparent
security, enthroned?" (Bury, J. B., *The Idea of Progress,* p. 352).
The price we pay for escaping from the illusion of finality is the
recognition that nothing, not even the belief that we have escaped
that illusion, is likely to endure. All philosophies based upon the

absolute and the unconditioned have their defects; but all philosophies based upon the universal relativity of things have their defects
also, a minor one being that they must be prepared, at the appropriate moment, to commit hara-kiri in deference to the ceaseless
change which they postulate.

(15) Belief in progress as a fact depends upon the standard of
value chosen for measuring it and upon the time perspective in which
it is measured. If we look back a hundred years, it is obvious that
there has been progress in the mastery of physical forces. If we look
back two thousand years, it is uncertain whether there has been
much if any progress in intelligence and the art of living. If we look
back two hundred and fifty thousand years, it is apparent that there
has been progress in all those aspects of life which civilized men
regard as valuable. All these judgments are based on standards
of value appreciable by the mind of civilized man. But if we take a
still longer perspective and estimate the universe as a whole, as an
omniscient intelligence indifferent to human values might estimate
it, in terms of cosmic energy, then progress and the very existence
of man himself become negligible and meaningless. In such a perspective we should see the whole life of man on the earth as a mere
momentary ripple on the surface of one of the minor planets in one
of the minor stellar systems.

Questions

1. *Thought* and *greatness* are the key words in the first sentence of
the opening paragraph of Becker's essay. What succeeding words, phrases,
and sentences are equivalents and instances of each term?

2. What is the function of Paragraph 2? What pattern of organization is Becker invoking in it: classification, chronology, or comparison?
To what extent does each of these patterns operate in the succeeding
paragraphs? What key words and phrases mark the chronological progression in the essay?

3. Where is the topic sentence or phrase for Paragraph 7? What are
the topic sentences or phrases for the next three paragraphs? (There may
be more than one to a paragraph.)

4. In which sentence does Becker pass judgment on the usefulness of
each of the three conceptions of history? In which does he pass judg-

ment on their validity? If he thinks none of the conceptions can be absolutely valid, which one does he think is most nearly valid and which one least?

5. Would the meaning of the essay be altered by the omission of Paragraph 1? Can you relate Becker's mood in the final paragraph to his assertion in the first that the notion of progress is an answer to an insoluble question?

6. Why do you suppose Becker chose to organize a large part of his essay chronologically?

7. Becker's evidence for the variant forms of the conception of progress consists mainly of references to leading thinkers of the past three centuries. What other kinds of evidence does he supply?

8. What is the irony of the phrase "engaging prospect" in Paragraph 7? Is there a clear indication in Becker's later discussion that he is being ironical here? Can you know from his earlier discussion that he is being ironical? By what modification can you eliminate the irony?

9. Is Becker's argument convincing, and are you persuaded in spite of yourself? Where do you find it weakest? Do you think it desirable or undesirable that he writes so impersonally in such an essay?

10. What ideas other than that of Progress seem to you worth examining in their historical development? Prepare an essay showing how one such idea was held at two or more different historical moments.

POINT OF VIEW AND ASSUMPTIONS

In a basic respect, point of view is a grammatical problem. If a writer begins an essay in the first person (*In my first year in high school, I* . . .) he should not ordinarily shift to another person later on (*Suddenly in your sophomore year you* . . .). This is a rule with exceptions, but it is a good rule to start with.

The broad meaning of point of view is the perspective from which a writer writes. In the so-called personal essay, he writes from either a real or an assumed personal viewpoint, whose visible mark is the grammatical first person (*In Moulmein, in Lower Burma, I was hated by large numbers of people,* writes George Orwell). In formal writing, the writer often effaces himself to a certain extent. When Carl Becker analyzes the notion of progress (in Section III), he removes himself from the essay grammatically. He never says, *I have been led to think* or *you will agree with me.* He speaks as though his words could belong to any intelligent, reflective person: *Although grounded in the nature of man as a conscious creature, the idea of progress belongs historically to the European tradition.* But a writer can never efface himself entirely. Whether he is freely expressing personal opinions or whether he is setting down the facts of a scientific experiment, he displays a point of view: passionate or patient, subjective or objective, emotional or logical, poetical or scientific, and so forth.

The grammatical person that a writer may employ or decline to employ does little more than begin to define a point of view. Perhaps a student is asked to write an essay about his high school days. He writes about the things he did and did not do: he did go to the Sophomore Hop, but he did not do much dancing there; he did do his homework, but he did not do it eagerly; he did go to football games, but he did not get into a frenzy about them. Gradually a point of view emerges of a rather aloof young boy. The more precise the detail, the more clearly his point of view will be distinguishable from that of another boy who did the same things but in a different spirit.

Because point of view may be assumed as well as real, a reader can never be certain that the point of view he observes in a piece of writing is genuine or artificial, serious or ironical, true or false.

But he has to make an educated guess, just as when listening to a politician say nice, intelligent things he has to decide whether the man means them or whether he is lying. The more aware the reader is of the point of view of a writer, the better able he will be to judge its consistency, strength, and tone. Ultimately, of course, he needs to understand point of view in order to understand the full meaning of an essay. The reader who fails to perceive the aloof schoolboy behind the details of what the schoolboy did and did not do has missed half the point—the point of view.

Suppose that a student writes an essay about his high school football days, when he was a starry-eyed boy who idealized the coach, idolized the captain of the team, and tried to be an alert, fearless, and self-reliant lineman. His point of view is clear, and something else may be too—his assumptions. He may not include in his essay his father's opinion that the battles of free enterprise are won on the football fields of Central High School. He may not say outright that sports build character. These things may be implicit in the self-reliance, courage, and alertness that he mentions. They are assumptions. He may be conscious of them; then again he may not be.

As terms, *point of view* and *assumptions* are sometimes used interchangeably. To say, *He is writing from the point of view of a Republican,* is probably to say, *His assumptions are those of a Republican.* Assumptions refer to the ideas that a person holds, consciously or unconsciously; point of view is a larger term and refers broadly to his ideas but more especially to his general perspective on things. In discussing a writer's ideas, it is generally useful to speak of his assumptions.

We are particularly aware of the assumptions of other people in arguments with them. If we are quarreling about civil rights, we may realize that the other side assumes that all men are created equal and that democracy means the obligation to tolerate. At the same time, the other side may realize that we assume that all men are not created equal and that democracy means the right to discriminate. If each person simply holds to his assumptions, the argument may end in a deadlock, but if the assumptions are themselves examined, the argument may get somewhere. "Of course," says the one person, "I realize that some people are born with more brains or better bodies than others. All I mean is that in the eyes of God, the potential Shakespeare does not deserve more than the potential farm laborer." "Well, I don't believe in God," says the other person, "but if you mean by 'being created equal' that every human life ought to be taken care of, I suppose I would agree. Nevertheless . . . ." And so the arguers might find that they agree in three-quarters of what they say, instead of totally disagree. In writing essays, the opportunity to recognize and challenge assumptions comes in a somewhat different way, for the writer has to imagine the views and reactions of his audience, and he also has to see his own assumptions by himself. If he is writing an essay on civil rights for an American audience, he will assume that democracy is the best form of government. But if he happens to be visiting a Communist country, he will have to argue the point. Again, if he is writing for an American audience, he may speak of the white race and the Negro race; and then suddenly he may ask himself: do I know what I mean by the word *race* or am I assuming a meaning that many other people assume too and that happens to be wrong? He goes off and reads some history and anthropology, and finds he has to write a new essay. And then he surrenders his finished essay to his audience, and he may be in trouble. For his readers inevitably come from somewhat different backgrounds from his, and they have a vantage point for recognizing assumptions that he was unaware of, for questioning assumptions that he thought would be acceptable, and for rejecting others that he argued. Then again they may be taken in by his assumptions, or they may consciously agree. If he has argued his case well, and understood both his own assumptions and those of his readers, he may persuade many people.

Being able to recognize assumptions is valuable in every sort of writing. If, instead of taking for granted that sports build character, the student had been aware of what he was assuming, he might have asked himself: do sports build character? Did the captain of the team become an egotist? Was one of the linemen a bully? Did the coach ever recommend dirty tricks? The answer might emerge: yes, sports build character—all kinds of character. At this point the student might be ready to write a more complex essay in which he

looks back upon the naive boy he was. He might avoid the first
person in the essay, referring to himself as *he* in order to suggest
how distant he feels from his younger self. His essay would have
two points of view.

If sports do build character (good and bad), the assumption becomes fact. Fact implies truth, whereas assumption implies question-
ableness. Some assumptions may be valid, others invalid, others impossible to judge adequately. What we today call an assumption may
once have been considered a fact (such as the notion that mankind
is progressing). What people today call a fact may once have been
merely an assumption (the notion that there are atomic particles).
In our sceptical modern world, the tendency is to believe that all
assertions are assumptions based upon more or less adequate evidence. One always has to leap from evidence to inference. Do
sports build good and bad character? Or is character formed in
preschool years? Or is it formed in the cradle? Or is it prefabricated
in the genes? Or is it formed in prayer? Our age is not so sceptical
that the Freudian psychologist is likely to admit that his views on
character are as half-baked as he thinks the sociologist's are; but it
is sceptical enough so that a reader who does not have a vested
interest in either psychology or sociology may question the assumptions of both.

DOWN AND OUT

George Orwell

Of Orwell's several autobiographical accounts, the most vivid is probably his *Down and Out in Paris and London,* of which the following is a chapter. Experiences such as those related here did much to sharpen his awareness of social injustice (already aroused by his experiences in India) and to convince him of the efficacy of socialism. Strongly anti-Fascist, he fought on the Republican side in the Spanish Civil War, during which he was severely wounded. While recuperating, he began meditating a new volume, *Homage to Catalonia,* which proved to be a detailed record of his hopes for Spain and of their brutal disappointment. (Further information on Orwell appears on pp. 109, 373.)

(1) I travelled to England third class via Dunkirk and Tilbury, which is the cheapest and not the worst way of crossing the Channel. You had to pay extra for a cabin, so I slept in the saloon, together with most of the third-class passengers. I find this entry in my diary for that day:

(2) "Sleeping in the saloon, twenty-seven men, sixteen women. Of the women, not a single one has washed her face this morning. The men mostly went to the bathroom; the women merely produced vanity cases and covered the dirt with powder. *Q.* A secondary sexual difference?"

(3) On the journey I fell in with a couple of Roumanians, mere children, who were going to England on their honeymoon trip. They asked innumerable questions about England, and I told them some

startling lies. I was so pleased to be getting home, after being hard up for months in a foreign city, that England seemed to me a sort of Paradise. There are, indeed, many things in England that make you glad to get home; bathrooms, armchairs, mint sauce, new potatoes properly cooked, brown bread, marmalade, beer made with veritable hops—they are all splendid, if you can pay for them. England is a very good country when you are not poor; and, of course, with a tame imbecile to look after, I was not going to be poor. The thought of not being poor made me very patriotic. The more questions the Roumanians asked, the more I praised England: the climate, the scenery, the art, the literature, the laws—everything in England was perfect.

(4) Was the architecture in England good? the Roumanians asked. "Splendid!" I said. "And you should just see the London statues! Paris is vulgar—half grandiosity and half slums. But London——"

(5) Then the boat drew alongside Tilbury pier. The first building we saw on the waterside was one of those huge hotels, all stucco and pinnacles, which stare from the English coast like idiots staring over an asylum wall. I saw the Roumanians, too polite to say anything, cocking their eyes at the hotel. "Built by French architects," I assured them; and even later, when the train was crawling into London through the eastern slums, I still kept it up about the beauties of English architecture. Nothing seemed too good to say about England, now that I was coming home and was not hard up any more.

(6) I went to B.'s office, and his first words knocked everything to ruins. "I'm sorry," he said; "your employers have gone abroad, patient and all. However, they'll be back in a month. I suppose you can hang on till then?"

(7) I was outside in the street before it even occurred to me to borrow some more money. There was a month to wait, and I had exactly nineteen and sixpence in hand. The news had taken my breath away. For a long time I could not make up my mind what to do. I loafed the day in the streets, and at night, not having the slightest notion of how to get a cheap bed in London, I went to a "family" hotel, where the charge was seven and sixpence. After paying the bill I had ten and twopence in hand.

(8) By the morning I had made my plans. Sooner or later I

should have to go to B. for more money, but it seemed hardly decent to do so yet, and in the meantime I must exist in some hole-and-corner way. Past experience set me against pawning my best suit. I would leave all my things at the station cloakroom, except my second-best suit, which I could exchange for some cheap clothes and perhaps a pound. If I was going to live a month on thirty shillings I must have bad clothes—indeed, the worse the better. Whether thirty shillings could be made to last a month I had no idea, not knowing London as I knew Paris. Perhaps I could beg, or sell boot-laces, and I remembered articles I had read in the Sunday papers about beggars who have two thousand pounds sewn into their trousers. It was, at any rate, notoriously impossible to starve in London, so there was nothing to be anxious about.

(9) To sell my clothes I went down into Lambeth, where the people are poor and there are a lot of rag shops. At the first shop I tried the proprietor was polite but unhelpful; at the second he was rude; at the third he was stone deaf, or pretended to be so. The fourth shopman was a large blond young man, very pink all over, like a slice of ham. He looked at the clothes I was wearing and felt them disparagingly between thumb and finger.

(10) "Poor stuff," he said, "very poor stuff, that is." (It was quite a good suit.) "What yer want for 'em?"

(11) I explained that I wanted some older clothes and as much money as he could spare. He thought for a moment, then collected some dirty-looking rags and threw them on to the counter. "What about the money?" I said, hoping for a pound. He pursed his lips, then produced *a shilling* and laid it beside the clothes. I did not argue —I was going to argue, but as I opened my mouth he reached out as though to take up the shilling again; I saw that I was helpless. He let me change in a small room behind the shop.

(12) The clothes were a coat, once dark brown, a pair of black dungaree trousers, a scarf and a cloth cap; I had kept my own shirt, socks and boots, and I had a comb and razor in my pocket. It gives one a very strange feeling to be wearing such clothes. I had worn bad enough things before, but nothing at all like these; they were not merely dirty and shapeless, they had—how is one to express it? —a gracelessness, a patina of antique filth, quite different from mere

shabbiness. They were the sort of clothes you see on a bootlace seller, or a tramp. An hour later, in Lambeth, I saw a hang-dog man, obviously a tramp, coming towards me, and when I looked again it was myself, reflected in a shop window. The dirt was plastering my face already. Dirt is a great respecter of persons; it lets you alone when you are well dressed, but as soon as your collar is gone it flies towards you from all directions.

(13) I stayed in the streets till late at night, keeping on the move all the time. Dressed as I was, I was half afraid that the police might arrest me as a vagabond, and I dared not speak to anyone, imagining that they must notice a disparity between my accent and my clothes. (Later I discovered that this never happened.) My new clothes had put me instantly into a new world. Everyone's demeanour seemed to have changed abruptly. I helped a hawker pick up a barrow that he had upset. "Thanks, mate," he said with a grin. No one had called me mate before in my life—it was the clothes that had done it. For the first time I noticed, too, how the attitude of women varies with a man's clothes. When a badly dressed man passes them they shudder away from him with a quite frank movement of disgust, as though he were a dead cat. Clothes are powerful things. Dressed in a tramp's clothes it is very difficult, at any rate for the first day, not to feel that you are genuinely degraded. You might feel the same shame, irrational but very real, your first night in prison.

(14) At about eleven I began looking for a bed. I had read about doss-houses (they are never called doss-houses, by the way), and I supposed that one could get a bed for fourpence or thereabouts. Seeing a man, a navvy or something of the kind, standing on the kerb in the Waterloo Road, I stopped and questioned him. I said I was stony broke and wanted the cheapest bed I could get.

(15) "Oh," said he, "you go to that 'ouse across the street there, with the sign 'Good Beds for Single Men.' That's a good kip [sleeping place], that is. I bin there myself on and off. You'll find it cheap *and* clean."

(16) It was a tall, battered-looking house, with dim lights in all the windows, some of which were patched with brown paper. I entered a stone passage-way, and a little etiolated boy with sleepy

eyes appeared from a door leading to a cellar. Murmurous sounds
came from the cellar, and a wave of hot air and cheese. The boy
yawned and held out his hand.

(17) "Want a kip? That'll be a 'og, guv'nor."

(18) I paid the shilling, and the boy led me up a rickety unlighted
staircase to a bedroom. It had a sweetish reek of paregoric and foul
linen; the windows seemed to be tight shut, and the air was almost
suffocating at first. There was a candle burning, and I saw that the
room measured fifteen feet square by eight high, and had eight
beds in it. Already six lodgers were in bed, queer lumpy shapes with
all their own clothes, even their boots, piled on top of them. Someone was coughing in a loathsome manner in one corner.

(19) When I got into the bed I found that it was as hard as a
board, and as for the pillow, it was a mere hard cylinder like a block
of wood. It was rather worse than sleeping on a table, because the
bed was not six feet long, and very narrow, and the mattress was
convex, so that one had to hold on to avoid falling out. The sheets
stank so horribly of sweat that I could not bear them near my nose.
Also, the bedclothes only consisted of the sheets and a cotton coun-
terpane, so that though stuffy it was none too warm. Several noises
recurred throughout the night. About once in an hour the man
on my left—a sailor, I think—woke up, swore vilely, and lighted
a cigarette. Another man, victim of bladder disease, got up and
noisily used his chamber-pot half a dozen times during the night.
The man in the corner had a coughing fit once in every twenty minutes, so regularly that one came to listen for it as one listens for
the next yap when a dog is baying the moon. It was an unspeakably
repellent sound; a foul bubbling and retching, as though the man's
bowels were being churned up within him. Once when he struck a
match I saw that he was a very old man, with a grey, sunken face
like that of a corpse, and he was wearing his trousers wrapped round
his head as a nightcap, a thing which for some reason disgusted me
very much. Every time he coughed or the other man swore, a sleepy
voice from one of the other beds cried out:

(20) "Shut up! Oh, for Christ's —— *sake* shut up!"

(21) I had about an hour's sleep in all. In the morning I was

woken by a dim impression of some large brown thing coming towards me. I opened my eyes and saw that it was one of the sailor's
feet, sticking out of bed close to my face. It was dark brown, quite
dark brown like an Indian's, with dirt. The walls were leprous, and
the sheets, three weeks from the wash, were almost raw umber
colour. I got up, dressed and went downstairs. In the cellar were a
row of basins and two slippery roller towels. I had a piece of soap
in my pocket, and I was going to wash, when I noticed that every
basin was streaked with grime—solid, sticky filth as black as boot-
blacking. I went out unwashed. Altogether, the lodging-house had
not come up to its description as cheap *and* clean. It was however,
as I found later, a fairly representative lodging-house.

(22) I crossed the river and walked a long way eastward, finally
going into a coffee-shop on Tower Hill. An ordinary London coffee-
shop, like a thousand others, it seemed queer and foreign after Paris.
It was a little stuffy room with the high-backed pews that were
fashionable in the 'forties, the day's menu written on a mirror with
a piece of soap, and a girl of fourteen handling the dishes. Navvies
were eating out of newspaper parcels, and drinking tea in vast saucer-
less mugs like china tumblers. In a corner by himself a Jew, muzzle
down in the plate, was guiltily wolfing bacon.

(23) "Could I have some tea and bread and butter?" I said to
the girl.

(24) She stared. "No butter, only marg," she said, surprised.
And she repeated the order in the phrase that is to London what
the eternal *coup de rouge* is to Paris: "Large tea and two slices!"

(25) On the wall beside my pew there was a notice saying
"Pocketing the sugar not allowed," and beneath it some poetic
customer had written:

He that takes away the sugar
Shall be called a dirty ——

but someone else had been at pains to scratch out the last word.
This was England. The tea-and-two-slices cost threepence halfpenny,
leaving me with eight and twopence.

Questions

1. The query on sex difference in Paragraph 2 is unconnected with the nominal subject of the essay, but Orwell's concern in it is typical. What is that general concern?

2. Orwell's point of view on the trip back to England finds expression in several details: his financial circumstance, his observation of the passengers in the morning, and his lies to the Rumanian couple. Define the several aspects of that point of view, and suggest if possible one characteristic that underlies all the details.

3. Orwell says in Paragraph 8 that he had nothing to be anxious about, though later he remarks that he was half afraid that the police would arrest him. What single attitude dominates the rest of his experience?

4. Orwell's situation in his experience was always ambiguous: he was a beggar and not a beggar. Where does he seem to succumb almost entirely to the point of view of a beggar? Where is he most conscious of his difference? Explain.

5. Orwell's point of view in writing his essay (as distinguished from undergoing the experience) comes across strongly in such a sentence as "I entered a stone passage-way, and a little etiolated boy with sleepy eyes appeared from a door leading to a cellar." Define that point of view and illustrate it with two or three other examples.

6. When Orwell thought that he had nothing to be anxious about, he was assuming certain things about human needs, desires, and dignity. What are they?

7. The fourth rag-shop owner, the women who shuddered, and the man on the curb in the Waterloo Road judged by appearances. What were their judgments, and what assumptions underlay them?

8. Orwell shows no particular interest in improving the lot of the people he is with, and at the outset he shows no interest in finding a temporary job for himself. Insofar as he is interested in human society, what appears to be his particular interest? Express his interest as an assumption that contrasts with the assumption a minister, a social worker, a politician, a capitalist, or a socialist might have.

9. Read E. M. Forster's essay in this section and discuss whether in any respects Orwell seems to exemplify the English character as Forster sees it.

PORRO UNUM . . .*

MAX BEERBOHM

Though Max Beerbohm (1872–1956) was knighted in 1939, his greatest impact as wit and satirist occurred in the two decades or so preceding World War I. Fastidious and irreverent, his essays and drawings early established him as something of an institution—the "incomparable Max." In 1898, he succeeded George Bernard Shaw as drama critic for a notable London weekly. He resigned in 1910, when he moved to Rapallo, Italy, where he lived principally until his death. Among his better-known works are *A Christmas Garland,* a series of parodies of contemporary authors: *Zuleika Dobson,* a brilliantly ironical novel of undergraduate life at Oxford (his own university); and *The Poet's Corner,* a collection of remarkable caricatures of nineteenth-century authors.

(1) By graceful custom, every newcomer to a throne in Europe pays a round of visits to his neighbours. When King Edward came back from seeing the Tsar at Reval, his subjects seemed to think that he had fulfilled the last demand on his civility. That was in the days of Abdul Hamid. None of us wished the King to visit Turkey. Turkey is not internationally powerful, nor had Abdul any Guelph blood in him; and so we were able to assert, by ignoring her and him, our humanitarianism and passion for liberty, quite safely, quite politely. Now that Abdul is deposed from "his infernal throne," it is taken as a matter of course that the King will visit his successor. Well, let His

---

* *Porro unum est necessarium:* But one thing is needful.

Reprinted from *Yet Again* by Max Beerbohm by permission of Alfred A. Knopf, Inc. Published 1951 by Alfred A. Knopf, Inc., and by permission of William Heinemann, Ltd., London.

Majesty betake himself and his tact and a full cargo of Victorian Orders to Constantinople, by all means. But, on the way, nestling in the very heart of Europe, perfectly civilised and strifeless, jewelled all over with freedom, is another country which he has not visited since his accession—a country which, oddly enough, none but I seems to expect him to visit. Why, I ask, should Switzerland be cold-shouldered?

(2) I admit she does not appeal to the romantic imagination. She never has, as a nation, counted for anything. Physically soaring out of sight, morally and intellectually she has lain low and said nothing. Not one idea, not one deed, has she to her credit. All that is worth knowing of her history can be set forth without compression in a few lines of a guide-book. Her one and only hero—William Tell—never, as we now know, existed. He has been proved to be a myth. Also, he is the one and only myth that Switzerland has managed to create. He exhausted her poor little stock of imagination. Living as pigmies among the blind excesses of Nature, living on sufferance there, animalculae, her sons have been overwhelmed from the outset, have had no chance whatsoever of development. Even if they had a language of their own, they would have no literature. Not one painter, not one musician, have they produced; only couriers, guides, waiters, and other parasites. A smug, tame, sly, dull, mercenary little race of men, they exist by and for the alien tripper. They are the fine flower of commercial civilisation, the shining symbol of international comity, and have never done anybody any harm. I cannot imagine why the King should not give them the incomparable advertisement of a visit.

(3) Not that they are badly in need of advertisement over here. Every year the British trippers to Switzerland vastly outnumber the British trippers to any other land—a fact which shows how little the romantic imagination tells as against cheapness and comfort of hotels and the notion that a heart strained by climbing is good for the health. And this fact does but make our Sovereign's abstention the more remarkable. Switzerland is not "smart," but a King is not the figure-head merely of his *entourage:* he is the whole nation's figure-head. Switzerland, alone among nations, is a British institution, and King Edward ought not to snub her. That we expect him to do so

without protest from us, seems to me a rather grave symptom of flunkeyism.

(4) Fiercely resenting that imputation, you proceed to raise difficulties. "Who," you ask, "would there be to receive the King in the name of the Swiss nation?" I promptly answer, "The President of the Swiss Republic." You did not expect that. You had quite forgotten, if indeed you had ever heard, that there was any such person. For the life of you, you could not tell me his name. Well, his name is not very widely known even in Switzerland. A friend of mine, who was there lately, tells me that he asked one Swiss after another what was the name of the President, and that they all sought refuge in polite astonishment at such ignorance, and, when pressed for the name, could only screw up their eyes, snap their fingers, and feverishly declare that they had it on the tips of their tongues. This is just as it should be. In an ideal republic there should be no one whose name might not at any moment slip the memory of his fellows. Some sort of foreman there must be, for the State's convenience; but the more obscure he be, and the more automatic, the better for the ideal of equality. In the Republics of France and of America the President is of an extrusive kind. His office has been fashioned on the monarchic model, and his whole position is anomalous. He has to try to be ornamental as well as useful, a symbol as well as a pivot. Obviously, it is absurd to single out one man as a symbol of the equality of all men. And not less unreasonable is it to expect him to be inspiring as a patriotic symbol, an incarnation of his country. Only an anointed king, whose forefathers were kings too, can be that. In France, where kings have been, no one can get up the slightest pretence of emotion for the President. If the President is modest and unassuming, and doesn't, as did the late M. Faure, make an ass of himself by behaving in a kingly manner, he is safe from ridicule: the amused smiles that follow him are not unkind. But in no case is any one proud of him. Never does any one see France in him. In America, where no kings have been, they are able to make a pretence of enthusiasm for a President. But no real chord of national sentiment is touched by this eminent gentleman who has no past or future eminence, who has been shoved forward for a space and will anon be sent packing in favour of some other upstart. Let

some princeling of a foreign State set foot in America, and lo! all
the inhabitants are tumbling over one another in their desire for
a glimpse of him—a desire which is the natural and pathetic outcome of their unsatisfied inner craving for a dynasty of their own.
Human nature being what it is, a monarchy is the best expedient,
all the world over. But, given a republic, let the thing be done thoroughly, let the appearance be well kept up, as in Switzerland. Let
the President be, as there, a furtive creature and insignificant, not
merely coming no man knows whence, nor merely passing no man
knows whither, but existing no man knows where; and existing not
even as a name—except on the tip of the tongue. National dignity,
as well as the republican ideal, is served better thus. Besides, it is
less trying for the President.

(5) And yet, stronger than all my sense of what is right and
proper is the desire in me that the President of the Swiss Republic
should, just for once, be dragged forth, blinking, from his burrow
in Berne (Berne is the capital of Switzerland), into the glare of
European publicity, and be driven in a landau to the railway station,
there to await the King of England and kiss him on either cheek
when he dismounts from the train, while the massed orchestras of all
the principal hotels play our national anthem—and also a Swiss
national anthem, hastily composed for the occasion. I want him to
entertain the King, that evening, at a great banquet, whereat His
Majesty will have the President's wife on his right hand, and will
make a brief but graceful speech in the Swiss language (English,
French, German, and Italian, consecutively) referring to the glorious
and never-to-be-forgotten name of William Tell (embarrassed silence), and to the vast number of his subjects who annually visit
Switzerland (loud and prolonged cheers). Next morning, let there
be a review of twenty thousand waiters from all parts of the country,
all the head-waiters receiving a modest grade of the Victorian Order.
Later in the day, let the King visit the National Gallery—a hall
filled with picture post-cards of the most picturesque spots in Switzerland; and thence let him be conducted to the principal factory of
cuckoo-clocks, and, after some of the clocks have been made to
strike, be heard remarking to the President, with a hearty laugh,
that the sound is like that of the cuckoo. How the second day of the

visit would be filled up, I do not know; I leave that to the President's discretion. Before his departure to the frontier, the King will of course be made honorary manager of one of the principal hotels.

(6) I hope to be present in Berne during these great days in the President's life. But, if anything happen to keep me here, I shall content myself with the prospect of his visit to London. I long to see him and his wife driving past, with the proper escort of Life Guards, under a vista of quadrilingual mottoes, bowing acknowledgments to us. I wonder what he is like. I picture him as a small spare man, with a slightly grizzled beard, and pleasant though shifty eyes behind a pince-nez. I picture him frock-coated, bowler-hatted, and evidently nervous. His wife I cannot at all imagine.

Questions

1. What point of view is implicit in the use of such phrases as "by graceful custom," "round of visits," "quite politely," and "cold-shouldered" (Paragraph 1)?

2. What attitude toward the King is expressed in the sentence "Well, let His Majesty . . ."? Distinguish it from the attitude towards Switzerland displayed in the succeeding sentence. Are the two attitudes irreconcilable? Are they, individually or together, consistent with the point of view implicit in the phrases mentioned in Question 1?

3. Compare the values implicit in such terms as "civility," "passion for liberty," and "strifeless" (Paragraph 1) with the values implicit in "not one idea" and "no literature" (Paragraph 2). What does your answer suggest generally about point of view in the two paragraphs? On the basis of your answer define the point of view from which the writer says that the Swiss are "the fine flower of commercial civilization." What accompanying phrases in the second paragraph support your interpretation?

4. What shift in point of view—if any—is implied by Beerbohm's abandonment of the first person plural for the first person singular at the end of the first paragraph?

5. What assumption about human nature does the writer entertain in his phrase in Paragraph 4, "human nature being what it is"? What are the assumed political values upon which he builds his argument in the paragraph?

6. Paragraph 5 differs from those before in lacking both argument and explicit evaluation. How, then, does it proceed? Examine some of the varying means within the paragraph by which Beerbohm establishes a point of view. (Consider "dragged forth, blinking, from his burrow," "Berne is the capital of Switzerland," "massed orchestras of all the principal hotels," "glorious . . . embarrassed.")

7. The humor in the essay rests mainly upon the interplay between Beerbohm's assumed points of view and his presumed actual point of view that underlies them. At what point in the essay are you first aware of the discrepancy? On what basis are you able to distinguish the assumed from the actual? At what points in the essay—if any—does irony disappear?

8. Relying upon your analysis in Question 7, describe what you think to be Beerbohm's own assumptions about the proper commercial, social, moral, cultural, and political conduct of man.

9. Beerbohm is humorous instead of serious, ironical instead of straightforward. What do you suppose his general point of view would be in any piece of writing, irrespective of its subject?

A SLIGHT SOUND AT EVENING

E. B. WHITE

The image of E. B. White as a New Yorker, writing for a periodical of that name, is hardly a complete one since there is also the White who has made his residence much of the time in Maine. Though the two images are not necessarily incompatible, they do reveal a continuing tension in his work between the urban and the rural, the city man as against his country counterpart. The interaction of the two becomes especially apparent in White's several essays on Thoreau, the most recent of which is represented below. (Further information on White appears on pp. 79, 137.)

Allen Cove, Summer, 1954

(1) In his journal for July 10–12, 1841, Thoreau wrote: "A slight sound at evening lifts me up by the ears, and makes life seem inexpressibly serene and grand. It may be in Uranus, or it may be in the shutter." The book into which he later managed to pack both Uranus and the shutter was published in 1854, and now, a hundred years having gone by, *Walden,* its serenity and grandeur unimpaired, still lifts us up by the ears, still translates for us that language we are in danger of forgetting, "which all things and events speak without metaphor, which alone is copious and standard."

(2) *Walden* is an oddity in American letters. It may very well be the oddest of our distinguished oddities. For many it is a great deal too odd, and for many it is a particular bore. I have not found it to be a well-liked book among my acquaintances, although usually spoken of with respect, and one literary critic for whom I have the

highest regard can find no reason for anyone's giving *Walden* a second thought. To admire the book is, in fact, something of an embarrassment, for the mass of men have an indistinct notion that its author was a sort of Nature Boy.

(3) I think it is of some advantage to encounter the book at a period in one's life when the normal anxieties and enthusiasms and rebellions of youth closely resemble those of Thoreau in that spring of 1845 when he borrowed an ax, went out to the woods, and began to whack down some trees for timber. Received at such a juncture, the book is like an invitation to life's dance, assuring the troubled recipient that no matter what befalls him in the way of success or failure he will always be welcome at the party—that the music is played for him, too, if he will but listen and move his feet. In effect, that is what the book is—an invitation, unengraved; and it stirs one as a young girl is stirred by her first big party bid. Many think it a sermon; many set it down as an attempt to rearrange society; some think it an exercise in nature-loving; some find it a rather irritating collection of inspirational puffballs by an eccentric show-off. I think it none of these. It still seems to me the best youth's companion yet written by an American, for it carries a solemn warning against the loss of one's valuables, it advances a good argument for travelling light and trying new adventures, it rings with the power of positive adoration, it contains religious feeling without religious images, and it steadfastly refuses to record bad news. Even its pantheistic note is so pure as to be noncorrupting—pure as the flute-note blown across the pond on those faraway summer nights. If our colleges and universities were alert, they would present a cheap pocket edition of the book to every senior upon graduating, along with his sheepskin, or instead of it. Even if some senior were to take it literally and start felling trees, there could be worse mishaps: the ax is older than the Dictaphone and it is just as well for a young man to see what kind of chips he leaves before listening to the sound of his own voice. And even if some were to get no farther than the table of contents, they would learn how to name eighteen chapters by the use of only thirty-nine words and would see how sweet are the uses of brevity.

(4) If Thoreau had merely left us an account of a man's life in

the woods or if he had simply retreated to the woods and there recorded his complaints about society, or even if he had contrived to include both records in one essay, *Walden* would probably not have lived a hundred years. As things turned out, Thoreau, very likely without knowing quite what he was up to, took man's relation to Nature and man's dilemma in society and man's capacity for elevating his spirit and he beat all these matters together, in a wild free interval of self-justification and delight, and produced an original omelette from which people can draw nourishment in a hungry day. *Walden* is one of the first of the vitamin-enriched American dishes. If it were a little less good than it is, or even a little less queer, it would be an abominable book. Even as it is, it will continue to baffle and annoy the literal mind and all those who are unable to stomach its caprices and imbibe its theme. Certainly the plodding economist will continue to have rough going if he hopes to emerge from. the book with a clear system of economic thought. Thoreau's assault on the Concord society of the mid-nineteenth century has the quality of a modern Western: he rides into the subject at top speed, shooting in all directions. Many of his shots ricochet and nick him on the rebound, and throughout the melee there is a horrendous cloud of inconsistencies and contradictions, and when the shooting dies down and the air clears, one is impressed chiefly by the courage of the rider and by how splendid it was that somebody should have ridden in there and raised all that ruckus.

(5) When he went to the pond, Thoreau struck an attitude and did so deliberately, but his posturing was not to draw the attention of others to him but rather to draw his own attention more closely to himself. "I learned this at least by my experiment: that if one advances confidently in the direction of his dreams, and endeavors to live the life which he has imagined, he will meet with a success unexpected in common hours." The sentence has the power to resuscitate the youth drowning in his sea of doubt. I recall my exhilaration upon reading it, many years ago, in a time of hesitation and despair. It restored me to health. And now in 1954 when I salute Henry Thoreau on the hundredth birthday of his book, I am merely paying off an old score—or an installment on it.

(6) In his journal for May 3–4, 1838—Boston to Portland—he

wrote: "Midnight—head over the boat's side—between sleeping and waking—with glimpses of one or more lights in the vicinity of Cape Ann. Bright moonlight—the effect heightened by seasickness." The entry illuminates the man, as the moon the sea on that night in May. In Thoreau the natural scene was heightened, not depressed, by a disturbance of the stomach, and nausea met its match at last. There was a steadiness in at least one passenger if there was none in the boat. Such steadiness (which in some would be called intoxication) is at the heart of *Walden*—confidence, faith, the discipline of looking always at what is to be seen, undeviating gratitude for the life-everlasting that he found growing in his front yard. "There is nowhere recorded a simple and irrepressible satisfaction with the gift of life, any memorable praise of God." He worked to correct that deficiency. *Walden* is his acknowledgment of the gift of life. It is the testament of a man in a high state of indignation because (it seemed to him) so few ears heard the uninterrupted poem of creation, the morning wind that forever blows. If the man sometimes wrote as though all his readers were male, unmarried, and well-connected, it is because he gave his testimony during the callow years, and, for that matter, never really grew up. To reject the book because of the immaturity of the author and the bugs in the logic is to throw away a bottle of good wine because it contains bits of the cork.

(7) Thoreau said he required of every writer, first and last, a simple and sincere account of his own life. Having delivered himself of this chesty dictum, he proceeded to ignore it. In his books and even in his enormous journal, he withheld or disguised most of the facts from which an understanding of his life could be drawn. *Walden,* subtitled "Life in the Woods," is not a simple and sincere account of a man's life, either in or out of the woods; it is an account of a man's journey into the mind, a toot on the trumpet to alert the neighbors. Thoreau was well aware that no one can alert his neighbors who is not wide-awake himself, and he went to the woods (among other reasons) to make sure that he would stay awake during his broadcast. What actually took place during the years 1845-47 is largely unrecorded, and the reader is excluded from the private life of the author, who supplies almost no gossip about himself, a great deal about his neighbors and about the universe.

(8) As for me, I cannot in this short ramble give a simple and sincere account of my own life, but I think Thoreau might find it instructive to know that this memorial essay is being written in a house that, through no intent on my part, is the same size and shape as his own domicile on the pond—about ten by fifteen, tight, plainly finished, and at a little distance from my Concord. The house in which I sit this morning was built to accommodate a boat, not a man, but by long experience I have learned that in most respects it shelters me better than the larger dwelling where my bed is, and which, by design, is a manhouse not a boathouse. Here in the boathouse I am a wilder and, it would appear, a healthier man, by a safe margin. I have a chair, a bench, a table, and I can walk into the water if I tire of the land. My house fronts a cove. Two fishermen have just arrived to spot fish from the air—an osprey and a man in a small yellow plane who works for the fish company. The man, I have noticed, is less well equipped than the hawk, who can dive directly on his fish and carry it away, without telephoning. A mouse and a squirrel share the house with me. The building is, in fact, a multiple dwelling, a semidetached affair. It is because I am semidetached while here that I find it possible to transact this private business with the fewest obstacles.

(9) There is also a woodchuck here, living forty feet away under the wharf. When the wind is right, he can smell my house; and when the wind is contrary, I can smell his. We both use the wharf for sunning, taking turns, each adjusting his schedule to the other's convenience. Thoreau once ate a woodchuck. I think he felt he owed it to his readers, and that it was little enough, considering the indignities they were suffering at his hands and the dressing-down they were taking. (Parts of *Walden* are pure scold.) Or perhaps he ate the woodchuck because he believed every man should acquire strict business habits, and the woodchuck was destroying his market beans. I do not know. Thoreau had a strong experimental streak in him. It is probably no harder to eat a woodchuck than to construct a sentence that lasts a hundred years. At any rate, Thoreau is the only writer I know who prepared himself for his great ordeal by eating a woodchuck; also the only one who got a hangover from drinking too much water. (He was drunk the whole time, though he seldom touched wine or coffee or tea.)

(10) Here in this compact house where I would spend one day as deliberately as Nature if I were not being pressed by the editor of a magazine, and with a woodchuck (as yet uneaten) for neighbor, I can feel the companionship of the occupant of the pondside cabin in Walden woods, a mile from the village, near the Fitchburg right of way. Even my immediate business is no barrier between us: Thoreau occasionally batted out a magazine piece, but was always suspicious of any sort of purposeful work that cut into his time. A man, he said, should take care not to be thrown off the track by every nutshell and mosquito's wing that falls on the rails.

(11) There has been much guessing as to why he went to the pond. To set it down to escapism is, of course, to misconstrue what happened. Henry went forth to battle when he took to the woods, and *Walden* is the report of a man torn by two powerful and opposing drives—the desire to enjoy the world (and not be derailed by a mosquito wing) and the urge to set the world straight. One cannot join these two successfully, but sometimes, in rare cases, something good or even great results from the attempt of the tormented spirit to reconcile them. Henry went forth to battle, and if he set the stage himself, if he fought on his own terms and with his own weapons, it was because it was his nature to do things differently from most men, and to act in a cocky fashion. If the pond and the woods seemed a more plausible site for a house than an in-town location, it was because a cowbell made for him a sweeter sound than a churchbell. *Walden,* the book, makes the sound of a cowbell, more than a churchbell, and proves the point, although both sounds are in it, and both remarkably clear and sweet. He simply preferred his churchbell at a little distance.

(12) I think one reason he went to the woods was a perfectly simple and commonplace one—and apparently he thought so, too. "At a certain season of our life," he wrote, "we are accustomed to consider every spot as the possible site of a house." There spoke the young man, a few years out of college, who had not yet broken away from home. He hadn't married, and he had found no job that measured up to his rigid standards of employment, and like any young man, or young animal, he felt uneasy and on the defensive until he had fixed himself a den. Most young men, of course, casting about for a site, are content merely to draw apart from their kinfolks.

Thoreau, convinced that the greater part of what his neighbors called good was bad, withdrew from a great deal more than family: he pulled out of everything for a while, to serve everybody right for being so stuffy, and to try his own prejudices on the dog.

(13) The house-hunting sentence above, which starts the chapter called "Where I Lived, and What I Lived For," is followed by another passage that is worth quoting here because it so beautifully illustrates the offbeat prose that Thoreau was master of, a prose at once strictly disciplined and wildly abandoned. "I have surveyed the country on every side within a dozen miles of where I live," continued this delirious young man. "In imagination I have bought all the farms in succession, for all were to be bought, and I knew their price. I walked over each farmer's premises, tasted his wild apples, discoursed on husbandry with him, took his farm at his price, at any price, mortgaging it to him in my mind; even put a higher price on it—took everything but a deed of it—took his word for his deed, for I dearly love to talk—cultivated it, and him too to some extent, I trust, and withdrew when I had enjoyed it long enough, leaving him to carry it on." A copy-desk man would get a double hernia trying to clean up that sentence for the management, but the sentence needs no fixing, for it perfectly captures the meaning of the writer and the quality of the ramble.

(14) "Wherever I sat, there I might live, and the landscape radiated from me accordingly." Thoreau, the home-seeker, sitting on his hummock with the entire State of Massachusetts radiating from him, is to me the most humorous of the New England figures, and *Walden* the most humorous of the books, though its humor is almost continuously subsurface and there is nothing deliberately funny anywhere, except a few weak jokes and bad puns that rise to the surface like the perch in the pond that rose to the sound of the maestro's flute. Thoreau tended to write in sentences, a feat not every writer is capable of, and *Walden* is, rhetorically speaking, a collection of certified sentences, some of them, it would now appear, as indestructible as they are errant. The book is distilled from the vast journals, and this accounts for its intensity: he picked out bright particles that pleased his eye, whirled them in the kaleidoscope of his content, and produced the pattern that has endured—the color, the form, the light.

(15) On this its hundredth birthday, Thoreau's *Walden* is pertinent and timely. In our uneasy season, when all men unconsciously seek a retreat from a world that has got almost completely out of hand, his house in the Concord woods is a haven. In our culture of gadgetry and the multiplicity of convenience, his cry "Simplicity, simplicity, simplicity!" has the insistence of a fire alarm. In the brooding atmosphere of war and the gathering radioactive storm, the innocence and serenity of his summer afternoons are enough to burst the remembering heart, and one gazes back upon that pleasing interlude —its confidence, its purity, its deliberateness—with awe and wonder, as one would look upon the face of a child asleep.

(16) "This small lake was of most value as a neighbor in the intervals of a gentle rain-storm in August, when, both air and water being perfectly still, but the sky overcast, midafternoon had all the serenity of evening, and the wood-thrush sang around, and was heard from shore to shore." Now, in the perpetual overcast in which our days are spent, we hear with extra perception and deep gratitude that song, tying century to century.

(17) I sometimes amuse myself by bringing Henry Thoreau back to life and showing him the sights. I escort him into a phone booth and let him dial Weather. "This is a delicious evening," the girl's voice says, "when the whole body is one sense, and imbibes delight through every pore." I show him the spot in the Pacific where an island used to be, before some magician made it vanish. "We know not where we are," I murmur. "The light which puts out our eyes is darkness to us. Only that day dawns to which we are awake." I thumb through the latest copy of *Vogue* with him. "Of two patterns which differ only by a few threads more or less of a particular color," I read, "the one will be sold readily, the other lie on the shelf, though it frequently happens that, after the lapse of a season, the latter becomes the most fashionable." Together we go outboarding on the Assabet, looking for what we've lost—a hound, a bay horse, a turtledove. I show him a distracted farmer who is trying to repair a hay baler before the thunder shower breaks. "This farmer," I remark, "is endeavoring to solve the problem of a livelihood by a formula more

complicated than the problem itself. To get his shoestrings he specu-
lates in herds of cattle."

(18) I take the celebrated author to Twenty-One for lunch, so
the waiters may study his shoes. The proprietor welcomes us. "The
gross feeder," remarks the proprietor, sweeping the room with his
arm, "is a man in the larva stage." After lunch we visit a classroom
in one of those schools conducted by big corporations to teach
their superannuated executives how to retire from business without serious injury to their health. (The shock to men's systems
these days when relieved of the exacting routine of amassing
wealth is very great and must be cushioned.) "It is not necessary,"
says the teacher to his pupils, "that a man should earn his living
by the sweat of his brow, unless he sweats easier than I do. We
are determined to be starved before we are hungry."

(19) I turn on the radio and let Thoreau hear Winchell beat the
red hand around the clock. "Time is but the stream I go a-fishing in,"
shouts Mr. Winchell, rattling his telegraph key. "Hardly a man
takes a half hour's nap after dinner, but when he wakes he holds
up his head and asks, 'What's the news?' If we read of one man
robbed, or murdered, or killed by accident, or one house burned,
or one vessel wrecked, or one steamboat blown up, or one cow
run over on the Western Railroad, or one mad dog killed, or one
lot of grasshoppers in the winter—we need never read of another. One is enough."

(20) I doubt that Thoreau would be thrown off balance by the
fantastic sights and sounds of the twentieth century. "The Concord
nights," he once wrote, "are stranger than the Arabian nights." A
four-engined airliner would merely serve to confirm his early
views on travel. Everywhere he would observe, in new shapes
and sizes, the old predicaments and follies of men—the despera-
tion, the impedimenta, the meanness—along with the visible
capacity for elevation of the mind and soul. "This curious world
which we inhabit is more wonderful than it is convenient; more
beautiful than it is useful; it is more to be admired and enjoyed
than used." He would see that today ten thousand engineers are
busy making sure that the world shall be convenient even if it is
destroyed in the process, and others are determined to increase

its usefulness even though its beauty is lost somewhere along the way.

(21) At any rate, I'd like to stroll about the countryside in Thoreau's company for a day, observing the modern scene, inspecting today's snowstorm, pointing out the sights and offering belated apologies for my sins. Thoreau is unique among writers in that those who admire him find him uncomfortable to live with— a regular hairshirt of a man. A little band of dedicated Thoreauvians would be a sorry sight indeed: fellows who hate compromise and have compromised, fellows who love wildness and have lived tamely, and at their side, censuring them and chiding them, the ghostly figure of this upright man, who long ago gave corroboration to impulses they perceived were right and issued warnings against the things they instinctively knew to be their enemies. I should hate to be called a Thoreauvian, yet I wince every time I walk into the barn I'm pushing before me, seventy-five feet by forty, and the author of *Walden* has served as my conscience through the long stretches of my trivial days.

(22) Hairshirt or no, he is a better companion than most, and I would not swap him for a soberer or more reasonable friend even if I could. I can reread his famous invitation with undiminished excitement. The sad thing is that not more acceptances have been received, that so many decline for one reason or another, pleading some previous engagement or ill health. But the invitation stands. It will beckon as long as this remarkable book stays in print— which will be as long as there are August afternoons in the intervals of a gentle rainstorm, as long as there are ears to catch the faint sounds of the orchestra. I find it agreeable to sit here this morning, in a house of correct proportions, and hear across a century of time his flute, his frogs, and his seductive summons to the wildest revels of them all.

Questions

1. In the process of implying his own point of view toward *Walden*, White alludes to a number of others. Limiting yourself to the first four paragraphs, how many different ones do you find? Do they seem to overlap?

2. White refers several times to the fact that his essay is a memorial one designed to appear in a magazine. What other bits of personal information does he give? Drawing upon all of them, can you make some sort of composite picture of the writer?

3. White's images are often distinctive. In Paragraph 4 *Walden* is described as an "original omelette . . . in a hungry day" and as "one of the first of the vitamin-enriched American dishes." In Paragraph 7 *Walden* becomes "a toot on the trumpet to alert the neighbors." Find other images of a similar nature. If you agree that White is writing a serious essay, how would you characterize the point of view he employs in such passages?

4. What assumptions about the good life for young men underlie White's assertions in Paragraph 3? Consider whether they are the same assumptions that underlie his later recommendation of *Walden* to "all men" in "our uneasy season" (Paragraph 15).

5. In Paragraphs 8 through 10 White reveals that he is composing his essay in a house similar in size and setting to Thoreau's. What other parallels between the two men are either stated or implied in the essay? To what extent would you say that White is writing from Thoreau's point of view?

6. Toward the end of the essay, White suggests what a "little band of dedicated Thoreauvians" would be like and suspects that he is one of them. Is there evidence in the essay that it is written, totally or in part, from the point of view of a Thoreauvian—one who hates compromise but has compromised, etc.?

7. Prepare an essay in which Thoreau, as White presents him, encounters some of the "fantastic sights and sounds of the twentieth century"—in a schoolroom, perhaps, or in front of a television set.

8. Make a case in opposition to Thoreau's doctrine of "Simplicity, simplicity, simplicity!" Examine your own assumptions with the care that you give to his.

STUDENT MOBS

J. B. PRIESTLEY

Born in Yorkshire, England, the son of a schoolmaster, J. B.
Priestley (1894—) received his education at Cambridge and
then settled in London, where he began a very long and full
career as a writer: initially as a reviewer and critic, then as
essayist and biographer and as novelist and playwright. He
has continued to write in all of these forms, as the occasion
and particular form seem to merge. Among his many novels
are *The Good Companions, Angel Pavement,* and *The
Shapes of Sleep;* his essay collections include *Apes and
Angels, Postscripts,* and *Delight.* He has written a portion
of his autobiography in *Midnight on the Desert.*

(1) Being a fair-minded man, I begin this piece by admitting
that I may have some slight prejudice against students. This is
stronger on the negative than on the positive side. It is not that
I dislike students as such; it is more that, unlike so many people,
remembering their youth, I don't regard student antics through a
nostalgic haze. True, I was a student myself once, but then by the
time I went up to Cambridge, in the Michaelmas Term of 1919,
I was a man not an overgrown boy, already in my twenty-sixth year
and a battered old soldier. I wanted to get on with my life and
not clown around with lads newly released from school and given
their first cheque-books.

(2) I didn't see then—and have never seen since—why young
men in universities, turning themselves into mischievous and sometimes dangerous mobs, should be treated indulgently, as if they

From *Moments and Other Pieces,* by J. B. Priestley. Reprinted by permission
of A. D. Peters & Co. and William Heinemann Ltd.

259

were quite different from mobs of garage hands, apprentice fitters, bus-drivers. Indeed, there is a case for more severity. Students are not supposed to be ignorant and stupid. If they are, then they should be sent home and not receive higher education at public expense. They are wasting not only their own but also other people's time, energy and money. There must be countries now in which peasants are going without substantial meals and some decent clothes so that a lot of lads can spend several years in universities. Such lads should begin to develop a sense of responsibility. They should be the last and not the first to create howling destructive mobs. They should be reading books, not burning them.

(3) It is not the occasional 'rags' that get out of hand I am thinking about now; it is the so-called 'demonstrations' that seem to make an appearance every few nights on the TV news. I do not care whose side they are supposed to be on, I am more and more depressed and revolted by these idiot processions, with their banners and slogans and mindless grinning faces, on their way to break windows, smash cars, burn furniture and books, terrify women and children, and to reduce international law, custom and sensible usages to chaos. In many instances, of course, these 'demonstrations' are anything but student improvisations, having been organized by governments on a secret rent-a-mob basis. Even where governments have apologized, it is hard to believe that the student mobs could not have been checked and dispersed before any real damage was done. And this is all part of the darkening picture.

(4) We live in a curious age. We are offered glimpses of a genuine world civilization slowly emerging—the UN special agencies, organizations like Oxfam,* and here and there, as I have seen for myself, remote enterprises, dedicated to healing or education, with international staffs of selfless enthusiasts. And such glimpses warm the heart and brighten hope. But along with these are sights and sounds that suggest that the whole fabric of civilization, the work of centuries, is rapidly being torn apart. Two official policies clash, and instantly embassies, consulates, centres of information services, are surrounded and then attacked by howling mobs of students,

* A famine-relief organization.

at once defying law, custom, usage. And that this may not be merely so many hot-headed lads escaping all control, that it may itself be part of government policy, mob antics as additional propaganda to deceive world opinion, makes our situation even worse. It is as if we were all compelled to exist now in a sinister circus. No doubt governments have always been dishonest and hypocritical, but now it is beginning to look as if power-mania is ready to destroy those long-accepted forms and civilities that make international relations possible. The time may soon come when ambassadors will have to move around in tanks, and embassies and consulates will have to be fortified or abandoned. And perhaps students on admittance will be given machine-guns and flame-throwers.

(5) There is something else, just as bad, perhaps even worse, and evidence of it is amply supplied to us by TV cameras and mikes. What we see in these student faces illuminated by burning cars and bonfires of books is not the glow of political enthusiasm but a frenzied delight in destruction. Whatever country or party they may be demonstrating for or against, what really inspires them is an urge towards violent demolition. They don't know—and may never know—how to make anything worth having, but they need no courses on wrecking and destroying. If degrees were given in window-smashing, car-overturning, furniture-firing, they would all have them with honours. They may still be weak in sciences and the arts, medicine and the law, but they already have Firsts in Hooliganism. I doubt if some of them even know which side they are shouting for, their minds having abandoned the intricate and tedious arguments of politics as they joyfully contemplate the destruction of other people's property. What sort of doctors and lawyers and chemists and teachers of languages they will make, we cannot tell; but there should be no shortage of recruits with degrees for demolition squads and wrecking crews. Soon there may appear on many a campus those huge iron balls with which New York keeps knocking itself down. At a signal from the Ministry of Foreign Affairs, out they will roll to demolish an embassy or two before it is time for any evening seminars.

(6) In this enthusiasm not for politics but for destruction

and violence, these students may be said to be taking their proper place, right up there in the van, giving a lead to youth everywhere. For we live, I repeat, in a curious age, which is trying hard to abolish want and disease but is also abolishing, without trying, any regard and respect for other people's possessions. And it is in the countries where lads are now most carefully and expensively nurtured that they proceed to knock hell out of everything. They may grow up under capitalism or socialism but what they really care about is vandalism. Now that they have sufficient money to take special trains to football matches, they will wreck them on the way back. Well-paid and full-fed youth has already done more damage than all the hungry millions of the Bleak Age. Towns that would not risk a penny rate for the arts are now having to face a bigger bill every year to restore public property that has been idiotically or malevolently destroyed. A woman who had taught in junior schools for forty years told me that the most recent children were far and away the most destructive she had ever known: they just wanted to smash things. It is as if creatures from other planets had arrived, taking the shape of playful kids who put things on the lines in the hope of de-railing expresses.

(7) It was rough in the North when I was a boy there. Boys came to elementary schools in clogs; on Saturday nights there were drunken fights, with much smashing of crockery, in streets 'back o' t'mill'; and when in my middle teens I played football (sometimes on grounds made out of cinder tips) in a local league, both players and spectators could be very rough indeed. But I don't recall any of this curiously malevolent destructiveness and this violence that mark our present time. If youngsters, together with their parents, were aggressively rough, it was because they knew no better, but I cannot remember any of the deeply disturbing psychopathic element that seems so common today. There might be fights between pugnacious equals but helpless people were not being half-killed merely to round off an evening's amusement. Our destructiveness and violence today do not seem to come from any surplus of energy but from a neurotic or even psychotic heartlessness, a cold disregard of other persons, a hatred of life. And something very much like it, only of course further developed and more subtle,

has crept like a huge cold serpent into too much of our fiction and drama. There are people among us who don't seem to belong to the human race. And while I won't join a mob to smash their windows, overturn their cars, burn their furniture and books, I'll be damned if I'll admire 'em.

(8) It is all very odd, bewildering, really rather frightening, for while we can just about deal with it today, what will it be like tomorrow? No sooner do we appear to have made the world safer than a strange half-mad gleam comes into its eyes. The young arrive eager not to create but to destroy. The students never march to build a house but only to knock one down. Like those sinister puffs of steam we notice in New York streets at night, threats of violence, puffing from some hell below, multiply even while we elaborate the techniques and apparatus of a world civilization. And though I am familiar with all the usual explanations—H-bomb, no religion, bad homes and irresponsible parents, dead-end jobs, boring environment, and the rest—I remain puzzled, never entirely convinced, still wondering if there might not be some unknown factor, a vast X in the dark. Meanwhile, I think I could take some newsreel footage showing me students making something instead of breaking something—or even just studying.

Questions

1. Priestley says that he does not dislike students as such, but he does have reservations about them quite aside from the issue of mob activity. Point out his reservations at two or three separate points in the essay.

2. "Students are ignorant and stupid, and this is why they have to be sent to the university at public expense." What contrasting assumptions about human nature, education, and society underlie this statement and Priestley's on the same point in Paragraph 2?

3. What sort of people are not depressed and revolted by student mobs? Would you say that all decent-minded people are on Priestley's side?

4. Priestley offers a glimpse of a future that he thinks would "warm the heart" (Paragraph 4), but it would chill the blood of a lot of people. What would the positive values of such people be?

5. Priestley takes potshots at New York City and contemporary

fiction and drama in Paragraphs 5 and 7. If the violent action in these places is not mainly produced by the younger generation, is Priestley contradicting himself? Discuss.

6. Priestley implies that power mania is worse than it used to be (Paragraph 4), but he has lived through two world wars. Can you show that he has these wars at the back of his mind throughout the essay?

7. In Paragraph 3 Priestley says that he finds student mobs depressing and revolting. In the last paragraph he finds them frightening. Which of the three adjectives do you think comes closest to defining his mood in the essay itself? Base your discussion on an analysis of Paragraphs 1 and 4.

8. From your own point of view, what sort of person does Priestley seem to be?

9. In March, 1967, there was riotous behavior by students at Long Island University and at Fort Lauderdale, Florida. The accounts in the *New York Times* may suggest whether the riots were like those that Priestley describes. Write a report, evaluating them according to Priestley's standards.

IMPRESSIONS OF JAPAN

WILLIAM FAULKNER

William Faulkner (1897–1962) is generally acknowledged to be among the greatest of American novelists. Born near Oxford, Mississippi, he passed most of his life there, and to good purpose, since he drew on its history and traditions in creating his mythical Yoknapatawpha County, the setting of much of his fiction—*The Sound and the Fury, Light in August, The Hamlet.* Though he restricted his scene, and by his subject matter encouraged a sociological interest in his work, his concern was ultimately with—in his own words—the "human heart in conflict with itself," the "old universal truths lacking which any story is ephemeral and doomed—love and honor and pity and pride and compassion and sacrifice." In 1951 he received a Nobel Prize. In 1955 he visited Japan, and at that time wrote the prose reprinted here.

(1) The engines are long since throttled back; the overcast sinks slowly upwards with no semblance whatever of speed until suddenly you see the aircraft's shadow scudding the cottony hillocks; and now speed has returned again, aircraft and shadow now rushing toward one another as toward one mutual headlong destruction.

(2) To break through the overcast and fling that shadow once more down, upon an island. It looks like land, like any other airfound landfall, yet you know it is an island, almost as if you saw both sea-bound flanks of it at the same instant, like a transparent slide; an island more miraculously found in the waste of water

than Wake or Guam even, since here is a civilization, an ordered and ancient homogeny of the human race.

(3) It is visible and audible, spoken and written too: a communication between man and man because human speaks it; you hear and see them. But to this one western ear and eye it means nothing because it resembles nothing which that western eye remembers; there is nothing to measure it against, nothing for memory and habit to say, "Why this looks like the word for house or home or happiness"; not even just cryptic but acrostic too, as though the splashed symbols of the characters held not mere communication but something urgent and important beyond just information, promising toward some ultimate wisdom or knowledge containing the secret of man's salvation. But then no more, because there is nothing for western memory to measure it against; so not the mind to listen but only the ear to hear that chirrup and skitter of syllables like the cries of birds in the mouths of children, like music in the mouths of women and young girls.

(4) The faces: Van Gogh and Manet would have loved them: that of the pilgrim with staff and pack and dusty with walking, mounting the stairs toward the Temple in the early sunlight; the Temple lay-brother or perhaps servant, his gown tucked about his thighs, squatting in the gate of the compound before beginning, or perhaps having already set it into motion, the day; that of the old woman vending peanuts beneath the gate for tourists to feed the pigeons with: a face worn with living and remembering, as though not one life had been long enough but rather every separate breath had been needed to etch into it all those fine and myriad lines; a face durable and now even a comfort to her, as if it had by now blotted up whatever had ever ached or sorrowed behind it, leaving it free now of the anguishes and the griefs and the enduring: here is one anyway who never read Faulkner and neither knows nor cares why he came to Japan nor gives one single damn what he thinks of Ernest Hemingway.

(5) He is much too busy to have time to bother about whether he is happy or not, quite dirty, perhaps five years old, pastless and apparently immune even from parents, playing in the gutter with the stub of a cigarette.

(6) The bowl of mountains containing the lake is as full of hard rapid air as the mouth of a wind-tunnel; for some time now we have been thinking that maybe it is already too late to take a reef in the mainsail: yet there it is. It is only a skiff yet to the western eye it is as invincibly and irrevocably alien as a Chinese junk, driven by a battered U.S. made outboard engine and containing a woman in a kimono beneath an open paper parasol such as would have excited no comment in a sunny reach of the English Thames, as fragile and invulnerable in the center of that hard blue bowl of wind as a butterfly in the eye of a typhoon.

(7) The geisha's mass of blueblack lacquered hair encloses the painted face like a helmet, surmounts, crowns the slender body's ordered and ritual posturing like a grenadier's bearskin busby, too heavy in appearance for that slender throat to bear, the painted fixed expressionless face immobile and immune also above the studied posturing: yet behind that painted and lifeless mask is something quick and alive and elfin: or more than elfin: puckish: or more than puckish even: sardonic and quizzical, a gift for comedy, and more: for burlesque and caricature: for a sly and vicious revenge on the race of men.

(8) Kimono. It covers her from throat to ankles; with a gesture as feminine as the placing of a flower or as female as the cradling of a child, the hands themselves can be concealed into the sleeves until there remains one unbroken chalice-shape of modesty proclaiming her femininity where nudity would merely parade her mammalian femaleness. A modesty which flaunts its own immodestness like the crimson rose tossed by no more than one white flick of hand, from the balcony window—modesty, than which there is nothing more immodest and which therefore is a woman's dearest possession; she should defend it with her life.

(9) Loyalty. In her western clothes, blouse and skirt, she is merely one dumpy and nondescript young woman though in kimono at the deft balanced rapid tripping glide she too comes into her own share of that national heritage of feminine magic. Though she has more than that; she partakes of her share of that other quality which women have in this land which was not given them by what they have on: loyalty, constancy, fidelity, not for, but at least one

hopes not without, reward. She does not speak my language nor I hers, yet in two days she knows my countryman's habit of waking soon after first light so that each morning when I open my eyes a coffee tray is already on the balcony table; she knows I like a fresh room to breakfast in when I return from walking, and it is so: the room done for the day and the table set and the morning paper ready; she asks without words why I have no clothes to be laundered today, and without words asks permission to sew the buttons and darn the socks; she calls me wise man and teacher, who am neither, when speaking of me to others; she is proud to have me for her client and, I hope, pleased that I try to deserve that pride and match with courtesy that loyalty. There is a lot of loose loyalty in this land. Even a little of it is too valuable to be ignored. I would wish that all of it were deserved or at least appreciated as I have tried to do.

(10) This is the same rice paddy which I know back home in Arkansas and Mississippi and Louisiana, where it replaces now and then the cotton. This one is merely a little smaller and a little more fiercely cultivated, right up to the single row of beans which line the very edge of the irrigation canals, the work here done by hand where in my country machines do it since we have more machines than we have people; nature is the same: only the economy is different.

(11) And the names are the same names too: Jonathan and Winesap and Delicious; the heavy August foliage is blue gray with the same spray which we use. But there the resemblance ceases: every single apple enclosed in this twist of paper until that whole tree to this western eye becomes significant and festive and cere-monial like the symbolical tree of the western rite of Christmas. Only it is more significant here: where in the West there is one small often artificial tree to a family, wrested from the living dirt to be decked in ritual tinsel and then to die as though the tree were not the protagonist of a rite but the victim of a sacrifice, here not one tree to a family but every tree of all is dressed and decked to proclaim and salute older gods than Christ: Demeter and Ceres.

(12) Briefer and faster now, toward the journey's nearing end: goldenrod, as evocative of dust and autumn and hay fever as ever in Mississippi, against a tall bamboo fence.

(13) The scenery is beautiful but the faces are better still.

(14) The swift supple narrow grace with which the young girl bows and in that same one glowing motion recovers, tougher through very tenderness than the rigid culture which bent her as is the willow bough itself to the hard gust which can never do more than sway it.

(15) The tools they use evoke the ones Noah must have built his ark with, yet the framework of the house seems to rise and stand without nails in the fitted joints nor even the need for nails, as if here were a magic, an art in the simple building of man's habitations which our western ancestors seemed to have lost somewhere when they moved.

(16) And always the water, the sound, the plash and drip of it, as if here were a people making constant oblation to water as some peoples do to what they call their luck.

(17) So kind the people that with three words the guest can go anywhere and live: Gohan; Sake; Arrigato. And one more word:

(18) Tomorrow now the aircraft lightens, a moment more and the wheels will wrench free of the ground, already dragging its shadow back toward the overcast before the wheels are even tucked up, into the overcast and then through it, the land, the island gone now which memory will always know though eye no longer remembers. Sayonara.

Questions

1. Try to relate the physical perspective on Japan in the first two paragraphs to the mental outlook of Paragraph 3 and to the general outlook that pervades the essay. At what points does Faulkner resume a comparable physical perspective?

2. In what different respects is Faulkner interested in the two men and the woman in Paragraph 4? His reference to the painters Van Gogh and Manet might seem to suggest that his interests are æsthetic. Are they? At what points in the first six paragraphs would you say Faulkner's interests are most explicitly æsthetic? How close does he seem to be to the people he describes in these paragraphs?

3. Is Faulkner's judgment upon the geisha in Paragraph 7 moral? Is it æsthetic? Does he disapprove more of the outward woman or the inward? What assumed values underlie his judgment?

4. What are the distinctions between *feminine* and *female* that Faulkner makes in Paragraph 8? What assumptions about women underlie the distinctions?

5. What aspects of rice paddies does Faulkner ignore that someone else might be preoccupied with? What is his broad interest in them? In what way might it be said that his interest in rice paddies is consistent with—perhaps the same as—his interest in the little boy in Paragraph 5?

6. What are the three or four assumed standards by which Faulkner passes judgment against the West in Paragraph 11? To what extent generally in the essay does he seem to praise Japan at the expense of the West?

7. The interests of another visitor to Japan might well have been predominantly philosophical, sociological, or cultural. What is Faulkner's predominant interest? Explain how it applies to Paragraphs 4 through 7.

8. Analyze the development of Faulkner's references to himself. Would you say that the changes make for inconsistency in point of view? What modification in point of view might have resulted had he used one or another of the forms of reference consistently?

9. Examine Paragraph 7 for its syntax, rhythm, and movement of thought. Express the effect of these factors as point of view.

10. Faulkner's subject is, in part, appearance and reality. Discuss its various aspects.

THE DANCE

D. H. LAWRENCE

Born and brought up in an ugly little mining village, Lawrence early witnessed the dehumanizing effects of industrialism, and much of his later effort was spent in battle against the conditions he found characteristic of modern industrial existence— mechanization, thwarting of the self, distortion of the human affections. He pursued the battle in a variety of literary forms: poetry, novels (*Women in Love, Lady Chatterley's Lover*), short stories, and essays. The ethos underlying his work is perhaps best suggested by his own words, "My great religion is a belief in the blood, the flesh, as being wiser than the intellect." Lawrence's literary friendships, at once intimate and stormy, included those with Aldous Huxley, Bertrand Russell, and Katherine Mansfield. (Further information on Lawrence appears on pp. 16, 382.)

(1) Maria had no real license for San Gaudenzio, yet the peasants always called for wine. It is easy to arrange in Italy. The penny is paid another time.

(2) The wild old road that skirts the lake-side, scrambling always higher as the precipice becomes steeper, climbing and winding to the villages perched high up, passes under the high boundary-wall of San Gaudenzio, between that and the ruined church. But the road went just as much between the vines and past the house as outside, under the wall; for the high gates were always open, and men or women and mules come into the property to call at the door of the homestead. There was a loud shout, "Ah—a—a—ah—

From *Twilight in Italy* by D. H. Lawrence. Reprinted by permission of The Viking Press, Inc., Laurence Pollinger, Ltd., and the Estate of the late Mrs. Frieda Lawrence. All rights reserved.

Mari—'a. O—O—Oh Pa'o'!" from outside, another wild, inarticu-
late cry from within, and one of the Fiori appeared in the doorway
to hail the newcomer.

(3) It was usually a man, sometimes a peasant from Mugiano,
high up, sometimes a peasant from the wilds of the mountain,
a wood-cutter, or a charcoal-burner. He came in and sat in the
house-place, his glass of wine in his hand between his knees, or
on the floor between his feet and he talked in a few wild phrases,
very shy, like a hawk indoors, and unintelligible in his dialect.

(4) Sometimes we had a dance. Then, for the wine to drink,
three men came with mandolins and guitars, and sat in a corner
playing their rapid tunes, while all danced on the dusty brick floor
of the little parlour. No strange women were invited, only men;
the young bloods from the big village on the lake, the wild men
from above. They danced the slow, trailing, lilting polka-waltz round
and round the small room, the guitars and mandolins twanging
rapidly, the dust rising from the soft bricks. There were only the
two Englishwomen: so men danced with men, as the Italians love
to do. They love even better to dance with men, with a dear blood-
friend, than with women.

(5) "It's better like this, two men?" Giovanni says to me, his
blue eyes hot, his face curiously tender.

(6) The wood-cutters and peasants take off their coats, their
throats are bare. They dance with strange intentness, particularly
if they have for partner an English Signora. Their feet in thick boots
are curiously swift and significant. And it is strange to see the Englishwomen, as they dance with the peasants, transfigured with a
kind of brilliant surprise. All the while the peasants are very cour-
teous, but quiet. They see the women dilate and flash, they think
they have found a footing, they are certain. So the male dancers
are quiet, but even grandiloquent, their feet nimble, their bodies
wild and confident.

(7) They are at a loss when the two English Signoras move together and laugh excitedly at the end of the dance.

(8) "Isn't it fine?"

(9) "Fine! Their arms are like iron, carrying you round."

(10) "Yes! Yes! And the muscles on their shoulders! I never
knew there were such muscles! I'm almost frightened."

(11) "But it's fine, isn't it? I'm getting into the dance."

(12) "Yes—yes—you've only to let them take you."

(13) Then the glasses are put down, the guitars give their strange, vibrant, almost painful summons, and the dance begins again.

(14) It is a strange dance, strange and lilting, and changing as the music changed. But it had always a kind of leisurely dignity, a trailing kind of polka-waltz, intimate, passionate, yet never hurried, never violent in its passion, always becoming more intense. The women's faces changed to a kind of transported wonder, they were in the very rhythm of delight. From the soft bricks of the floor the red ochre rose in a thin cloud of dust, making hazy the shadowy dancers; the three musicians, in their black hats and their cloaks, sat obscurely in the corner, making a music that came quicker and quicker, making a dance that grew swifter and more intense, more subtle, the men seeming to fly and to implicate other strange inter-rhythmic dance into the women, the women drifting and palpitating as if their souls shook and resounded to a breeze that was subtly rushing upon them, through them; the men worked their feet, their thighs swifter, more vividly, the music came to an almost intolerable climax, there was a moment when the dance passed into a possession, the men caught up the women and swung them from the earth, leapt with them for a second, and then the next phase of the dance had begun, slower again, more subtly interwoven, taking perfect, oh, exquisite delight in every interrelated movement, a rhythm within a rhythm, a subtle approaching and drawing nearer to a climax, nearer, till, oh, there was the surpassing lift and swing of the women, when the woman's body seemed like a boat lifted over the powerful, exquisite wave of the man's body, perfect, for a moment, and then once more the slow, intense, nearer movement of the dance began, always nearer, nearer, always to a more perfect climax.

(15) And the women waited as if in transport for the climax, when they would be flung into a movement surpassing all movement. They were flung, borne away, lifted like a boat on a supreme wave, into the zenith and nave of the heavens, consummate.

(16) Then suddenly the dance crashed to an end, and the dancers stood stranded, lost, bewildered, on a strange shore. The air was

full of red dust, half-lit by the lamp on the wall; the players in the corner were putting down their instruments to take up their glasses.

(17) And the dancers sat round the wall, crowding in the little room, faint with the transport of repeated ecstacy. There was a subtle smile on the face of the men, subtle, knowing, so finely sensual that the conscious eyes could scarcely look at it. And the women were dazed, like creatures dazzled by too much light. The light was still on their faces, like a blindness, a reeling, like a transfiguration. The men were bringing wine, on a little tin tray, leaning with their proud, vivid loins, their faces flickering with the same subtle smile. Meanwhile, Maria Fiori was splashing water, much water, on the red floor. There was the smell of water among the glowing transfigured men and women who sat gleaming in another world, round the walls.

(18) The peasants have chosen their women. For the dark, handsome Englishwoman, who looks like a slightly malignant Madonna, comes Il Duro; for the "bella bionda," the wood-cutter. But the peasants have always to take their turn after the young well-to-do men from the village below.

(19) Nevertheless, they are confident. They cannot understand the middle-class diffidence of the young men who wear collars and ties and finger-rings.

(20) The wood-cutter from the mountain is of medium height, dark, thin, and hard as a hatchet, with eyes that are black like the very flaming thrust of night. He is quite a savage. There is something strange about his dancing, the violent way he works one shoulder. He has a wooden leg, from the knee-joint. Yet he dances well, and is inordinately proud. He is fierce as a bird, and hard with energy as a thunderbolt. He will dance with the blonde Signora. But he never speaks. He is like some violent phenomenon rather than a person. The woman begins to wilt a little in his possession.

(21) "È bello—il ballo?" he asks at length, one direct, flashing question.

(22) "Si—molto bello," cries the woman, glad to have speech again.

(23) The eyes of the wood-cutter flash like actual possession.

He seems now to have come into his own. With all his senses, he is dominant, sure.

(24) He is inconceivably vigorous in body, and his dancing is almost perfect, with a little catch in it, owing to his lameness, which brings almost a pure intoxication. Every muscle in his body is supple as steel, supple, as strong as thunder, and yet so quick, so delicately swift, it is almost unbearable. As he draws near to the swing, the climax, the ecstasy, he seems to lie in wait, there is a sense of a great strength crouching ready. Then it rushes forth, liquid, perfect, transcendent, the woman swoons over in the dance, and it goes on, enjoyment, infinite, incalculable enjoyment. He is like a god, a strange natural phenomenon, most intimate and compelling, wonderful.

(25) But he is not a human being. The woman, somewhere shocked in her independent soul, begins to fall away from him. She has another being, which he has not touched, and which she will fall back upon. The dance is over, she will fall back on herself. It is perfect, too perfect.

(26) During the next dance, while she is in the power of the educated Ettore, a perfect and calculated voluptuary, who knows how much he can get out of this Northern woman and only how much, the wood-cutter stands on the edge of darkness, in the open doorway, and watches. He is fixed upon her, established, perfect. And all the while she is aware of the insistent hawk-like poising of the face of the wood-cutter, poised on the edge of the darkness, in the doorway, in possession, unrelinquishing.

(27) And she is angry. There is something stupid, absurd, in the hard, talon-like eyes watching so fiercely and so confidently in the doorway, sure, unmitigated. Has the creature no sense?

(28) The woman reacts from him. For some time she will take no notice of him. But he waits, fixed. Then she comes near to him, and his will seems to take hold of her. He looks at her with a strange, proud, inhuman confidence, as if his influence with her was already accomplished.

(29) "Venga—venga un po'," he says, jerking his head strangely to the darkness.

(30) "What?" she replies, and passes shaken and dilated and

brilliant, consciously ignoring him, passes away among the others, among those who are safe.

(31) There is food in the kitchen, great hunks of bread, sliced sausage that Maria has made, wine, and a little coffee. But only the quality come to eat. The peasants may not come in. There is eating and drinking in the little house, the guitars are silent. It is eleven o'clock.

(32) Then there is singing, the strange bestial singing of these hills. Sometimes the guitars can play an accompaniment, but usually not. Then the men lift up their heads and send out the high, half-howling music, astounding. The words are in dialect. They argue among themselves for a moment: will the Signora understand? They sing. The Signora does not understand in the least. So with a strange, slightly malignant triumph, the men sing all the verses of their song, sitting round the walls of the little parlour. Their throats move, their faces have a slight mocking style. The boy capers in the doorway like a faun, with glee, his straight black hair falling over his forehead. The elder brother sits straight and flushed, but even his eyes glitter with a kind of yellow light of laughter. Paolo also sits quiet, with the invisible smile on his face. Only Maria, large and active, prospering now, keeps collected, ready to order a shrill silence in the same way as she orders the peasants violently, to keep their places.

(33) The boy comes to me and says:

(34) "Do you know, Signore, what they are singing?"

(35) "No," I say.

(36) So he capers with furious glee. The men with the watch-ful eyes, all roused, sit round the wall and sing more distinctly:

"Si verrà la primavera
Fiorann'le mandoline,
Vienn' di basso le Trentine
Coi 'taliani far' l'amor."

But the next verses are so improper that I pretend not to understand. The women, with wakened, dilated faces, are listening, listening hard, their two faces beautiful in their attention, as if listening to something magical, a long way off. And the men sitting round the wall sing more plainly, coming nearer to the correct Italian. The song comes loud and vibrating and maliciously from their reedy throats, it penetrates everybody. The foreign women can understand the sound, they can feel the malicious, suggestive mockery. But they cannot catch the words. The smile becomes more dangerous on the faces of the men.

(37) Then Maria Fiori sees that I have understood, and she cries, in her loud, overriding voice:

(38) "Basta—basta."

(39) The men get up, straighten their bodies with a curious, offering movement. The guitars and mandolins strike the vibrating strings. But the vague Northern reserve has come over the English-women. They dance again, but without the fusion in the dance. They have had enough.

(40) The musicians are thanked, they rise and go into the night. The men pass off in pairs. But the wood-cutter, whose name and whose nickname I could never hear, still hovered on the edge of the darkness.

(41) Then Maria sent him also away, complaining that he was too wild, *proprio selvatico,* and only the "quality" remained, the well-to-do youths from below. There was a little more coffee, and a talking, a story of a man who had fallen over a declivity in a lonely part going home drunk in the evening, and had lain unfound for eighteen hours. Then a story of a donkey who had kicked a youth in the chest and killed him.

(42) But the women were tired, they would go to bed. Still the two young men would not go away. We all went out to look at the night.

(43) The stars were very bright overhead, the mountain opposite and the mountains behind us faintly outlined themselves on the sky. Below, the lake was a black gulf. A little wind blew cold from the Adige.

(44) In the morning the visitors had gone. They had insisted on staying the night. They had eaten eight eggs each and much bread at one o'clock in the morning. Then they had gone to sleep, lying on the floor in the sitting-room.

(45) In the early sunshine they had drunk coffee and gone down to the village on the lake. Maria was very pleased. She would have made a good deal of money. The young men were rich. Her cupidity seemed like her very blossom.

Questions

1. In Paragraph 1 Lawrence is perhaps a cynical, knowing observer of Italian life. What is he in Paragraph 2? Does the quick shift imply uncertainty of point of view, or what? In your answer, make use of what seems to you to be Lawrence's general point of view throughout the essay.

2. What seems to be the focus of Lawrence's attention in Paragraph 4: the visible scene? the kind of music? Italian custom and behavior? Which of these things—if any of them—preoccupies him in Paragraphs 3, 5, and 6? Taking the four paragraphs together, can you define Lawrence's dominant interest?

3. From what physical perspective is it likely that Lawrence is observing the dance in Paragraph 14? How much of the detail of the paragraph may be said to depend upon that perspective?

4. Paragraph 14 has interesting qualities: apparent contradictions (the dance is "leisurely" yet "intense," "had always a kind of . . . dignity" yet "passed into a possession," grows "swifter and more intense" at the same time that the women are "drifting"), extreme use of repetition and qualification ("a trailing kind of polka-waltz, intimate, passionate, yet never hurried, never violent in its passion, always becoming more intense"), odd metaphors ("women . . . palpitating," "worked . . . their thighs . . . more vividly"), the employment of one long sentence, covering most of the paragraph, to describe the dance. What point of view do these qualities establish? What relationship of Lawrence to the dancers is suggested in the following lines: "taking perfect, oh, exquisite delight . . . and drawing nearer to a climax, nearer, till, oh, there was the surpassing lift"?

5. At one point in Paragraphs 20 through 28 Lawrence speaks in a tone of voice—hence from a point of view—that is not his own. Where is it? How do you know? Where else in these same paragraphs might it be said that Lawrence comes close to assuming someone else's tone of voice? If it were asserted that in these paragraphs Lawrence's identity dissolves into that of one of the persons he describes, who do you suppose would be meant: the wood-cutter, the woman, or Ettore? Explain, discussing the values at issue in his preference.

6. What pejorative weight does Lawrence give to "bestial," "half-howling," and "malignant" in the long paragraph preceding the verse?

7. With your answers to previous questions in mind, what would you say are Lawrence's assumptions about the values that should govern human existence?

8. Lawrence avoids referring to himself in most of the essay, but he is very much present. What would you say is the most important way in which his presence is felt? Discuss.

NOTES ON THE ENGLISH CHARACTER

E. M. FORSTER

Forster's interest in the English character, reflected in the essay
that follows, has been a lasting one, and has influenced the
concerns of his fiction, where his habit is frequently to explore
his countrymen as they respond under the pressures of a foreign setting—Italy in both *Where Angels Fear to Tread* and
A Room with a View, India in *A Passage to India.* In *Howards End,* he shifts his focus to England, providing a penetrating glimpse into English social history of the late nineteenth
and early twentieth centuries. Forster himself has spent much
of his later life in leisurely retirement, at Abinger, a small
village in Surrey, and at Cambridge. (Further information on
Forster appears on pp. 188, 362.)

(1) *First Note.* I had better let the cat out of the bag at once and
record my opinion that the character of the English is essentially
middle-class. There is a sound historical reason for this, for, since
the end of the eighteenth century, the middle classes have been the
dominant force in our community. They gained wealth by the Industrial Revolution, political power by the Reform Bill of 1832; they
are connected with the rise and organization of the British Empire;
they are responsible for the literature of the nineteenth century. Solidity, caution, integrity, efficiency. Lack of imagination, hypocrisy.
These qualities characterize the middle classes in every country, but
in England they are national characteristics also, because only in
England have the middle classes been in power for one hundred and
fifty years. Napoleon, in his rude way, called us "a nation of shop-

keepers." We prefer to call ourselves "a great commercial nation"—
it sounds more dignified—but the two phrases amount to the same.
Of course there are other classes: there is an aristocracy, there are
the poor. But it is on the middle classes that the eye of the critic
rests—just as it rests on the poor in Russia and on the aristocracy
in Japan. Russia is symbolized by the peasant or by the factory
worker; Japan by the samurai; the national figure of England is Mr.
Bull with his top hat, his comfortable clothes, his substantial stomach, and his substantial balance at the bank. Saint George may caper
on banners and in the speeches of politicians, but it is John Bull who
delivers the goods. And even Saint George—if Gibbon is correct—
wore a top hat once; he was an army contractor and supplied indifferent bacon. It all amounts to the same in the end.

(2) *Second Note.* Just as the heart of England is the middle
classes, so the heart of the middle classes is the public-school system.
This extraordinary institution is local. It does not even exist all over
the British Isles. It is unknown in Ireland, almost unknown in Scot-
land (countries excluded from my survey), and though it may inspire
other great institutions—Aligarh, for example, and some of the
schools in the United States—it remains unique, because it was
created by the Anglo-Saxon middle classes, and can flourish only
where they flourish. How perfectly it expresses their character—far
better, for instance, than does the university, into which social and
spiritual complexities have already entered. With its boarding-
houses, its compulsory games, its system of prefects and fagging, its
insistence on good form and on *esprit de corps,* it produces a type
whose weight is out of all proportion to its numbers.

(3) On leaving his school, the boy either sets to work at once—
goes into the army or into business, or emigrates—or else proceeds
to the university, and after three or four years there enters some
other profession—becomes a barrister, doctor, civil servant, school-
master, or journalist. (If through some mishap he does not become
a manual worker or an artist.) In all these careers his education, or
the absence of it, influences him. Its memories influence him also.
Many men look back on their school days as the happiest of their
lives. They remember with regret that golden time when life, though
hard, was not yet complex; when they all worked together and

played together and thought together, so far as they thought at all; when they were taught that school is the world in miniature, and believed that no one can love his country who does not love his school. And they prolong that time as best they can by joining their Old Boys' society; indeed, some of them remain Old Boys and nothing else for the rest of their lives. They attribute all good to the school. They worship it. They quote the remark that "the battle of Waterloo was won on the playing-fields of Eton." It is nothing to them that the remark is inapplicable historically and was never made by the Duke of Wellington, and that the Duke of Wellington was an Irishman. They go on quoting it because it expresses their sentiments; they feel that if the Duke of Wellington didn't make it he ought to have, and if he wasn't an Englishman he ought to have been. And they go forth into a world that is not entirely composed of public-school men or even of Anglo-Saxons, but of men who are as various as the sands of the sea; into a world of whose richness and subtlety they have no conception. They go forth into it with well-developed bodies, fairly developed minds, and undeveloped hearts. And it is this undeveloped heart that is largely responsible for the difficulties of Englishmen abroad. An undeveloped heart—not a cold one. The difference is important, and on it my next note will be based.

(4) For it is not that the Englishman can't feel—it is that he is afraid to feel. He has been taught at his public school that feeling is bad form. He must not express great joy or sorrow, or even open his mouth too wide when he talks—his pipe might fall out if he did. He must bottle up his emotions, or let them out only on a very special occasion.

(5) Once upon a time (this is an anecdote) I went for a week's holiday on the Continent with an Indian friend. We both enjoyed ourselves and were sorry when the week was over, but on parting our behavior was absolutely different. He was plunged in despair. He felt that because the holiday was over all happiness was over until the world ended. He could not express his sorrow too much. But in me the Englishman came out strong. I reflected that we should meet again in a month or two, and could write in the interval if we had anything to say; and under these circumstances I could

not see what there was to make a fuss about. It wasn't as if we were parting forever or dying. "Buck up," I said, "do buck up." He refused to buck up, and I left him plunged in gloom.

(6) The conclusion of the anecdote is even more instructive. For when we met the next month our conversation threw a good deal of light on the English character. I began by scolding my friend. I told him that he had been wrong to feel and display so much emotion upon so slight an occasion; that it was inappropriate. The word "inappropriate" roused him to fury. "What?" he cried. "Do you measure out your emotions as if they were potatoes?" I did not like the simile of the potatoes, but after a moment's reflection I said, "Yes, I do; and what's more, I think I ought to. A small occasion demands a little emotion, just as a large occasion demands a great one. I would like my emotions to be appropriate. This may be measuring them like potatoes, but it is better than slopping them about like water from a pail, which is what you did." He did not like the simile of the pail. "If those are your opinions, they part us forever," he cried, and left the room. Returning immediately, he added: "No—but your whole attitude toward emotion is wrong. Emotion has nothing to do with appropriateness. It matters only that it shall be sincere. I happened to feel deeply. I showed it. It doesn't matter whether I ought to have felt deeply or not."

(7) This remark impressed me very much. Yet I could not agree with it, and said that I valued emotion as much as he did, but used it differently; if I poured it out on small occasions I was afraid of having none left for the great ones, and of being bankrupt at the crises of life. Note the word "bankrupt." I spoke as a member of a prudent middle-class nation, always anxious to meet my liabilities. But my friend spoke as an Oriental, and the Oriental has behind him a tradition, not of middle-class prudence, but of kingly munificence and splendour. He feels his resources are endless, just as John Bull feels his are finite. As regards material resources, the Oriental is clearly unwise. Money isn't endless. If we spend or give away all the money we have, we haven't any more, and must take the consequences, which are frequently unpleasant. But, as regards the resources of the spirit, he may be right. The emotions may be endless. The more we express them, the more we have to express.

> *True love in this differs from gold and clay,*
> *That to divide is not to take away,*

says Shelley. Shelley, at all events, believes that the wealth of the spirit is endless; that we may express it copiously, passionately, and always; and that we can never feel sorrow or joy too acutely.

(8) In the above anecdote, I have figured as a typical Englishman. I will now descend from that dizzy and somewhat unfamiliar height, and return to my business of note-taking. A note on the *slowness* of the English character. The Englishman appears to be cold and unemotional because he is really slow. When an event happens, he may understand it quickly enough with his mind, but he takes quite a while to feel it. Once upon a time a coach, containing some Englishmen and some Frenchmen, was driving over the Alps. The horses ran away, and as they were dashing across a bridge the coach caught on the stonework, tottered, and nearly fell into the ravine below. The Frenchmen were frantic with terror: they screamed and gesticulated and flung themselves about, as Frenchmen would. The Englishmen sat quite calm. An hour later the coach drew up at an inn to change horses, and by that time the situations were exactly reversed. The Frenchmen had forgotten all about the danger, and were chattering gaily; the Englishmen had just begun to feel it, and one had a nervous breakdown and was obliged to go to bed. We have here a clear physical difference between the two races—a difference that goes deep into character. The Frenchmen responded at once; the Englishmen responded in time. They were slow and they were also practical. Their instinct forbade them to throw themselves about in the coach, because it was more likely to tip over if they did. They had this extraordinary appreciation of *fact* that we shall notice again and again. When a disaster comes, the English instinct is to do what can be done first, and to postpone the feeling as long as possible. Hence they are splendid at emergencies. No doubt they are brave—no one will deny that—but bravery is partly an affair of the nerves, and the English nervous system is well equipped for meeting a physical emergency. It acts promptly and feels slowly. Such a combination is fruitful, and anyone who possesses it has gone a long way toward being brave. And when the action is over, then the Englishman can feel.

(9) There is one more consideration—a most important one. If the English nature is cold, how is it that it has produced a great literature that is particularly great in poetry? Judged by its prose, English literature would not stand in the first rank. It is its poetry that raises it to the level of Greek, Persian, or French. And yet the English are supposed to be so unpoetical. How is this? The nation that produced the Elizabethan drama and the Lake Poets cannot be a cold, unpoetical nation. We can't get fire out of ice. Since literature always rests upon national character, there must be in the English nature hidden springs of fire to produce the fire we see. The warm sympathy, the romance, the imagination, that we look for in Englishmen whom we meet, and too often vainly look for, must exist in the nation as a whole, or we could not have this outburst of national song. An undeveloped heart—not a cold one.

(10) The trouble is that the English nature is not at all easy to understand. It has a great air of simplicity, it advertises itself as simple, but the more we consider it, the greater the problems we shall encounter. People talk of the mysterious East, but the West also is mysterious. It has depths that do not reveal themselves at the first gaze. We know what the sea looks like from a distance: it is of one colour, and level, and obviously cannot contain such creatures as fish. But if we look into the sea over the edge of a boat, we see a dozen colours, and depth below depth, and fish swimming in them. That sea is the English character—apparently imperturbable and even. The depths and the colours are the English romanticism and the English sensitiveness—we do not expect to find such things, but they exist. And—to continue my metaphor—the fish are the English emotions, which are always trying to get up to the surface, but don't quite know how. For the most part we see them moving far below, distorted and obscure. Now and then they succeed and we exclaim, "Why, the Englishman has emotions! He· actually can feel!" And occasionally we see that beautiful creature the flying fish, which rises out of the water altogether into the air and the sunlight. English literature is a flying fish. It is a sample of the life that goes on day after day beneath the surface; it is a proof that beauty and emotion exist in the salt, inhospitable sea.

(11) And now let's get back to terra firma. The Englishman's attitude toward criticism will give us another starting-point. He is not

annoyed by criticism. He listens or not as the case may be, smiles and passes on, saying, "Oh, the fellow's jealous"; "Oh, I'm used to Bernard Shaw; monkey tricks don't hurt me." It never occurs to him that the fellow may be accurate as well as jealous, and that he might do well to take the criticism to heart and profit by it. It never strikes him—except as a form of words—that he is capable of improvement; his self-complacency is abysmal. Other nations, both Oriental and European, have an uneasy feeling that they are not quite perfect. In consequence they resent criticism. It hurts them; and their snappy answers often mask a determination to improve themselves. Not so the Englishman. He has no uneasy feeling. Let the critics bark. And the "tolerant humorous attitude" with which he confronts them is not really tolerant, because it is insensitive, and not really humorous, because it is bounded by the titter and the guffaw.

(12) Turn over the pages of *Punch*. There is neither wit, laughter, nor satire in our national jester—only the snigger of a suburban householder who can understand nothing that does not resemble himself. Week after week, under Mr. Punch's supervision, a man falls off his horse, or a colonel misses a golf ball, or a little girl makes a mistake in her prayers. Week after week ladies show not too much of their legs, foreigners are deprecated, originality condemned. Week after week a bricklayer does not do as much work as he ought and a futurist does more than he need. It is all supposed to be so good-tempered and clean; it is also supposed to be funny. It is actually an outstanding example of our attitude toward criticism: the middle-class Englishman, with a smile on his clean-shaven lips, is engaged in admiring himself and ignoring the rest of mankind. If, in those colourless pages, he came across anything that really was funny—a drawing by Max Beerbohm, for instance—his smile would disappear, and he would say to himself, "The fellow's a bit of a crank," and pass on.

(13) This particular attitude reveals such insensitiveness as to suggest a more serious charge: is the Englishman altogether indifferent to the things of the spirit? Let us glance for a moment at his religion—not, indeed, at his theology, which would not merit inspection, but at the action on his daily life of his belief in the

unseen. Here again his attitude is practical. But an innate decency comes out: he is thinking of others rather than of himself. Right conduct is his aim. He asks of his religion that it shall make him a better man in daily life; that he shall be more kind, more just, more merciful, more desirous to fight what is evil and to protect what is good. No one could call this a low conception. It is, as far as it goes, a spiritual one. Yet—and this seems to me typical of the race—it is only half the religious idea. Religion is more than an ethical code with a divine sanction. It is also a means through which man may get into direct connection with the divine, and, judging by history, few Englishmen have succeeded in doing this. We have produced no series of prophets, as has Judaism or Islam. We have not even produced a Joan of Arc, or a Savonarola. We have produced few saints. In Germany the Reformation was due to the passionate conviction of Luther. In England it was due to a palace intrigue. We can show a steady level of piety, a fixed determination to live decently according to our lights—little more.

(14) Well, it is something. It clears us of the charge of being an unspiritual nation. That facile contrast between the spiritual East and the materialistic West can be pushed too far. The West also is spiritual. Only it expresses its belief, not in fasting and visions, not in prophetic rapture, but in the daily round, the common task. An incomplete expression, if you like. I agree. But the argument underlying these scattered notes is that the Englishman is an incomplete person. Not a cold or an unspiritual one. But undeveloped, incomplete.

(15) The attitude of the average orthodox Englishman is often misunderstood. It is thought that he must know that a doctrine—say, like that of the Trinity—is untrue. Moslems in particular feel that his faith is a dishonest compromise between polytheism and monotheism. The answer to this criticism is that the average orthodox Englishman is no theologian. He regards the Trinity as a mystery that it is not his place to solve. "I find difficulties enough in daily life," he will say. "I concern myself with those. As for the Trinity, it is a doctrine handed down to me from my fathers, whom I respect, and I hope to hand it down to my sons, and that they will respect me. No doubt it is true, or it would not have been handed down.

And no doubt the clergy could explain it to me if I asked them; but, like myself, they are busy men, and I will not take up their time."

(16) In such an answer there is confusion of thought, if you like, but no conscious deceit, which is alien to the English nature. The Englishman's deceit is generally unconscious.

(17) For I have suggested earlier that the English are sometimes hypocrites, and it is now my duty to develop this rather painful subject. Hypocrisy is the prime charge that is always brought against us. The Germans are called brutal, the Spanish cruel, the Americans superficial, and so on; but we are perfide Albion, the island of hypocrites, the people who have built up an Empire with a Bible in one hand, a pistol in the other, and financial concessions in both pockets. Is the charge true? I think it is; but while making it we must be quite clear as to what we mean by hypocrisy. Do we mean *conscious* deceit? Well, the English are comparatively guiltless of this; they have little of the Renaissance villain about them. Do we mean *unconscious* deceit? Muddle-headedness? Of this I believe them to be guilty. When an Englishman has been led into a course of wrong action, he has nearly always begun by muddling himself. A public-school education does not make for mental clearness, and he possesses to a very high degree the power of confusing his own mind. We have seen this tendency at work in the domain of theology; how does it work in the domain of conduct?

(18) Jane Austen may seem an odd authority to cite, but Jane Austen has, within her limits, a marvellous insight into the English mind. Her range is limited, her characters never attempt any of the more scarlet sins. But she has a merciless eye for questions of conduct, and the classical example of two English people muddling themselves before they embark upon a wrong course of action is to be found in the opening chapters of *Sense and Sensibility*. Old Mr. Dashwood has just died. He has been twice married. By his first marriage he has a son, John; by his second marriage three daughters. The son is well off; the young ladies and their mother—for Mr. Dashwood's second wife survives him—are badly off. He has called his son to his death-bed and has solemnly adjured him to provide for the second family. Much moved, the young man promises, and mentally decides to give each of his sisters a thousand pounds; and

then the comedy begins. For he announces his generous intention to his wife, and Mrs. John Dashwood by no means approves of depriving their own little boy of so large a sum. The thousand pounds are accordingly reduced to five hundred. But even this seems rather much. Might not an annuity to the stepmother be less of a wrench? Yes—but though less of a wrench it might be more of a drain, for "she is very stout and healthy, and scarcely forty." An occasional present of fifty pounds will be better, "and will, I think, be amply discharging my promise to my father." Or, better still, an occasional present of fish. And in the end nothing is done, nothing; the four impecunious ladies are not even helped in the moving of their furniture.

(19) Well, are the John Dashwoods hypocrites? It depends upon our definition of hypocrisy. The young man could not see his evil impulses as they gathered force and gained on him. And even his wife, though a worse character, is also self-deceived. She reflects that old Mr. Dashwood may have been out of his mind at his death. She thinks of her own little boy—and surely a mother ought to think of her own child. She has muddled herself so completely that in one sentence she can refuse the ladies the income that would enable them to keep a carriage and in the next can say that they will not be keeping a carriage and so will have no expenses. No doubt men and women in other lands can muddle themselves, too, yet the state of mind of Mr. and Mrs. John Dashwood seems to me typical of England. They are slow—they take time even to do wrong; whereas people in other lands do wrong quickly.

(20) There are national faults as there are national diseases, and perhaps one can draw a parallel between them. It has always impressed me that the national diseases of England should be cancer and consumption—slow, insidious, pretending to be something else; while the diseases proper to the South should be cholera and plague, which strike at a man when he is perfectly well and may leave him a corpse by evening. Mr. and Mrs. John Dashwood are moral consumptives. They collapse gradually without realizing what the disease is. There is nothing dramatic or violent about their sin. You cannot call them villains.

(21) Here is the place to glance at some of the other charges

that have been brought against the English as a nation. They have, for instance, been accused of treachery, cruelty, and fanaticism. In these charges I have never been able to see the least point, because treachery and cruelty are conscious sins. The man knows he is doing wrong, and does it deliberately, like Tartuffe or Iago. He betrays his friend because he wishes to. He tortures his prisoners because he enjoys seeing the blood flow. He worships the Devil because he prefers evil to good. From villainies such as these the average Englishman is free. His character, which prevents his rising to certain heights, also prevents him from sinking to these depths. Because he doesn't produce mystics he doesn't produce villains either; he gives the world no prophets, but no anarchists, no fanatics—religious or political.

(22) Of course there are cruel and treacherous people in England —one has only to look at the police courts—and examples of public infamy can be found, such as the Amritsar massacre. But one does not look at the police courts or the military mind to find the soul of any nation; and the more English people one meets the more convinced one becomes that the charges as a whole are untrue. Yet foreign critics often make them. Why? Partly because they fix their eyes on the criminal classes, partly because they are annoyed with certain genuine defects in the English character, and in their irritation throw in cruelty in order to make the problem simpler. Moral indignation is always agreeable, but nearly always misplaced. It is indulged in both by the English and by the critics of the English. They all find it great fun. The drawback is that while they are amusing themselves the world becomes neither wiser nor better.

(23) The main point of these notes is that the English character is incomplete. No national character is complete. We have to look for some qualities in one part of the world and others in another. But the English character is incomplete in a way that is particularly annoying to the foreign observer. It has a bad surface—self-complacent, unsympathetic, and reserved. There is plenty of emotion further down, but it never gets used. There is plenty of brain power, but it is more often used to confirm prejudices than to dispel them. With such an equipment the Englishman cannot be popular. Only I would repeat: there is little vice in him and no real coldness. It is the machinery that is wrong.

(24) I hope and believe myself that in the next twenty years we shall see a great change, and that the national character will alter into something that is less unique but more lovable. The supremacy of the middle classes is probably ending. What new element the working classes will introduce one cannot say, but at all events they will not have been educated at public schools. And whether these notes praise or blame the English character—that is only incidental. They are the notes of a student who is trying to get at the truth and would value the assistance of others. I believe myself that the truth is great and that it shall prevail. I have no faith in official caution and reticence. The cats are all out of their bags, and diplomacy cannot recall them. The nations *must* understand one another, and quickly; and without the interposition of their governments, for the shrinkage of the globe is throwing them into one another's arms. To that understanding these notes are a feeble contribution—notes on the English character as it has struck a novelist.

Questions

1. Forster lets two cats out of the bag: at the beginning and at the end. With what seriousness does he use the expression on each occasion? What point of view is suggested? If you see a difference in point of view, which one would you say is more characteristic of the essay?

2. At the end of the essay Forster identifies his point of view as that of a novelist. What aspects of the form of the essay and the means of argument and illustration suggest a novelist's point of view rather than, say, a sociologist's?

3. The basic assumption of the essay is implicit in the title phrase "English character." State the assumption in terms broad enough to include French and American character as well. At what point in the essay does Forster himself most seriously challenge the assumption?

4. If before the end of the eighteenth century the dominant force in England was the aristocracy, what—according to Forster's reasoning in the second sentence of Paragraph 1—would have been the essential character of the English people then? State the assumption that underlies his reasoning. Can you think of a country where such an assumption would not apply?

5. Is the anecdote about the French and English people in the carriage funny because it is convincing or convincing because it is funny? Would its

illustrative value be seriously damaged if one of the Frenchmen had drunk to excess at the inn? To what extent would you say Forster's point depends upon the validity of the anecdote as he has told it?

6. How detailed is Forster's analogy between English poetry and a flying fish? How much further might it be extended before it became untenable? Why is it so convincing as it stands?

7. What assumptions about the relationship of character to behavior, action, and thought underlie Forster's discussion of the Englishman's response to criticism, his spirituality, and his theology? Can you think of any contrasting assumptions that would seem reasonable?

8. What does Forster assume about the relationship of literature to life when he uses *Punch* to support his argument? What contrasting assumption might preclude his using the magazine so? What slightly different assumption about the relationship of literature to life does Forster make in discussing *Sense and Sensibility*? Do you find one assumption more convincing than the other?

9. What elements in the earlier "notes" prepare the reader for the sense of urgency to which the essay rises at the end? How would you describe Forster's overall point of view in the essay?

10. Forster says that the English are solid, cautious, honest, efficient, unimaginative, and hypocritical. To what extent would you say that the same qualities characterize Americans? Does your answer suggest that Americans and English are very much alike, that a half-dozen terms are inadequate to define national character, or what? Discuss.

A VERY YOUNG PERSON

RUDYARD KIPLING

Rudyard Kipling (1865–1936) is best remembered for his poetry (*Barrack-Room Ballads*), short stories (*Soldiers Three*), and novels (*Kim*) relating to India. Born in Bombay, of English parents, he was sent to England for his education, but returned to India in preference to attending an English university. He became, at seventeen, a reporter for a local newspaper, and also began writing poetry and short stories, issuing no less than fifteen volumes in the years 1888–1891. These captured the life of India as no Western writer had previously and brought him early fame. Though he soon left India for world travel, a stay in the United States, and finally a home in England, he continued to draw on his early experiences, perhaps most memorably in the *Jungle Books* and *Kim*. He received a Nobel Prize in 1907.

Give me the first six years of a child's life and you can have the rest.

(1) Looking back from this my seventieth year, it seems to me that every card in my working life has been dealt me in such a manner that I had but to play it as it came. Therefore, ascribing all good fortune to Allah the Dispenser of Events, I begin:—

(2) My first impression is of daybreak, light and colour and golden and purple fruits at the level of my shoulder. This would be the memory of early morning walks to the Bombay fruit market with my *ayah* and later with my sister in her perambulator, and of our returns with our purchases piled high on the bows of it. Our

From *Something of Myself*, by Rudyard Kipling. Copyright 1937 by Caroline Kipling. Reprinted by permission of Mrs. George Bambridge and Doubleday & Co., Inc.

ayah was a Portuguese Roman Catholic who would pray—I beside her—at a wayside Cross. Meeta, my Hindu bearer, would sometimes go into little Hindu temples where, being below the age of caste, I held his hand and looked at the dimly seen, friendly Gods.

(3) Our evening walks were by the sea in the shadow of palm-groves which, I think, were called the Mahim Woods. When the wind blew the great nuts would tumble, and we fled—my *ayah* and my sister in her perambulator—to the safety of the open. I have always felt the menacing darkness of tropical eventides, as I have loved the voices of night-winds through palm or banana leaves, and the song of the tree-frogs.

(4) There were far-going Arab dhows on the pearly waters, and gaily dressed Parsees wading out to worship the sunset. Of their creed I knew nothing, nor did I know that near our little house on the Bombay Esplanade were the Towers of Silence, where their Dead are exposed to the waiting vultures on the rim of the towers, who scuffle and spread wings when they see the bearers of the Dead below. I did not understand my mother's distress when she found "a child's hand" in our garden, and said I was not to ask questions about it. I wanted to see that child's hand. But my *ayah* told me.

(5) In the afternoon heats before we took our sleep, she or Meeta would tell us stories and Indian nursery songs all unforgotten, and we were sent into the dining-room after we had been dressed, with the caution "Speak English now to Papa and Mamma." So one spoke "English," haltingly translated out of the vernacular idiom that one thought and dreamed in. The Mother sang wonderful songs at a black piano and would go out to Big Dinners. Once she came back, very quickly, and told me, still awake, that "the Big Lord Sahib" had been killed and there was to be no Big Dinner. This was Lord Mayo, assassinated by a native. Meeta explained afterwards that he had been "hit with a knife." Meeta unconsciously saved me from any night terrors or dread of the dark. Our *ayah,* with a servant's curious mixture of deep affection and shallow device, had told me that a stuffed leopard's head on the nursery wall was there to see that I went to sleep. But Meeta spoke of it scornfully as "the head of an animal," and I took it off my mind as a fetish, good or bad, for it was only some unspecified "animal."

(6) Far across green spaces round the house was a marvellous place filled with smells of paints and oils, and lumps of clay with which I played. That was the atelier of my Father's School of Art, and a Mr. "Terry Sahib" his assistant, to whom my small sister was devoted, was our great friend. Once, on the way there alone, I passed the edge of a huge ravine a foot deep, where a winged monster as big as myself attacked me, and I fled and wept. My Father drew for me a picture of the tragedy with a rhyme beneath:—

> There was a small boy in Bombay
> Who once from a hen ran away.
>   When they said: "You're a baby,"
>   He replied: "Well, I may be:
> But I don't like these hens of Bombay."

This consoled me. I have thought well of hens ever since.

(7) Then those days of strong light and darkness passed, and there was a time in a ship with an immense semi-circle blocking all vision on each side of her. (She must have been the old paddle-wheel P. & O. *Ripon.*) There was a train across a desert (the Suez Canal was not yet opened) and a halt in it, and a small girl wrapped in a shawl on the seat opposite me, whose face stands out still. There was next a dark land, and a darker room full of cold, in one wall of which a white woman made naked fire, and I cried aloud with dread, for I had never before seen a grate.

(8) Then came a new small house smelling of aridity and emptiness, and a parting in the dawn with Father and Mother, who said that I must learn quickly to read and write so that they might send me letters and books.

(9) I lived in that house for close on six years. It belonged to a woman who took in children whose parents were in India. She was married to an old Navy Captain, who had been a midshipman at Navarino, and had afterwards been entangled in a harpoon-line while whale-fishing, and dragged down till he miraculously freed himself. But the line had scarred his ankle for life—a dry, black scar, which I used to look at with horrified interest.

(10) The house itself stood in the extreme suburbs of Southsea,

next to a Portsmouth unchanged in most particulars since Trafalgar
—the Portsmouth of Sir Walter Besant's *By Celia's Arbour*. The
timber for a Navy that was only experimenting with iron-clads such
as the *Inflexible* lay in great booms in the Harbour. The little training-
brigs kept their walks opposite Southsea Castle, and Portsmouth
Hard was as it had always been. Outside these things lay the desolation of Hayling Island, Lumps Fort, and the isolated hamlet of
Milton. I would go for long walks with the Captain, and once he
took me to see a ship called the *Alert* (or *Discovery*) returned from
Arctic explorations, her decks filled with old sledges and lumber, and
her spare rudder being cut up for souvenirs. A sailor gave me a
piece, but I lost it. Then the old Captain died, and I was sorry, for
he was the only person in that house as far as I can remember who
ever threw me a kind word.

(11) It was an establishment run with the full vigour of the
Evangelical as revealed to the Woman. I had never heard of Hell,
so I was introduced to it in all its terrors—I and whatever luckless
little slavey might be in the house, whom severe rationing had led
to steal food. Once I saw the Woman beat such a girl who picked
up the kitchen poker and threatened retaliation. Myself I was regularly beaten. The Woman had an only son of twelve or thirteen as
religious as she. I was a real joy to him, for when his mother had
finished with me for the day he (we slept in the same room) took
me on and roasted the other side.

(12) If you cross-examine a child of seven or eight on his day's
doings (specially when he wants to go to sleep) he will contradict
himself very satisfactorily. If each contradiction be set down as a
lie and retailed at breakfast, life is not easy. I have known a certain
amount of bullying, but this was calculated torture—religious as
well as scientific. Yet it made me give attention to the lies I soon
found it necessary to tell: and this, I presume, is the foundation of
literary effort.

(13) But my ignorance was my salvation. I was made to read
without explanation, under the usual fear of punishment. And on
a day that I remember it came to me that "reading" was not "the
Cat lay on the Mat," but a means to everything that would make me
happy. So I read all that came within my reach. As soon as my

pleasure in this was known, deprivation from reading was added to my punishments. I then read by stealth and the more earnestly.

(14) There were not many books in that house, but Father and Mother as soon as they heard I could read sent me priceless volumes. One I have still, a bound copy of *Aunt Judy's Magazine* of the early 'seventies, in which appeared Mrs. Ewing's *Six to Sixteen.* I owe more in circuitous ways to that tale than I can tell. I knew it, as I know it still, almost by heart. Here was a history of real people and real things. It was better than Knatchbull-Hugesson's *Tales at Tea-time,* better even than *The Old Shikarri* with its steel engravings of charging pigs and angry tigers. On another plane was an old magazine with Wordsworth's "I climbed the dark brow of the mighty Helvellyn." I knew nothing of its meaning but the words moved and pleased. So did other extracts from the poems of "A. Tennyson."

(15) A visitor, too, gave me a little purple book of severely moral tendency called *The Hope of the Katzikopfs*—about a bad boy made virtuous, but it contained verses that began, "Farewell Rewards and Fairies," and ended with an injunction "To pray for the 'noddle' of William Churne of Staffordshire." This bore fruit afterwards.

(16) And somehow or other I came across a tale about a lion-hunter in South Africa who fell among lions who were all Free-masons, and with them entered into a confederacy against some wicked baboons. I think that, too, lay dormant until the *Jungle Books* began to be born.

(17) There comes to my mind here a memory of two books of verse about child-life which I have tried in vain to identify. One—blue and fat—described "nine white wolves" coming "over the wold" and stirred me to the deeps; and also certain savages who "thought the name of England was something that could not burn."

(18) The other book—brown and fat—was full of lovely tales in strange metres. A girl was turned into a water-rat "as a matter of course"; an Urchin cured an old man of gout by means of a cool cabbage-leaf, and somehow "forty wicked Goblins" were mixed up in the plot; and a "Darling" got out on the house-leads with a broom and tried to sweep stars off the skies. It must have been an unusual

book for that age, but I have never been able to recover it, any more than I have a song that a nursemaid sang at low-tide in the face of the sunset on Littlehampton Sands when I was less than six. But the impression of wonder, excitement and terror and the red bars of failing light is as clear as ever.

(19) Among the servants in the House of Desolation was one from Cumnor, which name I associated with sorrow and darkness and a raven that "flapped its wings." Years later I identified the lines: "And thrice the Raven flapped her wing Around the towers of Cumnor Hall." But how and where I first heard the lines that cast the shadow is beyond me—unless it be that the brain holds everything that passes within reach of the senses, and it is only ourselves who do not know this.

(20) When my Father sent me a *Robinson Crusoe* with steel engravings I set up in business alone as a trader with savages (the wreck parts of the tale never much interested me), in a mildewy basement room where I stood my solitary confinements. My apparatus was a cocoanut shell strung on a red cord, a tin trunk, and a piece of packing-case which kept off any other world. Thus fenced about, everything inside the fence was quite real, but mixed with the smell of damp cupboards. If the bit of board fell, I had to begin the magic all over again. I have learned since from children who play much alone that this rule of "beginning again in a pretend game" is not uncommon. The magic, you see, lies in the ring or fence that you take refuge in.

(21) Once I remember being taken to a town called Oxford and a street called Holywell, where I was shown an Ancient of Days who, I was told, was the Provost of Oriel; wherefore I never understood, but conceived him to be some sort of idol. And twice or thrice we went, all of us, to pay a day-long visit to an old gentleman in a house in the country near Havant. Here everything was wonderful and unlike my world, and he had an old lady sister who was kind, and I played in hot, sweet-smelling meadows and ate all sorts of things.

(22) After such a visit I was once put through the third degree by the Woman and her son, who asked me if I had told the old gentleman that I was much fonder of him than was the Woman's

son. It must have been the tail-end of some sordid intrigue or other —the old gentleman being of kin to that unhappy pair—but it was beyond my comprehension. My sole concern had been a friendly pony in the paddock. My dazed attempts to clear myself were not accepted and, once again, the pleasure that I was seen to have taken was balanced by punishments and humiliation—above all humiliation. That alternation was quite regular. I can but admire the infernal laborious ingenuity of it all. *Exempli gratia.* Coming out of church once I smiled. The Devil-Boy demanded why. I said I didn't know, which was child's truth. He replied that I *must* know. People didn't laugh for nothing. Heaven knows what explanation I put forward; but it was duly reported to the Woman as a "lie." Result, afternoon upstairs with the Collect to learn. I learned most of the Collects that way and a great deal of the Bible. The son after three or four years went into a Bank and was generally too tired on his return to torture me, unless things had gone wrong with him. I learned to know what was coming from his step into the house.

(23) But, for a month each year I possessed a paradise which I verily believe saved me. Each December I stayed with my Aunt Georgy, my mother's sister, wife of Sir Edward Burne-Jones, at The Grange, North End Road. At first I must have been escorted there, but later I went alone, and arriving at the house would reach up to the open-work iron bell-pull on the wonderful gate that let me into all felicity. When I had a house of my own, and The Grange was emptied of meaning, I begged for and was given that bell-pull for my entrance, in the hope that other children might also feel happy when they rang it.

(24) At The Grange I had love and affection as much as the greediest, and I was not very greedy, could desire. There were most wonderful smells of paints and turpentine whiffing down from the big studio on the first floor where my Uncle worked; there was the society of my two cousins, and a sloping mulberry tree which we used to climb for our plots and conferences. There was a rocking-horse in the nursery and a table that, tilted up on two chairs, made a toboggan-slide of the best. There were pictures finished or half finished of lovely colours; and in the rooms chairs and cupboards such as the world had not yet seen, for William Morris (our Deputy

"Uncle Topsy") was just beginning to fabricate these things. There was an incessant come and go of young people and grown-ups all willing to play with us—except an elderly person called "Browning" who took no proper interest in the skirmishes which happened to be raging on his entry. Best of all, immeasurably, was the beloved Aunt herself reading us *The Pirate* or *The Arabian Nights* of evenings, when one lay out on the big sofas sucking toffee, and calling our cousins "Ho, Son," or "Daughter of my Uncle" or "O True Believer."

(25) Often the Uncle, who had a "golden voice," would assist in our evening play, though mostly he worked at black and white in the middle of our riots. He was never idle. We made a draped chair in the hall serve for the seat of "Norna of the Fitful Head" and addressed her questions till the Uncle got inside the rugs and gave us answers which thrilled us with delightful shivers, in a voice deeper than all the boots in the world. And once he descended in broad daylight with a tube of "Mummy Brown" in his hand, saying that he had discovered it was made of dead Pharaohs and we must bury it accordingly. So we all went out and helped—according to the rites of Mizraim and Memphis, I hope—and—to this day I could drive a spade within a foot of where that tube lies.

(26) At bedtime one hastened along the passages, where unfinished cartoons lay against the walls. The Uncle often painted in their eyes first, leaving the rest in charcoal—a most effective presentation. Hence our speed to our own top-landing, where we could hang over the stairs and listen to the loveliest sound in the world— deep-voiced men laughing together over dinner.

(27) It was a jumble of delights and emotions culminating in being allowed to blow the big organ in the studio for the beloved Aunt, while the Uncle worked, or "Uncle Topsy" came in full of some business of picture-frames or stained glass or general denunciations. Then it was hard to keep the little lead weight on its string below the chalk mark, and if the organ ran out in squeals the beloved Aunt would be sorry. Never, *never* angry!

(28) As a rule Morris took no notice of anything outside what was in his mind at the moment. But I remember one amazing exception. My cousin Margaret and I, then about eight, were in the

nursery eating pork-dripping on brown bread, which is .a dish for the Gods, when we heard "Uncle Topsy" in the hall calling, as he usually did, for "Ned" or "Georgie." The matter was outside our world. So we were the more impressed when, not finding the grown-ups, he came in and said he would tell us a story. We settled ourselves under the table which we used for a toboggan-slide and he, bravely as ever, climbed on to our big rocking-horse. There, slowly surging back and forth while the poor beast creaked, he told us a tale full of fascinating horrors, about a man who was condemned to dream bad dreams. One of them took the shape of a cow's tail waving from a heap of dried fish. He went away as abruptly as he had come. Long afterwards, when I was old enough to know a maker's pains, it dawned on me that we must have heard the Saga of Burnt Njal, which was then interesting him. In default of grown-ups, and pressed by need to pass the story between his teeth and clarify it, he had used us.

(29) But on a certain day—one tried to fend off the thought of it—the delicious dream would end, and one would return to the House of Desolation, and for the next two or three mornings there cry on waking up. Hence more punishments and cross-examinations.

(30) Often and often afterwards, the beloved Aunt would ask me why I had never told anyone how I was being treated. Children tell little more than animals, for what comes to them they accept as eternally established. Also, badly-treated children have a clear notion of what they are likely to get if they betray the secrets of a prison-house before they are clear of it.

(31) In justice to the Woman I can say that I was adequately fed. (I remember a gift to her of some red "fruit" called "tomatoes" which, after long consideration, she boiled with sugar; and they were very beastly. The tinned meat of those days was Australian beef with a crumbly fat, and string-boiled mutton, hard to get down.) Nor was my life an unsuitable preparation for my future, in that it demanded constant wariness, the habit of observation, and attendance on moods and tempers; the noting of discrepancies between speech and action; a certain reserve of demeanour; and automatic suspicion of sudden favours. Brother Lippo Lippi, in his own harder case, as a boy discovered:—

Why, soul and sense of him grow sharp alike,
He learns the look of things and none the less
For admonition.

So it was with me.

(32) My troubles settled themselves in a few years. My eyes
went wrong, and I could not well see to read. For which reason I
read the more and in bad lights. My work at the terrible little day-
school where I had been sent suffered in consequence, and my
monthly reports showed it. The loss of "reading-time" was the worst
of my "home" punishments for bad school-work. One report was so
bad that I threw it away and said that I had never received it. But this
is a hard world for the amateur liar. My web of deceit was swiftly
exposed—the Son spared time after banking-hours to help in the
auto-da-fé—and I was well beaten and sent to school through the
streets of Southsea with the placard "Liar" between my shoulders.
In the long run these things, and many more of the like, drained
me of any capacity for real, personal hate for the rest of my days.
So close must any life-filling passion lie to its opposite. "Who having
known the Diamond will concern himself with glass?"

(33) Some sort of nervous breakdown followed for I imagined I
saw shadows and things that were not there, and they worried me
more than the Woman. The beloved Aunt must have heard of it,
and a man came down to see me as to my eyes and reported that I
was half-blind. This, too, was supposed to be "showing-off," and I
was segregated from my sister—another punishment—as a sort of
moral leper. Then—I do not remember that I had any warning—
the Mother returned from India. She told me afterwards that when
she first came up to my room to kiss me good-night, I flung up an
arm to guard off the cuff that I had been trained to expect.

(34) I was taken at once from the House of Desolation, and for
months ran wild in a little farmhouse on the edge of Epping Forest,
where I was not encouraged to refer to my guilty past. Except for
my spectacles, which were uncommon in those days, I was completely happy with my Mother and the local society, which included
for me a gipsy of the name of Saville, who told me tales of selling
horses to the ignorant; the farmer's wife; her niece Patty who turned

a kind blind eye on our raids into the dairy; the postman; and the farm-boys. The farmer did not approve of my teaching one of his cows to stand and be milked in the field. My Mother drew the line at my return to meals red-booted from assisting at the slaughter of swine, or reeking after the exploration of attractive muck-heaps. These were the only restrictions I recall.

(35) A cousin, afterwards to be a Prime Minister, would come down on visits. The farmer said that we did each other "no good." Yet the worst I can remember was our self-sacrificing war against a wasp's nest on a muddy islet in a most muddy pond. Our only weapons were switches of broom, but we defeated the enemy un-scathed. The trouble at home centered round an enormous current roly-poly—a "spotted dog" a foot long. We took it away to sustain us in action and we heard a great deal about it from Patty in the even-ing.

(36) Then we went to London and stayed for some weeks in a tiny lodging-house in the semi-rural Brompton Road, kept by an ivory-faced, lordly-whiskered ex-butler and his patient wife. Here, for the first time, it happened that the night got into my head. I rose up and wandered about that still house till daybreak, when I slipped out into the little brick-walled garden and saw the dawn break. All would have been well but for Pluto, a pet toad brought back from Epping Forest, who lived mostly in one of my pockets. It struck me that he might be thirsty, and I stole into my Mother's room and would have given him drink from a water-jug. But it slipped and broke and very much was said. The ex-butler could not understand why I had stayed awake all night. I did not know then that such night-wakings would be laid upon me through my life; or that my fortunate hour would be on the turn of sunrise, with a sou'-west breeze afoot.

(37) The sorely tried Mother got my sister and me season-tickets for the old South Kensington Museum which was only across the road. (No need in those days to caution us against the traffic.) Very shortly we two, on account of our regular attendance (for the weather had turned wet), owned that place and one policeman in special. When we came with any grown-ups he saluted us mag-nificently. From the big Buddha with the little door in his back, to

the towering dull-gilt ancient coaches and carven chariots in long
dark corridors—even the places marked "private" where fresh treasures were always being unpacked—we roved at will, and divided
the treasures child-fashion. There were instruments of music inlaid
with lapis, beryl and ivories; glorious gold-fretted spinets and clavi-
chords; the bowels of the great Glastonbury clock; mechanical
models; steel- and silver-butted pistols, daggers and arquebusses—
the labels alone were an education; a collection of precious stones
and rings—we quarrelled over those—and a big bluish book
which was the manuscript of one of Dickens' novels. That man
seemed to me to have written very carelessly; leaving out lots which
he had to squeeze in between the lines afterwards.

(38) These experiences were a soaking in colour and design
with, above all, the proper Museum smell; and it stayed with me. By
the end of that long holiday I understood that my Mother had
written verses, that my Father "wrote things" also; that books and
pictures were among the most important affairs in the world; that
I could read as much as I chose and ask the meaning of things from
anyone I met. I had found out, too, that one could take pen and
set down what one thought, and that nobody accused one of "showing off" by so doing. I read a good deal; *Sidonia the Sorceress;* Emerson's poems; and Bret Harte's stories; and I learned all sorts of
verses for the pleasure of repeating them to myself in bed.

Questions

1. The first six paragraphs describe things Kipling remembers from his
first years in India, but many of these things would be the same for an
adult. Where in these paragraphs does he observe specifically from a
child's point of view, where specifically from an adult's point of view?
Explain.

2. Kipling obviously recalls more of his youth in India than he has
chosen to describe. What bias seems to prevail in his choices? Make a
judgment on the extent to which that bias implies the presence of an overall point of view.

3. Describe the dominant point of view in Paragraphs 7 and 8. What is
the effect of the parentheses in Paragraph 7 with regard to point of view?
Describe the shift that occurs in Paragraph 9.

4. The point of view in Paragraph 11 is particularly complex. From what perspective does Kipling say, "I was a real joy to him" and "he . . . roasted the other side"? Analyze other phrases such as "an establishment run with the full vigour of the Evangelical" and "luckless little slavey," and sum up, if possible, the point of view of the paragraph.

5. From what special child's point of view did Kipling regard life in the house at Portsmouth? Isolate four or five of his characteristics, and compare them with the characteristics he displayed at the Grange.

6. If the woman in the house at Portsmouth had a theory of child-training, what was it? On what assumptions about the nature of children would it be based?

7. The proverb Kipling uses as prelude to his essay minimizes all but the first six years of a child's life, but Kipling writes in detail about experiences (at the Grange, at the Museum) that take him well beyond his sixth year. How would you justify this apparent discrepancy?

8. In Paragraph 12 and elsewhere, Kipling remarks upon the development of his literary interests. What general assumptions about the origin and nature of writing underlie them?

9. Had Kipling had other experiences he would have been a different kind of writer; had he had other experiences he would not have been a writer at all. Make an argument in support of each of these assertions. Which of the two seems to you more satisfactory?

10. Read Randall Jarrell's essay that follows, and compare his and Kipling's views on the educational process.

THE SCHOOLS OF YESTERYEAR
(A ONE-SIDED DIALOGUE)

RANDALL JARRELL

Randall Jarrell (1914–1965) was born and raised in Tennessee, received his education at Vanderbilt University, and subsequently taught at a number of colleges and universities. Though he worked also at translating and editing, it is as a literary and cultural critic (*Poetry and the Age, A Sad Heart at the Supermarket*) and, most of all, as a poet that he is remembered. His poetry appears in several volumes—*Blood for a Stranger, The Seven-League Crutches, The Woman at the Washington Zoo*. His one novel, *Pictures from an Institution,* has an academic setting and is a further instance of his concern with the state of modern culture.

UNCLE WADSWORTH (*a deep, slightly grained or corrugated, comfortable-sounding voice, accompanied by an accordion*); School days, school days, dear old golden rule—
ALVIN (*Alvin's voice is young*): Stop, Uncle Wadsworth!
UNCLE WADSWORTH: Why should I stop, Alvin boy?
ALVIN: Because it isn't *so,* Uncle Wadsworth. (*With scorn.*) Dear old golden rule days! That's just nostalgia, just sentimentality. The man that wrote that song was just too old to remember what it was really like. Why, kids hated school in those days—they used to play hookey all the time. It's different now. Children *like* to go to school now.
UNCLE WADSWORTH: Finished, Alvin boy?
ALVIN: Finished, Uncle Wadsworth.

UNCLE WADSWORTH: School days, school days, dear old golden rule days, Readin' and 'ritin' and 'rithmetic, Taught to—

ALVIN: Stop, Uncle Wadsworth!

UNCLE WADSWORTH: Why should I stop this time, Alvin boy?

ALVIN: Reading and writing and arithmetic! What a curriculum! Why, it sounds like it was invented by an illiterate. How could a curriculum like that prepare you for life? No civics, no social studies, no hygiene; no home economics, no manual training, no physical education! And extra-curricular activities—where were they?

UNCLE WADSWORTH: Where indeed? Where are the extra-curricular activities of yesteryear? Shall I go on, Alvin boy?

ALVIN: Go ahead, Uncle Wadsworth.

UNCLE WADSWORTH: School days, school days, dear old golden rule days, Readin' and 'ritin' and 'rithmetic, Taught to the tune of a hick'ry stick—

ALVIN: Stop! Stop! Stop, Uncle Wadsworth! (*He pants with emotion.*) Honestly, Uncle, I don't see how you can bear to say it. *Taught to the tune of a hickory stick!* . . . Imagine having to *beat* poor little children with a *stick!* Thank God those dark old days of ignorance and fear and compulsion are over, and we just appeal to the child's better nature, and get him to adjust, and try to make him see that what he likes to do is what we want him to do.

UNCLE WADSWORTH: Finished, Alvin boy?

ALVIN: Finished, Uncle Wadsworth.

UNCLE WADSWORTH: Well, so am I. I can't seem to get going in this song—every fifty yards I get a puncture and have to stop for air. You go on for a while and let me interrupt you. Go ahead, Alvin.

ALVIN: Go ahead where?

UNCLE WADSWORTH: Go ahead about those dark old days of ignorance and fear and compulsion. It makes my flesh creep—and I'm just like the fat boy, I *like* to have my flesh creep.

ALVIN: What fat boy?

UNCLE WADSWORTH: The one in *Pickwick Papers*. (*Silence from Alvin.*) You know, *Pickwick Papers*. (*Silence from Alvin.*) It's a book, son—a book by Charles Dickens. Ever read any Dickens?

ALVIN: Oh, sure. I read *The Tale of Two Cities* in high school. And *Oliver Twist*—well, really I didn't read it exactly, I read it in *Illustrated Classics*. And I saw *Great Expectations* in the movies.

UNCLE WADSWORTH: Why, you and Dickens are old friends. But go on about the—the schools of yesteryear.

ALVIN: Well, I will, Uncle Wadsworth. After all, it's only because I was lucky enough to be born now that I didn't have to go to one of those schools myself. I can just see myself trudging to school barefooted in my overalls—because they didn't even have school buses then, you know—

UNCLE WADSWORTH: Not a one! If a school bus had come for me I'd have thought it was a patrol wagon someone had painted orange for Hallowe'en.

ALVIN: Well, there I am trudging along, and I'm not only trudging, I'm *limping*.

UNCLE WADSWORTH: Stub your toe?

ALVIN (*with bitter irony*): Stub my toe! I'm limping because I'm *sore*—sore all over, where the teacher beat me.

UNCLE WADSWORTH: All over isn't where the teacher beat you, Alvin boy—I know.

ALVIN: All right, all right! And when I get to the school is it the Consolidated School? Is there a lunch-room and a 'chute-the-'chute and a jungle-gym? Is it—is it like schools ought to be? Uh-*uh!* That school has one room, and it's *red*.

UNCLE WADSWORTH: You mean that even in those days the Communists—

ALVIN: No, no, not Red, *red!* Red like a barn. And when I get inside, the teacher is an old maid that looks like a broomstick, or else a man that looks like a—that looks like Ichabod Crane. And then this Crane-type teacher says to me, real stern: "Alvin McKinley, stand up! Are you aware, Alvin, that it is *three minutes past seven?*"

UNCLE WADSWORTH: Three minutes past seven! What on earth are you and Ichabod Crane doing in school at that ungodly hour?

ALVIN: That's when school starts then! Or six, maybe. . . . Then he says, pointing his finger at me in a terrible voice: "Three minutes tardy! And what, Alvin, what did I warn you would happen to you if you ever again were so much as one minute tardy? What did I tell you that I would do to you?" And I say in a little meek voice, because I'm scared, I say: "Whip me." And he says: "YES, WHIP YOU!" And I say—

UNCLE WADSWORTH: You say, "Oh, *don't* whip pore Uncle Tom, massa! If only you won't whip him he won't never—"

ALVIN: Oh, stop it, Uncle Wadsworth! That's not what I say at all, and you know it. How can I tell about the schools of yesteryear if you won't be serious? Well, anyway, he says to me: "Have you anything to say for yourself?" And I say, "Please, Mr. Crane, it was four miles, and I had the cows to milk, and Ma was sick and I had to help Sister cook the hoe-cakes—"

UNCLE WADSWORTH: Hoe-cakes! (*With slow relish.*) Hoe-cakes. . . . Why, I haven't had any hoe-cakes since. . . . . How'd you hear about hoe-cakes, Alvin boy?

ALVIN: Uncle Wadsworth, if you keep interrupting me about irrevu— irrelevancies, how can I get anywhere?

UNCLE WADSWORTH: I apologize, Alvin; I am silent, Alvin.

ALVIN: Then he looks at me and he smiles like—like somebody in *Dick Tracy,* and he says: Alvin, *spare your breath."* And then he walks over to the corner next to the stove, and do you know what's in the corner?

UNCLE WADSWORTH: What's in the corner?

ALVIN: Sticks. Sticks of every size. Hundreds of sticks. And then he reaches down and takes the biggest one and—and—

UNCLE WADSWORTH: And—and—

ALVIN: And he *beats* me.

UNCLE WADSWORTH (*with a big sigh*): The Lord be praised! For a minute I was afraid he was going to burn you at the stake. But go ahead, Alvin.

ALVIN: Go ahead?

UNCLE WADSWORTH: It's still just ten minutes after seven. Tell me about your day—your school-day—your dear old golden rule day.

ALVIN: Well, then he says: "Take your Readers!" And I look around
and everybody in the room, from little kids just six years old
with their front teeth out to great big ones, grown men practically that look like they ought to be on the Chicago Bears—
everybody in the room picks up the same book and they all
start reading aloud out of the—*McGuffey Reader!* Ha-ha-ha! The
McGuffey Reader!

UNCLE WADSWORTH: And why, Alvin, do you laugh?

ALVIN: Because it's funny, that's why! The McGuffey Reader!

UNCLE WADSWORTH: Have you ever seen a McGuffey Reader, Alvin?

ALVIN: How could I of, Uncle Wadsworth? I didn't go to school
back in those days.

UNCLE WADSWORTH: Your account was so vivid that for a moment
I forgot. . . . You've never seen such a Reader. Well, I have.

ALVIN: Oh, sure—you used one in school yourself, didn't you?

UNCLE WADSWORTH: No, Alvin—strange as it seems, I did not;
nor did I ever shake the hand of Robert E. Lee, nor did I
fight in the War of 1812, nor did I get to see Adam and Eve and
the Serpent. My father used a McGuffey Reader; I did not.

ALVIN: I'm sorry, Uncle Wadsworth.

UNCLE WADSWORTH: No need, no need. . . . Alvin, if you will
go over to the bookcase and reach into the right hand corner of
the top shelf, you will find a book—a faded, dusty, red-brown
book.

ALVIN: Here it is. It's all worn, and there're gold letters on the
back, and it says *Appletons' Fifth Reader.*

UNCLE WADSWORTH: Exactly. *Appletons' Fifth Reader.* Week before last, at an antique-dealer's over near Hillsboro, side by side
with a glass brandy-flask bearing the features of the Father of
our Country, George Washington, I found this Reader.

ALVIN: Look how yellow the paper is! And brown spots all over
it. . . . Gee, they must have used it all over the country; it
says New York, Boston, and Chicago, 1880, and it was printed
in 1878 and 1879 too, and—look at the picture across from
it, it's one of those old engravings. I guess they didn't have
photographs in those days.

UNCLE WADSWORTH: Guess again, Alvin boy. And what is the
subject of this old engraving?

ALVIN: A girl with a bucket, and back behind her somebody's plow-
ing, and it's dawn. And there's some poetry underneath.
UNCLE WADSWORTH:

> *While the plowman near at hand*
> *Whistles o'er the furrowed land*
> *And the milkmaid singeth blithe. . . .*

ALVIN: That's right. You mean to say you *memorized* it?
UNCLE WADSWORTH: Fifty years ago, Alvin. Doesn't any of it have
a—a familiar ring?
ALVIN: Well, to tell the truth, Uncle Wadsworth. . . .
UNCLE WADSWORTH: What does it say in small letters down at
the right-hand corner of the page?
ALVIN: It says—*"L'Allegro,* page 420." *L'Allegro!* Sure! sure!
Why, I read it in sophomore English. We spent two whole days
on that poem and on—you know, that other one that goes with
it. They're by John Milton.
UNCLE WADSWORTH: Yes, Milton. And in that same—
ALVIN: But Uncle Wadsworth, you don't mean to say they had
Milton in a Fifth Reader! Why, we were sophomores in college,
and there were two football players that were juniors, and believe
me, it was all Dr. Taylor could do to get us through that poem.
How could little kids in the fifth grade read Milton?
UNCLE WADSWORTH: Sit down, Alvin. Do you remember reading,
at about the same time you read "L'Allegro," a poem called
"Elegy Written in a Country Churchyard"?
ALVIN: Well—
UNCLE WADSWORTH: Gray's "Elegy"?
ALVIN: Say me some, Uncle Wadsworth.
UNCLE WADSWORTH:

> *Full many a gem of purest ray serene*
> *The dark unfathom'd caves of ocean bear;*
> *Full many a flower is born to blush unseen*
> *And waste its sweetness on the desert air.*

ALVIN: Sure, I remember that one. I liked that one.
UNCLE WADSWORTH: Well, Alvin, that very poem—

ALVIN: Oh *no,* Uncle Wadsworth! You're not going to tell me that that poem was in a Fifth Reader!

UNCLE WADSWORTH: No, Alvin, I am not. I want you to . . . to steel yourself. That poem was not in Appletons' Fifth Reader, that poem was in Appletons' Fourth Reader. (*Alvin groans in awe.*) And Wordsworth—you studied Wordsworth in your sophomore English?

ALVIN (*lifelessly*): Uh-huh.

UNCLE WADSWORTH: There are four of Wordsworth's poems in Appletons' Fourth Reader.

ALVIN: I guess in the Sixth Reader they were reading Einstein.

UNCLE WADSWORTH: No, but in the Fifth Reader—run your eye down the table of contents, Alvin—there are selections by Addison, Bishop Berkeley, Bunyan, Byron, Coleridge, Carlyle, Cervantes, Coleridge—the whole *Ancient Mariner,* Alvin—Defoe, De Quincy, Dickens, Emerson, Fielding, Hawthorne, George Herbert, Hazlitt, Jefferson, Dr. Johnson, Shakespeare, Shelley, Sterne, Swift, Tennyson, Thoreau, Mark Twain—

ALVIN: It's hard to believe.

UNCLE WADSWORTH: And there are also selections from simpler writers—

ALVIN: Yeah, simple ones—

UNCLE WADSWORTH: Simpler writers such as Scott, Burns, Longfellow, Cooper, Audubon, Poe, Oliver Wendell Holmes, Benjamin Franklin, Washington Irving. Alvin, have you ever—at college perhaps—ever read anything by Goethe?

ALVIN: I don't *believe* so.

UNCLE WADSWORTH: Well, Alvin boy, if after milking the cow and baking the hoe-cakes, you had limped four miles barefoot to that one-room red schoolhouse of yours, and had been beaten by that Ichabod Crane of a teacher, you would still have got to read, in your Appletons' Fifth Reader, one poem and five pages of prose from Goethe's immortal *Wilhelm Meister.* . . . As it is you don't limp, nobody beats you, and you read—whom *do* you read, Alvin? Tell me some of the writers you read in the fifth grade.

ALVIN: I don't exactly remember their *names.*

UNCLE WADSWORTH: There in the bookcase—that red and yellow

and black book there—is the Fifth Reader of today. *Days and Deeds,* it is called; it is, I believe, the most popular Fifth Reader in the country. That's right, hand it over. Here on page 3 is its table of contents; come, Alvin, read out to me the names of the writers from whom the children of today get their knowledge of life and literature.

ALVIN: Well, the first one's Fletcher D. Slater, and then Nora Burglon, and Sterling North and Ruth G. Plowhead—

UNCLE WADSWORTH: Plowhead?

ALVIN: That's what it says. Then Ruth E. Kennell, Gertrude Robinson, Philip A. Rollins, J. Walker McSpadden, Merlin M.—

UNCLE WADSWORTH: You're sure you're not making up some of these names?

ALVIN: How could I? Merlin M. Taylor, Sanford Tousey, Gladys M. Wick, Marie Barton, Margaret Leighton, Edward C. James —no, Janes, Leonard K. Smith, P. L. Travers, Esther Shepherd, James C. Bowman, Dr. Seuss—

UNCLE WADSWORTH: Land! Land!

ALVIN: No, Seuss. Seuss.

UNCLE WADSWORTH: I speak figuratively. I mean that here, at last, is a name I recognize, the name of a well-known humorist and cartoonist.

ALVIN: Oh. Then there's Armstrong Sperry, Myra M. Dodds, Alden G. Stevens, Lavinia R. Davis, Lucy M. Crockett, Raymond Jannson, Hubert Evans, Ruth E. Tanner, Three Boy Scouts—

UNCLE WADSWORTH: Three Boy Scouts. An Indian, no doubt. . . . Never heard of him.

ALVIN: Heard of *them.* There're three of them.

UNCLE WADSWORTH: Three? Thirty! Three hundred! They're *all* Boy Scouts! Alvin, these are names only a mother could love— names only a mother would know. That they are honest names, respected names of worthy citizens, I have not the slightest doubt; but when I reflect that it is *these* names that have replaced those of Goethe, of Shakespeare, of Cervantes, of Dr. Johnson— of all the other great and good writers of the Appleton Fifth Reader—when I think of this, Alvin, I am confused, I am dismayed, I am *astounded.*

ALVIN: Uncle Wadsworth, you've got all red in the face.

UNCLE WADSWORTH: There are also in the Appleton Fifth Reader,
elaborate analyses of the style, rhetoric, and organization of
the literary works included; penetrating discussions of their logic;
highly technical instructions for reading them aloud in the most
effective way; discussions of etymology, spelling, pronunciation, the
general development of the English language. And, Alvin, these
are *not* written in the insipid baby-talk thought appropriate for
children today. Here, in a paragraph about *Don Quixote,* is one
of the Fifth Reader's typical discussions of logic: "The question
here involved is the old sophism of Eubulides. . . . Is a man a
liar who says that he tells lies? If he is, then he does not tell
lies; and if he does not tell lies, is he a liar? If not, then is not
his assertion a lie? . . . It will be noticed that the perplexity
comes from the fact of self-relation: the one assertion relates
to another assertion of the same person; and the one assertion
being conditioned upon the other, the difficulty arises. It is the
question of self-contradiction—of two mutually contradictory state-
ments, one must be false. It is a sophism, but one that continually
occurs among unsophisticated reasoners. It is also a practical
sophism, for it is continually being acted in the world around
us (e.g., a person seeks pleasure by such means that, while he
enjoys himself, he undermines his health, or sins against his
conscience, and thus draws inevitably on him physical suffering and
an uneasy soul). It is therefore well worthy of study in its purely
logical form. . . . All universal negative assertions (and a lie is a
negation) are liable to involve the assertion itself in self-contradiction."

ALVIN: Ohhhhh. . . . *Ohhhhh.* . . . If I'd gone to school then, I'd
have known what that means in the *fifth grade?*

UNCLE WADSWORTH: You'd have known it or you never would
have got into the sixth grade.

ALVIN: Then I'd be the oldest settler in the fifth grade, because
I'm a junior in college and I still can't understand it.

UNCLE WADSWORTH: Yes, it's surprising what those fifth-graders
were expected to know. The Reader contains a little essay called
"Hidden Beauties of Classic Authors," by a writer named N.
P. Willis.

ALVIN: N. P. Willis. . . . I guess he was Ruth G. Plowhead's grandpa.

UNCLE WADSWORTH: Yes, he isn't exactly a classic author himself. He tells you how he fell in love with Beaumont and Fletcher, and the *Faerie Queene,* and *Comus,* and *The Rape of the Lock;* he says that he knows "no more exquisite sensation than this warming of the heart to an old author; and it seems to me that the most delicious portion of intellectual existence is the brief period in which, one by one, the great minds of old are admitted with all their time-mellowed worth to the affections." Well, at the end of the essay there're some questions; what do you think is the first thing they ask those fifth graders?

ALVIN: What?

UNCLE WADSWORTH: "Have you read Milton's *Comus?*—Pope's *Rape of the Lock?*"

ALVIN: Now Uncle Wadsworth, you've got to admit that that's a terrible thing to ask a little boy in the fifth grade.

UNCLE WADSWORTH: *I* think it's a terrible thing. But they didn't. As a matter of fact, *I* think it's a terrible thing to ask a big boy in his junior year in college. How about it, Alvin? Have *you* read Milton's *Comus?* Pope's *Rape of the Lock?*

ALVIN: Well, to tell you the truth, Uncle Wadsworth—

UNCLE WADSWORTH: Tell ahead.

ALVIN: Well, to—well—well, it just isn't the *sort* of question you can answer yes or no. I *may* have read Milton's *Comus;* it's the kind of thing we read hundreds of things like in our sophomore survey course; I guess the chances are ten to one I read it, and a year ago I could have told you for certain whether or not I read it, but right now all I can say is if I didn't read it, it would surprise me a lot.

UNCLE WADSWORTH: And *The Rape of the Lock?*

ALVIN: No.

UNCLE WADSWORTH: *No?* You mean you *know* you didn't read it?

ALVIN: Uh-huh.

UNCLE WADSWORTH: How do you know?

ALVIN: I—

UNCLE WADSWORTH: Go on, go on.

ALVIN: Well Uncle Wadsworth, it seems to me that a book with a title like that, if I'd read it I'd remember it.

UNCLE WADSWORTH: Alvin, if you weren't my own nephew, I'd— I'd be proud to have invented you. . . . Here's another of those poems, the kind that *you* read in your sophomore year in college and that your great-grandfather read in the Fifth Reader. It's by George Herbert, the great religious poet George Herbert. Read it to me, Alvin; and when you've read it, tell me what it means.

ALVIN (*in careful singsong*): *Sunday*. By George Herbert.

> *O Day most calm, most bright!*
> *The fruit of this, the next world's bud;*
> *The endorsement of supreme delight,*
> *Writ by a Friend, and with his blood;*
> *The couch of Time*: *Care's calm and bay*:
> *The week were dark but for thy light;*
> *Thy torch doth show the way.*
>
> *The other days and thou*
> *Make up one man, whose face thou art,*
> *Knocking at heaven with thy brow:*
> *The working-days are the back part;*
> *The burden of the week lies there;*
> *Making the whole to stoop and bow,*
> *Till thy release appear.*
>
> *Man had—man had—*

Uncle Wadsworth, I'm all mixed up. I've *been* all mixed up. And if you ask me that fifth grade was mixed up too.

UNCLE WADSWORTH: Where did you first begin to feel confused?

ALVIN: I never did not feel confused.

UNCLE WADSWORTH: Surely the first line—

ALVIN: Yeah. Yeah. The first one was all right. *O Day most calm, most bright!* That means it's Sunday, and it's all calm and bright. Then it says, *the fruit of this*. . . . *The fruit of this*. What's the fruit of this?

UNCLE WADSWORTH: *The fruit of this, the next world's bud. World* is understood.

ALVIN: Understood?

UNCLE WADSWORTH: Yes. The fruit of this world and the bud of the next world.

ALVIN: Oh. . . . *The endorsement of supreme delight. (Pauses.) The endorsement of supreme delight.* . . . Uncle Wadsworth, a line like that—you've got to admit a line like that's *obscure.*

UNCLE WADSWORTH: It means that—it *says* that Sunday is like the endorsement of a check or note; because of the endorsement this supreme delight, our salvation, is negotiable, we can cash it.

ALVIN: Oh. . . . Like endorsing a check. *Writ by a Friend—Friend's* got a capital *F.* . . . Oh! That means it was written by a Quaker. (*Uncle Wadsworth laughs.*) But that's what it does mean. We live on a road named the Friendly Road because it goes to a Quaker church. If *Friend* doesn't mean *Quaker* why's it got a capital *F?*

UNCLE WADSWORTH: *Writ by a Friend, and with his blood.* If you're talking about church and Sunday and the next world, and mention a Friend who has written something with his blood, who is that Friend, Alvin?

ALVIN: Oh. . . . *The couch of Time; Care's calm and bay.* . . . (*Pauses.*) Uncle Wadsworth, do we *have* to read poetry?

UNCLE WADSWORTH: Of course not, Alvin. Nobody else does, why should we? Let's get back to prose. Here's the way the Fifth Reader talks about climbing a mountain: "Some part of the beholder, even some vital part, seems to escape through the loose grating of his ribs as he ascends. . . . He is more lone than you can imagine. There is less of substantial thought and fair understanding in him than in the plains where men inhabit. His reason is dispersed and shadowy, more thin and subtle, like the air. Vast, Titanic, inhuman Nature has got him at disadvantage, caught him alone, and pilfers him of some of his divine faculty. She does not smile on him as in the plains. She seems to say sternly, 'Why come ye here before your time? . . . Why seek me where I have not called you, and then

complain because you find me but a stepmother? Shouldst thou
freeze, or starve, or shudder thy life away, here is no shrine, nor
altar, nor any access to my ear. "Chaos and ancient Night,
I come no spy/ With purpose to explore or to disturb/ The
secrets of your realm—" ' "

ALVIN: Uncle Wadsworth, if the prose is like that, I'd just as
soon have stayed with the poetry. Didn't they have any plain
American writers in the Fifth Reader?

UNCLE WADSWORTH: Plain American writers? That was Thoreau
I was reading to you. Well, if he's too hard, here's what the
Fifth Reader has to say about him. It's talking about his account
of the battle between the black ants and the red: "The style
of this piece is an imitation of the heroic style of Homer's 'Iliad,'
and is properly a 'mock-heroic.' The intention of the author is
two-fold: half-seriously endowing the incidents of everyday
life with epic dignity, in the belief that there is nothing mean and
trivial to the poet and philosopher, and that it is the man that
adds dignity to the occasion, and not the occasion that dignifies
the man; half-satirically treating the human events alluded to as
though they were non-heroic, and only fit to be applied to the
events of animal life."

ALVIN (*wonderingly*): Why, it's just like old Taylor!

UNCLE WADSWORTH: Professor Taylor would lecture to you in that
style?

ALVIN: He'd get going that way, but pretty soon he'd see we didn't
know what he meant, and then he'd talk so we could understand
him. . . . Well, if the Fifth Reader sounds like that about
ants, I sure don't want to hear it about scansion and etymology!

UNCLE WADSWORTH: But Alvin, wouldn't you *like* to be able to
understand it? Don't you wish you'd had it in the fifth grade and
known what it was talking about?

ALVIN: Sure, sure! Would I have made old Taylor's eyes pop out!
All we ever had in the fifth grade was Boy Scouts going on
hikes, and kids going to see their grandmother for Thanksgiving;
it was easy.

UNCLE WADSWORTH: And interesting?

ALVIN: Nah, it was corny—the same old stuff; how can you make
stuff like that interesting?

UNCLE WADSWORTH: How indeed?

ALVIN: But how did things like Shakespeare and Milton and Dickens ever get in a Fifth Reader?

UNCLE WADSWORTH: Alvin, they've always *been* there. Yesterday, here in the United States, those things were in the Fifth Reader; today, everywhere else in the world, those things or their equivalent are in the Fifth Reader; it is only here in the United States, today, that the Fifth Reader consists of *Josie's Home Run,* by Ruth G. Plowhead, and *A Midnight Lion Hunt,* by Three Boy Scouts. I read, in a recent best-seller, this sentence: "For the first time in history Americans see their children getting less education than they got themselves." That may be; and for the first time in history Americans see a book on why their children can't read becoming a best-seller, being serialized in newspapers across the nation. Alvin, about school-buildings, health, lunches, civic responsibility, kindness, good humor, spontaneity, we have nothing to learn from the schools of the past; but about reading, with pleasure and understanding, the best that has been thought and said in the world—about *that* we have much to learn. The child who reads and understands the Appleton Fifth Reader is well on the way to becoming an educated, cultivated human being—and if he has to do it sitting in a one-room schoolhouse, if he has to do it sitting on a hollow log, he's better off than a boy sitting in the Pentagon reading *Days and Deeds.* There's a jug of cider in the ice-box, Alvin; you get it, I'll get the glasses; and let's drink a toast to—

ALVIN: To the Appleton Fifth Reader! long may she read! (*They drink.*)

UNCLE WADSWORTH: And now, Alvin, let us conclude the meeting with a song.

ALVIN: What song?

UNCLE WADSWORTH: What song? Alvin, can you ask? Start us off, Alvin!

ALVIN: School days, school days. . . .

BOTH: Dear old golden rule days. . . .

ALVIN: Louder, Uncle Wadsworth, louder!

BOTH: Readin' and 'ritin' and 'rithmetic
      Taught to the tune of a hick'ry stick. . . .

(*Alvin and Uncle Wadsworth and the accordion disappear into the distance.*)

Questions

1. What are some of the advantages with regard to point of view that Jarrell derives from writing his essay as though it were a playlet? What contributions are made by the stage directions italicized in the text?

2. What adjustments in attitude and point of view would have resulted had Alvin been speaking not to his Uncle Wadsworth, but to his father (himself a college graduate of old), to his pastor, or to his recent teacher, Professor Taylor? Would the tone of the whole have likely been the same in each instance? Explain.

3. How would you describe Alvin's abilities of self-expression as to precision, originality of statement, and range of allusion (Dick Tracy, Chicago Bears)? How would you relate your description to the sort of reading Alvin was given in the fifth grade? What assumption are you being asked to make about that relationship?

4. For perhaps half of the essay, Alvin is scornful of what he takes to be his uncle's schooling. What assumptions about student-teacher relations, a school's physical environment, and its curriculum are at the basis of Alvin's reaction?

5. Alvin expresses amazement at what "little kids in the fifth grade" were once expected to understand. Reread the series of excerpts from the *Appleton Fifth Reader* (pp. 311–18) and formulate the sort of assumptions that book makes about the potentiality of fifth-grade students. Do these assumptions seem realistic or far-fetched?

6. Alvin's misconceptions about the past are comic in effect; so are his frequent lapses of memory. But in what sense are they both serious in implication and attributable to more than simply the ignorance of youth? You might consider whether Alvin is remedying matters now that he is a junior in college and reading at last the materials contained in the *Appleton Fifth Reader*.

7. Professor Taylor—"old Taylor"—is several times mentioned. Infer and describe his daily trials and tribulations at the college.

8. Jarrell's subtitle reads "A One-Sided Dialogue," but recall Alvin's opening remark, "just nostalgia, just sentimentality." Is there evidence that Uncle Wadsworth is somewhat pompous and complacent? That his point

of view is not entirely to be trusted? That he is not entirely the spokesman for Jarrell's own views?

9. An interested party not represented in the essay is Alvin's fifth-grade teacher. Frame an argument as presented by Alvin's teacher in defense of Alvin's curriculum. Present it as part of a dialogue, the other speaker being Professor Taylor.

THE GENESIS OF A MOOD

JOSEPH WOOD KRUTCH

When Krutch published *The Modern Temper* in 1929, he
sought to provide a record not only of his own views and feelings but also those of the generation to which he belonged.
The opening chapter, offered here, was followed by others on
such themes as tragedy, science, and metaphysics. When the
book was reissued in 1956, Krutch noted that though he still
agreed with the diagnosis he had made earlier, he no longer
experienced the attendant despair. The movement of his views
can be traced in such later volumes as *The Great Chain of Life*
and *Human Nature and the Human Condition*. (Further information on Krutch appears on p. 206.)

(1) It is one of Freud's quaint conceits that the child in its mother's
womb is the happiest of living creatures. Into his consciousness
no conflict has yet entered, for he knows no limitations to his
desires and the universe is exactly as he wishes it to be. All his
needs are satisfied before even he becomes aware of them, and if
his awareness is dim that is but the natural result of a complete
harmony between the self and the environment, since, as Spencer
pointed out in a remote age, to be omniscient and omnipotent would
be to be without any consciousness whatsoever. The discomfort
of being born is the first warning which he receives that any event
can be thrust upon him; it is the first limitation of his omnipotence
which he perceives, and he is cast upon the shores of the world
wailing his protest against the indignity to which he has been
subjected. Years pass before he learns to control the expression

of enraged surprise which arises within him at every unpleasant fact with which he is confronted, and his parents conspire so to protect him that he will learn only by very slow stages how far is the world from his heart's desire.

(2) The cradle is made to imitate as closely as may be the conditions, both physical and spiritual, of the womb. Of its occupant no effort is demanded, and every precaution is taken to anticipate each need before it can arise. If, as the result of any unforeseen circumstance, any unsatisfied desire is born, he need only raise his voice in protest to cause the entire world in so far as he knows it—his nurse or his parents—to rush to his aid. The whole of his physical universe is obedient to his will and he is justified by his experience in believing that his mere volition controls his destiny. Only as he grows older does he become aware that there are wills other than his own or that there are physical circumstances rebellious to any human will. And only after the passage of many years does he become aware of the full extent of his predicament in the midst of a world which is in very few respects what he would wish it to be.

(3) As a child he is treated as a child, and such treatment implies much more than the physical coddling of which Freud speaks. Not only do those who surround him co-operate more completely than they ever will again to satisfy his wishes in material things, but they encourage him to live in a spiritual world far more satisfactory than their own. He is carefully protected from any knowledge of the cruelties and complexities of life; he is led to suppose that the moral order is simple and clear, that virtue triumphs, and that the world is, as the desires of whole generations of mankind have led them to try to pretend that it is, arranged according to a pattern which would seem reasonable and satisfactory to human sensibilities. He is prevented from realizing how inextricably what men call good and evil are intertwined, how careless is Nature of those values called mercy and justice and righteousness which men have come, in her despite, to value; and he is, besides, encouraged to believe in a vast mythology peopled with figments which range all the way from the Saints to Santa Claus and which represent projections of human wishes which the adult has come to recognize

as no more than projections but which he is willing that the child, for the sake of his own happiness, should believe real. Aware how different is the world which experience reveals from the world which the spirit desires, the mature, as though afraid that reality could not be endured unless the mind had been gradually inured to it, allow the child to become aware of it only by slow stages, and little by little he learns, not only the limitations of his will, but the moral discord of the world. Thus it is, in a very important sense, true that the infant does come trailing clouds of glory from that heaven which his imagination creates, and that as his experience accumulates he sees it fade away into the light of common day.

(4) Now races as well as individuals have their infancy, their adolescence, and their maturity. Experience accumulates not only from year to year but from generation to generation, and in the life of each person it plays a little larger part than it did in the life of his father. As civilization grows older it too has more and more facts thrust upon its consciousness and is compelled to abandon one after another, quite as the child does, certain illusions which have been dear to it. Like the child, it has instinctively assumed that what it would like to be true is true, and it never gives up any such belief until experience in some form compels it to do so. Being, for example, extremely important to itself, it assumes that it is extremely important to the universe also. The earth is the center of all existing things, man is the child and the protégé of those gods who transcend and who will ultimately enable him to transcend all the evils which he has been compelled to recognize. The world and all that it contains were designed for him, and even those things which seem noxious have their usefulness only temporarily hid. Since he knows but little he is free to imagine, and imagination is always the creature of desire.

I I

(5) The world which any consciousness inhabits is a world made up in part of experience and in part of fancy. No experience, and hence no knowledge, is complete, but the gaps which lie between

the solid fragments are filled in with shadows. Connections, explanations, and reasons are supplied by the imagination, and thus the world gets its patterned completeness from material which is spun out of the desires. But as time goes on and experience accumulates there remains less and less scope for the fancy. The universe becomes more and more what experience has revealed, less and less what imagination has created, and hence, since it was not designed to suit man's needs, less and less what he would have it be. With increasing knowledge his power to manipulate his physical environment increases, but in gaining the knowledge which enables him to do so he surrenders insensibly the power which in his ignorance he had to mold the universe. The forces of nature obey him, but in learning to master them he has in another sense allowed them to master him. He has exchanged the universe which his desires created, the universe made for man, for the universe of nature of which he is only a part. Like the child growing into manhood, he passes from a world which is fitted to him into a world for which he must fit himself.

(6) If, then, the world of poetry, mythology, and religion represents the world as a man would like to have it, while science represents the world as he gradually comes to discover it, we need only compare the two to realize how irreconcilable they appear. For the cozy bowl of the sky arched in a protecting curve above him he must exchange the cold immensities of space and, for the spiritual order which he has designed, the chaos of nature. God he had loved *because* God was anthropomorphic, because He was made in man's own image, with purposes and desires which were human and hence understandable. But Nature's purpose, if purpose she can be said to have, is no purpose of his and is not understandable in his terms. Her desire merely to live and to propagate in innumerable forms, her ruthless indifference to his values, and the blindness of her irresistible will strike terror to his soul, and he comes in the fullness of his experience to realize that the ends which he proposes to himself —happiness and order and reason—are ends which he must achieve, if he achieve them at all, in her despite. Formerly he had believed in even his darkest moments that the universe was rational if he could only grasp its rationality, but gradually he comes to suspect

that rationality is an attribute of himself alone and that there is no reason to suppose that his own life has any more meaning than the life of the humblest insect that crawls from one annihilation to another. Nature, in her blind thirst for life, has filled every possible cranny of the rotting earth with some sort of fantastic creature, and among them man is but one—perhaps the most miserable of all, because he is the only one in whom the instinct of life falters long enough to enable it to ask the question "Why?" As long as life is regarded as having been created, creating may be held to imply a purpose, but merely to have come into being is, in all likelihood, merely to go out of it also.

(7) Fortunately, perhaps, man, like the individual child, was spared in his cradle the knowledge which he could not bear. Illusions have been lost one by one. God, instead of disappearing in an instant, has retreated step by step and surrendered gradually his control of the universe. Once he decreed the fall of every sparrow and counted the hairs upon every head; a little later he became merely the original source of the laws of nature, and even today there are thousands who, unable to bear the thought of losing him completely, still fancy that they can distinguish the uncertain outlines of a misty figure. But the rôle which he plays grows less and less, and man is left more and more alone in a universe to which he is completely alien. His world was once, like the child's world, three-quarters myth and poetry. His teleological concepts molded it into a form which he could appreciate and he gave to it moral laws which would make it meaningful, but step by step the outlines of nature have thrust themselves upon him, and for the dream which he made is substituted a reality devoid of any pattern which he can understand.

(8) In the course of this process innumerable readjustments have been made, and always with the effort to disturb as little as possible the myth which is so much more full of human values than the fact which comes in some measure to replace it. Thus, for example, the Copernican theory of astronomy, removing the earth from the center of the universe and assigning it a very insignificant place among an infinitude of whirling motes, was not merely resisted as a fact but was, when finally accepted, accepted as far as possible without its implications. Even if taken entirely by itself and without the whole

system of facts of which it is a part, it renders extremely improbable the assumption, fundamental in most human thought, that the universe has man as its center and is hence understandable in his terms, but this implication was disregarded just as, a little later, the implications of the theory of evolution were similarly disregarded. It is not likely that if man had been aware from the very beginning that his world was a mere detail in the universe, and himself merely one of the innumerable species of living things, he would ever have come to think of himself, as he even now tends to do, as a being whose desires must be somehow satisfiable and whose reason must be matched by some similar reason in nature. But the myth, having been once established, persists long after the assumptions upon which it was made have been destroyed, because, being born of desire, it is far more satisfactory than any fact.

(9) Unfortunately, perhaps, experience does not grow at a constant, but at an accelerated, rate. The Greeks who sought knowledge, not through the study of nature but through the examination of their own minds, developed a philosophy which was really analogous to myth, because the laws which determined its growth were dictated by human desires and they discovered few facts capable of disturbing the pattern which they devised. The Middle Ages retreated still further into themselves, but with the Renaissance man began to surrender himself to nature, and the sciences, each nourishing the other, began their iconoclastic march. Three centuries lay between the promulgation of the Copernican theory and the publication of the *Origin of Species,* but in sixty-odd years which have elapsed since that latter event the blows have fallen with a rapidity which left no interval for recovery. The structures which are variously known as mythology, religion, and philosophy, and which are alike in that each has as its function the interpretation of experience in terms which have human values, have collapsed under the force of successive attacks and shown themselves utterly incapable of assimilating the new stores of experience which have been dumped upon the world. With increasing completeness science maps out the pattern of nature, but the latter has no relation to the pattern of human needs and feelings.

(10) Consider, for example, the plight of ethics. Historical criti-

cism having destroyed what used to be called by people of learning and intelligence "Christian Evidences," and biology having shown how unlikely it is that man is the recipient of any transcendental knowledge, there remains no foundation in authority for ideas of right and wrong; and if, on the other hand, we turn to the traditions of the human race anthropology is ready to prove that no consistent human tradition has ever existed. Custom has furnished the only basis which ethics have ever had, and there is no conceivable human action which custom has not at one time justified and at another condemned. Standards are imaginary things, and yet it is extremely doubtful if man can live well, either spiritually or physically, without the belief that they are somehow real. Without them society lapses into anarchy and the individual becomes aware of an intolerable disharmony between himself and the universe. Instinctively and emotionally he is an ethical animal. No known race is so low in the scale of civilization that it has not attributed a moral order to the world, because no known race is so little human as not to suppose a moral order so innately desirable as to have an inevitable existence. It is man's most fundamental myth, and life seems meaningless to him without it. Yet, as that systematized and cumulative experience which is called science displaces one after another the myths which have been generated by need, it grows more and more likely that he must remain an ethical animal in a universe which contains no ethical element.

I I I

(11) Mystical philosophers have sometimes said that they "accepted the universe." They have, that is to say, formed of it some conception which answered the emotional needs of their spirit and which brought them a sense of being in harmony with its aims and processes. They have been aware of no needs which Nature did not seem to supply and of no ideals which she too did not seem to recognize. They have felt themselves one with her because they have had the strength of imagination to make her over in their own image, and it is doubtful if any man can live at peace who does not thus feel himself at home. But as the world assumes the shape which sci-

ence gives it, it becomes more and more difficult to find such emotional correspondences. Whole realms of human feeling, like the realm of ethics, find no place for themselves in the pattern of nature and generate needs for which no satisfaction is supplied. What man knows is everywhere at war with what he wants.

(12) In the course of a few centuries his knowledge, and hence the universe of which he finds himself an inhabitant, has been completely revolutionized, but his instincts and his emotions have remained, relatively at least, unchanged. He is still, as he always was, adjusted to the orderly, purposeful, humanized world which all peoples unburdened by experience have figured to themselves, but that world no longer exists. He has the same sense of dignity to which the myth of his descent from the gods was designed to minister, and the same innate purposefulness which led him to attribute a purpose to nature, but he can no longer think in terms appropriate to either. The world which his reason and his investigation reveal is a world which his emotions cannot comprehend.

(13) Casually he accepts the spiritual iconoclasm of science, and in the detachment of everyday life he learns to play with the cynical wisdom of biology and psychology, which explain away the awe of emotional experience just as earlier science explained away the awe of conventional piety. Yet, under the stress of emotional crises, knowledge is quite incapable of controlling his emotions or of justifying them to himself. In love, he calls upon the illusions of man's grandeur and dignity to help him accept his emotions, and faced with tragedy he calls upon illusion to dignify his suffering; but lyric flight is checked by the rationality which he has cultivated, and in the world of metabolism and hormones, repressions and complexes, he finds no answer for his needs. He is feeling about love, for example, much as the troubadour felt, but he thinks about it in a very different way. Try as he may, the two halves of his soul can hardly be made to coalesce, and he cannot either feel as his intelligence tells him that he should feel or think as his emotions would have him think, and thus he is reduced to mocking his torn and divided soul. In the grip of passion he cannot, as some romanticist might have done, accept it with a religious trust in the mystery of love, nor yet can he regard it as a psychiatrist, himself quite free from

emotion, might suggest—merely as an interesting specimen of psychical botany. Man *qua* thinker may delight in the intricacies of psychology, but man *qua* lover has not learned to feel in its terms; so that, though complexes and ductless glands may serve to explain the feelings of another, one's own still demand all those symbols of the ineffable in which one has long ceased to believe.

(14) Time was when the scientist, the poet, and the philosopher walked hand in hand. In the universe which the one perceived the other found himself comfortably at home. But the world of modern science is one in which the intellect alone can rejoice. The mind leaps, and leaps perhaps with a sort of elation, through the immensities of space, but the spirit, frightened and cold, longs to have once more above its head the inverted bowl beyond which may lie whatever paradise its desires may create. The lover who surrendered himself to the Implacable Aphrodite or who fancied his foot upon the lowest rung of the Platonic ladder of love might retain his self-respect, but one can neither resist nor yield gracefully to a carefully catalogued psychosis. A happy life is a sort of poem, with a poem's elevation and dignity, but emotions cannot be dignified unless they are first respected. They must seem to correspond with, to be justified by, something in the structure of the universe itself; but though it was the function of religion and philosophy to hypostatize some such correspondence, to project a humanity upon nature, or at least to conceive of a humane force above and beyond her, science finds no justification for such a process and is content instead to show how illusions were born.

(15) The most ardent love of truth, the most resolute determination to follow nature no matter to what black abyss she may lead, need not blind one to the fact that many of the lost illusions had, to speak the language of science, a survival value. Either individuals or societies whose life is imbued with a cheerful certitude, whose aims are clear, and whose sense of the essential rightness of life is strong, live and struggle with an energy unknown to the skeptical and the pessimistic. Whatever the limitations of their intellects as instruments of criticism, they possess the physical and emotional vigor which is, unlike critical intelligence, analogous to the processes of nature. They found empires and conquer wildernesses, and they

pour the excess of their energy into works of art which the intelligence of more sophisticated peoples continues to admire even though it has lost the faith in life which is requisite for the building of a Chartres or the carving of a Venus de Milo. The one was not erected to a law of nature or the other designed to celebrate the libido, for each presupposed a sense of human dignity which science nowhere supports.

(16) Thus man seems caught in a dilemma which his intellect has devised. Any deliberately managed return to a state of relative ignorance, however desirable it might be argued to be, is obviously out of the question. We cannot, as the naïve proponents of the various religions, new and old, seem to assume, believe one thing and forget another merely because we happen to be convinced that it would be desirable to do so; and it is worth observing that the new psychology, with its penetrating analysis of the influence of desire upon belief, has so adequately warned the reason of the tricks which the will can play upon it that it has greatly decreased the possibility of beneficent delusion and serves to hold the mind in a steady contemplation of that from which it would fain escape. Weak and uninstructed intelligences take refuge in the monotonous repetition of once living creeds, or are even reduced to the desperate expedient of going to sleep amid the formulae of the flabby pseudo-religions in which the modern world is so prolific. But neither of these classes affords any aid to the robust but serious mind which is searching for some terms upon which it may live.

(17) And if we are, as by this time we should be, free from any teleological delusion, if we no longer make the unwarranted assumption that every human problem is somehow of necessity solvable, we must confess it may be that for the sort of being whom we have described no survival is possible in any form like that which his soul has now taken. He is a fantastic thing that has developed sensibilities and established values beyond the nature which gave him birth. He is of all living creatures the one to whom the earth is the least satisfactory. He has arrived at a point where he can no longer delude himself as to the extent of his predicament, and should he either become modified or disappear the earth would continue to spin and the grass to grow as it has always done. Of the thousands of

living species the vast majority would be as unaware of his passing as they are unaware now of his presence, and he would go as a shadow goes. His arts, his religions, and his civilizations—these are fair and wonderful things, but they are fair and wonderful to him alone. With the extinction of his poetry would come also the extinction of the only sensibility for which it has any meaning, and there would remain nothing capable of feeling a loss. Nothing would be left to label the memory of his discontent "divine," and those creatures who find in nature no lack would resume their undisputed possession of the earth.

(18) Anthropoid in form some of them might continue to be, and possessed as well of all of the human brain that makes possible a cunning adaptation to the conditions of physical life. To them nature might yield up subtler secrets than any yet penetrated; their machines might be more wonderful and their bodies more healthy than any yet known—even though there had passed away, not merely all myth and poetry, but the need for them as well. Cured of his transcendental cravings, content with things as they are, accepting the universe as experience had shown it to be, man would be freed of his soul and, like the other animals, either content or at least desirous of nothing which he might not hope ultimately to obtain.

(19) Nor can it be denied that certain adumbrations of this type have before now come into being. Among those of keener intellect there are scientists to whom the test tube and its contents are all-sufficient, and among those of coarser grain, captains of finance and builders of mills, there are those to whom the acquirement of wealth and power seems to constitute a life in which no lack can be perceived. Doubtless they are not new types; doubtless they have always existed; but may they not be the strain from which Nature will select the coming race? Is not their creed the creed of Nature, and are they not bound to triumph over those whose illusions are no longer potent because they are no longer really believed? Certain philosophers, clinging desperately to the ideal of a humanized world, have proposed a retreat into the imagination. Bertrand Russell in his popular essay, *A Free Man's Worship,* Unamuno and Santayana *passim* throughout their works, have argued that the way of salvation lay in a sort of ironic belief, in a determination to act as though

one still believed the things which once were really held true. But is not this a desperate expedient, a last refuge likely to appeal only to the leaders of a lost cause? Does it not represent the last, least substantial, phase of fading faith, something which borrows what little substance it seems to have from a reality of the past? If it seems half real to the sons of those who lived in the spiritual world of which it is a shadow, will it not seem, a little further removed, only a faint futility? Surely it has but little to oppose to those who come armed with the certitudes of science and united with, not fleeing from, the nature amid which they live.

(20) And if the dilemma here described is itself a delusion it is at least as vividly present and as terribly potent as those other delusions which have shaped or deformed the human spirit. There is no significant contemporary writer upon philosophy, ethics, or aesthetics whose speculations do not lead him to it in one form or another, and even the less reflective are aware of it in their own way. Both our practical morality and our emotional lives are adjusted to a world which no longer exists. In so far as we adhere to a code of conduct, we do so largely because certain habits still persist, not because we can give any logical reason for preferring them, and in so far as we indulge ourselves in the primitive emotional satisfactions—romantic love, patriotism, zeal for justice, and so forth—our satisfaction is the result merely of the temporary suspension of our disbelief in the mythology upon which they are founded. Traditionalists in religion are fond of asserting that our moral codes are flimsy because they are rootless; but, true as this is, it is perhaps not so important as the fact that our emotional lives are rootless too.

(21) If the gloomy vision of a dehumanized world which has just been evoked is not to become a reality, some complete readjustment must be made, and at least two generations have found themselves unequal to the task. The generation of Thomas Henry Huxley, so busy with destruction as never adequately to realize how much it was destroying, fought with such zeal against frightened conservatives that it never took time to do more than assert with some vehemence that all would be well, and the generation that followed either danced amid the ruins or sought by various compromises to save the remains of a few tottering structures. But neither patches

nor evasions will serve. It is not a changed world but a new one in which man must henceforth live if he lives at all, for all his premises have been destroyed and he must proceed to new conclusions. The values which he thought established have been swept away along with the rules by which he thought they might be attained.

(22) To this fact many are not yet awake, but our novels, our poems, and our pictures are enough to reveal that a generation aware of its predicament is at hand. It has awakened to the fact that both the ends which its fathers proposed to themselves and the emotions from which they drew their strength seem irrelevant and remote. With a smile, sad or mocking, according to individual temperament, it regards those works of the past in which were summed up the values of life. The romantic ideal of a world well lost for love and the classic ideal of austere dignity seem equally ridiculous, equally meaningless when referred, not to the temper of the past, but to the temper of the present. The passions which swept through the once major poets no longer awaken any profound response, and only in the bleak, tortuous complexities of a T. S. Eliot does it find its moods given adequate expression. Here disgust speaks with a robust voice and denunciation is confident, but ecstasy, flickering and uncertain, leaps fitfully up only to sink back among the cinders. And if the poet, with his gift of keen perceptions and his power of organization, can achieve only the most momentary and unstable adjustments, what hope can there be for those whose spirit is a less powerful instrument?

(23) And yet it is with such as he, baffled, but content with nothing which plays only upon the surface, that the hope for a still humanized future must rest. No one can tell how many of the old values must go or how new the new will be. Thus, while under the influence of the old mythology the sexual instinct was transformed into romantic love and tribal solidarity into the religion of patriotism, there is nothing in the modern consciousness capable of effecting these transmutations. Neither the one nor the other is capable of being, as it once was, the *raison d'être* of a life or the motif of a poem which is not, strictly speaking, derivative and anachronistic. Each is fading, each becoming as much a shadow as devotion to the cult of purification through self-torture. Either the instincts upon which

they are founded will achieve new transformations or they will remain merely instincts, regarded as having no particular emotional
significance in a spiritual world which, if it exists at all, will be as
different from the spiritual world of, let us say, Robert Browning
as that world is different from the world of Cato the Censor.

(24) As for this present unhappy time, haunted by ghosts from
a dead world and not yet at home in its own, its predicament is not,
to return to the comparison with which we began, unlike the predicament of the adolescent who has not yet learned to orient himself
without reference to the mythology amid which his childhood was
passed. He still seeks in the world of his experience for the values
which he had found there, and he is aware only of a vast disharmony.
But boys—most of them, at least—grow up, and the world of adult
consciousness has always held a relation to myth intimate enough
to make readjustment possible. The finest spirits have bridged the
gulf, have carried over with them something of a child's faith, and
only the coarsest have grown into something which was no more
than finished animality. Today the gulf is broader, the adjustment
more difficult, than ever it was before, and even the possibility of
an actual human maturity is problematic. There impends for the
human spirit either extinction or a readjustment more stupendous
than any made before.

Questions

1. Krutch discusses Freud's "quaint conceit" in the opening section.
What exactly is Krutch's application of it? How important is it to the development of the essay?

2. Krutch tends to summarize his general view in the third sentence of
the last paragraph of Section I. With the whole essay in mind, summarize
the "facts" that he thinks have been thrust on man and the "illusions" that
he thinks man has had to abandon. Can you sum up the predicament he
asserts man is left in?

3. Krutch tends to contrast terms like *fancy, mythology,* and *desire*
with another group of terms. List some. Considering each group separately, what are the common elements among the terms?

4. Krutch makes considerable use of the term *nature,* for example in
Paragraph 6. What meanings attach to the term as it is used throughout

the essay? What additional meanings can you associate with *nature* that Krutch seems to overlook?

5. Paragraphs 9 and 10 draw upon historical incidents for illustration. From what perspective, or point of view, in time does Krutch write? How characteristic is this of his perspective in the rest of the essay? Support your answer with particular instances.

6. It is commonly said that in Christian belief the notion of a God of Wrath preceded the notion of a God of Love. If this is so, what assumption of Krutch's is undercut? Consider especially his discussion in Paragraphs 5 and 6 of the essay.

7. In the opening sentence of Paragraph 4, Krutch makes an assumption about the course of racial history. Concede that his assumption is true, and argue from evidence in the essay that man is at the point of old age instead of on the verge of maturity, as is implied in the last paragraph of the essay. If the assumption is false, show to what extent Krutch's general argument in the essay is thereby damaged.

8. Krutch's outlook is pessimistic, and it is debatable whether a naturally pessimistic disposition led him to his views or whether his views led him into pessimism. Examine Section I of the essay for evidence of humor and wit (as in the opening sentence, where Krutch labels as a "quaint conceit" a view with which he entirely agrees). What does the evidence suggest about Krutch's character?

9. Read George Santayana's essay in Section I of the text, and discuss whether his views in it accord with those that Krutch ascribes to him in Paragraph 19 of the essay.

10. Compare Krutch's assumptions on the nature of historical development with those Carl Becker expresses in his essay on "Progress" (pp. 217–26).

STYLE AND TONE

In one respect, tone and style are the heart of every course in reading and writing; they underlie discussions of informality, simplicity, precision, and economy. But as qualities that the individual theme might possess—distinguishing its informality and simplicity from the same general qualities in another theme—they are usually the last things to receive attention.

Tone in writing may be thought of most easily as the writer's tone of voice; it is the attitude that he assumes toward his subject and his reader. The student who writes, *Say now, did it ever strike you that George Orwell and Carl Becker operate on the same wavelength,* is assuming a breezy tone. He might have said in a more subdued informal tone, *Offhand it might not seem so, but George Orwell and Carl Becker have a lot in common.* Or he might have chosen a more formal tone and said, *A careful comparison between George Orwell and Carl Becker displays many similarities. Say now* is colloquial; it serves to establish an air of familiar address, as though writer and reader were in conversation. *Strike you* is on the borderline between colloquial language and informal written language. *Operate on the same wavelength* is a vivid and jarring metaphor, in keeping with *strike you* and *say now.* The three phrases are the essential means by which the student establishes his breezy tone. The differing phrases in the other two versions are likewise the chief means by which individual tones are established. Sometimes in analyzing tone we merely want to be able to say that the tone is breezy because of the highly colloquial language (or serious, because of the generally formal language). Sometimes we want to know why a particular tone was adopted—perhaps to meet, or to counteract, a frivolous subject, occasion, audience (or a serious subject, occasion, audience). At other times we want to pass judgment upon the tone: it is vulgarly irreverent; it is stuffily reverent; it is confused; and so forth.

A writer establishes the tone of a piece of writing by a variety of means, some of them deliberate and artful, some of them unconscious and automatic. He knows, for instance, that *ain't* is customarily regarded as a vulgar colloquialism. If he uses it in a piece of writing, other than reportage of conversation, he can achieve certain effects: a tone of casual humor, or of disrespect, or of utter familiarity. Of course if he does not know about *ain't,* he cannot deliberately achieve these effects; he will probably produce a jumble of uncontrolled tones. Few students will have trouble controlling *ain't,* but other words are more difficult. What specific contrasts in tone are suggested by the following pairs: *say now—offhand; a lot in common— many similarities; strike you—careful comparison displays?*

Diction affects tone. Tone affects diction. The tone that a writer falls into may induce him—sometimes without his thinking about it—to choose one sort of word instead of another. It must have been easy for Abraham Lincoln, with his legal background and with a solemn occasion in mind, to find his formal, magisterial, abstractly metaphorical language: *Fourscore and seven years ago our fathers brought forth on this continent . . . .* How easy it is for all of us to use language unbecoming to our normal civilized selves when we are angry. More than diction is involved too. The long, balanced sentences of Lincoln contribute to his solemn tone, and the short, irregular phrases of an angry man suggest his tone. Diction may be the most obvious and most important element in tone, but sentence structure, rhythm, and sound are also significant. With all these elements, the degree of conscious control is variable. People cannot be entirely conscious in their writing.

Tone, it may appear, is closely allied with point of view. When we say that the tone of the Gettysburg Address is formal and magisterial, we suggest a point of view. But the distinction between tone and point of view is real. Tone is to be thought of as expressing the mood and manner of the writer; point of view is his stated or implied outlook. Tone may vary considerably within an essay, if only to avoid monotony. Point of view is more likely to remain constant, and changes in it will quickly raise the question of inconsistency.

Some years after George Santayana's death, Bertrand Russell said of him, *There was always something rather prim about Santayana. His clothes were always neat, and even in country lanes he wore patent-leather button boots. I think a person of sufficient intelligence might perhaps have guessed these characteristics from his literary style.* Any student who wants to may test his intelligence by reading the Santayana essay in Section I of this text, and he may be forced to decide that Russell is wrong. But whether Russell is wrong or right about Santayana, he is expressing a common opinion: the style is the man himself.

Like tone, style refers to the way a man writes rather than to what he writes about; and in analyzing it we examine the same features: diction, sentence structure, rhythm, sound. Used as an objective term, style is the sum of all the parts of a man's writing habits—in a given essay or in all his work. Consider the following passage in which D. H. Lawrence describes being in Sicily near Mount Etna.

Why can't one sit still? Here in Sicily it is so pleasant: the sunny Ionian sea, the changing jewel of Calabria, like a fire-opal moved in the light; Italy and the panorama of Christmas clouds, night with the dog-star laying a long, luminous gleam across the sea, as if baying at us, Orion marching above; how the dog-star Sirius looks at one, looks at one! he is the hound of heaven, green, glamorous and fierce!—and then oh regal evening star, hung westward flaring over the jagged dark precipices of tall Sicily: then Etna, that wicked witch, resting her thick white snow under heaven, and slowly slowly rolling her orange-colored smoke. They called her the Pillar of Heaven, the Greeks. It seems wrong at first, for she trails up in a long, magical, flexible line from the sea's edge to her blunt cone, and does not seem tall. She seems rather low, under heaven. But as one knows her better, oh awe and wizardry! Remote under heaven, aloof, so near, yet never with us. The painters try to paint her, and the photographers to photograph her, in vain. Because why? Because the near ridges, with their olives and white houses, these are with us. Because the river-bed, and Naxos under the lemon groves, Greek Naxos deep under dark-leaved, many-fruited lemon groves, Etna's skirts and skirt-bottoms, these still are our world, our own world. Even the high villages among the oaks, on Etna. But Etna herself, Etna of the snow and secret changing winds, she is beyond a crystal wall. When I look at her, low, white, witchlike under heaven, slowly rolling her orange smoke and giving sometimes a breath of rose-red flame, then I must look away from earth, into the ether, into the low empyrean. And there, in that remote region, Etna is alone. If you would see her, you must slowly take off your eyes from the world and go a naked seer to the strange chamber of the empyrean.*

We can describe the style of the passage in objective terms. Most of the vocabulary is the ordinary informal language of writing, but there are several unusual words of a somewhat poetical quality (*luminous, regal, awe, wizardry, seer, empyrean*), and there are words and phrases quite appropriate for informal speech (*can't . . . sit still, it is so pleasant, because why*). A similar wide range is observable in the sentence structures. There are long sentences (*When I look at her . . .*), short sentences (*She seems rather low, under heaven.*), grammatically incomplete sentences (*Because why?*), sentences of seemingly confused construction (*Here in Sicily . . .*). This last kind of sentence epitomizes the general style of the passage, for the overall variety of vocabulary and sentence suggests an almost helter-skelter piling of description. The second sentence (*Here in Sicily . . .*) is a series of non-parallel phrases and clauses tumbling over one another in a fairly simple way. Throughout the passage there are adjectives and other modifiers in profusion (*green, glamorous and fierce*), repeated sentence patterns (*Because why? Because . . . . Because . . .*), repeated language (*witch, wizardry, witchlike*). But doubtless the most striking stylistic feature of the passage is its richness of sensuous metaphor. Within the first lines we have *why can't one sit still, sunny . . . sea, jewel of Calabria, like a fire-opal, dog-star laying a . . . gleam, as if baying at us, Orion marching.*

All these elements of style are available for anyone to employ, and every writer with a notable style is likely to have his imitators. But it is one thing to write a paragraph imitating Lawrence's style and another thing to be able to sustain that style page after page. A particular mentality is required to pour out sensuous metaphor in the manner that Lawrence is capable of; another sort of mentality is required to pour out abstract diction. So when we read Lawrence, we infer the man behind the style. We may be mistaken in our inference, just as we may be mistaken when we infer character from a man's habits and gestures; but still we do it. What sort of man is Lawrence? The repetitions, the rapid shifts, the sensuousness, the underlying simplicity of his style suggest a man of passion, energy, volatility, impatience.

Because style and tone concern the way a writer writes instead of what he writes about, they may seem to be unrelated to meaning.

They may seem to be icing on the cake. But they themselves provide meanings that can support, contradict, or not have anything particularly to do with the ordinary meaning in an essay. Consider the Lawrence passage again. If we try to abstract from it a literal meaning, we have something like this: Lawrence says that Sicily is lovely, in particular Mount Etna, and that Mount Etna has a special, secret, aloof sort of fascination that requires one to turn away from the nearer world. But if we think of some of the metaphors that Lawrence uses to describe Etna, we see a fuller and somewhat different meaning. The intensity of *that wicked witch . . . rolling her orange-colored smoke* and *Etna's skirts and skirt-bottoms* and *low, white, witchlike . . . giving sometimes a breath of rose-red flame* suggests a feeling that is almost like physical passion for a woman. At the same time the intensity has an extravagance that makes it playful. The reader does not take *that wicked witch* entirely seriously. Much more obviously than in most writing, the meaning of the Lawrence passage resides in part in its style and tone. What the passage is about is Lawrence's feeling for Mount Etna, his intimate, intense, and playful passion for it. He is not primarily trying to describe a scene in a way that would satisfy a photographer.

Tone.   The following terms represent extremes between which a writer varies. Some of the terms are often applied to style. *Impersonal, formal, serious, reserved,* vs. *personal, informal, light, intimate.*

Style.   Some of the following terms are often applied to tone as well. *Learned, involved, didactic, elevated, allusive, poetical, elegant, ironical, witty,* vs. *simple, clear, plain, economical.*

DICTION
The following terms are commonly used to distinguish different sorts of words and phrases in English.

Anglo-Saxon vs. Latinate
The larger part of the vocabulary of English today derives from Anglo-Saxon. The words are generally short and simple: *I, dog,*

good, hit. There are, though, very many words drawn from Latin, and these tend to be longer: *ego, canine, excellent, assault*. Other words come from other languages such as French and Spanish. The word *assault* comes from Latin via French.

Colloquial vs. Informal vs. Formal
Colloquial language is language usually reserved for speech: *flicks, guts, screwball*. Informal language is language used in ordinarily careful speech and writing: *movie, bravery, crazy*. Formal language tends to be very careful, polite, and learned: *cinema, heroism, schizophrenic*. The line between formal and informal and between informal and colloquial is often blurred and frequently disappears.

Common vs. Special
All the examples of colloquial, informal, formal, Anglo-Saxon, and Latinate vocabulary above are common words in the sense of being in general use. There are various categories of words used by special groups or in special circumstances.
Slang is the newest colloquial speech: *pad* for *bed* is slang. *Archaism* refers to language once common but now rarely used: *ere* meaning *before* is archaic. *Jargon* is the technical language of a group: *identify, reject, regress, superego* are words with special meanings for psychologists. *Localism* refers to language that is used in a particular region: *down east* is a New England localism that refers to Maine.

Concrete vs. Abstract
To say that a man has *guts* or that he has *rocks in the head* is to use concrete diction—language referring to the physical world and physical sensation. To say that he is *brave* or is *crazy* is to use abstract diction—language referring to nonsensuous things. Probably all abstract diction derives from concrete diction. When we say that a man has *very deep* thoughts, we are using concrete diction that is so commonplace that we have to think twice to realize that it is concrete. When we say that a man has *profound* thoughts, we are using a word that is abstract

except to someone who knows Latin and remembers that it means "very deep."

Denotative vs. Connotative

Denotation refers to the basic meaning of a word, connotation to overtones of meaning in it. *Home* and *house* basically refer to the place where a person lives; the overtone of *home* is family and love, the overtone of *house* is physical structure.

Literal vs. Figurative

To speak literally is to mean exactly what you say; to speak figuratively is to use metaphor or irony or other such devices. *He speeded down the road* is literal; *he rocketed down the road* is figurative unless the man is using a rocket; *that's just fine and dandy* (said with a sneer) is figurative. Most literal language has figurative language buried in it: we say *down the road* but we do not literally mean "down"; the word down has simply lost its figurative strength in this usage.

THE BORE

W. Somerset Maugham

W. Somerset Maugham (1874–1965) was born in Paris, of
English parents, and spent much of a long life in travel. Orphaned at the age of ten, he studied medicine at his guardian's
insistence, but having qualified as a physician, he turned instead to writing, achieving early success as playwright (*A Man
of Honor, The Circle*) and novelist. He wrote voluminously
and in virtually every prose category—fictions large and small,
essays, memoirs. His best-known novels are probably *The
Moon and Sixpence,* a fictionalized biography of Gauguin, and
Of Human Bondage, a fictionalized account of his own early
years as a medical student. *The Summing-Up* and *Strictly Personal* offer reminiscences and reflections of an elderly, sometimes cynical, man of letters.

(1) We saw it coming from a good way off, two or three large
waves following one another, and it didn't look very alarming. It
came nearer, very quickly, with a roar like the roar of a stormy sea,
and I saw that the waves were much larger than I had thought. I
didn't like the look of them, and I tightened my belt so that my
trousers shouldn't slip down if I had to swim for it. Then in a moment the Bore was upon us. It was a great mass of water, eight, ten,
twelve feet high, and it was quite plain at once that no boat could
weather it. The first wave dashed over us, drenching us all and half
filling the boat with water, and then immediately another wave struck
us. The boatmen began to shout. They were prisoners from the up-

country jail and they wore their prison clothes. They lost control of the boat; the force of the water turned it round so that we were broadside on as we were carried on the crest of the Bore. Another wave dashed over us and we began to sink. Gerald, R. and I scrambled from beneath the awning under which we had been lying, and suddenly the boat gave way under us and we found ourselves in the water. It was surging and storming round us. My first impulse was to swim for the shore, but R. shouted to Gerald and me to cling to the boat. For two or three minutes we did this. I expected that the waves would pass as the Bore swept up the river and that in a few minutes at the outside we should find ourselves once more in calm water. I forgot that we were being carried along with the Bore. The waves kept dashing over us. We were hanging on to the gunwale and the base of the framework which supported the rattan mats of the awning. Then a bigger wave caught the boat, and it turned over, falling upon us, so that we lost our hold. There was nothing then but a slippery bottom to put our hands to, and as the keel came within reach we made a desperate grab at it. The boat continued to turn, like a wheel, and then we caught hold of the gunwale with a greater sense of security, only to feel the boat turn again, forcing us under water, and the whole business repeated itself.

(2) This went on for I don't know how long. I thought it was because we were all clinging to the side of the boat, and I tried to get some of the crew to go round to the other side; I thought that if half of us remained on one side while half went over to the other, we could keep the boat bottom down and so easily hang on; but I could make no one understand. The waves swept over us, and each time the gunwale slipped out of my hand I was pushed under, only to come up again as the keel gave me something to cling to.

(3) Presently I began to get terribly out of breath, and I felt my strength going. I knew I couldn't hold out much longer. I thought the best thing was to make a dash for the bank, but Gerald begged me to try to hold on. The bank now didn't look more than forty or fifty yards away. We were still being carried along among the seething, pounding waves. The boat went round and round and we all scrambled round it like squirrels in a cage. I swallowed a good deal of water. I felt I was very nearly done. Gerald stayed near me and two or three times gave me a hand. He couldn't do much, for as the

side of the boat fell over us we were equally helpless. Then, I don't know why, for three or four minutes the boat held keel downwards, and we were able to hold on and rest. I thought the danger was past. It was a precious thing to be able to get one's breath. But on a sudden the boat rolled right round again, and the same thing repeated itself. The few moments' respite had helped me, and I was able to struggle a little longer. Then again I became terribly out of breath and I felt as weak as a rat. My strength was gone, and I didn't know if I had enough now to try to swim for the shore. Gerald by this time was nearly as exhausted as I was. I told him my only chance was to try to get ashore. I suppose we were in deeper water then, for it seemed that the waves were not so turbulent. On the other side of Gerald were two of the crew, and somehow they understood that we were down and out. They made signs to us that now we could risk making for the bank. I was dreadfully tired. They caught hold of a thin mattress as it floated past us, it was one of those that we had been lying on, and they made it into a roll which they used as a life-belt. It didn't look as though it would be much use, but I took hold of it with one hand, and with the other struck out for the shore. The two men came with Gerald and me. One of them swam by my side. I don't quite know how we reached it. Suddenly Gerald cried out that he could touch the bottom. I put down my legs, but could feel nothing. I swam a few more strokes, and then, trying again, my feet sank into thick mud. I was thankful to feel its beastly softness. I floundered on, and there was the bank, black mud into which we sank up to the knees.

(4) We scrambled up with the help of roots of dead trees that stuck out of the mud, and when we came to the top found a little flat of tall rank grass. We sank down and for a while lay there stretched out and exhausted. We were so tired that we couldn't move. We were covered with black mud from head to foot. After a time we stripped off our things and I made myself a loin cloth out of my dripping shirt. Then Gerald had a heart attack. I thought he was going to die. I could do nothing but let him lie still and tell him it would pass over. I don't know how long we lay there, the better part of an hour, I should think, and I don't know how long we were in the water. At last R. came along in a canoe and fetched us off.

(5) When we got to the Dyak long-house on the other side where

we were to spend the night, although we were caked with mud from top to toe, and were in the habit of having a swim three or four times a day, we couldn't bring ourselves to go into the river, but washed ourselves perfunctorily in a pail. None of us said anything, but we certainly all felt that we didn't want to have anything more to do with the river that night.

(6) Looking back, I was surprised to notice that not at any moment had I been at all frightened. I suppose the struggle was so severe that there was no time for any emotion, and even when I felt my strength going and thought that in a moment or two I should have to give up, I am not conscious that I had any feeling of fear or even distress at the thought of death by drowning. I was so tired that it seemed to me rather in the nature of a relief. Later in the evening when I was sitting in a dry sarong in the Dyak house and from it saw the yellow moon lying on her back it gave me a keen, almost a sensual pleasure. I couldn't help thinking that I might at that moment have been a corpse floating along with the tide up the river. And next morning when we started off again to go down stream I found an added pleasure in the cheerful sky and the sunshine and the greenness of the trees. The air was singularly good to breathe.

Questions

1. What do you think is Maugham's intention in describing this episode? To what extent would that intention be affected if the final paragraph were omitted?

2. To what effect in point of view does Maugham use the grammatical first person singular in the sketch?

3. Analyze Paragraph 1 for its range of diction and its sentence rhythms. Are they stylistically consistent with one another?

4. What contributions do Maugham's metaphors make to the dramatic quality of the episode? Assess the character of the more notable metaphors throughout the sketch.

5. Characterize the transitions within Paragraph 4. Are they of the same sort as those between paragraphs?

6. The style changes somewhat in the last two paragraphs. What are the noticeable changes and to what do you attribute them?

7. On the basis of your answers to the preceding questions, characterize the general tone of the sketch and state its contribution to Maugham's intention, which you assessed in Question 1.

8. In "Shooting an Elephant" in this section, George Orwell describes a moment of physical danger to himself. Compare his and Maugham's attitudes and their stylistic handling of the situations.

9. Does Maugham's style suggest more the man or more the craftsman? Is the style noticeable or not noticeable, conscious or self-conscious? Discuss.

FIRST START IN LIFE

H. G. Wells

Born in Bromley, a London suburb, H. G. Wells (1866–1946) was the son of a small shopkeeper; his mother had been a ladies' maid. He began working at the age of thirteen, and with the aid of a scholarship attended the Royal College of Science, graduating with first-class honors. He taught science for a time, turned to journalism, joined the Fabian Society (a socialist group that also included George Bernard Shaw), and began writing novels: science fiction *(The War of the Worlds, The Invisible Man)*, still read today, and more realistic novels of everyday life *(Mr. Polly*—which draws on his experiences touched upon below). Wells' best novel is probably *Tono Bungay,* in which he satirizes modern business ethics; he is also the author of *The Outline of History,* a popular account of world history from a distinctly rationalist point of view.

(1) My first start in life was rather hastily improvised. My mother had a second cousin, Thomas Pennicott, "Uncle Tom" we called him, who had always been very much in the margin of her world. I think he had admired her and been perhaps helped by her when they were young folk at Midhurst. He was one of the witnesses to her marriage. He was a fat, round-faced, clean-shaven, black-haired man, illiterate, good humoured and shrewd. He had followed the ruling tendency in my mother's family to keep inns, and he had kept the Royal Oak opposite the South Western Railway Station at Windsor to such good effect, that he was able to buy and rebuild a riverside inn, called Surly Hall, much affected by the Eton wet-bobs,

From *Experiment in Autobiography* by H. G. Wells, The Macmillan Company, 1934. Reprinted by permission of the Executors of the Estate of H. G. Wells.

during the summer term. He built it as a gabled house and the gables were decorated with blue designs and mottoes glorifying Eton in the Latin tongue, very elegant and correct. The wet-bobs rowed up in the afternoons and choked the bar and swarmed over the lawn, vociferously consuming squashed flies and other strangely named refreshments. There was a ferry, a number of tethered punts and boats, green tables under the trees, a decaying collection of stuffed birds, ostrich eggs, wampum and sundries, in an outhouse of white plaster and tarred weather boarding, called the Museum, an eyot and a willow-bordered paddock for campers. Surly Hall has long since disappeared from the banks of the Thames, though I believe that Monkey Island, half a mile further up, still carries on.

(2) It was Uncle Tom's excellent custom to invite Sarah's boys for the holidays; it was not an invariable custom but it happened most years, and we had a thoroughly healthy and expansive three weeks or a month, hanging about his licensed premises in an atmosphere faintly flavoured by sawdust and beer. My brothers' times fell into the Royal Oak days, but my lot was to visit Surly Hall for the last three of my school years. There I learnt to punt, paddle and row, but the current was considered too swift for me to attempt swimming without anyone to teach me. I did not learn to swim until I was past thirty.

(3) My uncle was a widower, but he had two grown-up daughters in their early twenties, Kate and Clara; they shared the duties of the one or two barmaids he also employed. They all found me a very amusing temporary younger brother. Kate was the serious sister, a blonde with intellectual aspirations, and she did very much to stimulate me to draw and read. There was a complete illustrated set of Dickens which I read in abundantly, and a lot of bound up *Family Heralds,* in which I best remember a translation of Eugene Sue's *Mysteries of Paris,* which seemed to me at the time, the greatest romance in the world. All these young women encouraged me to talk, because I said such unexpected things. They pretended to flirt with me, they used me as a convenient chaperon when enterprising men customers wanted to gossip on the lawn in the twilight, and Miss King, the chief barmaid, and Clara became competitive for my sentimental devotion. It all helped to educate me.

(4) One day there appeared on the lawn a delightful vision in fluttering muslin, like one of the ladies in Botticelli's *Primavera*. It was that great actress, Ellen Terry, then in her full loveliness, who had come to Surly Hall to study a part and presently be visited there by Mr. Henry Irving. I ceased to consider myself engaged to Miss King forthwith; I had pledged myself heedlessly; and later on I was permitted to punt the goddess about, show her where white lilies were to be found and get her a great bunch of wet forget-me-nots. There was an abundance of forget-me-nots among the sedges, and in a bend above us were smooth brown water surfaces under great trees and a spread of yellow (and some white) water-lilies in which dragon-flies hovered. It was far finer, I thought, than the Keston Fish Ponds, which had hitherto been the most beautiful place in my world, and at Keston there was no boat with oars, paddle and boat-hook complete, in which I could muck about for hours together.

(5) Often when I was going for walks along the rather trite and very pebbly footpaths about Bromley, thirty miles away, I would let my imagination play with the idea that round the next corner and a little further on and then a bit more, I should find myself with a cry of delighted recognition on the road that led immediately to Surly Hall in summer and all its pleasantness. And how was I to suspect that Uncle Tom was losing money and his temper over the place, having borrowed to rebuild it rather too pretentiously, and that he was quarrelling with both his daughters about their lovers and that dark-eyed Clara, dreadfully bored and distressed tempera-mentally, was taking to drink? I knew nothing of all that, nor how grely and dismally the Thames sluices by these riverside inns in the winter months.

(6) But this is a mere glimpse of summer paradise on the way to my first start in life. My mother, I think I have made it clear, was within her limits a very determined little woman. Almost as unques-tioning as her belief in Our Father and Our Saviour, was her belief in drapers. I know not whether that heartless trifler of her early years was a draper, but she certainly thought that to wear a black coat and tie behind a counter was the best of all possible lots attain-able by man—at any rate by man at our social level. She had bound my brother Frank, resisting weakly, to Mr. Crowhurst in the Mar-

ket Square, Bromley, for five years and she had bound my brother Freddy to Mr. Sparrowhawk of the Pavement for four, to obey those gentlemen as if they were parents and learn the whole art and mystery of drapery from them, and she was now making a very resolute attempt to incarcerate me and determine my future in the same fashion. It did not dawn upon her that my queer gifts of drawing and expression were of any value at all. But as poor father was to be all alone in Atlas House now—the use he made of his eight years of solitude does not concern this story—a Bromley shop was no longer a suitable soil in which to pop me in order to grow up the perfect draper. She did not like to send me away where there was no one to look after me, for she knew there are dangers that waylay the young who are not supervised. So she found a hasty solution to her problem by sending me on trial, with a view to apprenticeship, to Messrs. Rodgers and Denyer of Windsor, opposite the Castle. There my morals would be under the observation of Surly Hall. And from Messrs. Rodgers and Denyer I got my first impressions of the intensely undesirable life for which she designed me. I had no idea of what I was in for. I went to my fate as I was told, unquestioningly, as my brothers had done before me.

(7) I am told that for lots of poor boys, leaving school and going into employment about thirteen or fourteen is a very exhilarating experience. But that is because they get pay, freedom in the evening and on Sundays, and an enhanced dietary. And they are released from the irksomeness of lessons and school tasks. But I had rather liked lessons and school tasks and drapers' apprentices did not get pay. An immense fuss, entirely unjustifiable, was made about the valuable trade apprentices were going to learn, and in the past the parents of the victim, if he "lived in," usually paid a premium of forty or fifty pounds or so for his immolation. I knew that the new start meant a farewell to many childish things. I had seen both my brothers pass in servitude, and I can still remember my brother Freddy having a last game of "marble runs" with toy bricks on the tilted kitchen table, a game of which he was particularly fond, before he submitted to the yoke of Mr. Sparrowhawk and began that ritual of stock-keeping, putting things away, tidying things up, bending over the counter, being attentive and

measuring off, that lasted thereafter for forty-odd years of his life. He knew what he was going to, did my brother Fred; and that game was played with sacrificial solemnity. "I enjoyed that game," said Freddy, who has always displayed a certain gentle stoicism. "It's supper time Bert. . . . Let's put the things away."

(8) Now it was my turn to put the things away, put the books away, give up drawing and painting and every sort of free delight, stop writing stories and imitations of *Punch,* give up all vain hopes and dreams, and serve an employer.

(9) I hated this place into which I had been put from the outset, but I was far too childish, as yet, to make any real resistance to the closing in of the prison about me. But I would not, I could not, give myself satisfactorily to this strange restricted life. It was just by the luck of that incapacity that the prison rejected me.

(10) I was set down from Uncle Pennicott's dog-cart, with a small portmanteau containing all my earthly goods, at the side door of the establishment of Messrs. Rodgers and Denyer, I was taken up a narrow staircase to the men's dormitory, in which were eight or ten beds and four miserable wash-hand stands, and I was shown a dismal little sitting room with a ground glass window opening on a blank wall, in which the apprentices and assistants might "sit" of an evening, and then I was conducted downstairs to an underground dining-room, lit by naked gas-jets and furnished with two long tables covered with American cloth, where the eating was to be done. Then I was introduced to the shop and particularly to the cash desk, where it had been arranged for the first year of my apprenticeship that I was to sit on a tall stool and receive money, give change, enter the amount on a sheet and stamp receipts. I was further instructed in a ritual of dusting and window cleaning. I was to come down at half past seven in the morning, I learnt, without fail, dust, clean windows, eat a bread-and-butter breakfast at half past eight, prepare my cash sheet and so to the routine of the day. I had to add up my cash at the end of the day, count the money in the till, make sheet and cash agree, help to wrapper-up and sweep out the shop, and so escape at half-past seven or eight to drink the delights of freedom until ten, when I had to be in. Lights out at half past ten. And this was to go on day

after day—for ever it seemed to me—with an early closing day once a week at five, and Sunday free.

(11)   I did not rise to these demands upon me. My mind withdrew itself from my duties. I did my utmost to go on living within myself and leave my duties to do themselves. My disposition to reverie increased. I dusted abominably; whenever I could manage it I did not dust at all. I smuggled books into my desk or did algebraic problems from my battered Todhunter's Large Algebra; I gave change absent-mindedly and usually I gave inaccurate change, and I entered wrong figures on the cash sheet out of sheer slovenliness.

(12)   The one bright moment during the day was when the Guards fifes and drums went past the shop and up to the Castle. These fifes and drums swirled me away campaigning again. Dispatch riders came headlong from dreamland, brooking no denial from the shopwalker. "Is General Bert Wells here? The Prussians have landed!"

(13)   I obeyed, I realize, all the impulses of a developing claustrophobia during that first phase of servitude. I would abandon my desk to sneak down into the warehouse, where I spent an unconscionable time seated in a convenient place of reflection, reading. Or I just stood about down there behind stacks of unpacked bales.

(14)   As the afternoon dragged on, the hour of reckoning when the cash sheet was added up drew near. It never by any chance corresponded with the money in the till. There had to be a checking of bills, a scrutiny of figures. Wrong sums had been set down. The adding had been wild work. At first the total error would be anything —more or less. After some weeks it became constantly a shortage. The booking clerk, and one of the partners who did the business correspondence and supervised things, would stay late to wrestle with the problem. They were impatient and reproachful. I had, to stay too, profoundly apathetic. Either I was giving change in excess, or in some way the money was seeping away. I did not care a rap. I had always hated money sums and long additions and now I detested them. I just wanted to get out of that shop before it was ten o'clock and time to return to the house. I did not realize the dreadful suspicions that were gathering above my head, nor the tempta-

tion my inaccuracies were offering to anyone who had access to my desk while I was at meals or otherwise absent. Nobody thought of that, unless perhaps it was the booking clerk.

(15) Every early closing night, every Sunday, at every opportunity I had, I cut off to Surly Hall and took refuge with my cousins. I went with joy, and returned with heavy feet. I did not want to talk about business there and when they asked me how I was getting on I said "Oh all right," and turned the talk to more agreeable topics. I did the long two miles from Windsor to and fro after dark for the one or two bright hours I spent there. My cousin Kate or Miss King would play the piano and sing. They would talk to me as though I was not the lowest thing on earth. There, I was still esteemed clever, and the queer things I said were applauded. My cousins, delighted at my appreciation, sang "Sweet Dreamland Faces," and "Juanita," to me and I sat on a little stool close to the piano in a state of rapt appreciation—of the music, the shaded lamp, the comfort and the ease of it.

(16) In this world of gramophones, pianolas and the radio, it is worth noting that at the age of thirteen I had heard no music at all except an occasional brass band, the not very good music of hymn singing and organ voluntaries in Bromley Church and these piano songs at Surly Hall.

(17) Then came a terrible inquisition at the shop. I was almost charged with pilfering. But my uncle Tom defended me stoutly. "You better not go saying *that*," said my uncle Tom, and indeed, except that there was now a continual shortage in the cash desk, there was no evidence against me. I had no expensive vices; I had no criminal associates, I was extremely shabby and untidy; no marked money—if they used marked money—or indeed any money except the weekly sixpence allowed me for pocket money, had ever been found upon me and my bearing was one of unconscious but convincing rectitude. Indeed I never realized fully what all the fuss was about until afterwards. Yet the fact remains that as a cash desk clerk I had leaked abominably and somebody—I suppose— had got away with the leakage.

(18) It was plain also that I shirked all my other tasks. And while my start in life was thus already faltering, I had some sort

of difference with the junior porter, which resulted in a conspicuous black eye for me. It was a gross breach of social conventions for an apprentice to fight a porter. I had great difficulty in explaining that black eye to my own satisfaction at Surly Hall. Moreover the clothes I had come to Windsor in were anything but stylish, and Mr. Denyer, the most animated of the partners, liked the look of me less and less. I wore a black velvet cap with a peak and that was all wrong. It became plain that my mother's first attempt to give me a start in life had failed. I was not starting. I was not fitted, said Messrs. Rodgers and Denyer, with perfect truth, to be a draper. I was not refined enough.

(19) I do not recall that at Windsor from first to last I made more than the slightest effort to do what was expected of me. It was not so much a resistance as an aversion. And it is a queer thing about that place that though I stayed there a couple of months, I do not remember the name of a single individual except one assistant named Nash, who happened to be the son of a Bromley draper and wore a long moustache. But all the other figures who sat with him at the downstairs dinner table are now blank nameless figures. Did I look at them? Did I listen to them? Nor can I remember the positions of the counters or the arrangements of the goods in the shop. I made no friends. Mr. Denyer, young Mr. Rodgers and old Mr. Rodgers left impressions, because they were like great pantomime heads always looking for me and saying disagreeable things to me, and I was always engaged in getting away from them. They disliked me; I think everybody in that place came to dislike me as a tiresome boring little misfit who made trouble and didn't do his share and was either missing when he was wanted or in the way when he wasn't. My self-conceit, I suppose, has blotted out all the other humiliating details from my memory. I do not even remember whether I felt any chagrin at my failure. All that seems effaced beyond recall. And yet that nocturnal tramp along the Maidenhead Road, which I took whenever I could, is real and living to me still. I could draw a map of the whole way down the hill and through Clewer. I could show where the road was wider and where it narrowed down.

(20) Like most undernourished growing boys I was cowardly and

I found the last stretch from Clewer to the inn terrifyingly dark and lonely. It was black on the moonless nights and eerie by moonlight and often it was misty from the river. My imagination peopled the dark fields on either hand with crouching and pursuing foes. Chunks of badly trimmed hedge took on formidable shapes. Sometimes I took to my heels and ran. For a week or so that road was haunted by a rumour of an escaped panther—from Lady Florence Dixie's riverside home, the Fisheries. That phantom panther waited for me patiently; it followed me like a noiseless dog, biding its time. And one night on the other side of the hedge a sleeping horse sighed deeply, a gigantic sigh, and almost frightened me out of my wits.

(21) But nothing of that sort kept me from going at every opportunity to Surly Hall, where there was something to touch my imagination and sustain my self-respect. I was hanging on subconsciously long before I held on consciously, to that life of books and expression and creative living from which the close exactions and economies of employment for private profit were sucking me down. And nothing that my mother and cousins could say to move and encourage me, could induce me to fix my attention on the little flimsy bits of paper with carbon duplicates, that were being slapped down at the guichet of the cash desk.

(22) "One eleven half—two and six. Quick please."

Questions

1. Define the tone of Paragraph 1 on the basis of answers to the following questions. What is the general level of diction, and how much variation is there from that level? How complex are the sentence structures? On what basis is the paragraph developed? How striking are the metaphors?

2. Define the differences in tone and style that result from the following revision of the sixth sentence in Paragraph 1: He built it as a gabled house and decorated the gables with blue designs and mottoes glorifying Eton in the Latin tongue; he considered the effect to be very elegant and correct. Is the paragraph as a whole closer to the original or to the revision?

3. From what points of view does Wells speak of "a delightful vision in fluttering muslin," "that great actress," "I had pledged myself heedlessly,"

and "later on I was permitted to punt the goddess about" (Paragraph 4)? What contribution do the shifts make to the tone of the paragraph?

4. With what degree of seriousness does Wells speak of "summer paradise," "belief in Our Father and Our Savior," "belief in drapers," and "heartless trifler" (Paragraph 6)?

5. Where in Paragraphs 6 through 10 does Wells use a prison metaphor? What contribution do these metaphors make to the tone of Paragraph 7? Does that tone dominate the paragraph?

6. How would you account for the difference in structure and rhythm of the sentences in Paragraph 10 from those in Paragraph 11? Would you say that the structure and rhythm of Paragraphs 10, 11, or 1 is characteristic of the essay as a whole?

7. On the basis of your answers to the previous questions, characterize Wells' style, considering how ironical and metaphorical it is, how varied and complex, etc.

8. Wells is treating a serious occasion in his life, and such things as the thievery and his fears at night might add to the seriousness. What is the precise kind of seriousness that his tone and style establish?

9. Purely on the basis of his style, what might you infer about H. G. Wells the man?

10. Describe the character of the young Wells, as he appears from his behavior and from what the older Wells says about him. Does he seem to have any qualities in common with the older Wells you have inferred in Question 9?

VOLTAIRE AND FREDERICK THE GREAT

E. M. FORSTER

Witty, gentle, intimate, Forster's style lends itself admirably to the informal essay, of which he is an established master. As in the selection that follows, he can treat a subject that he finds rich in serious implication and yet retain a whimsical distance. At the same time, his interest in character types and their interplay, and in historical anecdote and its possibilities of universal relevance, suggests the presence of the novelist within the essayist. Forster's concern with techniques of fiction is a continuing one and achieves formal expression in his classic of criticism, *Aspects of the Novel*. (Further information on Forster appears on pp. 188, 280.)

(1) Two hundred years ago a Frenchman paid a visit to a German. It is a famous visit. The Frenchman was delighted to come to Germany, his German host delighted to welcome him. They were more than polite to one another, they were enthusiastic, and each thought, "I am sure we are going to be friends for ever." Yet the visit was a disaster. They still talk about it in Germany to-day, and they say it was the Frenchman's fault. And they still talk about it in France. And I'm going to talk about it now, partly because it makes such a good story, and partly because it contains a lesson for us all, even though it did happen two hundred years back.

(2) The Frenchman was Voltaire. People to-day sometimes think of Voltaire as a person who sneered at everything, and made improper jokes. He was much more than that, he was the greatest man of his age, indeed he was one of the greatest men whom

From *Two Cheers for Democracy*, copyright, 1951, by E. M. Forster. Reprinted by permission of Harcourt, Brace & World, Inc., and Edward Arnold Ltd.

European civilisation has produced. If I had to name two people to speak for Europe at the Last Judgment I should choose Shakespeare and Voltaire—Shakespeare for his creative genius, Voltaire for his critical genius and humanity. Voltaire cared for the truth, he believed in tolerance, he pitied the oppressed, and since he was a forceful character he was able to drive his ideas home. They happen to be my own ideas, and like many other small people I am thankful when a great person comes along and says for me what I can't say properly for myself. Voltaire speaks for the thousands and thousands of us who hate injustice and work for a better world.

(3) What did he do? He wrote enormously: plays (now forgotten); short stories, and some of them are still read—especially that masterpiece, *Candide*. He was a journalist, and a pamphleteer, he dabbled in science and philosophy, he was a good popular historian, he compiled a dictionary, and he wrote hundreds of letters to people all over Europe. He had correspondents everywhere, and he was so witty, so up-to-date, so on the spot that kings and emperors were proud to get a letter from Voltaire and hurried to answer it with their own hand. He is not a great creative artist. But he is a great man with a powerful intellect and a warm heart, enlisted in the service of humanity. That is why I rank him with Shakespeare as a spiritual spokesman for Europe. Two hundred years before the Nazis came, he was the complete anti-Nazi.

(4) I am so fond of him that I should like to add he had a perfect character. Alas, he hadn't! He was a bundle of contradictions and nerves. Although he loved truth he often lied. Although he loved humanity he was often malicious. Though generous he was a money-maker. He was a born tease. He had no dignity. And he was no beauty to look at either—a gibbering monkey of a man, very small, very thin, with a long sharp nose, a bad complexion and beady black eyes. He overdressed, as little people sometimes do, and his wig was so large that it seemed to extinguish him.

(5) That is the Frenchman who sets out for Berlin on June 13, 1751; the German whom he is about to visit is Frederick the Great, King of Prussia.

(6) Frederick is one of the founders of modern Germany, and Hitler has made a careful study of him. He plunged Europe into

wars to advance his ambitions. He believed in force and fraud and cruelty, and in doing everything himself. He had a genius for organising, he preferred to employ inferior men, and he despised the human race. That is the dividing line between him and Voltaire. Voltaire believed in humanity. Frederick did not. "You don't know this damned race of men," he once exclaimed. "You don't know them. I do." He was a cynic, and having had a very unhappy childhood he felt till the end of his life that he had not been properly appreciated; and we know how dangerous such men can be, and what miseries they can bring upon themselves and others.

(7) But there was another side to Frederick. He was a cultivated, sensitive gentleman. He was a good musician, he had read widely, and he had made a careful study of French. He even composed a number of French poems—they are not good, still they serve to show that to him German wasn't everything. He was, in this way, more civilised than Hitler. There was no Nordic purity nonsense about him. He did not think that Germany was destined to rule the world: he knew that the world is a very complicated place, and that we have to live and let live in it; he even believed in freedom of speech. "People can say what they like as long as I do what I like" was the way he put it. One day, as he went through Berlin he saw a caricature of himself on a wall, and all he said was: "Oh—hang it down lower so that it can be seen better."

(8) The visit began in a whirl of compliments. Voltaire called Frederick "The Solomon of the North," Frederick declared that of all his victorious titles the most precious was Possessor of Voltaire. He made his guest a court official, housed him royally, gave him a handsome salary, and promised an extra salary to his niece, Madame Denis, if she would come to keep house for him. (We shall hear more of poor Madame Denis in a minute.) Witty conversation, philosophic discussion, delicious food—Frederick liked good food, though he was careful to get it cheap. Everything seemed perfect—but! Not long after his arrival, Voltaire wrote a letter to a friend in France in which the ominous little word "But" keeps occurring.

(9) "The supper parties are delicious. The King is the life of the company. But. I have operas and comedies, reviews and con-

certs, my studies and books. But, but. Berlin is fine, the princesses charming, the maids of honour handsome. But." We can interpret this But. It is the instinctive protest of the free man who finds himself in the power of a tyrant. Voltaire, for all his faults, was a free man. Frederick had charm and intelligence. But—he was a tyrant.

(10) The visit went very slowly. Voltaire did several tiresome things. He got mixed up in a shady financial transaction, he quarrelled with another Frenchman who was in the king's service, he drank too much chocolate, and when the king rationed him he revenged himself by taking the wax candles out of the candlesticks and selling them. All very undignified. And—worst of all—he laughed at the king's French poems. Frederick, like Hitler, fancied himself as an artist, and he had often employed his guest to polish his verses up. Now he was told that the tiresome little monkey was poking fun at him and quoting him all over the place—a serious matter this, for some of the poems were imprudent, and intended for private circulation only. The Solomon of the North was vexed. He thought: "No doubt my visitor is a genius, but he is making more trouble than he's worth, and he's disloyal." And Voltaire thought: "No doubt my host is a mighty monarch, but I would rather worship him from a distance." He left Berlin, after a stay of two years, which had gradually become more and more uncomfortable for both parties.

(11) But that is not the end. The real bust-up was yet to come. It occurred at Frankfurt, where Voltaire was waiting for Madame Denis to join him. Frankfurt did not belong to the King of Prussia. He had no legal authority there at all, but he had his "Gestapo" and he worked through them to interfere with personal liberty. He discovered that Voltaire had taken away from Berlin (it seems by accident) a copy of the wretched French poems, flew into a passion and ordered Voltaire's luggage to be searched. As always, he employed second-rate people and they went too far. They not only searched Voltaire's luggage but they imprisoned him and bullied him night and day in the hope of extracting information which would please their royal master. It is an incredible affair, a real foretaste of Nazi methods. Voltaire tried to escape; he was stopped at the gates of Frankfurt and dragged back, and Madame Denis, who

now arrived to join her uncle, was also arrested and ill-treated. Madame Denis was a stout, emotional lady, with some pretensions as an actress. She was not one to suffer in silence and she soon made Europe ring with her protests. Voltaire's health broke down and he feigned to be more ill than he really was: he ran from his tormentors into an inner room and gasped "Will you not even allow me to be sick?" His secretary rushed up to assist him, and Voltaire, while making all the motions of vomiting, whispered in his ear, "I am pretending! I am pretending!" He loved fooling people; he could be mischievous even in his misery, and this is to me an endearing trait.

(12) Frederick saw things had gone too far. Voltaire and his niece were released, and in later years the two great men corresponded almost as enthusiastically as before. But they were careful not to meet and Voltaire at all events had learnt a lesson. Berlin had taught him that if a man believes in liberty and variety and tolerance and sympathy he cannot breathe the air of the totalitarian state. It all may seem nice upon the surface—But! The tyrant may be charming and intelligent—but! The machinery may work perfectly—but! Something is missing: the human spirit is missing. Voltaire kept faith with the human spirit. He fought its battle against German dictatorship two hundred years before our time.

Questions

1. Select the two paragraphs most different from each other in their diction. Analyze them and describe the overall range of diction in the essay.

2. Would you say that Forster's sentence rhythms are graceful, energetic, conversational, or what? Examine the first two paragraphs, analyzing such features as the employment of idiomatic phrases, ease or abruptness of transition, and use of series.

3. The organization of the essay is systematic. Describe it, and argue whether it seems to be in keeping with the style of transition and sentence phrasing (Question 2).

4. Forster's judgments are sometimes blunt, as when he says that Frederick the Great was a tyrant. Elsewhere he is subtle. Examine the means by which he expresses his opinions in Paragraph 10.

5. Examine the essay for its most notable metaphors, and assess their general quality.

6. Forster wrote this essay when European civilization was on the verge of being destroyed by Germany under Hitler. His accents are not the accents of doom, hysteria, or exhortation. What precisely are they? What is their range?

7. On the basis of your answers to previous questions, characterize Forster's style. Does the man behind the style seem very much like Voltaire?

8. Carl Becker, in an essay in this section, is writing history too, and like Forster he has a point to make and anecdotes to relate. But he is a professional historian, and Forster an amateur. What distinguishes their approaches, aside from the fact that the very nature of Becker's discussion does not allow him to elaborate his stories?

THE PATRON AND THE CROCUS

The daughter of Sir Leslie Stephen, himself a notable essayist, critic, and editor, Virginia Woolf was brought up in an atmosphere flavored largely by literary matters. Educated informally at home and given the freedom of her father's books, she early began to write, did many reviews for magazines and newspapers when still in her twenties, and later, with her husband Leonard Woolf, established the Hogarth Press. Under their supervision, the Press grew in size and prestige: it published the works of such distinguished authors as E. M. Forster, T. S. Eliot, and Katherine Mansfield. "The Patron and the Crocus" is but one expression of Virginia Woolf's lifelong concern with the nature of art, of the artist, and of his relationship to his audience. (Further information on Virginia Woolf appears on p. 104.)

(1) Young men and women beginning to write are generally given the plausible but utterly impracticable advice to write what they have to write as shortly as possible, as clearly as possible, and without other thought in their minds except to say exactly what is in them. Nobody ever adds on these occasions the one thing needful: "And be sure you choose your patron wisely," though that is the gist of the whole matter. For a book is always written for somebody to read, and, since the patron is not merely the paymaster, but also in a very subtle and insidious way the instigator and inspirer of what is written, it is of the utmost importance that he should be a desirable man.

From *The Common Reader* by Virginia Woolf, copyright 1958, by Leonard Woolf. Reprinted by permission of Harcourt, Brace & World, Inc., and Leonard Woolf.

(2) But who, then, is the desirable man—the patron who will cajole the best out of the writer's brain and bring to birth the most varied and vigorous progeny of which he is capable? Different ages have answered the question differently. The Elizabethans, to speak roughly, chose the aristocracy to write for and the playhouse public. The eighteenth-century patron was a combination of coffee-house wit and Grub Street bookseller. In the nineteenth century the great writers wrote for the half-crown magazines and the leisured classes. And looking back and applauding the splendid results of these different alliances, it all seems enviably simple, and plain as a pike-staff compared with our own predicament—for whom should we write? For the present supply of patrons is of unexampled and bewildering variety. There is the daily Press, the weekly Press, the monthly Press; the English public and the American public; the best-seller public and the worst-seller public; the high-brow public and the red-blood public; all now organised self-conscious entities capable through their various mouthpieces of making their needs known and their approval or displeasure felt. Thus the writer who has been moved by the sight of the first crocus in Kensington Gardens has, before he sets pen to paper, to choose from a crowd of competitors the particular patron who suits him best. It is futile to say, "Dismiss them all; think only of your crocus," because writing is a method of communication; and the crocus is an imperfect crocus until it has been shared. The first man or the last may write for himself alone, but he is an exception and an unenviable one at that, and the gulls are welcome to his works if the gulls can read them.

(3) Granted, then, that every writer has some public or other at the end of his pen, the high-minded will say that it should be a submissive public, accepting obediently whatever he likes to give it. Plausible as the theory sounds, great risks are attached to it. For in that case the writer remains conscious of his public, yet is superior to it—an uncomfortable and unfortunate combination, as the works of Samuel Butler, George Meredith, and Henry James may be taken to prove. Each despised the public; each desired a public; each failed to attain a public; and each wreaked his failure upon the public by a succession, gradually increasing in intensity, of an-

gularities, obscurities, and affectations which no writer whose patron was his equal and friend would have thought it necessary to
inflict. Their crocuses, in consequence, are tortured plants, beautiful
and bright, but with something wry-necked about them, malformed,
shrivelled on the one side, overblown on the other. A touch of the
sun would have done them a world of good. Shall we then rush to
the opposite extreme and accept (if in fancy alone) the flattering
proposals which the editors of the *Times* and the *Daily News* may
be supposed to make us—"Twenty pounds down for your crocus in
precisely fifteen hundred words, which shall blossom upon every
breakfast table from John o' Groats to the Land's End before nine
o'clock to-morrow morning with the writer's name attached?"

(4) But will one crocus be enough, and must it not be a very brilliant yellow to shine so far, to cost so much, and to have one's name
attached to it? The Press is undoubtedly a great multiplier of crocuses. But if we look at some of these plants, we shall find that they
are only very distantly related to the original little yellow or purple
flower which pokes up through the grass in Kensington Gardens
early in March every year. The newspaper crocus is an amazing
but still a very different plant. It fills precisely the space allotted to
it. It radiates a golden glow. It is genial, affable, warm-hearted. It
is beautifully finished, too, for let nobody think that the art of "our
dramatic critic" of the *Times* or of Mr. Lynd of the *Daily News* is
an easy one. It is no despicable feat to start a million brains running at nine o'clock in the morning, to give two million eyes something bright and brisk and amusing to look at. But the night comes
and these flowers fade. So little bits of glass lose their lustre if you
take them out of the sea; great prima donnas howl like hyenas if
you shut them up in telephone boxes; and the most brilliant of
articles when removed from its element is dust and sand and the
husks of straw. Journalism embalmed in a book is unreadable.

(5) The patron we want, then, is one who will help us to preserve our flowers from decay. But as his qualities change from age
to age, and it needs considerable integrity and conviction not to be
dazzled by the pretentions or bamboozled by the persuasions of the
competing crowd, this business of patron-finding is one of the tests
and trials of authorship. To know whom to write for is to know

how to write. Some of the modern patron's qualities are, however, fairly plain. The writer will require at this moment, it is obvious, a patron with the book-reading habit rather than the play-going habit. Nowadays, too, he must be instructed in the literature of other times and races. But there are other qualities which our special weaknesses and tendencies demand in him. There is the question of indecency, for instance, which plagues us and puzzles us much more than it did the Elizabethans. The twentieth-century patron must be immune from shock. He must distinguish infallibly between the little clod of manure which sticks to the crocus of necessity, and that which is plastered to it out of bravado. He must be a judge, too, of those social influences which inevitably play so large a part in modern literature, and able to say which matures and fortifies, which inhibits and makes sterile. Further, there is emotion for him to pronounce on, and in no department can he do more useful work than in bracing a writer against sentimentality on the one hand and a craven fear of expressing his feeling on the other. It is worse, he will say, and perhaps more common, to be afraid of feeling than to feel too much. He will add, perhaps, something about language, and point out how many words Shakespeare used and how much grammar Shakespeare violated, while we, though we keep our fingers so demurely to the black notes on the piano, have not appreciably improved upon *Antony and Cleopatra*. And if you can forget your sex altogether, he will say, so much the better; a writer has none. But all this is by the way—elementary and disputable. The patron's prime quality is something different, only to be expressed perhaps by the use of that convenient word which cloaks so much—atmosphere. It is necessary that the patron should shed and envelop the crocus in an atmosphere which makes it appear a plant of the very highest importance, so that to misrepresent it is the one outrage not to be forgiven this side of the grave. He must make us feel that a single crocus, if it be a real crocus, is enough for him; that he does not want to be lectured, elevated, instructed, or improved; that he is sorry that he bullied Carlyle into vociferation, Tennyson into idyllics, and Ruskin into insanity; that he is now ready to efface himself or assert himself as his writers require; that he is bound to them by a more than maternal tie; that they are twins indeed, one dying if the other dies, one flourishing if the other flourishes; that the fate of literature depends upon their happy alliance—all of which proves, as we began by saying, that the choice of a patron is of the highest importance. But how to choose rightly? How to write well? Those are the questions.

Questions

1. Mrs. Woolf organizes her essay in a quasilogical pattern. She sets up a question—how to choose a patron—and answers it by a process of elimination. Assuming that she is not really interested in logic, explain the selection and arrangement of material on other grounds.

2. At what point does the word *patron* begin to take on a meaning somewhat beyond the ordinary dictionary meaning, and what is the meaning that Mrs. Woolf attaches to it? At what point does the crocus become a work of art?

3. What special qualities does Mrs. Woolf want to attribute to art by calling it a crocus rather than, for example, a mirror? What effect does she achieve when she has the editor of the *Daily News* say, "Twenty pounds down for your crocus"?

4. Examine the elaboration of the image of the crocus for its various contributions to the tone of the essay.

5. Are the metaphors of patron and crocus supported by a profusion of briefer metaphors no less original, or do they stand amid several mainly conventional ones? Examine Paragraphs 4 and 5.

6. There is a good deal of formality in Mrs. Woolf's diction and in her phrasing, as a glance at the first half of Paragraph 3 shows. But the overall effect is not formal. Examine the whole of Paragraph 3.

7. Analyze the irony in Paragraph 4, and try to understand Mrs. Woolf's meaning. Define the quality of the irony. Is it bitter, sarcastic, playful, diffuse, or what?

8. Characterize Mrs. Woolf's style on the basis of your answers to the preceding questions. Do you think that the sex of the writer is not apparent in it, or do you have the impression of a woman writing?

9. Mrs. Woolf begins her essay by asking who the best patron is (the opening of Paragraph 2), and she ends it by asking the same question. Has the intervening material primarily provided an exercise for her style, or has she said something? Who is her patron? Write an essay on the issue.

SHOOTING AN ELEPHANT

GEORGE ORWELL

Orwell's experiences in India, as a youth and later as a member
of the Indian Imperial Police, gave him firsthand knowledge of
both Indian and Anglo-Indian life; they also turned him into
a sharply critical commentator on British imperialism, which
he came to characterize as "very largely a racket." His first
novel, *Burmese Days,* presents a devastating picture of the
hypocrisy and futility of English colonial existence. "Shooting
an Elephant," written several years after Orwell had left India
for Europe, may be profitably compared with another of his
essays, "Marrakech" (Section II), written slightly later. Both
suggest why he has been called the "conscience of his generation." (Further information on Orwell appears on pp. 109,
235.)

(1) In Moulmein, in Lower Burma, I was hated by large numbers of people—the only time in my life that I have been important enough for this to happen to me. I was sub-divisional police
officer of the town, and in an aimless, petty kind of way anti-
European feeling was very bitter. No one had the guts to raise a riot,
but if a European woman went through the bazaars alone somebody would probably spit betel juice over her dress. As a police
officer I was an obvious target and was baited whenever it seemed
safe to do so. When a nimble Burman tripped me up on the football
field and the referee (another Burman) looked the other way, the
crowd yelled with hideous laughter. This happened more than
once. In the end the sneering yellow faces of young men that met

me everywhere, the insults hooted after me when I was at a safe distance, got badly on my nerves. The young Buddhist priests were the worst of all. There were several thousands of them in the town and none of them seemed to have anything to do except stand on street corners and jeer at Europeans.

(2) All this was perplexing and upsetting. For at that time I had already made up my mind that imperialism was an evil thing and the sooner I chucked up my job and got out of it the better. Theoretically—and secretly, of course—I was all for the Burmese and all against their oppressors, the British. As for the job I was doing, I hated it more bitterly than I can perhaps make clear. In a job like that you see the dirty work of Empire at close quarters. The wretched prisoners huddling in the stinking cages of the lock-ups, the grey, cowed faces of the long-term convicts, the scarred buttocks of the men who had been flogged with bamboos—all these oppressed me with an intolerable sense of guilt. But I could get nothing into perspective. I was young and ill-educated and I had had to think out my problems in the utter silence that is imposed on every Englishman in the East. I did not even know that the British Empire is dying, still less did I know that it is a great deal better than the younger empires that are going to supplant it. All I knew was that I was stuck between my hatred of the empire I served and my rage against the evil-spirited little beasts who tried to make my job impossible. With one part of my mind I thought of the British Raj as an unbreakable tyranny, as something clamped down, in *saecula saeculorum,* upon the will of prostrate peoples; with another part I thought that the greatest joy in the world would be to drive a bayonet into a Buddhist priest's guts. Feelings like these are the normal by-products of imperialism; ask any Anglo-Indian official, if you can catch him off duty.

(3) One day something happened which in a roundabout way was enlightening. It was a tiny incident in itself, but it gave me a better glimpse than I had had before of the real nature of imperialism—the real motives for which despotic governments act. Early one morning the sub-inspector at a police station the other end of the town rang me up on the 'phone and said that an elephant was ravaging the bazaar. Would I please come and do something about it?

I did not know what I could do, but I wanted to see what was happening and I got on to a pony and started out. I took my rifle, an old .44 Winchester and much too small to kill an elephant, but I thought the noise might be useful *in terrorem*. Various Burmans stopped me on the way and told me about the elephant's doings. It was not, of course, a wild elephant, but a tame one which had gone "must." It had been chained up, as tame elephants always are when their attack of "must" is due, but on the previous night it had broken its chain and escaped. Its mahout, the only person who could manage it when it was in that state, had set out in pursuit, but had taken the wrong direction and was now twelve hours' journey away, and in the morning the elephant had suddenly reappeared in the town. The Burmese population had no weapons and were quite helpless against it. It had already destroyed somebody's bamboo hut, killed a cow and raided some fruit-stalls and devoured the stock; also it had met the municipal rubbish van and, when the driver jumped out and took to his heels, had turned the van over and inflicted violences upon it.

(4) The Burmese sub-inspector and some Indian constables were waiting for me in the quarter where the elephant had been seen. It was a very poor quarter, a labyrinth of squalid bamboo huts, thatched with palm-leaf, winding all over a steep hillside. I remember that it was a cloudy, stuffy morning at the beginning of the rains. We began questioning the people as to where the elephant had gone and, as usual, failed to get any definite information. That is invariably the case in the East, a story always sounds clear enough at a distance, but the nearer you get to the scene of events the vaguer it becomes. Some of the people said that the elephant had gone in one direction, some said that he had gone in another, some professed not even to have heard of any elephant. I had almost made up my mind that the whole story was a pack of lies, when we heard yells a little distance away. There was a loud, scandalized cry of "Go away, child! Go away this instant!" and an old woman with a switch in her hand came round the corner of a hut, violently shooing away a crowd of naked children. Some more women followed, clicking their tongues and exclaiming; evidently there was something that the children ought not to have seen. I

rounded the hut and saw a man's dead body sprawling in the mud. He was an Indian, a black Dravidian coolie, almost naked, and he could not have been dead many minutes. The people said that the elephant had come suddenly upon him round the corner of the hut, caught him with its trunk, put its foot on his back and ground him into the earth. This was the rainy season and the ground was soft, and his face had scored a trench a foot deep and a couple of yards long. He was lying on his belly with arms crucified and head sharply twisted to one side. His face was coated with mud, the eyes wide open, the teeth bared and grinning with an expression of unendurable agony. (Never tell me, by the way, that the dead look peaceful. Most of the corpses I have seen looked devilish.) The friction of the great beast's foot had stripped the skin from his back as neatly as one skins a rabbit. As soon as I saw the dead man I sent an orderly to a friend's house nearby to borrow an elephant rifle. I had already sent back the pony, not wanting it to go mad with fright and throw me if it smelt the elephant.

(5) The orderly came back in a few minutes with a rifle and five cartridges, and meanwhile some Burmans had arrived and told us that the elephant was in the paddy fields below, only a few hundred yards away. As I started forward practically the whole population of the quarter flocked out of the houses and followed me. They had seen the rifle and were all shouting excitedly that I was going to shoot the elephant. They had not shown much interest in the elephant when he was merely ravaging their homes, but it was different now that he was going to be shot. It was a bit of fun to them, as it would be to an English crowd; besides they wanted the meat. It made me vaguely uneasy. I had no intention of shooting the elephant—I had merely sent for the rifle to defend myself if necessary —and it is always unnerving to have a crowd following you. I marched down the hill, looking and feeling a fool, with the rifle over my shoulder and an ever-growing army of people jostling at my heels. At the bottom, when you got away from the huts, there was a metalled road and beyond that a miry waste of paddy fields a thousand yards across, not yet ploughed, but soggy from the first rains and dotted with coarse grass. The elephant was standing eight yards from the road, his left side towards us. He took not the slight-

est notice of the crowd's approach. He was tearing up bunches of grass, beating them against his knees to clean them and stuffing them into his mouth.

(6) I had halted on the road. As soon as I saw the elephant I knew with perfect certainty that I ought not to shoot him. It is a serious matter to shoot a working elephant—it is comparable to destroying a huge and costly piece of machinery—and obviously one ought not to do it if it can possibly be avoided. And at that distance, peacefully eating, the elephant looked no more dangerous than a cow. I thought then and I think now that his attack of "must" was already wearing off; in which case he would merely wander harmlessly about until the mahout came back and caught him. Moreover, I did not in the least want to shoot him. I decided that I would watch him for a little while to make sure that he did not turn savage again, and then go home.

(7) But at that moment I glanced round at the crowd that had followed me. It was an immense crowd, two thousand at the least and growing every minute. It blocked the road for a long distance on either side. I looked at the sea of yellow faces above the garish clothes—faces all happy and excited over this bit of fun, all certain that the elephant was going to be shot. They were watching me as they would watch a conjurer about to perform a trick. They did not like me, but with the magical rifle in my hands I was momentarily worth watching. And suddenly I realized that I should have to shoot the elephant after all. The people expected it of me and I had got to do it; I could feel their two thousand wills pressing me forward, irresistibly. And it was at this moment, as I stood there with the rifle in my hands, that I first grasped the hollowness, the futility of the white man's dominion in the East. Here was I, the white man with his gun, standing in front of the unarmed native crowd— seemingly the leading actor of the piece; but in reality I was only an absurd puppet pushed to and fro by the will of those yellow faces behind. I perceived in this moment that when the white man turns tyrant it is his own freedom that he destroys. He becomes a sort of hollow, posing dummy, the conventionalized figure of a sahib. For it is the condition of his rule that he shall spend his life in trying to impress the "natives," and so in every crisis he has got

to do what the "natives" expect of him. He wears a mask; and his face grows to fit it. I had got to shoot the elephant. I had committed myself to doing it when I sent for the rifle. A sahib has got to act like a sahib; he has got to appear resolute, to know his own mind and do definite things. To come all that way, rifle in hand, with two thousand people marching at my heels, and then to trail feebly away, having done nothing—no, that was impossible. The crowd would laugh at me. And my whole life, every white man's life in the East, was one long struggle not to be laughed at.

(8) But I did not want to shoot the elephant. I watched him beating his bunch of grass against his knees, with that preoccupied grandmotherly air that elephants have. It seemed to me that it would be murder to shoot him. At that age I was not squeamish about killing animals, but I had never shot an elephant and never wanted to. (Somehow it always seems worse to kill a *large* animal.) Besides, there was the beast's owner to be considered. Alive, the elephant was worth at least a hundred pounds; dead, he would only be worth the value of his tusks, five pounds, possibly. But I had got to act quickly. I turned to some experienced-looking Burmans who had been there when we arrived, and asked them how the elephant had been behaving. They all said the same thing: he took no notice of you if you left him alone, but he might charge if you went too close to him.

(9) It was perfectly clear to me what I ought to do. I ought to walk up to within, say, twenty-five yards of the elephant and test his behavior. If he charged, I could shoot; if he took no notice of me, it would be safe to leave him until the mahout came back. But also I knew that I was going to do no such thing. I was a poor shot with a rifle and the ground was soft mud into which one would sink at every step. If the elephant charged and I missed him, I should have about as much chance as a toad under a steam-roller. But even then I was not thinking particularly of my own skin, only of the watchful yellow faces behind. For at that moment, with the crowd watching me, I was not afraid in the ordinary sense, as I would have been if I had been alone. A white man mustn't be frightened in front of "natives"; and so, in general, he isn't frightened. The sole

thought in my mind was that if anything went wrong those two thousand Burmans would see me pursued, caught, trampled on and reduced to a grinning corpse like that Indian up the hill. And if that happened it was quite probable that some of them would laugh. That would never do. There was only one alternative. I shoved the cartridges into the magazine and lay down on the road to get a better aim.

(10) The crowd grew very still, and a deep, low, happy sigh, as of people who see the theatre curtain go up at last, breathed from innumerable throats. They were going to have their bit of fun after all. The rifle was a beautiful German thing with cross-hair sights. I did not then know that in shooting an elephant one would shoot to cut an imaginary bar running from ear-hole to ear-hole. I ought, therefore, as the elephant was sideways on, to have aimed straight at his ear-hole; actually I aimed several inches in front of this, thinking the brain would be further forward.

(11) When I pulled the trigger I did not hear the bang or feel the kick—one never does when a shot goes home—but I heard the devilish roar of glee that went up from the crowd. In that instant, in too short a time, one would have thought, even for the bullet to get there, a mysterious, terrible change had come over the elephant. He neither stirred nor fell, but every line of his body had altered. He looked suddenly stricken, shrunken, immensely old, as though the frightful impact of the bullet had paralysed him without knocking him down. At last, after what seemed a long time—it might have been five seconds, I dare say—he sagged flabbily to his knees. His mouth slobbered. An enormous senility seemed to have settled upon him. One could have imagined him thousands of years old. I fired again into the same spot. At the second shot he did not collapse but climbed with desperate slowness to his feet and stood weakly upright, with legs sagging and head drooping. I fired a third time. That was the shot that did for him. You could see the agony of it jolt his whole body and knock the last remnant of strength from his legs. But in falling he seemed for a moment to rise, for as his hind legs collapsed beneath him he seemed to tower upward like a huge rock toppling, his trunk reaching skywards like a tree.

He trumpeted, for the first and only time. And then down he came, his belly towards me, with a crash that seemed to shake the ground even where I lay.

(12) I got up. The Burmans were already racing past me across the mud. It was obvious that the elephant would never rise again, but he was not dead. He was breathing very rhythmically with long rattling gasps, his great mound of a side painfully rising and falling. His mouth was wide open—I could see far down into caverns of pale pink throat. I waited a long time for him to die, but his breathing did not weaken. Finally I fired my two remaining shots into the spot where I thought his heart must be. The thick blood welled out of him like red velvet, but still he did not die. His body did not even jerk when the shots hit him, the tortured breathing continued without a pause. He was dying, very slowly and in great agony, but in some world remote from me where not even a bullet could damage him further. I felt that I had got to put an end to that dreadful noise. It seemed dreadful to see the great beast lying there, powerless to move and yet powerless to die, and not even to be able to finish him. I sent back for my small rifle and poured shot after shot into his heart and down his throat. They seemed to make no impression. The tortured gasps continued as steadily as the ticking of a clock.

(13) In the end I could not stand it any longer and went away. I heard later that it took him half an hour to die. Burmans were bringing dahs and baskets even before I left, and I was told they had stripped his body almost to the bones by the afternoon.

(14) Afterwards, of course, there were endless discussions about the shooting of the elephant. The owner was furious, but he was only an Indian and could do nothing. Besides, legally I had done the right thing, for a mad elephant has to be killed, like a mad dog, if its owner fails to control it. Among the Europeans opinion was divided. The older men said I was right, the younger men said it was a damn shame to shoot an elephant for killing a coolie, because an elephant was worth more than any damn Coringhee coolie. And afterwards I was very glad that the coolie had been killed; it put me legally in the right and it gave me a sufficient pretext for

shooting the elephant. I often wondered whether any of the others grasped that I had done it solely to avoid looking a fool.

Questions

1. What sort of tone would such language as "guts," "hideous," "sneering," and "hooted" (Paragraph 1) ordinarily help to establish? Why do these words fail to contribute to such a tone in the context of the paragraph?

2. Define the difference in tone that results from the following revision of the first two sentences in the essay: In Moulmein, in Lower Burma, anti-European feeling, although expressed in an aimless, petty kind of way, was very bitter. I myself, as subdivisional police officer of the town, held —for the only time in my life—an important enough position to be hated by large numbers of people.

3. What variety in diction do you observe in Paragraph 2? Can you account for it? Identify the level of formality of those words and phrases that seem to you to establish the dominant tone of the paragraph.

4. Analyze the diction, sentence construction, and metaphorical language of the two passages describing the dead coolie and the dying elephant. Compare the tones of the two passages, especially in respect to the contribution of each to the seriousness of the descriptions.

5. On the basis of your answers to previous questions, what would you say Orwell's style is: simple, formal, flexible, complex, colorful? What might you infer about the man from his style?

6. Orwell says a good many unpleasant things about himself in the essay. What are the most important ones? Do they add up to a general impression of an unpleasant person? Why or why not?

7. Taking the subject of Orwell's essay to be "the real nature of imperialism—the real motive for which despotic governments act" (Paragraph 3), would you say he is most convincing in his emotional appeal or his rational evidence? Explain.

8. Suppose someone said that Orwell's essay is only superficially about the real nature of imperialism. What evidence could you offer that it is basically about something else?

THE RETURN JOURNEY

D. H. LAWRENCE

Lawrence's incessant wanderings, which took up the last ten years of his life, had a number of causes, among them the search for a climate suitable to his delicate health and a general disgust with things English. Though he found few places satisfactory for very long, his travels did give him rich materials for his writings: the novels, *Kangaroo,* set in Australia, and *The Plumed Serpent,* set in Mexico; the essays that make up *Sea and Sardinia, Mornings in Mexico,* and *Etruscan Places.* The following excerpt from *Twilight in Italy,* written at a somewhat earlier period, makes clear the degree and quality of Lawrence's investment in foreign settings. (Further information on Lawrence appears on pp. 16, 271.)

(1) When one walks, one must travel west or south. If one turn northward or eastward it is like walking down a cul-de-sac, to the blind end.

(2) So it has been since the Crusaders came home satiated, and the Renaissance saw the western sky as an archway into the future. So it is still. We must go westwards and southwards.

(3) It is a sad and gloomy thing to travel even from Italy into France. But it is a joyful thing to walk south to Italy, south and west. It is so. And there is a certain exaltation in the thought of going west, even to Cornwall, to Ireland. It is as if the magnetic poles were south-west and north-east, for our spirits, with the south-west, under the sunset, as the positive pole. So whilst I walk through Switzerland, though it is a valley of gloom and depression,

From *Twilight in Italy* by D. H. Lawrence. Reprinted by permission of The Viking Press, Inc., Laurence Pollinger, Ltd., and the estate of the late Mrs. Frieda Lawrence.

382

a light seems to flash out under every footstep, with the joy of progression.

(4) It was Sunday morning when I left the valley where the Italians lived. I went quickly over the stream, heading for Lucerne. It was a good thing to be out of doors, with one's pack on one's back, climbing uphill. But the trees were thick by the roadside; I was not yet free. It was Sunday morning, very still.

(5) In two hours I was at the top of the hill, looking out over the intervening valley at the long lake of Zurich, spread there beyond with its girdle of low hills, like a relief-map. I could not bear to look at it, it was so small and unreal. I had a feeling as if it were false, a large relief-map that I was looking down upon, and which I wanted to smash. It seemed to intervene between me and some reality. I could not believe that that was the real world. It was a figment, a fabrication, like a dull landscape painted on a wall, to hide the real landscape.

(6) So I went on, over to the other side of the hill, and I looked out again. Again there were the smoky-looking hills and the lake like a piece of looking-glass. But the hills were higher: that big one was the Rigi. I set off down the hill.

(7) There was fat agricultural land and several villages. And church was over. The church-goers were all coming home: men in black broadcloth and old chimney-pot silk hats, carrying their umbrellas; women in ugly dresses, carrying books and umbrellas. The streets were dotted with these black-clothed men and stiff women, all reduced to a Sunday nullity. I hated it. It reminded me of that which I knew in my boyhood, that stiff, null "propriety" which used to come over us, like a sort of deliberate and self-inflicted cramp, on Sundays. I hated these elders in black broadcloth, with their neutral faces, going home piously to their Sunday dinners. I hated the feeling of these villages, comfortable, well-to-do, clean, and proper.

(8) And my boot was chafing two of my toes. That always happens. I had come down to a wide, shallow valley-bed, marshy. So about a mile out of the village I sat down by a stone bridge, by a stream, and tore up my handkerchief, and bound up the toes. And as I sat binding my toes, two of the elders in black, with um-

brellas under their arms, approached from the direction of the village.

(9) They made me so furious, I had to hasten to fasten my boot, to hurry on again, before they should come near me. I could not bear the way they walked and talked, so crambling and material and mealy-mouthed.

(10) Then it did actually begin to rain. I was just going down a short hill. So I sat under a bush and watched the trees drip. I was so glad to be there, homeless, without place or belonging, crouching under the leaves in the copse by the road, that I felt I had, like the meek, inherited the earth. Some men went by, with their coat-collars turned up, and the rain making still blacker their black broadcloth shoulders. They did not see me. I was as safe and separate as a ghost. So I ate the remains of my food that I had bought in Zurich, and waited for the rain.

(11) Later, in the wet Sunday afternoon, I went on to the little lake, past many inert, neutral, material people, down an ugly road where trams ran. The blight of Sunday was almost intolerable near the town.

(12) So on I went, by the side of the steamy, reedy lake, walking the length of it. Then suddenly I went in to a little villa by the water for tea. In Switzerland every house is a villa.

(13) But this villa was kept by two old ladies and a delicate dog, who must not get his feet wet. I was very happy there. I had good jam and strange honey-cakes for tea, that I liked, and the little old ladies pattered round in a great stir, always whirling like two dry leaves after the restless dog.

(14) "Why must he not go out?" I said.

(15) "Because it is wet," they answered, "and he coughs and sneezes."

(16) "Without a handkerchief, that is not *angenehm,*" I said.

(17) So we became bosom friends.

(18) "You are Austrian?" they said to me.

(19) I said I was from Graz; that my father was a doctor in Graz, and that I was walking for my pleasure through the countries of Europe.

(20) I said this because I knew a doctor from Graz who was

always wandering about, and because I did not want to be myself, an Englishman, to these two old ladies. I wanted to be something else. So we exchanged confidences.

(21) They told me, in their queer, old, toothless fashion, about
their visitors, a man who used to fish all day, every day for three
weeks, fish every hour of the day, though many a day he caught
nothing—nothing at all—still he fished from the boat; and so on,
such trivialities. Then they told me of a third sister who had
died, a third little old lady. One could feel the gap in the house.
They cried; and I, being an Austrian from Graz, to my astonishment felt my tears slip over on to the table. I also *was* sorry, and
I would have kissed the little old ladies to comfort them.

(22) "Only in heaven it is warm, and it doesn't rain, and no
one dies," I said, looking at the wet leaves.

(23) Then I went away. I would have stayed the night at this
house: I wanted to. But I had developed my Austrian character
too far.

(24) So I went on to a detestable brutal inn in the town. And the
next day I climbed over the back of the detestable Rigi, with its
vile hotel, to come to Lucerne. There, on the Rigi, I met a lost
young Frenchman who could speak no German, and who said he
could not find people to speak French. So we sat on a stone
and became close friends, and I promised faithfully to go and
visit him in his barracks in Algiers: I was to sail from Naples to
Algiers. He wrote me the address on his card, and told me he had
friends in the regiment, to whom I should be introduced, and we
could have a good time, if I would stay a week or two, down
there in Algiers.

(25) How much more real Algiers was than the rock on the Rigi
where we sat, or the lake beneath, or the mountains beyond. Algiers
is very real, though I have never seen it, and my friend is my friend
for ever, though I have lost his card and forgotten his name. He
was a Government clerk from Lyons, making this his first foreign
tour before he began his military service. He showed me his "circular excursion ticket." Then at last we parted, for he must get to
the top of the Rigi, and I must get to the bottom.

(26) Lucerne and its lake were as irritating as ever—like the

wrapper round milk chocolate. I could not sleep even one night there: I took the steamer down the lake, to the very last station. There I found a good German inn, and was happy.

(27) There was a tall thin man, whose face was red and inflamed from the sun. I thought he was a German tourist. He had just come in; and he was eating bread and milk. He and I were alone in the eating-room. He was looking at an illustrated paper.

(28) "Does the steamer stop here all night?" I asked him in German, hearing the boat bustling and blowing her steam on the water outside, and glancing round at her lights, red and white, in the pitch darkness.

(29) He only shook his head over his bread and milk, and did not lift his face.

(30) "Are you English, then?" I said.

(31) No one but an Englishman would have hidden his face in a bowl of milk, and have shaken his red ears in such painful confusion.

(32) "Yes," he said, "I am."

(33) And I started almost out of my skin at the unexpected London accent. It was as if one suddenly found oneself in the Tube.

(34) "So am I," I said. "Where have you come from?"

(35) Then he began, like a general explaining his plans, to tell me. He had walked round over the Furka Pass, had been on foot four or five days. He had walked tremendously. Knowing no German, and nothing of the mountains, he had set off alone on this tour: he had a fortnight's holiday. So he had come over the Rhone Glacier across the Furka and down from Andermatt to the Lake. On this last day he had walked about thirty mountain miles.

(36) "But weren't you tired?" I said, aghast.

(37) He was. Under the inflamed redness of his sun- and wind- and snow-burned face he was sick with fatigue. He had done over a hundred miles in the last four days.

(38) "Did you enjoy it?" I asked.

(39) "Oh yes. I wanted to do it all." He wanted to do it, and he *had* done it. But God knows what he wanted to do it for. He had now one day at Lucerne, one day at Interlaken and Berne, then London.

(40) I was sorry for him in my soul, he was so cruelly tired, so perishingly victorious.

(41) "Why did you do so much?" I said. "Why did you come on foot all down the valley when you could have taken the train? Was it worth it?"

(42) "I think so," he said.

(43) Yet he was sick with fatigue and over-exhaustion. His eyes were quite dark, sightless: he seemed to have lost the power of seeing, to be virtually blind. He hung his head forward when he had to write a postcard, as if he felt his way. But he turned his postcard so that I should not see to whom it was addressed; not that I was interested; only I noticed his little, cautious, English movement of privacy.

(44) "What time will you be going on?" I asked.

(45) "When is the first steamer?" he said, and he turned out a guidebook with a time-table. He would leave at about seven.

(46) "But why so early?" I said to him.

(47) He must be in Lucerne at a certain hour, and at Interlaken in the evening.

(48) "I suppose you will rest when you get to London?" I said.

(49) He looked at me quickly, reservedly.

(50) I was drinking beer: I asked him wouldn't he have something. He thought a moment, then said he would have another glass of hot milk. The landlord came—"And bread?" he asked.

(51) The Englishman refused. He could not eat, really. Also he was poor; he had to husband his money. The landlord brought the milk and asked me, when would the gentleman want to go away. So I made arrangements between the landlord and the stranger. But the Englishman was slightly uncomfortable at my intervention. He did not like me to know what he would have for breakfast.

(52) I could feel so well the machine that had him in its grip. He slaved for a year, mechanically, in London, riding in the Tube, working in the office. Then for a fortnight he was let free. So he rushed to Switzerland, with a tour planned out, and with just enough money to see him through, and to buy presents at Interlaken: bits of the edelweiss pottery: I could see him going home with them.

(53) So he arrived, and with amazing, pathetic courage set forth

on foot in a strange land, to face strange landlords, with no language but English at his command, and his purse definitely limited. Yet he wanted to go among the mountains, to cross a glacier. So he had walked on and on, like one possessed, ever forward. His name might have been Excelsior, indeed.

(54) But then, when he reached his Furka, only to walk along the ridge and to descend on the same side! My God, it was killing to the soul. And here he was, down again from the mountains, beginning his journey home again: steamer and train and steamer and train and Tube, till he was back in the machine.

(55) It hadn't let him go, and he knew it. Hence his cruel self-torture of fatigue, his cruel exercise of courage. He who hung his head in his milk in torment when I asked him a question in German, what courage had he not needed to take this his very first trip out of England, alone, on foot!

(56) His eyes were dark and deep with unfathomable courage. Yet he was going back in the morning. He was going back. All he had courage for was to go back. He would go back, though he died by inches. Why not? It was killing him, it was like living loaded with irons. But he had the courage to submit, to die that way, since it was the way allotted to him.

(57) The way he sank on the table in exhaustion, drinking his milk, his will nevertheless, so perfect and unblemished, triumphant, though his body was broken and in anguish, was almost too much to bear. My heart was wrung for my countryman, wrung till it bled.

(58) I could not bear to understand my countryman, a man who worked for his living, as I had worked, as nearly all my countrymen work. He would not give in. On his holiday he would walk, to fulfil his purpose, walk on; no matter how cruel the effort were, he would not rest, he would not relinquish his purpose nor abate his will, not by one jot or tittle. His body must pay whatever his will demanded, though it were torture.

(59) It all seemed to me so foolish. I was almost in tears. He went to bed. I walked by the dark lake, and talked to the girl in the inn. She was a pleasant girl: it was a pleasant inn, a homely place. One could be happy there.

(60) In the morning it was sunny, the lake was blue. By night I should be nearly at the crest of my journey. I was glad.

(61) The Englishman had gone. I looked for his name in the book. It was written in a fair, clerkly hand. He lived at Streatham. Suddenly I hated him. The dogged fool, to keep his nose on the grindstone like that. What was all his courage but the very tip-top of cowardice? What a vile nature—almost Sadish, proud, like the infamous Red Indians, of being able to stand torture.

(62) The landlord came to talk to me. He was fat and comfortable and too respectful. But I had to tell him all the Englishman had done, in the way of a holiday, just to shame his own fat, ponderous, inn-keeper's luxuriousness that was too gross. Then all I got out of his enormous comfortableness was:

(63) "Yes, that's a *very* long step to take."

(64) So I set off myself, up the valley between the close, snow-topped mountains, whose white gleamed above me as I crawled, small as an insect, along the dark, cold valley below.

(65) There had been a cattle fair earlier in the morning, so troops of cattle were roving down the road, some with bells tang-tanging, all with soft faces and startled eyes and a sudden swerving of horns. The grass was very green by the roads and by the streams; the shadows of the mountain slopes were very dark on either hand overhead, and the sky with snowy flanks and tips was high up.

(66) Here, away from the world, the villages were quiet and obscure—left behind. They had the same fascinating atmosphere of being forgotten, left out of the world, that old English villages have. And buying apples and cheese and bread in a little shop that sold everything and smelled of everything, I felt at home again.

Questions

1. What effects do you think Lawrence achieves by his formal diction, his repetitiveness, and his variety in sentence length in the first three paragraphs? Do these effects in any way contribute to or qualify the believability of what he is affirming?

2. How strongly does Lawrence's feeling of hatred come across in

Paragraph 7? Base your answer on an examination of the stylistic features of the paragraph.

3. Compare the diction and sentence rhythms of Paragraph 10 with those in Paragraph 3. Which would you say are more typical of the essay as a whole?

4. Identify the point of view and tone of each of the following fragments from Paragraphs 12 through 24: "In Switzerland every house is a villa"; "a delicate dog, who must not get his feet wet"; "Without a handkerchief, that is not *angenehm*"; "So we became bosom friends"; "in their queer, old, toothless fashion"; "Only in heaven it is warm"; "So I went on to a detestable brutal inn."

5. Examine Lawrence's machine metaphor in the passage on the Englishman. What sort of machine is it? What does it stand for? How clearly can it be seen? How forceful is it?

6. On the basis of your answers to previous questions, characterize Lawrence's style. Does your description differ in significant respects from the account of his style in the Introduction to this section of the text?

7. Lawrence displays a considerable range of feeling in the essay. Describe it, and discuss the character of the man that seems to emerge.

8. Explain why, to you, Lawrence's opinions about the churchgoers and the Englishman are either convincing or unconvincing.

THE AMERICAN POLITICAL TRADITION

CARL BECKER

Probably the most shaping influence on Becker's thought occurred during his student days at the University of Wisconsin,
where he studied with the great historian Frederick Jackson
Turner, sharing daily, as he later wrote, in "the inestimable
privilege of watching an original and penetrating intelligence
at work." From Turner's theories about the frontier, Becker
gained a lasting interest in American history and particularly
in American democracy, subjects he returned to in many essays (some collected in *Every Man His Own Historian* and
New Liberties for Old) and in a number of books (*The Eve
of the Revolution, The Declaration of Independence, Modern
Democracy*). His last work, *Freedom and Responsibility in the
American Way of Life,* from which the following is a selection, was originally a series of lectures he delivered at the
University of Michigan. (Further information on Becker
appears on p. 217.)

(1) On certain conventional occasions we rise and sing to the
land of the free and the home of the brave, land of the Pilgrim's
pride, land where our fathers died. No doubt there is as much symbolic
truth in these phrases as one can reasonably expect to find in a patriotic hymn. But it is worth noting that in all the stages of our history
our fathers, if we go back a few generations, mostly died somewhere else. We are a collection of people from all the nations of
Europe, and even of the world—people who have in successive generations come here in order to escape oppression or to improve the

Reprinted from *Freedom and Responsibility in the American Way of Life* by
Carl Becker, by permission of Alfred A. Knopf, Inc. Copyright 1945 by Alfred
A. Knopf, Inc., and the University of Michigan.

material conditions of life. Goethe expressed this general feeling
when he exclaimed: "America, you have it better!" I once asked a
Greek who had recently come to this country how he liked it here.
He agreed with Goethe. "I like it fine," he said. "I am a Greek Jew.
So what? No one asks am I a Greek Jew. In America is everything
better for poor people like me." This is the essential fact: in America everything has always been better for poor people. It is this conviction, no doubt, that makes us a united nation, although by all the
rules known to an Adolf Hitler we should be neither united nor a
nation. Native- and foreign-born alike are united by the profound
conviction that America has the best of it. We are attached to the
U.S.A. less for what it is than for what it has to offer, less because
of its sacred rills and templed hills than because it is the place in
the world where all comers can find the best opportunity to do what
they like and get what they want. In this sense it has always been,
and has always been thought by the peoples of Europe to be, the
land of the free because it is the land of opportunity.

(2) It was in this light—a somewhat too glamorous light, no
doubt—that the first settlers looked to the new world of America.
John Winthrop tells us that he and his associates decided to remove
from England for two reasons mainly. One was that they wished to
escape from the hopeless struggle with bishops and king in order to
establish a "due form of government both civil and ecclesiastical."
The other was that he (and no doubt other men in his position)
found "his means heer soe shortened as he shall not be able to continue in that place and employment where he now is." Winthrop
was a man of substantial estate, and if his means were shortened,
how much more so were those of ordinary men! "This lande," he
says, "grows weary of her inhabitants, soe as man is heer of less
price amongst us than a horse or sheep. . . . We stand here striving
for places of habitation . . . and in ye mean tyme suffer a whole
continent as fruitful and convenient for the use of man to lie waste
without any improvement." To be free of oppression or to better
their fortunes—for these reasons chiefly the first settlers came to
America, and from that time to this the poor and oppressed classes
of Europe have continued to come for the same reasons.

(3) The first settlers found plenty of freedom in the new world—

so much indeed that in the first years it nearly wiped them out. But they were for the most part a hardy lot. As William Bradford said: "They are too delicate and unfitte to beginne new Plantations and Collonies that cannot endure the biting of a muskeeto." They stuck it out, the hardy ones, enduring all things—the mosquitoes and the Indians, the climate, even in some winters near starvation. They stuck it out and established the form of government that seemed to them due and proper. No doubt they were still subjects of the king and limited by the terms of royal charters, but king and Parliament and bishops were three thousand miles away, and efforts on their part to interfere with the due form of government could be ignored or, with sufficient ingenuity, made of slight effect. And if there were in any colony men too cantankerous to submit to the due form of government, they could always get out. In the New World men did not need to stand striving for places of habitation. And so Anne Hutchinson, who, "speaking from a mere motion of the spirit," criticized the ministers for preaching a covenant of works, and Roger Williams, who believed in soul liberty and even went so far as to say that the land belonged to the Indians, got out of Massachusetts Bay, or were forced out, and went to Rhode Island, where another due form of government was easily improvised and set up. And then there was Thomas Hooker, who had no great objection to the due form of government in Massachusetts Bay, but who found his town second to Boston and himself overtopped in influence by Winthrop and Cotton. He and the people of Newtown, therefore, as we are told, began to "have a hankering" after the Connecticut Valley; and in 1634 they requested from the General Court permission to leave Massachusetts Bay, advancing three reasons—"their want of accommodation for their cattle, the fruitfulness and commodiousness of Connecticut, and the *strong bent of their spirits to remove thither.*"

(4) The migration of the people of Newtown to the Connecticut Valley was in miniature a repetition of the migration of the first settlers from England to the New World and the prototype of all the later migrations from the older settlements to the uninhabited hinterland. Whenever people in the older settlements found the conditions of life unsatisfactory, whether for lack of accommodation for their cattle or some other reason, they were apt to have a "hanker-

ing" for some more fruitful and commodious region farther west. Nothing then restrained them from following the "strong bent of their spirits"; and so for three centuries the frontier of settlement was always moving on—into the upcountry of Virginia, into western New York and Pennsylvania, over the Alleghenies into the vast and fertile woodland and prairie country of the Middle West, across the Rockies to the Pacific coast. The difficulties and hardships encountered in this quest for new fortunes were many, and the conditions of life on the edge of the frontier were often hazardous and always bleak and primitive. But every successive frontier was a new "new world" which offered to its first settlers essentially the same advantages that New England and Virginia offered to the first settlers from England. It offered them freedom—free land, so that they need not stand striving for places of habitation; freedom from the social and religious conventions and restraints of a more settled society; and freedom within broad limits to establish a due form of government, a government that seemed to them suitable and adequate for people living on terms of equality and in something close to a primitive state of nature.

(5) The decisive factors in securing so much freedom and equality for the people of the United States were the country's geographic isolation from Europe, its vast extent, and its rich and seemingly unlimited natural resources. It is related that an Englishman riding from New York to San Francisco, having after a two days' journey finally arrived at Santa Fe, remarked that the discovery of America by Columbus seemed in no way remarkable, since it was difficult to see how anyone could have missed it. The people of the United States have never been troubled by the problem of *Lebensraum*. There has always been room enough; until recently there has always been (and this is the essential point) plenty of free or relatively free land to be had for the taking. Speculators have done their best at various times to buy it up and hold it for monopoly prices, but with slight success. There was always too much of it, and the consequence is that for the greater part of its history the United States has been predominantly a nation of small farmers owning their land in fee simple—farmers to whom the term "tenant" or "peasant" was unknown and to whom it was in no sense applicable.

(6) Benjamin Franklin, with his sure grasp of economic influences, foresaw this development. He noted the fact that industrialized cities of the European type, with their hopelessly impoverished working classes crowded together in slums, could never develop in America so long as any man with a little gumption could go elsewhere and become the independent owner of a farm. It was this situation that defeated every attempt to transplant and perpetuate in the New World the aristocratic social structure and upperclass political domination that prevailed in the old. In Franklin's time there were, it is true, pale replicas of the English class system in most of the colonies. Political control and social prestige were the prerogatives of a few interrelated landowning and merchant families —people of comparative wealth, living in fine houses, who preserved the social amenities and were conversant with the ideas then current among the educated upper classes in England. They thought of themselves as "the better sort" and looked with benevolent condescension on the "populace" of small farmers in the country and artisans and mechanics in the towns. "A poor man," according to a Philadelphia humorist writing in 1775, "has rarely the honor of speaking to a gentleman on any terms and never with familiarity but for a few weeks before election. How many . . . mechanics have been made happy within this fortnight by a shake of the hand, a pleasing smile, and a little familiar chat with gentlemen who have not for these seven years past condescended to look at them."* But, for all that, poverty and servility in the European sense were virtually unknown, and any young man of character and ability could, as the saying was, "get ahead" and "make something of himself"—could acquire an education (perhaps, signing himself Cassius, write a piece for the newspaper describing a certain condescension in gentlemen), could acquire a little property, and so edge himself, or at all events his children, into the reserved precincts of the "better sort." Even this mild species of unstable distinctions was seriously impaired by the American Revolution, which was as much an uprising of the populace against the better sort as it was an uprising of the better sort against British control, and it virtually

* Charles and Mary Beard, *The Rise of American Civilization,* I, 131.

disappeared as a political force in 1828 with the election of Andrew Jackson.

(7) The election of Jackson represented the triumph of the masses over the classes, of the agricultural democracy of the newer West and South over the industrial and moneyed aristocracy of the older East, of the untutored backwoodsman over the cultivated and fastidious gentleman and scholar. At the inaugural reception given by the new president, so we are told, "the White House was invaded by a mob of men, women, and boys who stood on chairs in their muddy boots, fought for the refreshments, and trod glass and porcelain underfoot. 'It would have done Mr. Wilberforce's heart good,' wrote an onlooker, 'to have seen a stout black wench eating in this free country a jelly with a gold spoon in the President's house.' Jackson was glad to escape by a window; and the mob was drawn off like flies to honey, by tubs of punch being placed on the lawn. Washington society thought of the Tuileries on the 10th of August, and shuddered."† This episode may be taken to symbolize the fact that the Middle West was emerging as the central and dominant political force in the United States, and that the rough-and-ready and unabashed freedom and equality of the frontier would make short shrift of ceremony, of distinctions of rank and office, and of the inherited European code of gentility and good manners so highly prized and carefully observed by the better sort.

(8) Such were the essential aspects of the historical experience of the American people that have had a fundamental influence in shaping their ideas about freedom and equality, the function of the government, and the liberty and responsibility of the individual. Since there was for so long a time more fertile land than there were people to cultivate it, it was always relatively easy for the common man to make his own way and pay his own score, unassisted by *noblesse oblige* or communal charity and without benefit of a watchful, paternalistic government: always relatively easy, therefore, for the common man to be and to feel independent, a free man and be damned to you, stranger! Since the people were always on the move from the more settled to the undeveloped regions of the country,

† Samuel Eliot Morison and Henry Steele Commager, *The Growth of the American Republic,* 355 [Edition of 1930].

successive generations of common men were forced to discard settled customs and fixed habits, to break with family ties and old associations, and, relying on their own initiative and common sense, to
reshape social institutions and forms of governments to suit the
practical needs of life in new and relatively primitive conditions. In
few countries have the common people been so little hampered by
tradition in their thought and action, or had so often to adapt their
lives to new and often hazardous conditions, or had so often the
opportunity to follow the bent of their spirits in framing fundamental
constitutional laws and new forms of governments. It is this peculiar historical experience that has disposed the American people
to emphasize the freedom and responsibility of the individual and to
minimize the function and authority of the government: that is to
say, to take it for granted that freedom of thought and conduct is
the natural right of the individual, and that government, so far from
being something transcendent or divine, is essentially a homespun
affair, a convenient committee appointed by the people to perform
certain specified communal services, and in the nature of the case
bound not to go beyond its instructions.

(9) This conception of the function of government and the freedom and responsibility of the individual, although firmly enough
grounded in the historical experience of the American people, is also
supported by a political philosophy—a philosophy clearly formulated at the very time when the United States became an independent
nation, and purporting to set forth the imprescriptible rights of all
men and the essential purpose of all just governments. The confidence of the people of the United States in the rightness of their
institutions and freedoms, sufficiently great in any case, is therefore
all the greater because they can be reminded every Fourth of July
that their institutions and freedoms are the kind of institutions and
freedoms best suited to all mankind because prescribed by the law
of nature and the will of God.

(10) The natural rights political philosophy was of European
origin. The Protestant Reformation was based on the doctrine of
justification by faith—the doctrine that the individual becomes a
good man by adhering to the law of God rather than by submitting
to the laws and conventions of society. In the seventeenth century

this doctrine was employed to justify the English revolution against the established authority of church and king, and at that time the law of God was often identified with the law of nature. But it was in the eighteenth century, in connection with the revolt against the despotic power of kings claiming to rule by divine right and supported by a privileged aristocracy of priests and nobles, that the natural rights philosophy was the most clearly formulated, and was given official sanction, as one may say, by the French Declaration of the Rights of Man and the Citizen and the American Declaration of Independence.

(11) In the Declaration of Independence Jefferson expressed what he called "the common sense of the subject" in the following brief passage:

We hold these truths to be self-evident; that all men are created equal; that they are endowed by their Creator with inherent and unalienable rights; that among these are life, liberty, and the pursuit of happiness; that to secure these rights governments are instituted among men, deriving their just powers from the consent of the governed; that whenever any form of government becomes destructive of these ends, it is the right of the people to alter or to abolish it, and to institute a new government, laying its foundation on such principles and organizing its powers in such form as to them shall seem most likely to effect their safety and happiness.

(12) This statement may be reduced to four fundamental principles: (1) that the universe, including man, is subject to the law of nature, which is a revelation of the will of God; (2) that all men have certain natural or God-given rights; (3) that governments exist to secure these rights; and (4) that all just governments derive their authority from the consent of the governed.

(13) This is the essence of the political philosophy formulated in the eighteenth century to justify the liberal-democratic revolution of modern times. It was revolutionary only in the sense that it was a reinterpretation in secular and liberal terms of the Christian doctrine of the origin, nature, and destiny of man. It denied that man is naturally prone to evil and error, and for that reason incapable,

apart from the compulsion of state and church, of arriving at the truth or living the good life. It affirmed, on the contrary, that men are endowed by their Creator with reason in order that they may progressively discover that which is true, and with conscience in order that they may be disposed, in the measure of their enlightenment, to follow that which is good. If Jefferson and his contemporaries entertained a somewhat too optimistic faith in the natural intelligence and goodness of men, the reason is that they were living at a time when in most countries men were too much governed— a time when the oppressions suffered by the majority of men were those imposed by the organized authority of church and state. For the majority of men, liberty could therefore be most easily conceived in terms of the emancipation of the individual from governmental constraint, and in order to justify such emancipation it was necessary to assume that men were by nature sufficiently rational and sufficiently good for the restraints of law and custom safely to be reduced to a minimum.

(14) For Jefferson and his contemporaries the essential freedoms were, naturally enough, those which had been the most commonly denied. Of these, there were three principal ones—freedom of opinion in order that the truth might prevail; freedom of occupation and economic enterprise in order that careers might be open to talent; and freedom from arbitrary government in order that no man might be compelled against his will. These freedoms were precisely what Jefferson meant by "liberty" as one of the inherent and inalienable rights of man, and it was through the fullest enjoyment of these freedoms that the "pursuit of happiness" would be the most likely to result in the greatest happiness for the greatest number of men. And so we arrive at the central idea of the natural rights philosophy in respect to the function of government and the freedom and responsibility of the individual: the happy idea that the best way to secure the inalienable rights of man is just to leave the individual as free as possible to do what he likes, and that accordingly no form of government can secure them so well as the one that governs least.

(15) The natural rights philosophy made its way in America with far less opposition than it did in Europe. It was accepted as a con-

venient theory for justifying the political separation of the American
colonies from Great Britain; but with that object attained no further
revolution of serious import, such as occurred in France, was required to bring the social and political institutions of the United
States into harmony with the philosophy that presided at its birth
as an independent nation. The state and Federal constitutions were
scarcely more than a codification of colonial institutions with the
Parliament and king left out, and the natural rights philosophy of
the Declaration of Independence was accepted without much opposition as the obvious and necessary foundation of the new political
structure. If the colonies had ever been governed by a king, it was
only by a king *in absentia* exercising a merely nominal control. Mon-
archical absolutism and the theory of divine right, the vested interest
of a ruling landed aristocracy based on birth, the moral and political
influence of an organized state religion—none of these obstacles to
political and social democracy, which had to be overcome in all
European countries, was ever in any real sense a part of the American political practice or tradition. The people of the United States
never had to live with the resistant survivals of an *ancien régime:*
never had, like the British, to place a king in cold storage in order
to keep a Pretender off their backs, or, like the French, to make
terms with powerful royalist and clerical parties openly or secretly
bent on destroying the republic. The natural rights philosophy was
therefore accepted by the people of the United States, as one may
say, without debate and by a rising vote. It seemed to them, as Jefferson said, merely the "common sense of the subject"; and it seemed
to them the common sense of the subject because it was scarcely
more than an ideological description of institutions and a way of life
to which they had long been accustomed and to which they were
entirely devoted.

Questions

1. Becker begins with a general statement of the condition of American life, turns to historical evidence of it, interrupts to restate the condition, continues with the evidence, and so forth. Outline his discussion
briefly, showing that it is essentially in two parts. Describe the overall
organization.

2. Becker shifts his grammatical point of view a few times in the essay. Examine the variations and the general usage, and state what they imply about his overall point of view.

3. Examine the transitions from paragraph to paragraph. How helpful are they in terms of idea and organization? What is their character stylistically?

4. In the first four paragraphs Becker occasionally quotes without using quotation marks. What effects of tone does he achieve?

5. Analyze the level of diction in Paragraph 4 and the quality of the metaphorical language. Analyze the sentence structure and rhythm of the paragraph. Are the several elements congruent stylistically?

6. What range of tone do you observe throughout the entire essay? Compare especially the first and last paragraphs, and see also Question 5. Does the tone, along with its changes, suggest anything about Becker's own commitment to the ideals he is writing about?

7. A scholar's style is expected to be prosaic rather than poetical, objective rather than personal, somewhat formal rather than colloquial. Is Becker's style chiefly this conventional one, or does it display some distinction of an individual mind? Assess the evidence from your answers to previous questions.

8. In Paragraph 6 Becker agrees with Benjamin Franklin that the "industrialized cities of the European type, with their hopelessly impoverished working classes crowded together in slums, could never develop in America so long as any man with a little gumption could go elsewhere and become the independent owner of a farm." Do the slums of Harlem destroy Becker's point? Does the fact that some of these slums are being removed, chiefly through the efforts of government, destroy the point? Discuss.

9. There is evidence that the agricultural democracy of the West and South has still to win the battle with the industrial and moneyed aristocracy of the East (Paragraph 7). Many accounts of the Kennedy campaign of 1960 and of the Goldwater campaign of 1964 discuss this matter. Write a report of one such discussion.

QUINCY

HENRY ADAMS

Descended from two presidents, the son of a famous diplomat, Henry Adams (1838–1918) studied at Harvard and the University of Berlin and spent the Civil War years in London as secretary to his father, then Minister to England. Always diffident about his own accomplishments, he nevertheless taught history at Harvard, edited the influential *North American Review,* wrote novels, biographies, historical essays, and a massive nine-volume *History of the United States During the Administrations of Jefferson and Madison.* His most famous works, written in old age, were intended as contrasts: *Mont-Saint-Michel and Chartres,* in which he explores the unified, coherent civilization of the Middle Ages, and *The Education of Henry Adams,* in which he ponders the complexities of modern existence by a study of his own past. What follows is the opening chapter of the *Education.*

(1) Under the shadow of Boston State House, turning its back on the house of John Hancock, the little passage called Hancock Avenue runs, or ran, from Beacon Street, skirting the State House grounds, to Mount Vernon Street, on the summit of Beacon Hill; and there, in the third house below Mount Vernon Place, February 16, 1838, a child was born, and christened later by his uncle, the minister of the First Church after the tenets of Boston Unitarianism, as Henry Brooks Adams.

(2) Had he been born in Jerusalem under the shadow of the Temple and circumcised in the Synagogue by his uncle the high priest, under the name of Israel Cohen, he would scarcely have been

From *The Education of Henry Adams* by Henry Adams. Reprinted by permission of the Houghton Mifflin Company and Constable & Co., Ltd.

more distinctly branded, and not much more heavily handicapped in the races of the coming century, in running for such stakes as the century was to offer; but, on the other hand, the ordinary traveller, who does not enter the field of racing, finds advantage in being, so to speak, ticketed through life, with the safeguards of an old, established traffic. Safeguards are often irksome, but sometimes convenient, and if one needs them at all, one is apt to need them badly. A hundred years earlier, such safeguards as his would have secured any young man's success; and although in 1838 their value was not very great compared with what they would have had in 1738, yet the mere accident of starting a twentieth-century career from a nest of associations so colonial—so troglodytic—as the First Church, the Boston State House, Beacon Hill, John Hancock and John Adams, Mount Vernon Street and Quincy, all crowding on ten pounds of unconscious babyhood, was so queer as to offer a subject of curious speculation to the baby long after he had witnessed the solution. What could become of such a child of the seventeenth and eighteenth centuries, when he should wake up to find himself required to play the game of the twentieth? Had he been consulted, would he have cared to play the game at all, holding such cards as he held, and suspecting that the game was to be one of which neither he nor any one else back to the beginning of time knew the rules or the risks or the stakes? He was not consulted and was not responsible, but had he been taken into the confidence of his parents, he would certainly have told them to change nothing as far as concerned him. He would have been astounded by his own luck. Probably no child, born in the year, held better cards than he. Whether life was an honest game of chance, or whether the cards were marked and forced, he could not refuse to play his excellent hand. He could never make the usual plea of irresponsibility. He accepted the situation as though he had been a party to it, and under the same circumstances would do it again, the more readily for knowing the exact values. To his life as a whole he was a consenting, contracting party and partner from the moment he was born to the moment he died. Only with that understanding—as a consciously assenting member in full partnership with the society of his age— had his education an interest to himself or to others.

(3) As it happened, he never got to the point of playing the game at all; he lost himself in the study of it, watching the errors of the players; but this is the only interest in the story, which otherwise has no moral and little incident. A story of education—seventy years of it—the practical value remains to the end in doubt, like other values about which men have disputed since the birth of Cain and Abel; but the practical value of the universe has never been stated in dollars. Although every one cannot be a Gargantua-Napoleon-Bismarck and walk off with the great bells of Notre Dame, every one must bear his own universe, and most persons are moderately interested in learning how their neighbors have managed to carry theirs.

(4) This problem of education, started in 1838, went on for three years, while the baby grew, like other babies, unconsciously, as a vegetable, the outside world working as it never had worked before, to get his new universe ready for him. Often in old age he puzzled over the question whether, on the doctrine of chances, he was at liberty to accept himself or his world as an accident. No such accident had ever happened before in human experience. For him, alone, the old universe was thrown into the ash-heap and a new one created. He and his eighteenth-century, troglodytic Boston were suddenly cut apart—separated forever—in act if not in sentiment, by the opening of the Boston and Albany Railroad; the appearance of the first Cunard steamers in the bay; and the telegraphic messages which carried from Baltimore to Washington the news that Henry Clay and James K. Polk were nominated for the Presidency. This was in May, 1844; he was six years old; his new world was ready for use, and only fragments of the old met his eyes.

(5) Of all this that was being done to complicate his education, he knew only the color of yellow. He first found himself sitting on a yellow kitchen floor in strong sunlight. He was three years old when he took this earliest step in education; a lesson of color. The second followed soon; a lesson of taste. On December 3, 1841, he developed scarlet fever. For several days he was as good as dead, reviving only under the careful nursing of his family. When he began to recover strength, about January 1, 1842, his hunger must have been stronger than any other pleasure or pain, for while in after life he

retained not the faintest recollection of his illness, he remembered quite clearly his aunt entering the sick-room bearing in her hand a saucer with a baked apple.

(6) The order of impressions retained by memory might naturally be that of color and taste, although one would rather suppose that the sense of pain would be first to educate. In fact, the third recollection of the child was that of discomfort. The moment he could be removed, he was bundled up in blankets and carried from the little house in Hancock Avenue to a larger one which his parents were to occupy for the rest of their lives in the neighboring Mount Vernon Street. The season was mid-winter, January 10, 1842, and he never forgot his acute distress for want of air under his blankets, or the noises of moving furniture.

(7) As a means of variation from a normal type, sickness in childhood ought to have a certain value not to be classed under any fitness or unfitness of natural selection; and especially scarlet fever affected boys seriously, both physically and in character, though they might through life puzzle themselves to decide whether it had fitted or unfitted them for success; but this fever of Henry Adams took greater and greater importance in his eyes, from the point of view of education, the longer he lived. At first, the effect was physical. He fell behind his brothers two or three inches in height, and proportionally in bone and weight. His character and processes of mind seemed to share in this fining-down process of scale. He was not good in a fight, and his nerves were more delicate than boys' nerves ought to be. He exaggerated these weaknesses as he grew older. The habit of doubt; of distrusting his own judgment and of totally rejecting the judgment of the world; the tendency to regard every question as open; the hesitation to act except as a choice of evils; the shirking of responsibility; the love of line, form, quality; the horror of ennui; the passion for companionship and the antipathy to society—all these are well-known qualities of New England character in no way peculiar to individuals but in this instance they seemed to be stimulated by the fever, and Henry Adams could never make up his mind whether, on the whole, the change of character was morbid or healthy, good or bad for his purpose. His brothers were the type; he was the variation.

(8) As far as the boy knew, the sickness did not affect him at all, and he grew up in excellent health, bodily and mental, taking life as it was given; accepting its local standards without a difficulty, and enjoying much of it as keenly as any other boy of his age. He seemed to himself quite normal, and his companions seemed always to think him so. Whatever was peculiar about him was education, not character, and came to him, directly or indirectly, as the result of that eighteenth-century inheritance which he took with his name.

(9) The atmosphere of education in which he lived was colonial, revolutionary, almost Cromwellian, as though he were steeped, from his greatest grandmother's birth, in the odor of political crime. Resistance to something was the law of New England nature; the boy looked out on the world with the instinct of resistance; for numberless generations his predecessors had viewed the world chiefly as a thing to be reformed, filled with evil forces to be abolished, and they saw no reason to suppose that they had wholly succeeded in the abolition; the duty was unchanged. That duty implied not only resistance to evil, but hatred of it. Boys naturally look on all force as an enemy, and generally find it so, but the New Englander, whether boy or man, in his long struggle with a stingy or hostile universe, had learned also to love the pleasure of hating; his joys were few.

(10) Politics, as a practice, whatever its professions, had always been the systematic organization of hatreds, and Massachusetts politics had been as harsh as the climate. The chief charm of New England was harshness of contrasts and extremes of sensibility—a cold that froze the blood, and a heat that boiled it—so that the pleasure of hating—one's self if no better victim offered—was not its rarest amusement; but the charm was a true and natural child of the soil, not a cultivated weed of the ancients. The violence of the contrast was real and made the strongest motive of education. The double exterior nature gave life its relative values. Winter and summer, cold and heat, town and country, force and freedom, marked two modes of life and thought, balanced like lobes of the brain. Town was winter confinement, school, rule, discipline; straight, gloomy streets, piled with six feet of snow in the middle; frosts that made the snow sing under wheels or runners; thaws when the streets be-

came dangerous to cross; society of uncles, aunts, and cousins who expected children to behave themselves, and who were not always gratified; above all else, winter represented the desire to escape and go free. Town was restraint, law, unity. Country, only seven miles away, was liberty, diversity, outlawry, the endless delight of mere sense impressions given by nature for nothing, and breathed by boys without knowing it.

(11) Boys are wild animals, rich in the treasures of sense, but the New England boy had a wider range of emotions than boys of more equable climates. He felt his nature crudely, as it was meant. To the boy Henry Adams, summer was drunken. Among senses, smell was the strongest—smell of hot pine-woods and sweet-fern in the scorching summer noon; of new-mown hay; of ploughed earth; of box hedges; of peaches, lilacs, syringas; of stables, barns, cowyards; of salt water and low tide on the marshes; nothing came amiss. Next to smell came taste, and the children knew the taste of everything they saw or touched; from pennyroyal and flagroot to the shell of a pignut and the letters of a spelling-book—the taste of A-B, AB, suddenly revived on the boy's tongue sixty years afterwards. Light, line, and color as sensual pleasures, came later and were as crude as the rest. The New England light is glare, and the atmosphere harshens color. The boy was a full man before he ever knew what was meant by atmosphere; his idea of pleasure in light was the blaze of a New England sun. His idea of color was a peony, with the dew of early morning on its petals. The intense blue of the sea, as he saw it a mile or two away, from the Quincy hills; the cumuli in a June afternoon sky; the strong reds and greens and purples of colored prints and children's picture-books, as the American colors then ran; these were ideals. The opposites or antipathies, were the cold grays of November evenings, and the thick, muddy thaws of Boston winter. With such standards, the Bostonian could not but develop a double nature. Life was a double thing. After a January blizzard, the boy who could look with pleasure into the violent snow-glare of the cold white sunshine, with its intense light and shade, scarcely knew what was meant by tone. He could reach it only by education.

(12) Winter and summer, then, were two hostile lives, and bred

two separate natures. Winter was always the effort to live; summer was tropical license. Whether the children rolled in the grass, or waded in the brook, or swam in the salt ocean, or sailed in the bay, or fished for smelts in the creeks, or netted minnows in the salt-marshes, or took to the pine-woods and the granite quarries, or chased muskrats and hunted snapping-turtles in the swamps, or mushrooms or nuts on the autumn hills, summer and country were always sensual living, while winter was always compulsory learning. Summer was the multiplicity of nature; winter was school.

(13) The bearing of the two seasons on the education of Henry Adams was no fancy; it was the most decisive force he ever knew; it ran through life, and made the division between its perplexing, warring, irreconcilable problems, irreducible opposites, with grow-ing emphasis to the last year of study. From earliest childhood the boy was accustomed to feel that, for him, life was double. Winter and summer, town and country, law and liberty, were hostile, and the man who pretended they were not, was in his eyes a school-master—that is, a man employed to tell lies to little boys. Though Quincy was but two hours' walk from Beacon Hill, it belonged in a different world. For two hundred years, every Adams, from father to son, had lived within sight of State Street, and sometimes had lived in it, yet none had ever taken kindly to the town, or been taken kindly by it. The boy inherited his double nature. He knew as yet nothing about his great-grandfather, who had died a dozen years before his own birth: he took for granted that any great-grandfather of his must have always been good, and his enemies wicked; but he divined his great-grandfather's character from his own. Never for a moment did he connect the two ideas of Boston and John Adams; they were separate and antagonistic; the idea of John Adams went with Quincy. He knew his grandfather John Quincy Adams only as an old man of seventy-five or eighty who was friendly and gentle with him, but except that he heard his grandfather always called "the President," and his grandmother "the Madam," he had no reason to suppose that his Adams grandfather differed in character from his Brooks grandfather who was equally kind and benevolent. He liked the Adams side best, but for no other reason than that it reminded him of the country, the summer,

and the absence of restraint. Yet he felt also that Quincy was in a way inferior to Boston, and that socially Boston looked down on Quincy. The reason was clear enough even to a five-year old child. Quincy had no Boston style. Little enough style had either; a simpler manner of life and thought could hardly exist, short of cave-dwelling. The flint-and-steel with which his grandfather Adams used to light his own fires in the early morning was still on the mantelpiece of his study. The idea of a livery or even a dress for servants, or of an evening toilette, was next to blasphemy. Bathrooms, water-supplies, lighting, heating, and the whole array of domestic comforts, were unknown to Quincy. Boston had already a bathroom, a water-supply, a furnace, and gas. The superiority of Boston was evident, but a child liked it no better for that.

(14) The magnificence of his grandfather Brooks's house in Pearl Street or South Street has long ago disappeared, but perhaps his country house at Medford may still remain to show what impressed the mind of a boy in 1845 with the idea of city splendor. The President's place at Quincy was the larger and older and far the more interesting of the two; but a boy felt at once its inferiority in fashion. It showed plainly enough its want of wealth. It smacked of colonial age, but not of Boston style or plush curtains. To the end of his life he never quite overcame the prejudice thus drawn in with his childish breath. He never could compel himself to care for nineteenth-century style. He was never able to adopt it, any more than his father or grandfather or great-grandfather had done. Not that he felt it as particularly hostile, for he reconciled himself to much that was worse; but because, for some remote reason, he was born an eighteenth-century child. The old house at Quincy was eighteenth century. What style it had was in its Queen Anne mahogany panels and its Louis Seize chairs and sofas. The panels belonged to an old colonial Vassall who built the house; the furniture had been brought back from Paris in 1789 or 1801 or 1817, along with porcelain and books and much else of old diplomatic remnants; and neither of the two eighteenth-century styles—neither English Queen Anne nor French Louis Seize—was comfortable for a boy, or for any one else. The dark mahogany had been painted white to suit daily life in winter gloom. Nothing seemed to favor,

for a child's objects, the older forms. On the contrary, most boys, as well as grown-up people, preferred the new, with good reason, and the child felt himself distinctly at a disadvantage for the taste.

(15) Nor had personal preference any share in his bias. The Brooks grandfather was as amiable and as sympathetic as the Adams grandfather. Both were born in 1767, and both died in 1848. Both were kind to children, and both belonged rather to the eighteenth than to the nineteenth centuries. The child knew no difference between them except that one was associated with winter and the other with summer; one with Boston, the other with Quincy. Even with Medford, the association was hardly easier. Once as a very young boy he was taken to pass a few days with his grandfather Brooks under charge of his aunt, but became so violently homesick that within twenty-four hours he was brought back in disgrace. Yet he could not remember ever being seriously homesick again.

(16) The attachment to Quincy was not altogether sentimental or wholly sympathetic. Quincy was not a bed of thornless roses. Even there the curse of Cain set its mark. There as elsewhere a cruel universe combined to crush a child. As though three or four vigorous brothers and sisters, with the best will, were not enough to crush any child, every one else conspired towards an education which he hated. From cradle to grave this problem of running order through chaos, direction through space, discipline through freedom, unity through multiplicity, has always been, and must always be, the task of education, as it is the moral of religion, philosophy, science, art, politics, and economy; but a boy's will is his life, and he dies when it is broken, as the colt dies in harness, taking a new nature in becoming tame. Rarely has the boy felt kindly towards his tamers. Between him and his master has always been war. Henry Adams never knew a boy of his generation to like a master, and the task of remaining on friendly terms with one's own family, in such a relation, was never easy.

(17) All the more singular it seemed afterwards to him that his first serious contact with the President should have been a struggle of will, in which the old man almost necessarily defeated the boy, but instead of leaving, as usual in such defeats, a lifelong sting, left rather an impression of as fair treatment as could be expected from

a natural enemy. The boy met seldom with such restraint. He could not have been much more than six years old at the time—seven at the utmost—and his mother had taken him to Quincy for a long stay with the President during the summer. What became of the rest of the family he quite forgot; but he distinctly remembered standing at the house door one summer morning in a passionate outburst of rebellion against going to school. Naturally his mother was the immediate victim of his rage; that is what mothers are for, and boys also; but in this case the boy had his mother at unfair disadvantage, for she was a guest, and had no means of enforcing obedience. Henry showed a certain tactical ability by refusing to start, and he met all efforts at compulsion by successful, though too vehement protest. He was in fair way to win, and was holding his own, with sufficient energy, at the bottom of the long staircase which led up to the door of the President's library, when the door opened, and the old man slowly came down. Putting on his hat, he took the boy's hand without a word, and walked with him, paralyzed with awe, up the road to the town. After the first moments of consternation at this interference in a domestic dispute, the boy reflected that an old gentleman close on eighty would never trouble himself to walk near a mile on a hot summer morning over a shadeless road to take a boy to school, and that it would be strange if a lad imbued with the passion of freedom could not find a corner to dodge around, somewhere before reaching the school door. Then and always, the boy insisted that this reasoning justified his apparent submission; but the old man did not stop, and the boy saw all his strategical points turned, one after another, until he found himself seated inside the school, and obviously the centre of curious if not malevolent criticism. Not until then did the President release his hand and depart.

(18) The point was that this act, contrary to the inalienable rights of boys, and nullifying the social compact, ought to have made him dislike his grandfather for life. He could not recall that it had this effect even for a moment. With a certain maturity of mind, the child must have recognized that the President, though a tool of tyranny, had done his disreputable work with a certain intelligence. He had shown no temper, no irritation, no personal feeling, and

had made no display of force. Above all, he had held his tongue.
During their long walk he had said nothing; he had uttered no
syllable of revolting cant about the duty of obedience and the
wickedness of resistance to law, he had shown no concern in the
matter; hardly even a consciousness of the boy's existence. Probably his mind at that moment was actually troubling itself little
about his grandson's iniquities, and much about the iniquities of
President Polk, but the boy could scarcely at that age feel the
whole satisfaction of thinking that President Polk was to be the
vicarious victim of his own sins, and he gave his grandfather
credit for intelligent silence. For this forbearance he felt instinctive
respect. He admitted force as a form of right; he admitted even
temper, under protest; but the seeds of a moral education would at
that moment have fallen on the stoniest soil in Quincy, which is,
as every one knows, the stoniest glacial and tidal drift known in
any Puritan land.

(19) Neither party to this momentary disagreement can have felt
rancor, for during these three or four summers the old President's
relations with the boy were friendly and almost intimate. Whether
his older brothers and sisters were still more favored he failed to
remember, but he was himself admitted to a sort of familiarity
which, when in his turn he had reached old age, rather shocked
him, for it must have sometimes tried the President's patience. He
hung about the library; handled the books; deranged the papers;
ransacked the drawers; searched the old purses and pocketbooks
for foreign coins; drew the swordcane; snapped the travelling-
pistols; upset everything in the corners, and penetrated the President's dressing-closet where a row of tumblers, inverted on the
shelf, covered caterpillars which were supposed to become moths
or butterflies, but never did. The Madam bore with fortitude the
loss of the tumblers which her husband purloined for these hatch-
eries; but she made protest when he carried off her best cut-glass
bowls to plant with acorns or peachstones that he might see the
roots grow, but which, she said, he commonly forgot like the caterpillars.

(20) At that time the President rode the hobby of tree-culture,
and some fine old trees should still remain to witness it, unless they

have been improved off the ground; but his was a restless mind, and although he took his hobbies seriously and would have been annoyed had his grandchild asked whether he was bored like an English duke, he probably cared more for the processes than for the results, so that his grandson was saddened by the sight and smell of peaches and pears, the best of their kind, which he brought up from the garden to rot on his shelves for seed. With the inherited virtues of his Puritan ancestors, the little boy Henry conscientiously brought up to him in his study the finest peaches he found in the garden, and ate only the less perfect. Naturally he ate more by way of compensation, but the act showed that he bore no grudge. As for his grandfather, it is even possible that he may have felt a certain self-reproach for his temporary rôle of schoolmaster—seeing that his own career did not offer proof of the worldly advantages of docile obedience—for there still exists somewhere a little volume of critically edited Nursery Rhymes with the boy's name in full written in the President's trembling hand on the fly-leaf. Of course there was also the Bible, given to each child at birth, with the proper inscription in the President's hand on the fly-leaf; while their grandfather Brooks supplied the silver mugs.

(21) So many Bibles and silver mugs had to be supplied, that a new house, or cottage, was built to hold them. It was "on the hill," five minutes' walk above the "old house," with a far view eastward over Quincy Bay, and northward over Boston. Till his twelfth year, the child passed his summers there, and his pleasures of childhood mostly centered in it. Of education he had as yet little to complain. Country schools were not very serious. Nothing stuck to the mind except home impressions, and the sharpest were those of kindred children; but as influences that warped a mind, none compared with the mere effect of the back of the President's bald head, as he sat in his pew on Sundays, in line with that of President Quincy, who, though some ten years younger, seemed to children about the same age. Before railways entered the New England town, every parish church showed half-a-dozen of these leading citizens, with gray hair, who sat on the main aisle in the best pews, and had sat there, or in some equivalent dignity, since the time of St. Augustine, if not since the glacial epoch. It was unusual for boys to sit behind

a President grandfather, and to read over his head the tablet in memory of a President great-grandfather, who had "pledged his life, his fortune, and his sacred honor" to secure the independence of his country and so forth, but boys naturally supposed, without much reasoning, that other boys had the equivalent of President grandfathers, and that churches would always go on, with the bald-headed leading citizens on the main aisle, and Presidents or their equivalents on the walls. The Irish gardener once said to the child: "You'll be thinkin' you'll be President too!" The casuality of the remark made so strong an impression on his mind that he never forgot it. He could not remember ever to have thought on the subject; to him, that there should be a doubt of his being President was a new idea. What had been would continue to be. He doubted neither about Presidents nor about Churches, and no one suggested at that time a doubt whether a system of society which had lasted since Adam would outlast one Adams more.

(22) The Madam was a little more remote than the President, but more decorative. She stayed much in her own room with the Dutch tiles, looking out on her garden with the box walks, and seemed a fragile creature to a boy who sometimes brought her a note or a message, and took distinct pleasure in looking at her delicate face under what seemed to him very becoming caps. He liked her refined figure; her gentle voice and manner; her vague effect of not belonging there, but to Washington or to Europe, like her furniture, and writing-desk with little glass doors above and little eighteenth-century volumes in old binding, labelled "Peregrine Pickle" or "Tom Jones" or "Hannah More." Try as she might, the Madam could never be Bostonian, and it was her cross in life, but to the boy it was her charm. Even at that age, he felt drawn to it. The Madam's life had been in truth far from Boston. She was born in London in 1775, daughter of Joshua Johnson, an American merchant, brother of Governor Thomas Johnson of Maryland; and Catherine Nuth, of an English family in London. Driven from England by the Revolutionary War, Joshua Johnson took his family to Nantes, where they remained till the peace. The girl Louisa Catherine was nearly ten years old when brought back to London, and her sense of nationality must have been confused; but the influence of the Johnsons and

the services of Joshua obtained for him from President Washington the appointment of Consul in London on the organization of the Government in 1790. In 1794 President Washington appointed John Quincy Adams Minister to The Hague. He was twenty-seven years old when he returned to London, and found the Consul's house a very agreeable haunt. Louisa was then twenty.

(23) At that time, and long afterwards, the Consul's house, far more than the Minister's, was the centre of contact for travelling Americans, either official or other. The Legation was a shifting point, between 1785 and 1815; but the Consulate, far down in the City, near the Tower, was convenient and inviting; so inviting that it proved fatal to young Adams. Louisa was charming, like a Romney portrait, but among her many charms that of being a New England woman was not one. The defect was serious. Her future mother-in-law, Abigail, a famous New England woman whose authority over her turbulent husband, the second President, was hardly so great as that which she exercised over her son, the sixth to be, was troubled by the fear that Louisa might not be made of stuff stern enough, or brought up in conditions severe enough, to suit a New England climate, or to make an efficient wife for her paragon son, and Abigail was right on that point, as on most others where sound judgment was involved; but sound judgment is sometimes a source of weakness rather than of force, and John Quincy already had reason to think that his mother held sound judgments on the subject of daughters-in-law which human nature, since the fall of Eve, made Adams helpless to realize. Being three thousand miles away from his mother, and equally far in love, he married Louisa in London, July 26, 1797, and took her to Berlin to be the head of the United States Legation. During three or four exciting years, the young bride lived in Berlin; whether she was happy or not, whether she was content or not, whether she was socially successful or not, her descendants did not surely know; but in any case she could by no chance have become educated there for a life in Quincy or Boston. In 1801 the overthrow of the Federalist Party drove her and her husband to America, and she became at last a member of the Quincy household, but by that time her children needed all her attention, and she remained there with occasional

winters in Boston and Washington, till 1809. Her husband was made Senator in 1803, and in 1809 was appointed Minister to Russia. She went with him to St. Petersburg, taking her baby, Charles Francis, born in 1807; but broken-hearted at having to leave her two older boys behind. The life at St. Petersburg was hardly gay for her; they were far too poor to shine in that extravagant society; but she survived it, though her little girl baby did not, and in the winter of 1814–15, alone with the boy seven years old, crossed Europe from St. Petersburg to Paris, in her travelling-carriage, passing through the armies, and reaching Paris in the *Cent Jours* after Napoleon's return from Elba. Her husband next went to England as Minister, and she was for two years at the Court of the Regent. In 1817 her husband came home to be Secretary of State, and she lived for eight years in F Street, doing her work of entertainer for President Monroe's administration. Next she lived four miserable years in the White House. When that chapter was closed in 1829, she had earned the right to be tired and delicate, but she still had fifteen years to serve as wife of a Member of the House, after her husband went back to Congress in 1833. Then it was that the little Henry, her grandson, first remembered her, from 1843 to 1848, sitting in her panelled room, at breakfast, with her heavy silver teapot and sugar-bowl and cream-jug, which still exist somewhere as an heirloom of the modern safety-vault. By that time she was seventy years old or more, and thoroughly weary of being beaten about a stormy world. To the boy she seemed singularly peaceful, a vision of silver gray, presiding over her old President and her Queen Anne mahogany; an exotic, like her Sèvres china; an object of deference to every one, and of great affection to her son Charles; but hardly more Bostonian than she had been fifty years before, on her wedding-day, in the shadow of the Tower of London.

   (24) Such a figure was even less fitted than that of her old husband, the President, to impress on a boy's mind, the standards of the coming century. She was Louis Seize, like the furniture. The boy knew nothing of her interior life, which had been, as the venerable Abigail, long since at peace, foresaw, one of severe stress and little pure satisfaction. He never dreamed that from her might come some of those doubts and self-questionings, those hesitations, those

rebellions against law and discipline, which marked more than one of her descendants; but he might even then have felt some vague instinctive suspicion that he was to inherit from her the seeds of the primal sin, the fall from grace, the curse of Abel, that he was not of pure New England stock, but half exotic. As a child of Quincy he was not a true Bostonian, but even as a child of Quincy he inherited a quarter taint of Maryland blood. Charles Francis, half Marylander by birth, had hardly seen Boston till he was ten years old, when his parents left him there at school in 1817, and he never forgot the experience. He was to be nearly as old as his mother had been in 1845, before he quite accepted Boston, or Boston quite accepted him.

(25) A boy who began his education in these surroundings, with physical strength inferior to that of his brothers, and with a certain delicacy of mind and bone, ought rightly to have felt at home in the eighteenth century and should, in proper self-respect, have rebelled against the standards of the nineteenth. The atmosphere of his first ten years must have been very like that of his grandfather at the same age, from 1767 till 1776, barring the battle of Bunker Hill, and even as late as 1846, the battle of Bunker Hill remained actual. The tone of Boston society was colonial. The true Bostonian always knelt in self-abasement before the majesty of English standards; far from concealing it as a weakness, he was proud of it as his strength. The eighteenth century ruled society long after 1850. Perhaps the boy began to shake it off rather earlier than most of his mates.

(26) Indeed this prehistoric stage of education ended rather abruptly with his tenth year. One winter morning he was conscious of a certain confusion in the house on Mount Vernon Street, and gathered from such words as he could catch, that the President, who happened to be then staying there, on his way to Washington, had fallen and hurt himself. Then he heard the word paralysis. After that day he came to associate the word with the figure of his grandfather, in a tall-backed, invalid armchair, on one side of the spare bedroom fireplace, and one of his old friends, Dr. Parkman or P. P. F. Degrand, on the other side, both dozing.

(27) The end of this first, or ancestral and Revolutionary, chapter

came on February 21, 1848—and the month of February brought life and death as a family habit—when the eighteenth century, as an actual and living companion, vanished. If the scene on the floor of the House, when the old President fell, struck the still simple-minded American public with a sensation unusually dramatic, its effect on a ten-year-old boy, whose boy-life was fading away with the life of his grandfather, could not be slight. One had to pay for Revolutionary patriots; grandfathers and grandmothers; Presidents; diplomats; Queen Anne mahogany and Louis Seize chairs, as well as for Stuart portraits. Such things warp young life. Americans commonly believed that they ruined it, and perhaps the practical common-sense of the American mind judged right. Many a boy might be ruined by much less than the emotions of the funeral service in the Quincy church, with its surroundings of national respect and family pride. By another dramatic chance it happened that the clergyman of the parish, Dr. Lunt, was an unusual pulpit orator, the ideal of a somewhat austere intellectual type, such as the school of Buckminster and Channing inherited from the old Congregational clergy. His extraordinarily refined appearance, his dignity of manner, his deeply cadenced voice, his remarkable English and his fine appreciation, gave to the funeral service a character that left an overwhelming impression on the boy's mind. He was to see many great functions—funerals and festivals—in after-life, till his only thought was to see no more, but he never again witnessed anything nearly so impressive to him as the last services at Quincy over the body of one President and the ashes of another.

(28) The effect of the Quincy service was deepened by the official ceremony which afterwards took place in Faneuil Hall, when the boy was taken to hear his uncle, Edward Everett, deliver a Eulogy. Like all Mr. Everett's orations, it was an admirable piece of oratory, such as only an admirable orator and scholar could create; too good for a ten-year-old boy to appreciate at its value; but already the boy knew that the dead President could not be in it, and had even learned why he would have been out of place there; for knowledge was beginning to come fast. The shadow of the War of 1812 still hung over State Street; the shadow of the Civil War to come had already begun to darken Faneuil Hall. No rhetoric could have reconciled Mr. Everett's audience to his subject. How could

he say there, to an assemblage of Bostonians in the heart of mercantile Boston, that the only distinctive mark of all the Adamses, since old Sam Adams's father a hundred and fifty years before, had been their inherited quarrel with State Street, which had again and again broken out into riot, bloodshed, personal feuds, foreign and civil war, wholesale banishments and confiscations, until the history of Florence was hardly more turbulent than that of Boston? How could he whisper the word Hartford Convention before the men who had made it? What would have been said had he suggested the chance of Secession and Civil War?

(29) Thus already, at ten years old, the boy found himself standing face to face with a dilemma that might have puzzled an early Christian. What was he?—where was he going? Even then he felt that something was wrong, but he concluded that it must be Boston. Quincy had always been right, for Quincy represented a moral principle—the principle of resistance to Boston. His Adams ancestors must have been right, since they were always hostile to State Street. If State Street was wrong, Quincy must be right! Turn the dilemma as he pleased, he still came back on the eighteenth century and the law of Resistance; of Truth; of Duty, and of Freedom. He was a ten-year-old priest and politician. He could under no circumstances have guessed what the next fifty years had in store, and no one could teach him; but sometimes, in his old age, he wondered—and could never decide—whether the most clear and certain knowledge would have helped him. Supposing he had seen a New York stock-list of 1900, and had studied the statistics of railways, telegraphs, coal, and steel—would he have quitted his eighteenth-century, his ancestral prejudices, his abstract ideals, his semi-clerical training, and the rest, in order to perform an expiatory pilgrimage to State Street, and ask for the fatted calf of his grandfather Brooks and a clerkship in the Suffolk Bank?

(30) Sixty years afterwards he was still unable to make up his mind. Each course had its advantages, but the material advantages, looking back, seemed to lie wholly in State Street.

Questions

1. Adams identifies several opposing forces at work in his education: the eighteenth and the twentieth centuries, Quincy and Boston, winter

and summer, force and freedom, Adams and State Street, Boston and Maryland. Explain the meaning of each term as Adams uses it.

2. Define Adams' broad assumptions about free will and determinism with regard to the autonomy of the individual person versus the controlling influences of nature, social environment, and physical health, and with regard to the influence of individual men upon history versus the inevitability of historical currents. Consider especially the discussions in Paragraphs 2 and 3.

3. Show how the point of view that Adams adopts toward himself in the essay is consonant with his views and assumptions that Questions 1 and 2 have explored. In what sense does the point of view that he maintains toward himself commit him to a certain tone in the essay? What other tones is he thereby committed not to use?

4. Examine Adams' use of the metaphor of the card game in Paragraphs 2 and 3. Would you say that it makes mainly for brevity, clarity, humor, or irony? Does he at any point carry the metaphor too far? Does he use it contradictorily? What aspects of a card game could he probably not employ, given his particular application of the metaphor?

5. Examine the metaphorical language, irony, paradox, and humor in Paragraph 10. How forceful and original are they?

6. Contrast the sentence structure and rhythm in Paragraph 10 with the structure and rhythm of the opening paragraph. What is the particular appropriateness of tone that results in each case?

7. Characterize the diction in Paragraph 13 according to four or five of the categories set forth in the Introduction to this section of the text.

8. Identify the several ironical touches by which Adams introduces humor into the account of his clash with his grandfather. Assuming that he might have treated the situation comically, explain why he does not.

9. What tone governs the following passages: "He was a ten-year-old priest and politician" (Paragraph 29) and "he was to inherit from her the seeds of primal sin, the fall from grace, the curse of Abel" (Paragraph 24)? Analyze the method by which Adams achieves that tone. What parallel do you find between his method here and in Paragraph 7? How would you explain the difference in tone?

10. Can you relate Adams' style in any way to the sort of person he describes himself as being in Paragraph 7 (in the sentence beginning "The habit of doubt . . .")?

EDUCATION BY POETRY:
A MEDITATIVE MONOLOGUE

ROBERT FROST

One of the most accomplished of modern American poets, Robert Frost (1874–1963) was born in San Francisco and then brought as a youth to New England, where he lived and worked—as mill hand, teacher, and farmer—most of his life. More than a regionalist, he wrote deceptively simple poetry that used the settings and often the postures of the area he knew best to present emotions and states of mind common to all men. Among his many honors were four Pulitzer Prizes for poetry and several commendations from Congress; and he is well-remembered both for his poetry readings and for such informal addresses as the following, delivered at Amherst College and taken down in shorthand by a member of the audience.

(1) I am going to urge nothing in my talk. I am not an advocate. I am going to consider a matter, and commit a description. And I am going to describe other colleges than Amherst. Or, rather say all that is good can be taken as about Amherst; all that is bad will be about other colleges.

(2) I know whole colleges where all American poetry is barred— whole colleges. I know whole colleges where all contemporary poetry is barred.

(3) I once heard of a minister who turned his daughter—his poetry-writing daughter—out on the street to earn a living, because

"Education by Poetry" from *The Amherst Graduates' Quarterly,* February, 1931. Copyright 1931, by Robert Frost. Reprinted by permission of the Amherst Alumni News and Holt, Rinehart & Winston, Inc., New York.

he said there should be no more books written; God wrote one book, and that was enough. (My friend George Russell, "Æ", has read no literature, he protests, since just before Chaucer.)

(4) That all seems sufficiently safe, and you can say one thing for it. It takes the onus off the poetry of having to be used to teach children anything. It comes pretty hard on poetry, I sometimes think,—what it has to bear in the teaching process.

(5) Then I know whole colleges where, though they let in older poetry, they manage to bar all that is poetical in it by treating it as something other than poetry. It is not so hard to do that. Their reason I have often hunted for. It may be that these people act from a kind of modesty. Who are professors that they should attempt to deal with a thing as high and as fine as poetry? Who are *they*? There is a certain manly modesty in that.

(6) That is the best general way of settling the problem; treat all poetry as if it were something else than poetry, as if it were syntax, language, science. Then you can even come down into the American and into the contemporary without any special risk.

(7) There is another reason they have, and that is that they are, first and foremost in life, markers. They have the marking problem to consider. Now, I stand here a teacher of many years' experience and I have never complained of having had to mark. I had rather mark anyone for anything—for his looks, carriage, his ideas, his correctness, his exactness, anything you please,—I would rather give him a mark in terms of letters, A, B, C, D, than have to use adjectives on him. We are all being marked by each other all the time, classified, ranked, put in our place, and I see no escape from that. I am no sentimentalist. You have got to mark, and you have got to mark, first of all, for accuracy, for correctness. But if I am going to give a mark, that is the least part of my marking. The hard part is the part beyond that, the part where the adventure begins.

(8) One other way to rid the curriculum of the poetry nuisance has been considered. More merciful than the others it would neither abolish nor denature the poetry, but only turn it out to disport itself, with the plays and games—in no wise discredited, though given no credit for. Anyone who liked to teach poetically could take his subject, whether English, Latin, Greek or French, out into the

nowhere along with the poetry. One side of a sharp line would be left to the rigorous and righteous; the other side would be assigned to the flowery where they would know what could be expected of them. Grade marks where more easily given, of course, in the courses concentrating on correctness and exactness as the only forms of honesty recognized by plain people; a general indefinite mark of X in the courses that scatter brains over taste and opinion. On inquiry I have found no teacher willing to take position on either side of the line, either among the rigors or among the flowers. No one is willing to admit that his discipline is not partly in exactness. No one is willing to admit that his discipline is not partly in taste and enthusiasm.

(9) How shall a man go through college without having been marked for taste and judgment? What will become of him? What will his end be? He will have to take continuation courses for college graduates. He will have to go to night schools. They are having night schools now, you know, for college graduates. Why? Because they have not been educated enough to find their way around in contemporary literature. They don't know what they may safely like in the libraries and galleries. They don't know how to judge an editorial when they see one. They don't know how to judge a political campaign. They don't know when they are being fooled by a metaphor, an analogy, a parable. And metaphor is, of course, what we are talking about. Education by poetry is education by metaphor.

(10) Suppose we stop short of imagination, initiative, enthusiasm, inspiration and originality—dread words. Suppose we don't mark in such things at all. There are still two minimal things, that we have got to take care of, taste and judgment. Americans are supposed to have more judgment than taste, but taste is there to be dealt with. That is what poetry, the only art in the colleges of arts, is there for. I for my part would not be afraid to go in for enthusiasm. There is the enthusiasm like a blinding light, or the enthusiasm of the deafening shout, the crude enthusiasm that you get uneducated by poetry, outside of poetry. It is exemplified in what I might call "sunset raving." You look westward toward the sunset, or if you get up early enough, eastward toward the sunrise, and you rave. It is oh's and ah's with you and no more.

(11) But the enthusiasm I mean is taken through the prism of the intellect and spread on the screen in a color, all the way from hyperbole at one end—or overstatement, at one end—to understatement at the other end. It is a long strip of dark lines and many colors. Such enthusiasm is one object of all teaching in poetry. I heard wonderful things said about Virgil yesterday, and many of them seemed to me crude enthusiasm, more like a deafening shout, many of them. But one speech had range, something of overstatement, something of statement, and something of understatement. It had all the colors of an enthusiasm passed through an idea.

(12) I would be willing to throw away everything else but that: enthusiasm tamed by metaphor. Let me rest the case there. Enthusiasm tamed to metaphor, tamed to that much of it. I do not think anybody ever knows the discreet use of metaphor, his own and other people's, the discreet handling of metaphor, unless he has been properly educated in poetry.

(13) Poetry begins in trivial metaphors, pretty metaphors, "grace" metaphors, and goes on to the profoundest thinking that we have. Poetry provides the one permissible way of saying one thing and meaning another. People say, "Why don't you say what you mean?" We never do that, do we, being all of us too much poets. We like to talk in parables and in hints and in indirections—whether from diffidence or some other instinct.

(14) I have wanted in late years to go further and further in making metaphor the whole of thinking. I find some one now and then to agree with me that all thinking, except mathematical thinking, is metaphorical, or all thinking except scientific thinking. The mathematical might be difficult for me to bring in, but the scientific is easy enough.

(15) Once on a time all the Greeks were busy telling each other what the All was—or was like unto. All was three elements, air, earth, and water (we once thought it was ninety elements; now we think it is only one). All was substance, said another. All was change, said a third. But best and most fruitful was Pythagoras' comparison of the universe with number. Number of what? Number of feet, pounds, and seconds was the answer, and we had science and all that has followed in science. The metaphor has held and held,

breaking down only when it came to the spiritual and psychological or the out of the way places of the physical.

(16) The other day we had a visitor here, a noted scientist, whose latest word to the world has been that the more accurately you know where a thing is, the less accurately you are able to state how fast it is moving. You can see why that would be so, without going back to Zeno's problem of the arrow's flight. In carrying numbers into the realm of space and at the same time into the realm of time you are mixing metaphors, that is all, and you are in trouble. They won't mix. The two don't go together.

(17) Let's take two or three more of the metaphors now in use to live by. I have just spoken of one of the new ones, a charming mixed metaphor right in the realm of higher mathematics and higher physics: that the more accurately you state where a thing is, the less accurately you will be able to tell how fast it is moving. And, of course, everything is moving. Everything is an event now. Another metaphor. A thing, they say, is an event. Do you believe it is? Not quite. I believe it is almost an event. But I like the comparison of a thing with an event.

(18) I notice another from the same quarter. "In the neighborhood of matter space is something like curved." Isn't that a good one! It seems to me that that is simply and utterly charming—to say that space is something like curved in the neighborhood of matter. "Something like."

(19) Another amusing one is from—what is the book?—I can't say it now; but here is the metaphor. Its aim is to restore you to your ideas of free will. It wants to give you back your freedom of will. All right, here it is on a platter. You know that you can't tell by name what persons in a certain class will be dead ten years after graduation, but you can tell actuarially how many will be dead. Now, just so this scientist says of the particles of matter flying at a screen, striking a screen; you can't tell what individual particles will come, but you can say in general that a certain number will strike in a given time. It shows, you see, that the individual particle can come freely. I asked Bohr about that particularly, and he said, "Yes, it is so. It can come when it wills and as it wills; and the action of the individual particle is unpredictable. But it is not so of

the action of the mass. There you can predict." He says, "That
gives the individual atom its freedom, but the mass its necessity."

(20) Another metaphor that has interested us in our time and
has done all our thinking for us is the metaphor of evolution. Never
mind going into the Latin word. The metaphor is simply the metaphor of the growing plant or of the growing thing. And somebody
very brilliantly, quite a while ago, said that the whole universe, the
whole of everything, was like unto a growing thing. That is all. I
know the metaphor will break down at some point, but it has not
failed everywhere. It is a very brilliant metaphor, I acknowledge,
though I myself get too tired of the kind of essay that talks about
the evolution of candy, we will say, or the evolution of elevators—
the evolution of this, that, and the other. Everything is evolution. I
emancipate myself by simply saying that I didn't get up the metaphor and so am not much interested in it.

(21) What I am pointing out is that unless you are at home in
the metaphor, unless you have had your proper poetical éducation
in the metaphor, you are not safe anywhere. Because you are not
at ease with figurative values: you don't know the metaphor in its
strength and its weakness. You don't know how far you may expect
to ride it and when it may break down with you. You are not safe
in science; you are not safe in history. In history, for instance—to
show that is the same in history as elsewhere—I heard somebody
say yesterday that Aeneas was to be likened unto (those words,
"likened unto"!) George Washington. He was that type of national
hero, the middle-class man, not thinking of being a hero at all, bent
on building the future, bent on his children, his descendants. A
good metaphor, as far as it goes, and you must know how far. And
then he added that Odysseus should be likened unto Theodore
Roosevelt. I don't think that is so good. Someone visiting Gibbon at
the point of death, said he was the same Gibbon as of old, still at
his parallels.

(22) Take the way we have been led into our present position
morally, the world over. It is by a sort of metaphorical gradient.
There is a kind of thinking—to speak metaphorically—there is a
kind of thinking you might say was endemic in the brothel. It is
always there. And every now and then in some mysterious way it

becomes epidemic in the world. And how does it do so? By using all the good words that virtue has invented to maintain virtue. It uses honesty, first,—frankness, sincerity—those words; picks them up, uses them. "In the name of honesty, let us see what we are." You know. And then it picks up the word joy. "Let us in the name of joy, which is the enemy of our ancestors, the Puritans . . . Let us in the name of joy, which is the enemy of the kill-joy Puritan . . ." You see. "Let us," and so on. And then, "In the name of health . . ." Health is another good word. And that is the metaphor Freudianism trades on, mental health. And the first thing we know, it has us all in up to the top knot. I suppose we may blame the artists a good deal, because they are great people to spread by metaphor. The stage too—the stage is always a good intermediary between the two worlds, the under and the upper,—if I may say so without personal prejudice to the stage.

(23) In all this I have only been saying that the devil can quote Scripture, which simply means that the good words you have lying around the devil can use for his purposes as well as anybody else. Never mind about my morality. I am not here to urge anything. I don't care whether the world is good or bad—not on any particular day.

(24) Let me ask you to watch a metaphor breaking down here before you.

(25) Somebody said to me a little while ago, "It is easy enough for me to think of the universe as a machine, as a mechanism."

(26) I said, "You mean the universe is like a machine?"

(27) He said, "No. I think it is one . . . Well, it is like . . ."

(28) "I think you mean the universe is like a machine."

(29) "All right. Let it go at that."

(30) I asked him, "Did you ever see a machine without a pedal for the foot, or a lever for the hand, or a button for the finger?"

(31) He said, "No—no."

(32) I said, "All right. Is the universe like that?"

(33) And he said, "No. I mean it is like a machine, only . . ."

(34) ". . . it is different from a machine," I said.

(35) He wanted to go just that far with that metaphor and no further. And so do we all. All metaphor breaks down somewhere.

That is the beauty of it. It is touch and go with the metaphor, and until you have lived with it long enough you don't know when it is going. You don't know how much you can get out of it and when it will cease to yield. It is a very living thing. It is a life itself.

(36) I have heard this ever since I can remember, and ever since I have taught: the teacher must teach the pupil to think. I saw a teacher once going around in a great school and snapping pupils' heads with thumb and finger and saying, "Think." That was when thinking was becoming the fashion. The fashion hasn't yet quite gone out.

(37) We still ask boys in college to think, as in the nineties, but we seldom tell them what thinking means; we seldom tell them it is just putting this and that together; it is just saying one thing in terms of another. To tell them is to set their feet on the first rung of a ladder the top of which sticks through the sky.

(38) Greatest of all attempts to say one thing in terms of another is the philosophical attempt to say matter in terms of spirit, or spirit in terms of matter, to make the final unity. That is the greatest attempt that ever failed. We stop just short there. But it is the height of poetry, the height of all thinking, the height of all poetic thinking, that attempt to say matter in terms of spirit and spirit in terms of matter. It is wrong to call anybody a materialist simply because he tries to say spirit in terms of matter, as if that were a sin. Materialism is not the attempt to say all in terms of matter. The only materialist—be he poet, teacher, scientist, politician, or statesman —is the man who gets lost in his material without a gathering metaphor to throw it into shape and order. He is the lost soul.

(39) We ask people to think, and we don't show them what thinking is. Somebody says we don't need to show them how to think; bye and bye they will think. We will give them the forms of sentences and, if they have any ideas, then they will know how to write them. But that is preposterous. All there is to writing is having ideas. To learn to write is to learn to have ideas.

(40) The first little metaphor . . . Take some of the trivial ones. I would rather have trivial ones of my own to live by than the big ones of other people.

(41) I remember a boy saying, "He is the kind of person that

wounds with his shield." That may be a slender one, of course. It goes a good way in character description. It has poetic grace. "He is the kind that wounds with his shield."

(42) The shield reminds me—just to linger a minute—the shield reminds me of the inverted shield spoken of in one of the books of the *Odyssey,* the book that tells about the longest swim on record. I forget how long it lasted—several days, was it?—but at last as Odysseus came near the coast of Phoenicia, he saw it on the horizon "like an inverted shield."

(43) There is a better metaphor in the same book. In the end Odysseus comes ashore and crawls up the beach to spend the night under a double olive tree, and it says, as in a lonely farmhouse where it is hard to get fire—I am not quoting exactly—where it is hard to start the fire again if it goes out, they cover the seeds of fire with ashes to preserve it for the night, so Odysseus covered himself with the leaves around him and went to sleep. There you have something that gives you character, something of Odysseus himself. "Seeds of fire." So Odysseus covered the seeds of fire in himself. You get the greatness of his nature.

(44) But these are slighter metaphors than the ones we live by. They have their charm, their passing charm. They are as it were the first steps toward the great thoughts, grave thoughts, thoughts lasting to the end.

(45) The metaphor whose manage we are best taught in poetry—that is all there is of thinking. It may not seem far for the mind to go but it is the mind's furthest. The richest accumulation of the ages is the noble metaphors we have rolled up.

(46) I want to add one thing more that the experience of poetry is to anyone who comes close to poetry. There are two ways of coming close to poetry. One is by writing poetry. And some people think I want people to write poetry, but I don't; that is, I don't necessarily. I only want people to write poetry if they want to write poetry. I have never encouraged anybody to write poetry that did not want to write it, and I have not always encouraged those who did want to write it. That ought to be one's own funeral. It is a hard, hard life, as they say.

(47) (I have just been to a city in the West, a city full of poets,

a city they have made safe for poets. The whole city is so lovely that you do not have to write it up to make it poetry; it is ready-made for you. But, I don't know—the poetry written in that city might not seem like poetry if read outside the city. It would be like the jokes made when you were drunk; you have to get drunk again to appreciate them.)

(48) But as I say, there is another way to come close to poetry, fortunately, and that is in the reading of it, not as linguistics, not as history, not as anything but poetry. It is one of the hard things for a teacher to know how close a man has come in reading poetry. How do I know whether a man has come close to Keats in reading Keats? It is hard for me to know. I have lived with some boys a whole year over some of the poets and I have not felt sure whether they have come near what it was all about. One remark sometimes told me. One remark was their mark for the year; had to be—it was all I got that told me what I wanted to know. And that is enough, if it was the right remark, if it came close enough. I think a man might make twenty fool remarks if he made one good one some time in the year. His mark would depend on that good remark.

(49) The closeness—everything depends on the closeness with which you come, and you ought to be marked for the closeness, for nothing else. And that will have to be estimated by chance remarks, not by question and answer. It is only by accident that you know some day how near a person has come.

(50) The person who gets close enough to poetry, he is going to know more about the word *belief* than anybody else knows, even in religion nowadays. There are two or three places where we know belief outside of religion. One of them is at the age of fifteen to twenty, in our self-belief. A young man knows more about himself than he is able to prove to anyone. He has no knowledge that any-body else will accept as knowledge. In his foreknowledge he has something that is going to believe itself into fulfilment, into acceptance.

(51) There is another belief like that, the belief in someone else, a relationship of two that is going to be believed into fulfilment. That is what we are talking about in our novels, the belief of love. And the

disillusionment that the novels are full of is simply the disillusionment from disappointment in that belief. That belief can fail, of course.

(52) Then there is a literary belief. Every time a poem is written, every time a short story is written, it is written not by cunning, but by belief. The beauty, the something, the little charm of the thing to be, is more felt than known. There is a common jest, one that always annoys me, on the writers, that they write the last end first, and then work up to it; that they lay a train toward one sentence that they think is pretty nice and have all fixed up to set like a trap to close with. No, it should not be that way at all. No one who has ever come close to the arts has failed to see the difference between things written that way, with cunning and device, and the kind that are believed into existence, that begin in something more felt than known. This you can realize quite as well—not quite as well, perhaps, but nearly as well—in reading as you can in writing. I would undertake to separate short stories on that principle; stories that have been believed into existence and stories that have been cunningly devised. And I could separate the poems still more easily.

(53) Now I think—I happen to think—that those three beliefs that I speak of, the self-belief, the love-belief, and the art-belief, are all closely related to the God-belief, that the belief in God is a relationship you enter into with Him to bring about the future.

(54) There is a national belief like that, too. One feels it. I have been where I came near getting up and walking out on the people who thought that they had to talk against nations, against nationalism, in order to curry favor with internationalism. Their metaphors are all mixed up. They think that because a Frenchman and an American and an Englishman can all sit down on the same platform and receive honors together, it must be that there is no such thing as nations. That kind of bad thinking springs from a source we all know. I should want to say to anyone like that: "Look! First I want to be a person. And I want you to be a person, and then we can be as interpersonal as you please. We can pull each other's noses—do all sort of things. But, first of all, you have got to have the personality. First of all, you have got to have the nations and then they can be as international as they please with each other."

(55) I should like to use another metaphor on them. I want my palette, if I am a painter, I want my palette on my thumb or on my chair, all clean, pure, separate colors. Then I will do the mixing on the canvas. The canvas is where the work of art is, where we make the conquest. But we want the nations all separate, pure, distinct, things as separate as we can make them; and then in our thoughts, in our arts, and so on, we can do what we please about it.

(56) But I go back. There are four beliefs that I know more about from having lived with poetry. One is the personal belief, which is a knowledge that you don't want to tell other people about because you cannot prove that you know. You are saying nothing about it till you see. The love belief, just the same, has that same shyness. It knows it cannot tell; only the outcome can tell. And the national belief we enter into socially with each other, all together, party of the first part, party of the second part, we enter into that to bring the future of the country. We cannot tell some people what it is we believe, partly, because they are too stupid to understand and partly because we are too proudly vague to explain. And anyway it has got to be fulfilled, and we are not talking until we know more, until we have something to show. And then the literary one in every work of art, not of cunning and craft, mind you, but of real art; that believing the thing into existence, saying as you go more than you even hoped you were going to be able to say, and coming with surprise to an end that you foreknew only with some sort of emotion. And then finally the relationship we enter into with God to believe the future in—to believe the hereafter in.

Questions

1. What variety of meanings does Frost attach to the matter of *marking* in Paragraphs 7 through 10? What does he mean by "enthusiasm tamed by metaphor" (Paragraph 12)?

2. At the beginning of Paragraph 14, Frost says, "I have wanted in late years to go further and further in making metaphor the whole of thinking." Does he mean that the theory of evolution as applied to the origin of man—instead of to the making of candy—is in fact a metaphor instead of the truth? (See Paragraph 20.) Does he mean that the

theory of subatomic particles is merely metaphorical? (See the whole central discussion from Paragraph 14 onward.) Discuss the issue.

3. Summarize the sort of education that Frost thinks a person can get through poetry.

4. The essay divides into three, four, or five main parts. Analyze and explain their ordering.

5. Examine the repetition that Frost employs in the first four paragraphs. What effects does he achieve by it? Relate these effects to the subtitle of the essay.

6. In what differing tones of voice does Frost say, "We are all being marked by each other all the time" (Paragraph 7), "But I like the comparison of a thing with an event" (Paragraph 17), "It seems to me that that is simply and utterly charming" (Paragraph 18), and "Its aim is to restore you to your ideas of free will" (Paragraph 19)? How do you know?

7. Compare and contrast the sentence structure and rhythm of the last paragraph with the structure and rhythm of the first paragraphs. The contrasts help establish the variation in mood throughout the essay. Define the broad progression of mood.

8. In Paragraphs 13 Frost speaks of "trivial metaphors, pretty metaphors, 'grace' metaphors." To what extent does he employ such metaphors in his prose? Analyze the character of the metaphorical language in one of the longer paragraphs.

9. How would you describe Frost's point of view in the essay? Saying that it is a poet's hardly begins to describe it. Questions 5 through 8 will help.

10. On the basis of your answers to previous questions, define Frost's style. What inferences about the man would you make from it?

11. Write an essay comparing the views of human knowledge expressed by Frost and by George Santayana in "Imagination" (Section I).

MEMORIES OF THE PAST

HENRY JAMES

Henry James (1843–1916), probably the most influential of
modern novelists, was born in New York City and educated
both in the United States and abroad. He early felt the
attraction of Europe, with its ancient and established cultures, and in his thirties he chose to make it his home. There
he wrote his many essays, short stories, and novels—*The
Portrait of a Lady, The Ambassadors, The Wings of the
Dove*—in a style subtle, refined, and increasingly intricate
and complex. Its quality at perhaps its highest development
can be experienced in the following selection, the opening of
A Small Boy and Others, which is the first volume of an
autobiography James began in old age but left incomplete at
his death.

(1) In the attempt to place together some particulars of the early
life of William James and present him in his setting, his immediate
native and domestic air, so that any future gathered memorials of
him might become the more intelligible and interesting, I found
one of the consequences of my interrogation of the past assert itself
a good deal at the expense of some of the others. For it was to memory in the first place that my main appeal for particulars had to be
made; I had been too near a witness of my brother's beginnings of
life, and too close a participant, by affection, admiration and sympathy, in whatever touched and moved him, not to feel myself in
possession even of a greater quantity of significant truth, a larger
handful of the fine substance of history, than I could hope to ex-

press or apply. To recover anything like the full treasure of scattered, wasted circumstance was at the same time to live over the spent experience itself, so deep and rich and rare, with whatever sadder and sorer intensities, even with whatever poorer and thinner passages, after the manner of every one's experience; and the effect of this in turn was to find discrimination among the parts of my subject again and again difficult—so inseparably and beautifully they seemed to hang together and the comprehensive case to decline mutilation or refuse to be treated otherwise than handsomely. This meant that aspects began to multiply and images to swarm, so far at least as they showed, to appreciation, as true terms and happy values; and that I might positively and exceedingly rejoice in my relation to most of them, using it for all that, as the phrase is, it should be worth. To knock at the door of the past was in a word to see it open to me quite wide—to see the world within begin to "compose" with a grace of its own round the primary figure, see it people itself vividly and insistently. Such then is the circle of my commemoration and so much these free and copious notes a labor of love and loyalty. We were, to my sense, the blest group of us, such a company of characters and such a picture of differences, and withal so fused and united and interlocked, that each of us, to that fond fancy, pleads for preservation, and that in respect to what I speak of myself as possessing I think I shall be ashamed, as of a cold impiety, to find any element altogether negligible. To which I may add perhaps that I struggle under the drawback, innate and inbred, of seeing the whole content of memory and affection in each enacted and recovered moment, as who should say, in the vivid image and the very scene; the light of the only terms in which life has treated me to experience. And I cherish the moment and evoke the image and repaint the scene; though meanwhile indeed scarce able to convey how prevailingly and almost exclusively, during years and years, the field was animated and the adventure conditioned for me by my brother's nearness and that play of genius in him of which I had never had a doubt from the first.

(2) The "first" then—since I retrace our steps to the start, for the pleasure, strangely mixed though it be, of feeling our small feet plant themselves afresh and artlessly stumble forward again—the

first began long ago, far off, and yet glimmers at me there as out
of a thin golden haze, with all the charm, for imagination and memory, of pressing pursuit rewarded, of distinctness in the dimness,
of the flush of life in the grey, of the wonder of consciousness in
everything; everything having naturally been all the while but the
abject little matter of course. Partly doubtless as the effect of a life,
now getting to be a tolerably long one, spent in the older world, I
see the world of our childhood as very young indeed, young with
its own juvenility as well as with ours; as if it wore the few and
light garments and had gathered in but the scant properties and
breakable toys of the tenderest age, or were at the most a very un-
formed young person, even a boisterous hobbledehoy. It exhaled at
any rate a simple freshness, and I catch its pure breath, at our infantile Albany, as the very air of long summer afternoons—occasions tasting of ample leisure, still bookless, yet beginning to be
bedless, or cribless; tasting of accessible garden peaches in a liberal
backward territory that was still almost part of a country town;
tasting of many-sized uncles, aunts, cousins, of strange legendary
domestics, inveterately but archaically Irish, and whose familiar
remarks and "criticism of life" were handed down, as well as of
dim family ramifications and local allusions—mystifications always
—that flowered into anecdote as into small hard plums; tasting
above all of a big much-shaded savory house in which a softly-sigh-
ing widowed grandmother, Catherine Barber by birth, whose attitude was a resigned consciousness of complications and accretions,
dispensed an hospitality seemingly as joyless as it was certainly
boundless. What she *liked,* dear gentle lady of many cares and anxieties, was the "fiction of the day," the novels, at that time promptly
pirated, of Mrs. Trollope and Mrs. Gore, of Mrs. Marsh, Mrs. Hub-
back and the Misses Kavanagh and Aguilar, whose very names are
forgotten now, but which used to drive her away to quiet corners
whence her figure comes back to me bent forward on a table with
the book held out at a distance and a tall single candle placed, apparently not at all to her discomfort, in that age of sparer and
braver habits, straight between the page and her eyes. There is a
very animated allusion to one or two of her aspects in the fragment
of a "spiritual autobiography," the reminiscences of a so-called

Stephen Dewhurst printed by W. J. (1885) in The Literary Remains of Henry James; a reference which has the interest of being
very nearly as characteristic of my father himself (which his references in almost any connection were wont to be) as of the person
or the occasion evoked. I had reached my sixteenth year when she
died, and as my only remembered grandparent she touches the
chord of attachment to a particular vibration. She represented for
us in our generation the only English blood—that of both her own
parents—flowing in our veins; I confess that out of that association,
for reasons and reasons, I feel her image most beneficently bend.
We were, as to three parts, of two other stocks; and I recall how
from far back I reflected—for I see I must have been always reflecting—that, mixed as such a mixture, our Scotch with our Irish,
might be, it had had still a grace to borrow from the third infusion
or dimension. If I could freely have chosen moreover it was precisely from my father's mother that, fond votary of the finest faith
in the vivifying and characterizing force of mothers, I should have
wished to borrow it; even while conscious that Catherine Barber's
own people had drawn breath in American air for at least two generations before her. Our father's father, William James, an Irishman
and a Protestant born (of county Cavan) had come to America, a
very young man and then sole of his family, shortly after the Revolutionary War; my father, the second son of the third of the mar-
riages to which the country of his adoption was liberally to help
him, had been born in Albany in 1811. Our maternal greatgrandfather on the father's side, Hugh Walsh, had reached our shores
from a like Irish home, Killyleagh, county Down, somewhat earlier,
in 1764, he being then nineteen; he had settled at Newburgh-on-
the-Hudson, half way to Albany, where some of his descendants till
lately lingered. Our maternal greatgrandfather on the mother's side
—that is our mother's mother's father, Alexander Robertson of Pol-
mont near Edinburgh—had likewise crossed the sea in the mid-
century and prospered in New York very much as Hugh Walsh was
prospering and William James was still more markedly to prosper,
further up the Hudson; as unanimous and fortunate beholders of
the course of which admirable stream I like to think of them. I find
Alexander Robertson inscribed in a wee New York directory of the

close of the century as Merchant; and our childhood in that city was passed, as to some of its aspects, in a sense of the afterglow, reduced and circumscribed, it is true, but by no means wholly inanimate, of his shining solidity.

(3) The sweet taste of Albany probably lurked most in its being our admired antithesis to New York; it was holiday, whereas New York was home; at least that presently came to be the relation, for to my very very first fleeting vision, I apprehend, Albany itself must have been the scene exhibited. Our parents had gone there for a year or two to be near our grandmother on their return from their first (that is our mother's first) visit to Europe, which had quite immediately followed my birth, which appears to have lasted some year and a half, and of which I shall have another word to say. The Albany experiment would have been then their first founded housekeeping, since I make them out to have betaken themselves for the winter following their marriage to the ancient Astor House—not indeed at that time ancient, but the great and appointed modern hotel of New York, the only one of such pretensions, and which somehow continued to project its massive image, that of a great square block of granite with vast dark warm interiors, across some of the later and more sensitive stages of my infancy. Clearly—or I should perhaps rather say dimly—recourse to that hospitality was again occasionally had by our parents; who had originally had it to such a happy end that on January 9th, 1842, my elder brother had come into the world there. It remained a tradition with him that our fathers' friend from an early time, R. W. Emerson, then happening to be in New York and under that convenient roof, was proudly and pressingly "taken upstairs" to admire and give his blessing to the lately-born babe who was to become the second American William James. The blessing was to be renewed, I may mention, in the sense that among the impressions of the next early years I easily distinguish that of the great and urbane Emerson's occasional presence in Fourteenth Street, a center of many images, where the parental tent was before long to pitch itself and rest awhile. I am interested for the moment, however, in identifying the scene of our very first perceptions—of my very own at least, which I can here best speak for.

(4) One of these, and probably the promptest in order, was that of my brother's occupying a place in the world to which I couldn't at all aspire—to any approach to which in truth I seem to myself ever conscious of having signally forfeited a title. It glimmers back to me that I quite definitely and resignedly thought of him as in the most exemplary manner already beforehand with me, already seated at his task when the attempt to drag me crying and kicking to the first hour of my education failed on the threshold of the Dutch House in Albany after the fashion I have glanced at in a collection of other pages than these (just as I remember to have once borrowed a hint from our grandmother's "interior" in a work of imagination). That failure of my powers or that indifference to them, my retreat shrieking from the Dutch House, was to leave him once for all already there an embodied demonstration of the possible— already wherever it might be that there was a question of my arriving, when arriving at all, belatedly and ruefully; as if he had gained such an advance of me in his sixteen months' experience of the world before mine began that I never for all the time of childhood and youth in the least caught up with him or overtook him. He was always round the corner and out of sight, coming back into view but at his hours of extremest ease. We were never in the same schoolroom, in the same game, scarce even in step together or in the same phase at the same time; when our phases overlapped, that is, it was only for a moment—he was clean out before I had got well in. How far he had really at any moment dashed forward it is not for me now to attempt to say; what comes to me is that I at least hung inveterately and woefully back, and that this relation alike to our interests and to each other seemed proper and preappointed. I lose myself in wonder at the loose ways, the strange process of waste, through which nature and fortune may deal on occasion with those whose faculty for application is all and only in their imagination and their sensibility. There may be during those bewildered and brooding years so little for them to "show" that I liken the individual dunce —as he so often must appear—to some commercial traveler who has lost the key to his packed case of samples and can but pass for a fool while other exhibitions go forward.

(5) I achieve withal a dim remembrance of my final submission,

though it is the faintest ghost of an impression and consists but of the bright blur of a dame's schoolroom, a mere medium for small piping shuffling sound and suffered heat, as well as for the wistfulness produced by "glimmering squares" that were fitfully screened, though not to any revival of cheer, by a huge swaying, yet dominant object. This dominant object, the shepherdess of the flock, was Miss Bayou or Bayhoo—I recover but the alien sound of her name, which memory caresses only because she may have been of like race with her temple of learning, which faced my grandmother's house in North Pearl Street and really justified its exotic claim by its yellow archaic gable-end: I think of the same as of brick baked in the land of dikes and making a series of small steps from the base of the gable to the point. These images are subject, I confess, to a soft confusion—which is somehow consecrated, none the less, and out of which, with its shade of contributory truth, some sort of scene insists on glancing. The very flush of the uneven bricks of the pavement lives in it, the very smell of the street cobbles, the imputed grace of the arching umbrage—I see it all as from under trees; the form of Steuben Street, which crossed our view, as steep even to the very essence of adventure, with a summit, and still more with a nethermost and riskiest incline, very far away. There lives in it the aspect of the other house—the other and much smaller than my grandmother's, conveniently near it and within sight; which was pinkish-red picked out with white, whereas my grandmother's was greyish-brown and very grave, and which must have stood back a little from the street, as I seem even now to swing, or at least to perch, on a relaxed gate of approach that was conceived to work by an iron chain weighted with a big ball; all under a spreading tree again and with the high, oh so high white stone steps (mustn't they have been marble?) and fan-lighted door of the pinkish-red front behind me. I lose myself in ravishment before the marble and the pink. There were other houses too—one of them the occasion of the first "paid" visit that struggles with my twilight of social consciousness; a call with my father, conveying me presumably for fond exhibition (since if my powers were not exhibitional my appearance and my long fair curls, of which I distinctly remember the lachrymose sacrifice, suppositiously were), on one of our aunts,

the youngest of his three sisters, lately married and who, predestined to an early death, hovers there for me, softly spectral, in
long light "front" ringlets, the fashion of the time and the capital
sign of all our paternal aunts seemingly; with the remembered en-
hancement of her living in Elk Street, the name itself vaguely por-
tentous, as through beasts of the forest not yet wholly exorcised,
and more or less under the high brow of that Capitol which, as
aloft somewhere and beneath the thickest shades of all, loomed,
familiar yet impressive, at the end of almost any Albany vista of
reference. I have seen other capitols since, but the whole majesty
of the matter must have been then distilled into my mind—even
though the connection was indirect and the concrete image, that of
the primitive structure, long since pretentiously and insecurely
superseded—so that, later on, the impression was to find itself, as
the phrase is, discounted. Had it not moreover been reinforced at
the time, for that particular Capitoline hour, by the fact that our
uncle, our aunt's husband, was a son of Mr. Martin Van Buren,
and that *he* was the President? This at least led the imagination
on—or leads in any case my present imagination of that one; minis-
tering to what I have called the soft confusion.

(6) The confusion clears, however, though the softness remains,
when, ceasing to press too far backward, I meet the ampler light of
conscious and educated little returns to the place; for the education
of New York, enjoyed up to my twelfth year, failed to blight its
romantic appeal. The images I really distinguish flush through the
maturer medium, but with the sense of them only the more won-
drous. The other house, the house of my parents' limited early
sojourn, becomes that of those of our cousins, numerous at that
time, who pre-eminently figured for us; the various brood presided
over by my father's second sister, Catherine James, who had married
at a very early age Captain Robert Temple, U.S.A. Both these
parents were to die young, and their children, six in number, the
two eldest boys, were very markedly to people our preliminary
scene; this being true in particular of three of them, the sharply
differing brothers and the second sister, Mary Temple, radiant and
rare, extinguished in her first youth, but after having made an impression on many persons, and on ourselves not least, which was to

become in the harmonious circle, for all time, matter of sacred legend and reference, of associated piety. Those and others with them were the numerous dawnings on which in many cases the deepening and final darknesses were so soon to follow: our father's family was to offer such a chronicle of early deaths, arrested careers, broken promises, orphaned children. It sounds cold-blooded, but part of the charm of our grandmother's house for us—or I should perhaps but speak for myself—was in its being so much and so sociably a nurseried and playroomed orphanage. The children of her lost daughters and daughters-in-law overflowed there, mainly as girls; on whom the surviving sons-in-law and sons occasionally and most trustingly looked in. Parentally bereft cousins were somehow more thrilling than parentally provided ones; and most thrilling when, in the odd fashion of that time, they were sent to school in New York as a preliminary to their being sent to school in Europe. They spent scraps of holidays with us in Fourteenth Street, and I think my first childish conception of the enviable lot, formed amid these associations, was to be so little fathered or mothered, so little sunk in the short range, that the romance of life seemed to lie in some constant improvisation, by vague over-hovering authorities, of new situations and horizons. We were intensely domesticated, yet for the very reason perhaps that we felt our young bonds easy; and they were *so* easy compared to other small plights of which we had stray glimpses that my first assured conception of true richness was that we should be sent separately off among cold or even cruel aliens in order to be there thrillingly homesick. Homesickness was a luxury I remember craving from the tenderest age—a luxury of which I was unnaturally, or at least prosaically, deprived. Our motherless cousin Augustus Barker came up from Albany to the Institution Charlier—unless it was, as I suspect, a still earlier specimen, with a name that fades from me, of that type of French establishment for boys which then and for years after so incongruously flourished in New York; and though he professed a complete satisfaction with pleasures tasted in our innocent society I felt that he was engaged in a brave and strenuous adventure while we but hugged the comparatively safe shore.

Questions

1. Consider the following revision of the first two sentences in James' sketch: In preparing an account of the early years of William James that might be helpful to later biographers, I found that my closeness to him in those years resulted in my having more material about him than I could well use. What differences do you observe in diction, sentence rhythm, and meaning? What is the broad difference in tone?

2. Justify the variety in sentence length in the first two paragraphs according to the material that James is treating. Explain how the general length and complexity of his sentences serve his broad intentions in the sketch.

3. By what reorganization of material about Catherine Barber might James have strengthened his pictorial image of her? What do you think his intention is in the way in which he does handle his material?

4. Judge the following metaphors on the basis of originality, effectiveness, and consistency with the general tone of the surrounding writing: "larger handful of the fine substance of history" (Paragraph 1), "the first . . . glimmers at me there as out of a thin golden haze" (Paragraph 2), "she touches the chord of attachment to a particular vibration" (Paragraph 2), and "liken the . . . dunce . . . to some commercial traveler who has lost the key to his packed case of samples" (Paragraph 4).

5. Examine the image of light in the final paragraph. Discuss its meaning, its relationship to other images in the paragraph, and its appropriateness to the sketch as a whole.

6. Describe the narrative flow of the essay. It may be particularly helpful to examine the relationship of "the sweet taste of Albany" (the opening of Paragraph 3) to material in the preceding paragraph, and also the basis on which James proceeds from subject to subject in Paragraph 5.

7. On the basis of your answers to previous questions, characterize James' style. Show how it contributes to the meaning of the sketch.

8. What sort of man does James seem to be? Base your answer on what he says about himself and also on his style.

9. Is the sketch effective as a piece of recollection? Discuss.